The Genealogy of Cities

The Genealogy of Cities

Charles P. Graves Jr.
Foreword by David Grahame Shane

The Kent State University Press
Kent, Ohio

Library of Congress Catalog Card Number 2008001521
ISBN 978-0-87338-939-6
Manufactured in China

Published with the generous support of the Graham Foundation.

Library of Congress Cataloging-in-Publication Data
Graves, Charles P., 1952–
The genealogy of cities / Charles P. Graves ; foreword by David Grahame Shane.
p. cm.
Includes bibliographical references and index.
ISBN 978-0-87338-939-6 (hardcover : alk. paper) ∞
1. City planning—History—Maps. 2. Cities and towns—Growth—History—Maps.
3. Cities and towns—Genealogy—Maps. I. Title.
G1046.G45G7 2008
307.76022'3—dc22 2008001521

British Library Cataloging-in-Publication data are available.

13 12 11 10 09 5 4 3 2 1

Contents

Foreword

David Grahame Shane

In the 1960s U.S. architects employed figure/ground techniques to represent a city's spatial organization in high-contrast black-and-white drawings. This technique attempted to represent clearly the void space of the city where activities took place. The coding, in patterns of black and white and in plan, severely limited the information these drawings could convey. In using figure/ground techniques, urban designers limited themselves to the plan in an effort to compress all the other information into a singe surface. It took weeks for a draftsperson to draw a city plan with pen and ink. During this time he would become intimately familiar with every little street, nook, and cranny of the city, researching which urban actor created each urban fragment. The exercise of drawing the plan became a kind of contemplative practice in itself, Zenlike in its calm concentration and attention to detail. Day after day the draftsperson would sit with seemingly little progress as a vast amount of information was compressed into an apparently simple plan.

The heritage of these drawings stretches back to Roque's map of London from 1746 and Nolli's plan of Rome from 1748. This was a transitional drawing technique from an age before engineers in the 1800s perfected accurate three-dimensional representational system within grid coordinates. Similarly the figure/ground drawings in the 1960s represent a transitional phase before the introduction of the age of computerization, with CAD, GPS, and satellite imaging creating the multiple layers of Google Earth in the early 2000s. Professors Jim Tice and Eric Steiner of Oregon University, for instance, have put the Nolli Map online as an interactive web resource (http://nolli.uoregon.edu/).

Contextual urban designers adopted figure/ground representational system as a critique of the "tabula rasa" techniques of modernism and U.S. urban renewal. Developing theories of Camillo Sitte from 1890s Vienna, such Cornell University contextualists as Colin Rowe, Fred Koetter, Stuart Cohen, Wayne Copper, Steven Peterson, and Tom Schumaker created an innovative postmodern system of urban analysis. The spatial coding system was briefly popular and influenced the urban analysis of James Stirling, O. M. Ungers, Leon and Rob Krier, Peter Eisenman, Danny Liebeskind, Stephen Holl, Bernard Tschumi, and Rem Koolhaas, among others. But the technique fell rapidly out of favor by the late 1970s except in urban design studios, where it continued as one method of representing the complexity of the city. Brian McGrath's *Transparent Cities* (1994) shows the sophistication and sensitivity that was possible in this system of deeply layered, figure/ground drawings.

Charles Graves's collection of figure/ground drawings in *A Genealogy of Cities* offers a rare chance to reexamine this transitional urban coding system in a variety of cities from around the globe. Graves, who studied under Colin Rowe at Cornell, has collected an extensive variety of plans that show different patterns of growth over time. Urban actors manipulated growth, leaving the traces of their concerns and preferences in the code, direction, and patterns of urban growth. The Graves collection shows the shifting choices of urban actors who controlled the sequence and pattern of growth in different cities at various times.

This collection of drawings offers evidence that urban actors generally began by creating a clearly controlled enclave with distinct boundaries. Actors surrounded the "urbs"—the hamlet, village, town, or city—by a hedge, ditch, moat, or wall. Other actors preferred linear organizational structures around a village main street that often linked two attractors, sometimes an older settlement to a new satellite. This linear arrangement of the armature, like the enclave system, needed constant monitoring and feedback to maintain its structure over time. Some actors began with linear structures, skipping the enclave stage, while other actors rapidly expanded the linear systems into a network containing multiple actors without a single dominant center.

Graves's collection reveals the patterns left by a three-stage narrative of city growth, variously described as premodern, modern, and postmodern or preindustrial, industrial, and postindustrial. Each set of actors interacted with earlier actors and transformed these patterns by their interventions, resulting in a complex and multilayered hybrid city. Over time the center of the city might shift from the original enclave to an armature and then to a satellite or multiple satellites. A close reading of figure/ground patterns in the Graves drawings reveals how actors switched codes and patterns of growth in cities over time.

In addition, Graves has invented a very useful way of cataloging the urban elements used to assemble these plans, indicated by small icons before each section, alerting the reader as to which element is under consideration in each section. These icons make the organization of his material extremely clear, easy to use, and elegant.

This book will prove to be very important as a repository of accurately and beautifully drawn plans of cites from around the world, all drawn at a standard scale. These drawings will be invaluable as a modern reference book for urban designers who have to grapple with the issue of scale and precedents in creating new urban places. These precedents will also be helpful for teachers of urban design in-studio, especially when associated with modern mapping and cartographic techniques, from Google to photos from Flickr.

Preface and Acknowledgments

The Genealogy of Cities has been a work in progress for almost nine years. While I was sitting with Colin Rowe one evening, he asked the question: "So Charles, where's the book?" My master's thesis under Rowe was an investigation in urban scale comparison, and he was always asking for an expanded, book-length version. Although there have been many twists and turns along the way, my primary goal has always been to produce a book that lets readers contemplate, compare, contrast, and consider how cities originated in their plan structure and growth.

In *Roma Interrotta* (London: Architectural Design, 1979), editor Michael Graves gave architects from around the world one of the twelve sections of the 1748 map of Rome by Giambattista Nolli. From their assigned section of the map, Rowe and his associates produced a design that was at the forefront of an urban design style called contextualism. This invited competition and set the stage for figure/ground investigation in urban design. That same year I was studying with Rowe at Cornell University and finishing my thesis, "Manhattan: A Measure." Since my time at Cornell, contextualism has been replaced by a succession of urban design styles. To paraphrase something Colin Rowe *might* have said, "The Zeitgeist of urban design is reflected in the times we live in. Time to move on!"

Even though current approaches to urban design can seem quite radical, they still deal with the same issue of the past: understanding the city fabric. But the figure/ground can only do so much. I believe that one of the most important steps in urban design is understanding the origins and makeup of a city.

In *Recombinant Urbanism: Conceptual Modeling in Architecture, Urban Design, and City Theory* (London: Academy Press, 2005), David Grahame Shane approaches the study of urban design at a global level, while weaving into the text urban history, financial and global influences, and new urban studies. *The Genealogy of Cities,* written as a tool for understanding city makeup, could act as a companion to Shane's text, with *Recombinant Urbanism* providing the urban theory and *The Genealogy of Cities* providing the city templates. Ideally, readers will see other possibilities while studying these city plans, add to the tools in this book, and, in time, enlarge the continuing study of cities and their designs.

Many deserve recognition for helping me produce this book, including Steven K. Peterson for his words of wisdom; Marcello Fantoni, Michael Dennis, and Edward Jones for their letters of support; my family, friends, and colleagues for their words of encouragement; Tatiana for enduring the long days and evenings I spent working on the drawings; and Lillian, my daughter.

I also want to acknowledge my friend and colleague, David Grahame Shane, for graciously agreeing to write the foreword to this book and for all the time he spent questioning my ideas.

I'd like to thank Jonathan Jackson of WSDIA for all his input on design and layout as well as the architecture students who assisted me: Chris Pless, Kyle May, Lance Wyse, and Michelle Murnane. Thank you to Will Underwood, Joanna H. Craig, Mary D. Young, Rebekah Cotton, Christine Brooks, and Darryl Crosby of the Kent State University Press for agreeing to publish my "not-your-standard-size" book.

I gratefully acknowledge the American Institute of Architects/American Architectural Foundation for awarding me a Fellowship for Advanced Study and

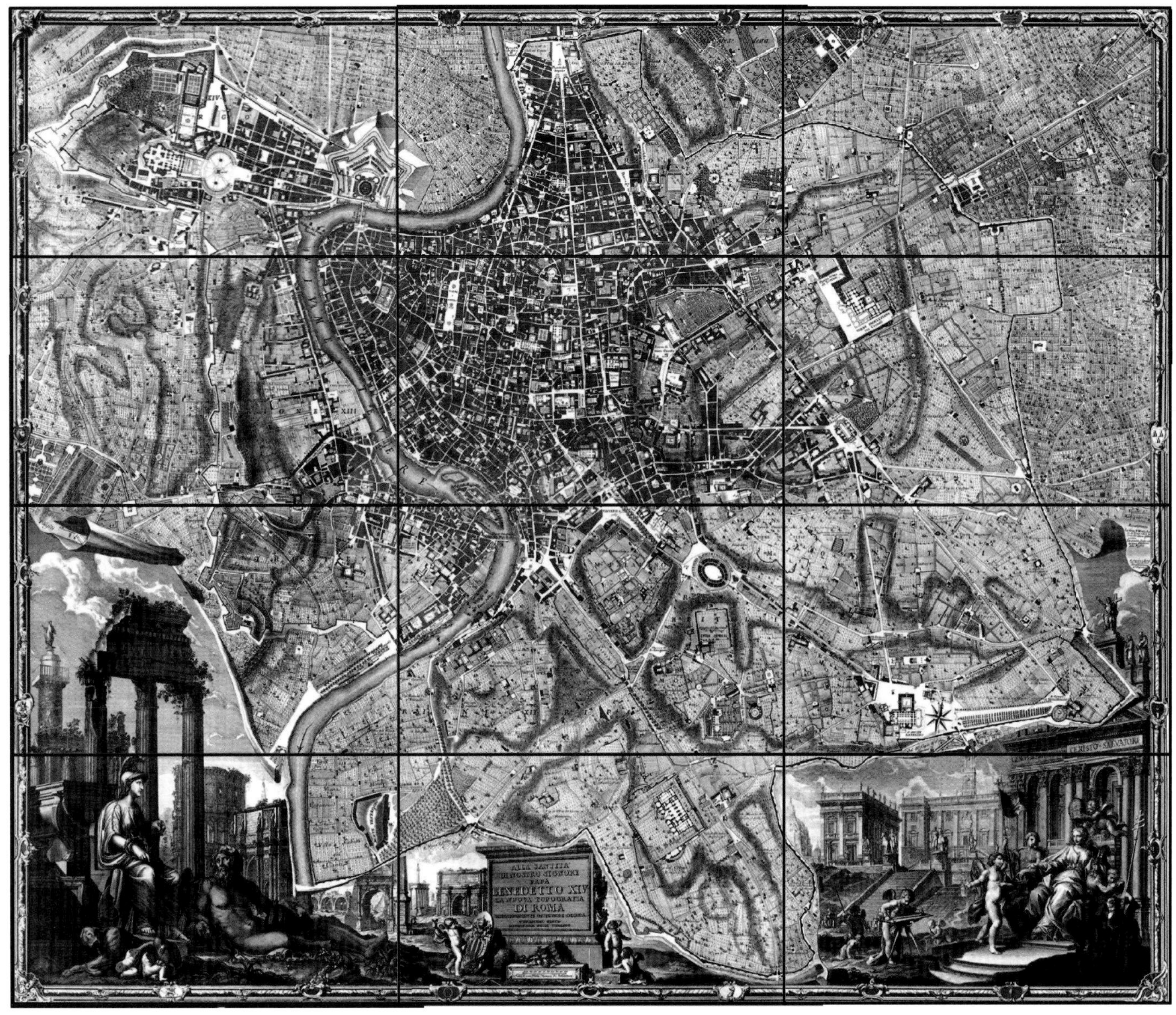

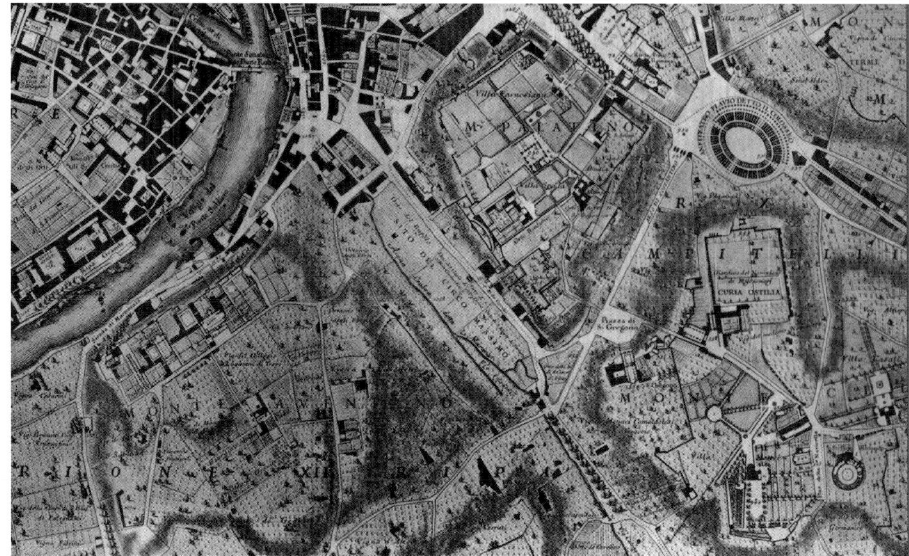

Top left: 1748 map of Rome by Giambattista Nolli.

Top right: Quadrant 8 detail from Nolli's map of Rome.

Lower right: Colin Rowe and group, "Solution for 'Roma Interotta,' quadrant 8, of the 1748 Map of Rome by Giambattista Nolli" (1979).

Research in Urban Design, which funded a year of city research and plan making. My thanks, too, extend to the Grahame Foundation for a generous grant that helped in the publication of this book.

And finally, I dedicate this book to three important people who passed away during its production. To Colin Rowe, who taught me; to my father, Charles P. Graves Sr., who had faith in me; and to Richard Role, who spent many evenings with me discussing the direction this book should take. These three men were always there to answer my questions, cheer me on, and push me toward completion.

Introduction

Early in my career teaching urban design, I came across two articles by Elbert Peets, "The Background of L'Enfant's Plan" and "The Genealogy of L'Enfant's Design of Washington."[1] In these articles, Peets traces the historic architectural and city scale fabric, which he considers a precedent for L'Enfant's design of Washington, D.C. L'Enfant's direct influences are Versailles and John Evelyn's plan for rebuilding London after the fire of 1666, according to Peets. In "The Background of L'Enfant's Plan," Peets's drawings compare streets, relationships and distances of block-shaped triangles, and scale comparisons of building fabric. In "The Genealogy of L'Enfant's Design of Washington," Peets further traces the genealogy of Washington, D.C., outlining Roman legionary camps, hunting forests, and early French town plans. Through this genealogical analysis, the observer can see a portion of the design process that may have influenced L'Enfant's design for Washington, D.C. It was Peets's process of tracing the genealogy that led me to consider the possibility of a pattern or typology for city designs and eventually to research and write this book.

Judging Size and Scale at an Urban Level

"If, as the philosophers maintain, the city is like some large house, and the house is in turn like some small city, cannot the various parts of the house—atria, loggias, dining rooms, porticoes and so on—be considered miniature buildings?"

—Leon Battista Alberti, *On the Art of Building in Ten Books*

Alberti describes the ability to mentally change scale when visualizing the design of urban architecture. Thus, streets can be seen as hallways, city squares as public living rooms, and the surrounding urban fabric as walls to the room. Some of the first steps in designing a building are (1) to investigate a suitable scale and massing that an architectural structure should have in relation to its design site or context, and (2) to study an appropriate function and sequencing of spaces. These processes of scaling, massing, and sequencing also occur in urban design. Similarly, as the architect studies precedents to implement a design, the urban designer researches and surveys urban precedents in the early stages of a project. This book is a companion to these processes, meant to help urban designers comprehend scale relationships at a city level; understand the historic sequence or growth, following the processes that have evolved to create the city fabric of today; and ultimately aid in future urban designs.

Whether our surroundings are stationary or moving through space—cars passing, people walking, wind blowing, doors opening—we tend to experience them based on our own size. The amount we can hold in our hand, the distance we cover in one stride, and how much we can see all depend on our physical size. All of these experiences are typically tangible and within our human grasp, but, outside the realm of our immediate space, it is sometimes difficult for urban designers to realize just how large or small architectural form or space should be and what type of spatial sequencing should occur. By comparing and contrasting, we can begin to understand the correct proportions needed to create habitable and pleasing urban space.

To fully understand the process of designing cities, it is important to study the pattern of existing cities—the individual parts that go into their makeup, the ensemble of architecture, and the structured landscape that has influenced urban

Types of plans Elbert Peets considered precedents for L'Enfant's design of Washington, D.C. From Peets, "The Background of L'Enfant's Plan" and "The Genealogy of L'Enfant's Design of Washington."

Below: Peets's "family tree" for Washington, D.C.

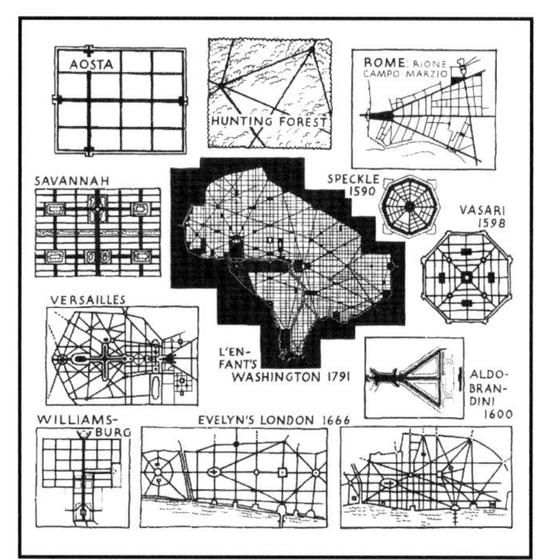

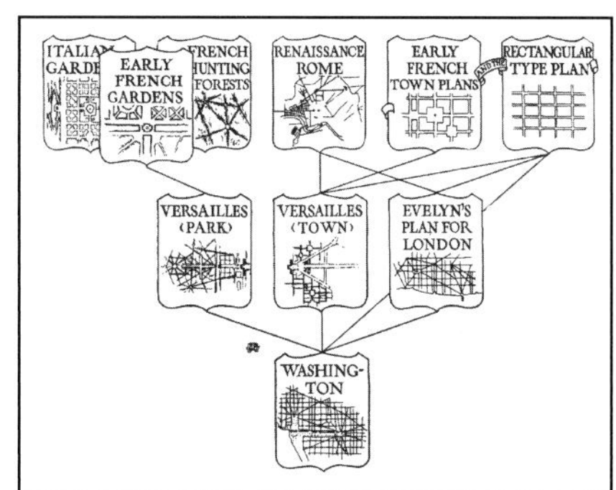

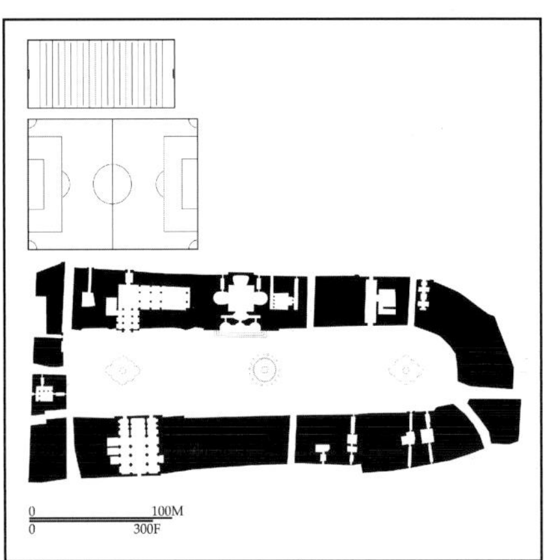

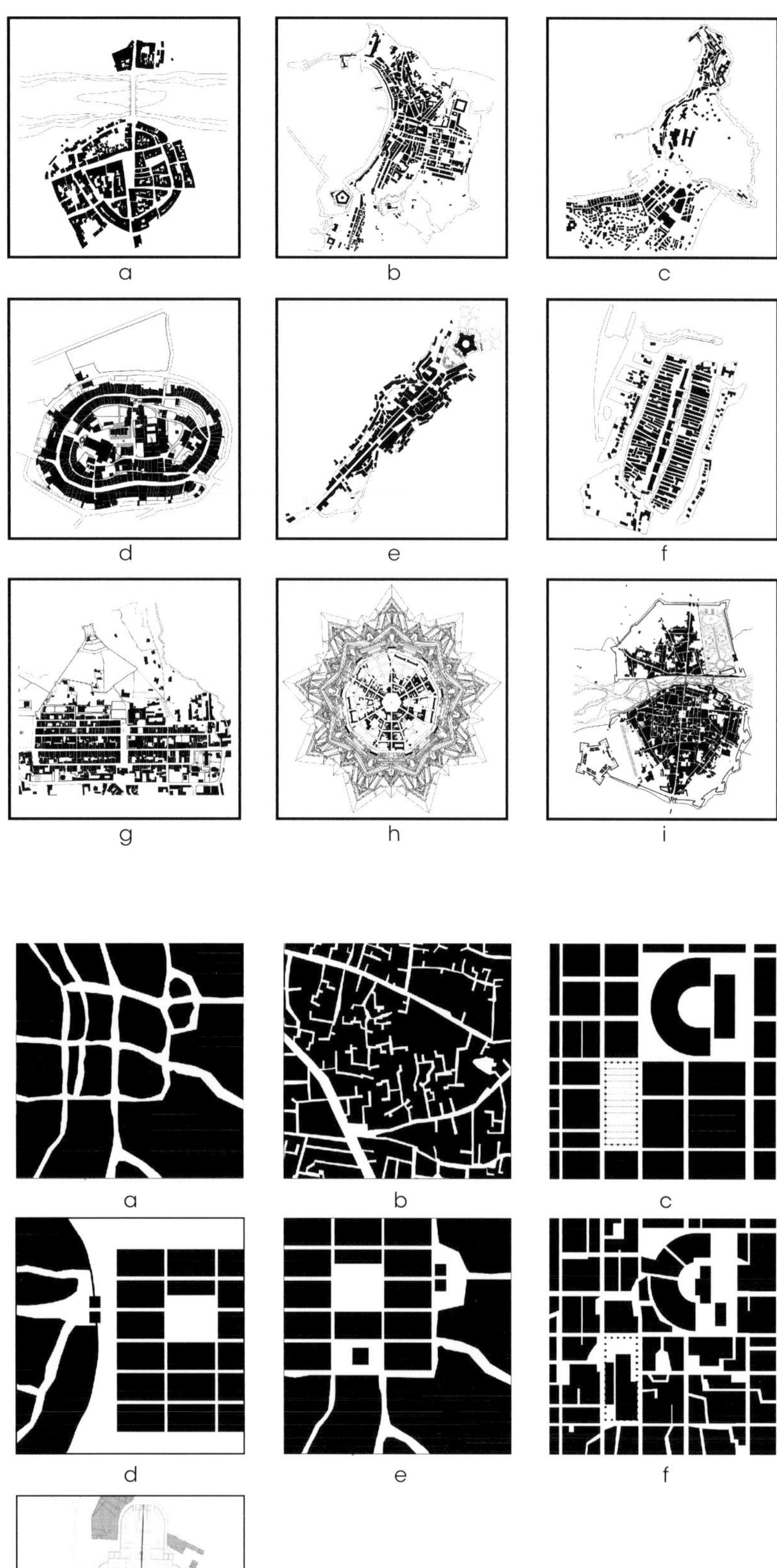

Above: Similar to a ruler used to measure personal space, large familiar spaces can be used to gauge the size of big urban spaces. Compare this piece of city fabric, Piazza Navona in Rome, to an American football field (160 ft. x 360 ft.) and an international football (soccer) field (90 m x 120 m).

Center top: Characteristic topographical and man-made circumstances for uban settlements and subsequent growth. a) riverbank origin; b) seafront; c) peninsular; d) hilltop; e) ridgetop; f) island; g) stepped hillside or flat open space; h) defensive wall as set constraint; i) a possible combination of any of the above.

Center bottom: Growth patterns for natural and planned cities (letters correspond to list in text).

designs. This procedure of study occurs through four methods: scale comparison, growth comparison over time, spatial sequency, and analysis. This book includes examples of these architectural elements, comparing, contrasting, and analyzing cities and their forming fabric with the intent of producing an urban atlas of historic city plans. It also enables the user to study a city plan, understand its influences or precedents as well as its unique characteristics, and, in due course, design better urban spaces. My research focused on gathering pertinent historic city plans. These original plans were drawn in various media, sizes, and scales. To facilitate an easy understanding of the drawings, I have redrawn every city plan to scale in a figure/ground format.[2]

The chapters of this book begin by explaining and illustrating the typological makeup and chronological typology of each phase of city structure throughout history, beginning with a series of ancient city plans and ending with proposals for modern cities. The appendix is meant to help in analysis and cross-reference.

Determinants for Urban Form and Setting

In *History of Urban Form: Before the Industrial Revolutions,* A. E. J. Morris says there are two types of urban form: organic and planned.[3] Rather than "organic," however, I prefer the term "natural." Natural urban form develops on its own, without predetermined intervention, while "planned" urban form results directly from intervention. Urban form originates in one of two ways: from the natural attributes of the area, including climate, topography, available building materials, and availability of permanent potable water; and from human intervention, including economics, politics, religion, or man-made property boundaries, defense, aggrandizement, rectilinear gridiron, urban mobility, aesthetics, legislation, urban infrastructure, social grouping, religious grouping, ethnic grouping, and leisure.

With an increase in population and changes in mechanization and transportation, the idea of city size we have today is much larger than the cities of our forefathers. London in 1300 had 100,000 people; in 1800, 960,000; and in 2000, 7,322,400. We typically define urban settings as the following:

- Hamlet has a population of fewer than 500.
- Village has a population of 500 or more.
- Town has a population of 5,000 or more.
- City has a population of 250,000 or more.
- Metropolis has a population of 2 million or more.
- Megalopolis has a population of 100 million or more.

In general there are nine topographical and man-made conditions for urban settlement and growth. Cities are formed on riverbanks, seafronts, peninsulas, hilltops, ridgetops, islands, hillsides, or open spaces, with defensive walls as a constraint, or in any combination of these.

The growth patterns for natural and planned cities are the following:

- Western European urbanism providing street frontage for plot development (a)
- Islamic urban form with housing on cul-de-sacs (b)
- Planned urban form employing the gridiron (c)
- Natural growth nucleus with planned gridiron extension (d)
- Planned gridiron nucleus with natural growth extension (e)
- Western European setting whereby an early medieval natural growth pattern is superimposed on the gridiron of a deserted Roman city (f)
- Complex of axial geometric spaces and forms that can be read on the outside as well as the inside (g)

Accurate Map Making of City Plans in History

One of the first precisely rendered city plans is the Forma Urbis Romae, an enormous map of Rome carved between 203 and 211 BC and measuring approximately 18 by 13 meters (60 by 43 feet). This plan, covering an entire wall inside the Templum in Rome, illustrated the ground plan of every architectural attribute in the ancient city—from large public monuments to small structures, rooms, and even staircases. Today only fragments of the plan exist.

The process of accurately recording a city in plan seems to have been dormant in the time between the Forma Urbis Romae and the beginning of the Renaissance, when Leonardo de Vinci, residing in Florence from 1501 to 1507, was commissioned to create a plan for Imola, Italy. It is said that Leonardo and his apprentices climbed the city towers and used a triangulation method for finding accurate points in space.

Included here are details of three city plans of Rome, representing the area around the Piazza Navona and the Pantheon. The first portion, drawn by Leonardo Buffalini in 1551, depicts both the outline of city blocks and in some cases the existing ground-floor plans. Compare this to the plan drawn by Giambattista

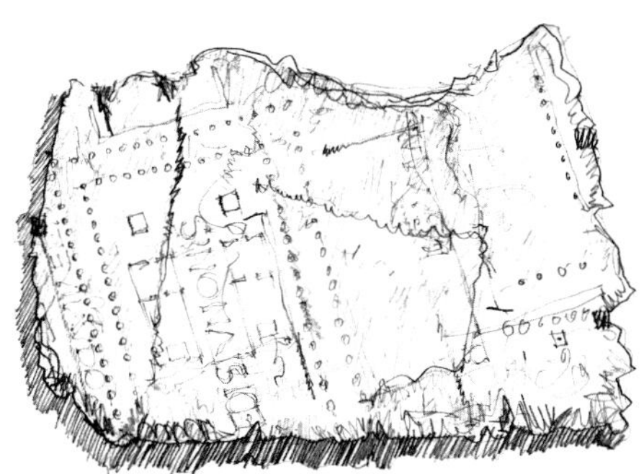

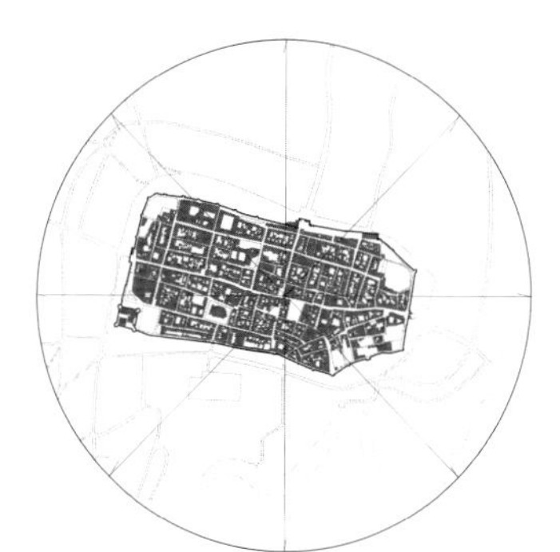

Far left: Sketch of a detail of the Forma Urbis Romae, carved ca. 203–211 AD.

Left: Town plan of Imola, Italy, based on a plan drawn by Leonardo da Vinci in 1502.

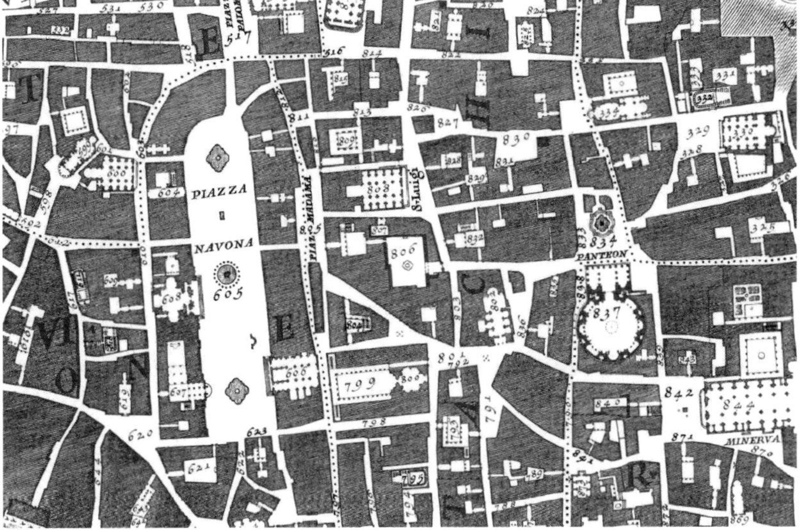

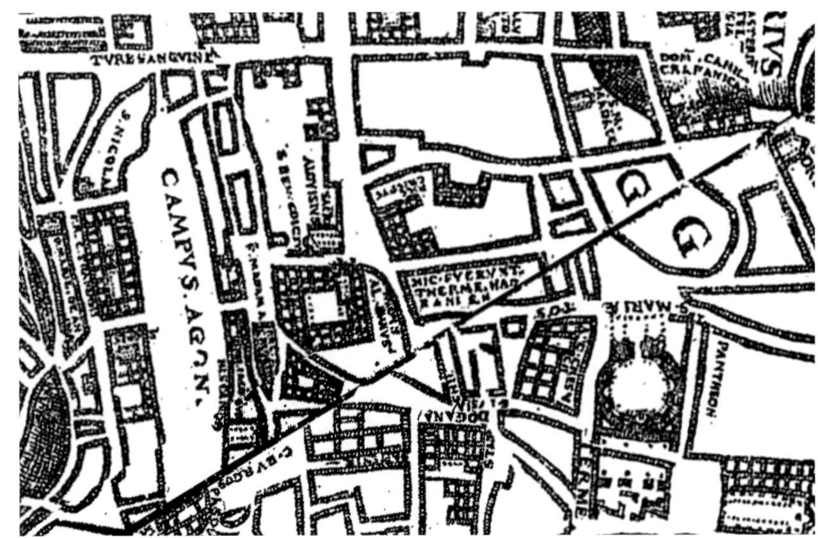

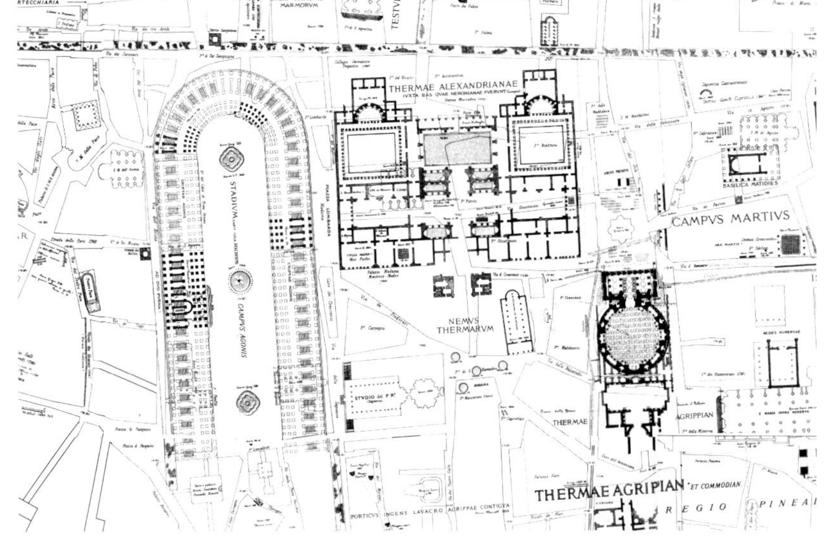

Top: Pianta di Roma, Giambattista Nolli (1748).

Center: Pianta di Roma, Leonardo Buffalini (1551).

Bottom: *Forma Urbis Romae,* Rodolfo Lanciani (1893–1901).

Nolli in 1748, where Nolli more accurately lays out the block footprints and records plans of buildings that were considered public/private spaces (such as churches, that were open to the public by day but locked at night). The open public urban space is shown as white, the semi-public/private space is rendered as ground-floor plans, and the private space appears as hatched form. The last plan in this series was drawn by Rodolfo Lanciani between 1893 and 1901 and is like an x-ray of Rome, showing three color-coded layers, with the ancient parts in black, the modern parts in red, and the planned changes delineated in thin blue lines.

The Choice of City Maps and Drawing Standards

Two major endeavors were integral in making this book. First was the research and collection of city plans. These plans had to be accurate and were typically dated prior to World War II so that the early fabric of these cities, before they were destroyed and rebuilt, could be investigated. Second, I had to redraw all the city plans to establish a common ground for comparison. The sources for the city plans varied, but two examples are Karl Baedeker's travel guides (ca. 1909) and an atlas published by the Society of Diffusion for Useful Knowledge (ca. 1840).

The city fabric can be broken into many conditions, but since this book deals with city plans, or two-dimensional images, it does not address the three-dimensional aspects, such as skylines and raised or terraced urban settings. These plans represent the following drawing types in this book:

- Outline of the block as a solid mass
- Outline of the block with a division of property lines
- Footprint of the buildings with possible property divisions and foliage (as a gray mass)
- Footprint of the buildings with key public and private buildings shown in ground plan, possible property division, and foliage (as a gray mass) (City plans with buildings shown in ground plan are commonly known as Nolli plans)

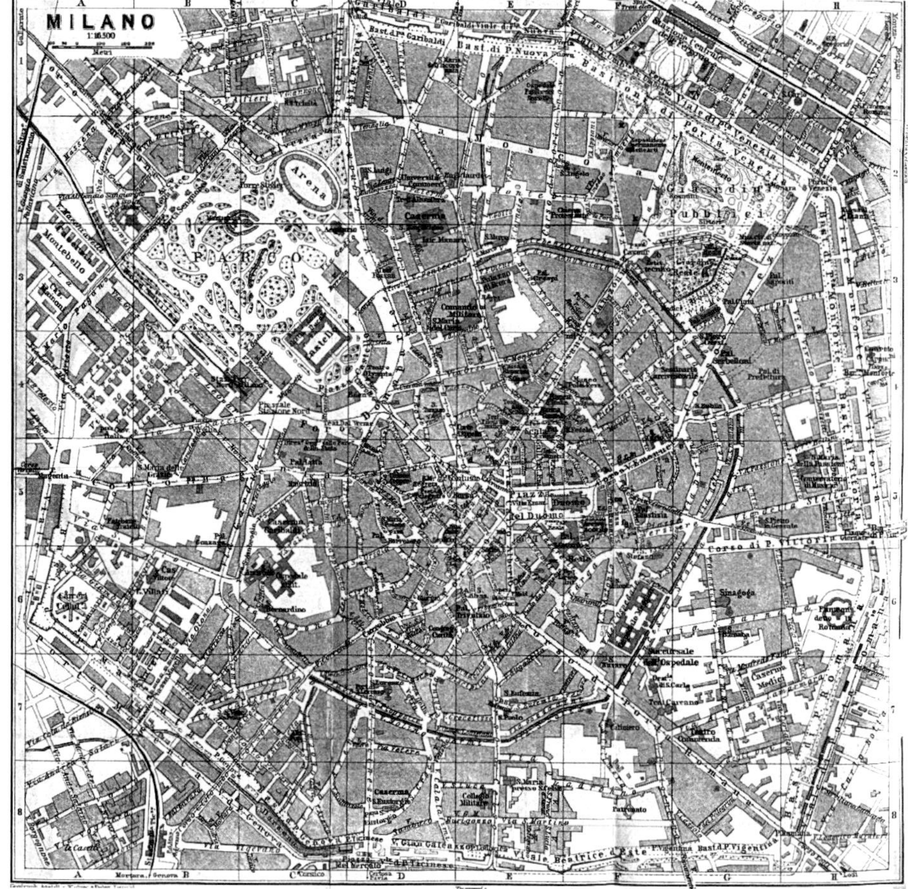

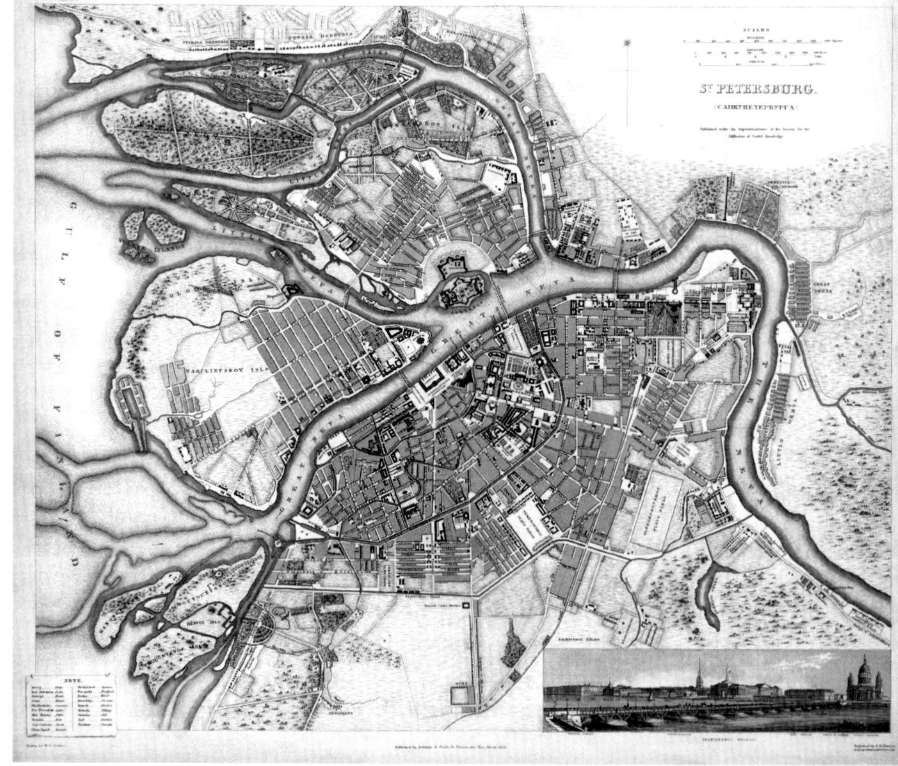

Top right: Milan, as depicted in *Baedeker's Travel Guides: Central Italy* (1913).

Bottom right: A plan of St. Petersburg, Russia, that appeared in an atlas published by the Society of Diffusion for Useful Knowledge (1834).

a

b

c

d

The drawing standards in this book are based on one of the following types: (a) outline of the block as a solid mass; (b) outline of the block with a division of property lines; (c) the footprint of the buildings with possible property divisions and foliage (as a gray mass); and (d) footprint of the buildings (with key public/private buildings shown in ground plan, commonly referred to as Nolli plans) with possible property division and foliage (as a gray mass).

Notes

1. "The Background of L'Enfant's Plan" and "The Genealogy of L'Enfant's Design of Washington" are reprinted in *On the Art of Designing Cities: Selected Essays of Elbert Peets,* ed. Paul D. Spreiregen (Cambridge, Mass.: MIT Press, 1968).

2. To understand the intrinsic advantage of the figure/ground as a comparative analytical drawing device, read Wayne Cooper, "The Figure/Ground," *Cornell Journal of Architecture* 2 (1982): 42–53.

3. A. E. J. Morris, *History of Urban Form : Before the Industrial Revolutions* (Harlow, England: Longman Scientific and Technical, 1994), 9–18.

Historical Typologies for Urban Settings

Imbedded in the following discussion of urban history, and, importantly, depicted at the bottom of each of the city plans, are twenty-eight typological icons representing various periods in the history of urban design and planning. These simple drawn icons allow the user to identify the plan's historical period and to cross-reference it against the Appendix, where all the city plans (in print and on the CD) are listed alphabetically and with the appropriate period icon.

Early Cities

Before 10,000 BC, humans were hunters and gatherers who sought shelter in natural formations. Later, in the proto-Neolithic and Neolithic periods, when humans began cultivating land and tending animals, they moved to permanent settlements, or villages. Around 3,500–3,000 BC, during the Bronze Age, the first urban civilizations were established. These higher cultures grew around functions of "socio-political or religious control; [their] chief purpose was to enhance the power of various leaders and institutions by demonstrating their jurisdiction over segments of domestic and ceremonial space."[1]

Planning in the early villages (10,000–3,500 BC) was a result of "distributing power among social institutions (lineages, council of elders, secret societies, etc.)."[2] The village community consisted of perhaps three to thirty families, possibly related, who used land, sometimes held communally, for cultivation and pasturage. This community type probably began in what is now Iraq and Iran, and its formation seems to have corresponded with the transformation of nomadic hunting to agriculture. The archetypal village was small, with homes situated together for sociability and defense, and surrounding land was farmed.[3]

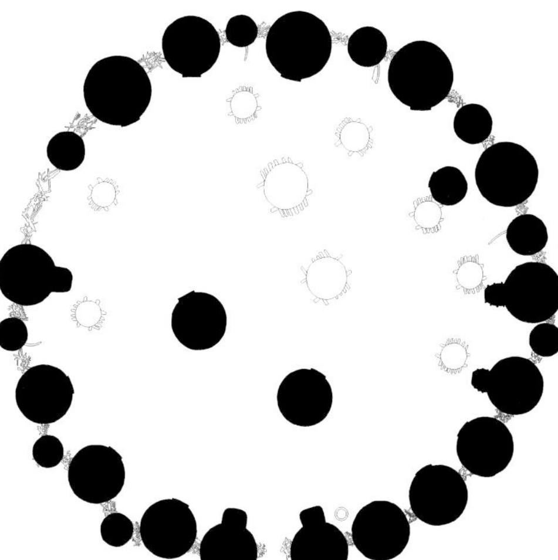

Right: Plan of Massa Homestead, Cameroon.

Left: Plan of Batoufam Village, Cameroon.

Early permanent villages varied depending on the setting. Although it may be imprudent to categorize these early settlements, it is possible to see a structure in their layout. One of the most common shapes was a circle, as found in Cameroon, and another was a clustering, with the central cluster typically delegated to the head of the village and his immediate family. Without a written record from the period, experts cannot determine whether this shape occurred due to some symbolic relationship or whether it was just a natural phenomenon.[4]

One criterion of a city is that it is a place of permanence. Many historians view human burial places as the first cities, because this was the only place where early,

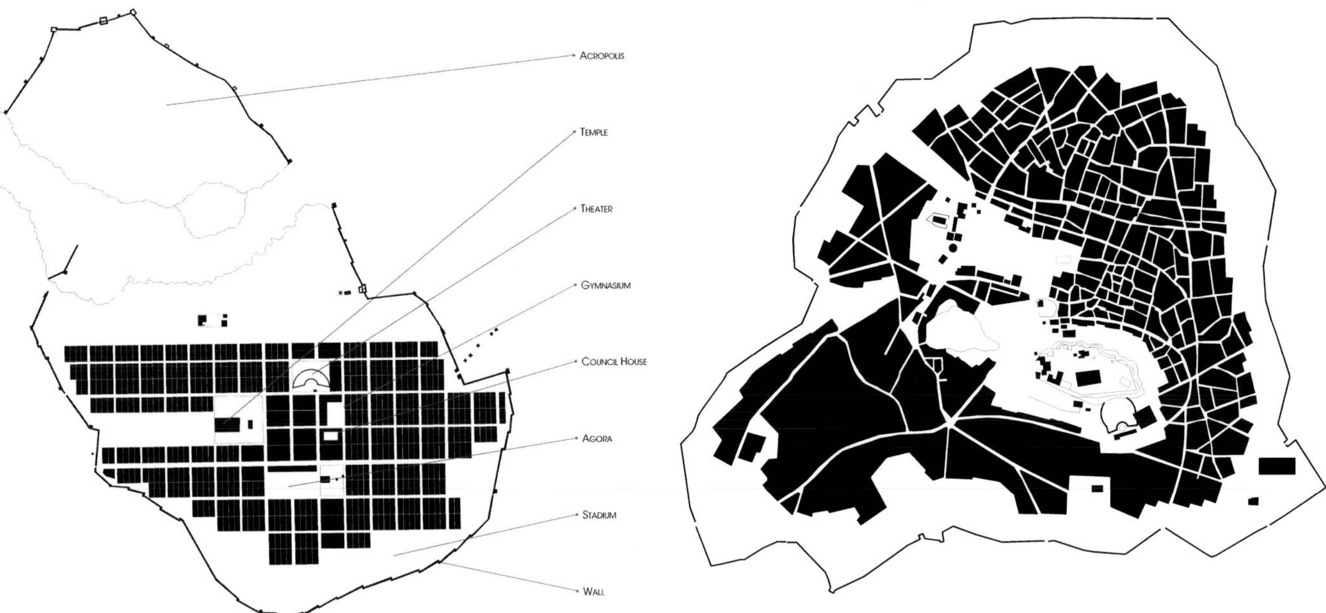

Top left: Plan of ancient Athens, with the Acropolis located in the white area toward the center.

Top right: Plan of Priene depicts various elements that make up the structure of a typical Greek colonial town.

nomadic man paused permanently. Aldo Rossi, a twentieth-century Italian architect, defined the city not only as a place of permanence but also as a locus of memory. If one accepts this definition, then the burial ground can be interpreted as a city, for it is a place of permanence, a place that marks the remembrance of the dead.

Greek Cities

There are generally two types of Greek cities: the parent, free-form type and the colonial city. Parent cities lacked an overall definite layout, whereas colonial cities were built on a structured, preplanned grid. Typically, both parent and colonial cities had a central area, an acropolis, that was located on an elevation, or plateau, and acted as a natural fortification. These sites, classically located on a natural rock citadel, contained temples and offered refuge from attack. Houses were built around the plateau and spread outward from the rock fortress. Eventually a surrounding wall was built and the settlement became a fortified town. “The Acropolis was the core of the town, and the town was the core of the city-state, which included both town and country.”[5]

A movement toward colonial cities occurred when the parent cities became too crowded to house all of their occupants. The Mediterranean coasts were the perfect sites for these Greek new towns. Although the parent cities were situated inland for protection, the emerging preference was for towns by the sea, allowing for easy trade and permitting escape in an emergency. Hippodamus was the first known city planner to introduce an orderly gridiron plan for building colonial Greek towns. This plan type provided an orderliness and expediency to the layout and construction that had been absent before. Colonial cities contained all the basic elements of a Greek city: walls, temples, theater, gymnasium, numerous official buildings, and the Agora, or gathering place. The wall layout generally followed the lay of the land and was usually irregular in shape.

The plan for the colonial city occurred from the inside out, a major difference from the later Roman grid-plan town. The Greeks began by laying out the grid of their streets and ended by constructing the walls, whereas the Romans began with the layout and construction of the walls and then proceeded with the street plans.

Roman

Imperial

While the Roman legion town was typically constructed using an orthogonal grid and laid out as a whole city unit, classical Rome was built over time from monumental buildings of formal geometric design. Both types of towns were influenced by their typography, but, while the Roman legion town was typically built on a flat terrain, the city of Rome conformed to its famous seven hills, weaving in, out, and over the land.

Imperial Roman style is a separate design entity, different from colonial towns and the towns from the Greek culture. It is a complex of geometric forms, allow-

Right: The Baths of Caracalla shown in a model of Rome at the time of Constantine, ca. 212–216 AD, as seen in the Museum of Roman Culture, Rome.

Far right: Imperial Rome constructed after a plan by Luigi Canina (1795–1856).

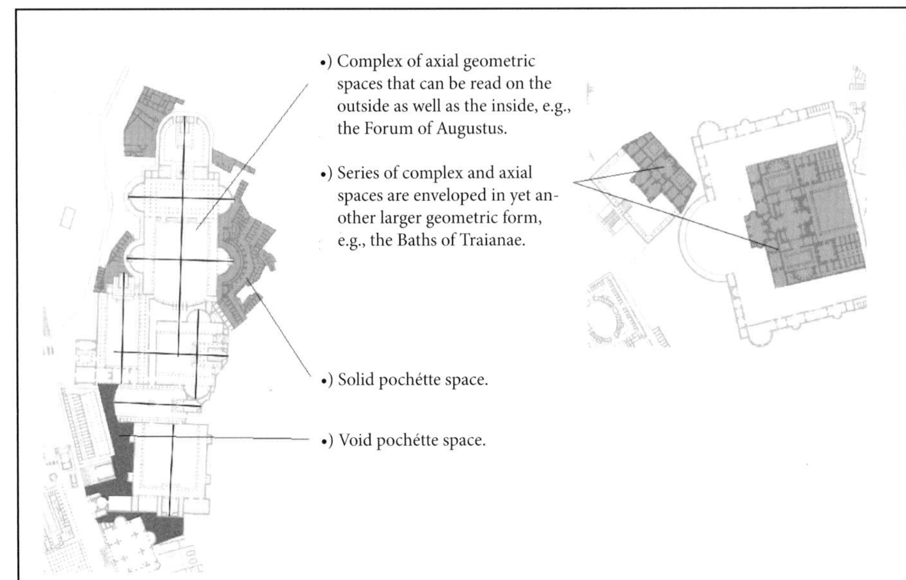

Bottom right: Monumental geometric forms within imperial Rome relate to each other on axial terms and create fields or zones of buildings.

ing for a multidirectional layout that conforms to the terrain of shifting valleys and peaks. To understand its geometric structure, one can study the two types of imperial Roman monuments. The first is a series of axial geometric spaces that can be seen on the outside as well as the inside (e.g., the Forum). The second structure is similar to the first, but the series of complex axial spaces is enveloped in yet another larger geometric form, giving the reading that the interior spaces are carved, verses the first type, which are added. These shapes can either stand alone or be knit together. The monumental geometric forms relate to each other on axial terms, creating fields, or zones, of buildings. Where these fields intersect, they create seemingly leftover, unordered space, which at times becomes either solid or void poché, or space.

Legion Towns

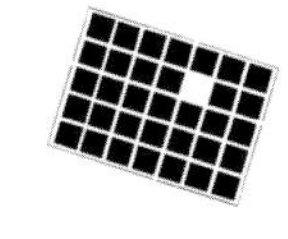

Roman legion towns, or *castra,* began to develop as the Roman Empire expanded its borders beyond the city of Rome. Roman legion towns were typically in the shape of a rectangle or square for purposes of defense. A town in the shape of a circle allowed an attacking army to concentrate their forces equally, while a rectilinear shape required the attacking army to divide its troops. Roman towns, however, were not usually created for defensive reasons but for offensive ones. As the empire grew, outposts had to be established to protect the conquered land. Though economic and political reasons customarily determined the location, also important were straight, flat roads so that people could easily approach one of the city's four gates.

The grid design is usually attributed to the Greeks, but in the Bronze Age, circa 1400–800 BC, between the Po River and the Apennine Mountains there existed more than 100 settlements planned on a grid. One of the largest of these was Terramara of Castallazzo di Fontanellato, located just west of Parma. This village was rectilinear and had two major cross streets with an internal open area that is similar to the forum found in the later Roman legion towns.

As the Romans began to expand their territory and sent out their legions, they set up campsites in the region in which they planned to focus their conquest. For expediency, they followed a set plan. These campsites were typically the foundations for more permanent settlements.

Permanent urban settlements, nearly always located near a water source, tended to follow a set of guidelines for design and layout. The shape, typically rectilinear, varied in size depending on the importance of the settlement. Located within the rectangle were two cross streets—the *decumanus,* running east and west, and the *cardo,* running north and south—which formed the infrastructure for the street organization. At or near the street intersection was the forum. Secondary streets completed the grid structure and formed blocks called *insulae.* Elements of the typical Roman legion town included: a wall with a series of towers, four gates, the

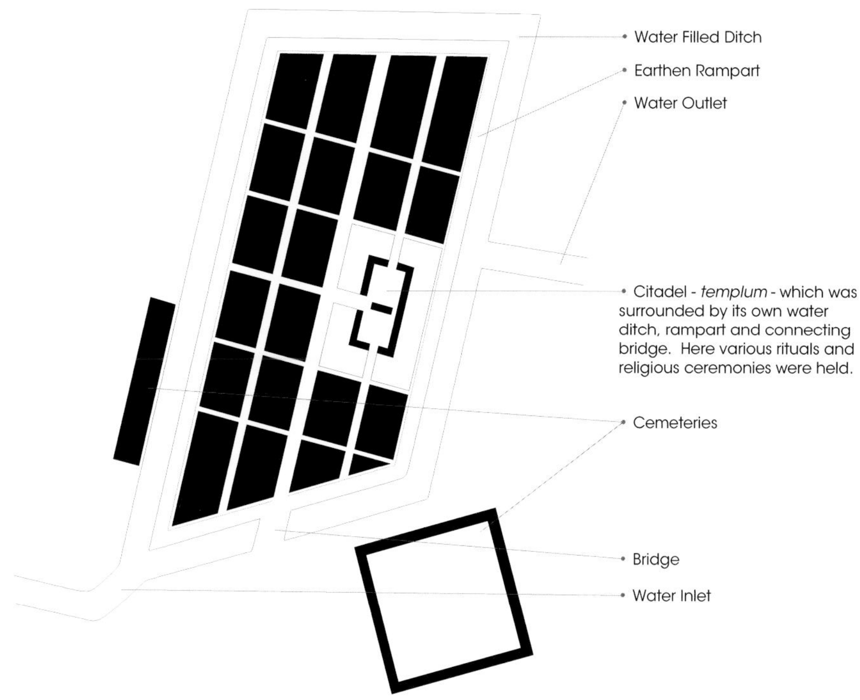

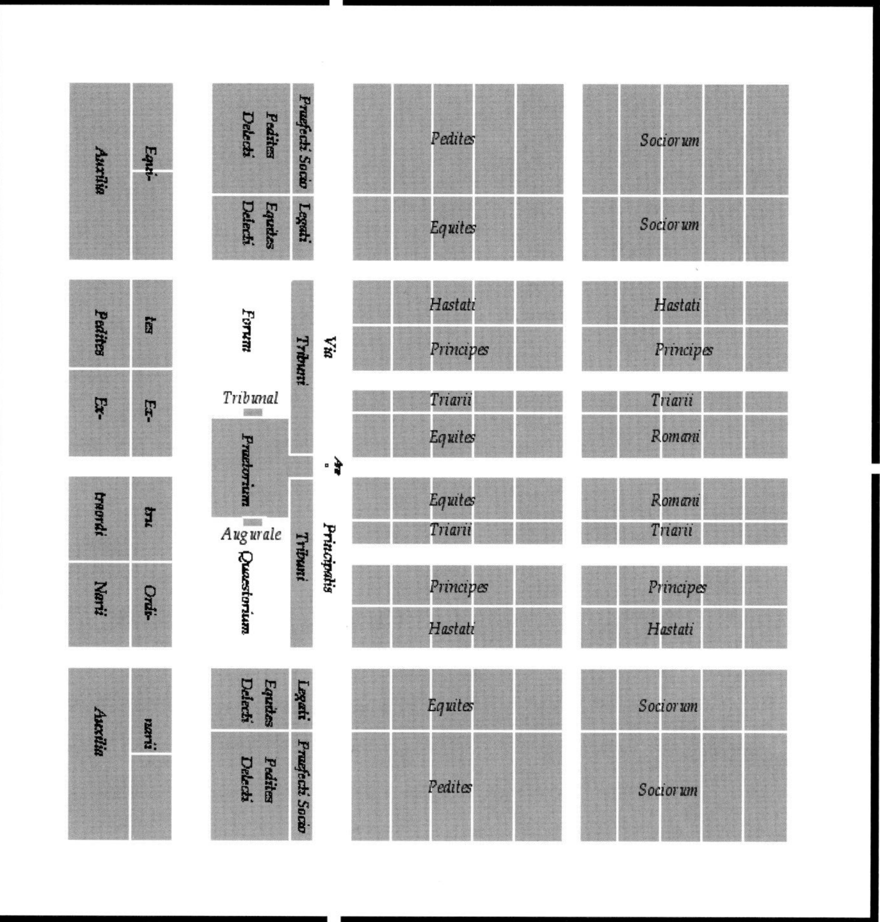

Top: Plan of Terramara of Castallazzo di Fontanellato, located just west of Parma, Italy.

Left: Typical Roman military encampment as described by Polybius, ca. 203–120 BC.

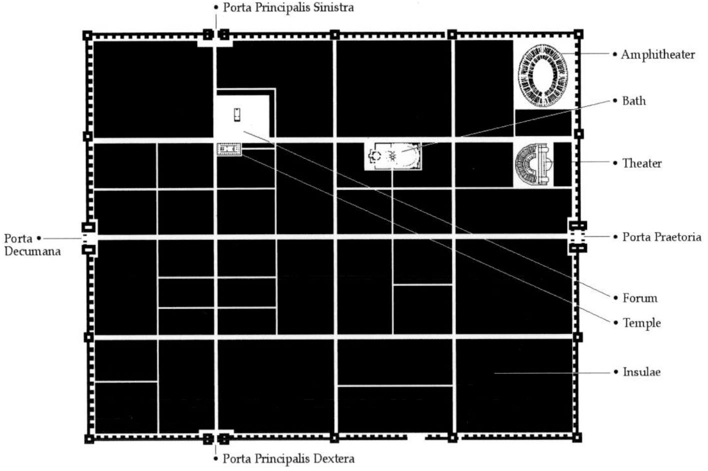

Top left: Typical layout of a Roman legion town depicting various city elements.

Top right: Plan of Arezzo, Italy, 1909, illustrates the original Roman town in black. Note the unstructured shape.

Bottom right: Plan of Como, Italy, 1950, shows the city conforming to the lake. The lake on the north side of the town is oriented toward the north-west.

cardo and *decumanus, insulae,* forum, temples, theater, public bath, and, located either inside or outside the walls, an amphitheater and coliseum.

The layout of Roman legion towns was not random; it was based on long-standing beliefs. The Romans, as early as the Etruscans, believed that two axes, crossing each other at right angles, divided the heavens into four parts. The intersecting axes pointed toward the four cardinal points, with the *cardo* stretching from the north to south and the *decumanus* from east to west. A city conceived and laid out according to this division, or *templum,* was considered sacred, and all Roman cities were built accordingly, although city planners did not always strictly follow the rectilinear form.[6] The layout was not always on a true north-south grid, and at times the town structure appeared almost amorphous in shape. The town of Como, for example, conforms to the water's edge and Arezzo to the hills.

The Romans followed a grid system for laying out the towns and the countryside as well. The common unit of measurement for the countryside was a square called a *centuria quadrata,* with each side measuring 20 *actus* (776 yards). The area, 200 *jugera* (0.75 acre), corresponded to the amount of land a man and two oxen could plow in one day. The Romans clung to this formula, which restricted their freedom and forced them into an endless repetition of the same plan. There were three types of Roman legion towns:

- *Coloniae,* either newly formed or native settlements allied to Rome with full Roman privilege and status;
- *Municipia,* generally important tribal centers with formal Roman status but whose residents had only partial rights of Roman citizenship; and
- *Civitas,* administration and market centers for minor districts, which were designed in the castra shape.

Non-Western Urbanism

According to Stefano Bianca, "In every genuine cultural tradition, architecture and urban form can be seen as natural expression of prevailing spiritual values and beliefs, which are intimately related to the microcosmos of man-made material structures." He contends that it is not important if these arise out of traditions and daily practices that relate to spiritual principles, but that it is a reflection of "the difference between consciously planned, often 'monumental' works of art, and the more modest vernacular architecture built by the inhabitants themselves or by anonymous craftsmen."[7] This idea is important in studying non-Western urban forms, which fall into three general categories, or regions: the Arab world, India, and China.

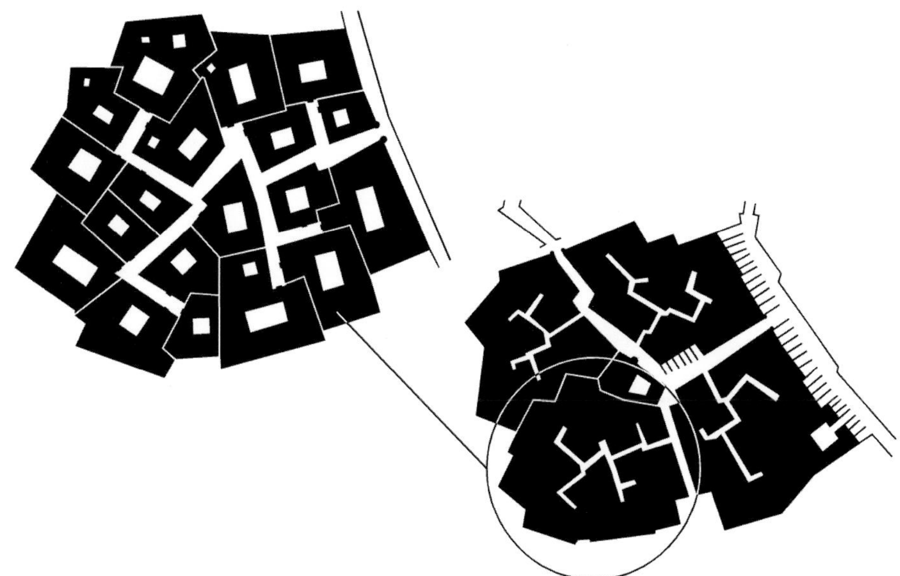

A common structure of a residential area in a predominantly Muslim African city that is composed of individual accessible cluster units. Note the market stalls along the main road at right and a pocket of stalls just inside the residential area. The detail shows a typical cluster of courtyard houses built around a dead-end alley.

The Arab World

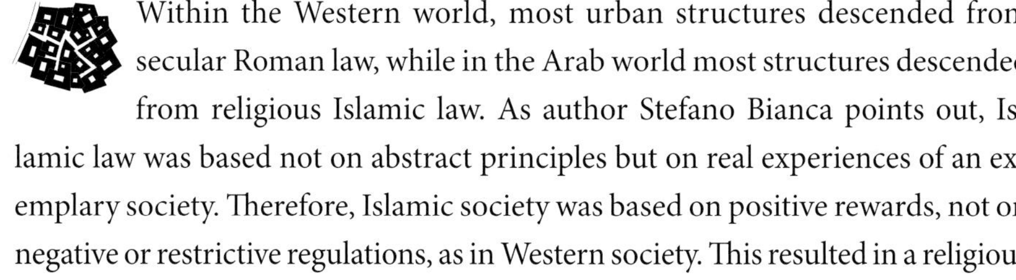

Within the Western world, most urban structures descended from secular Roman law, while in the Arab world most structures descended from religious Islamic law. As author Stefano Bianca points out, Islamic law was based not on abstract principles but on real experiences of an exemplary society. Therefore, Islamic society was based on positive rewards, not on negative or restrictive regulations, as in Western society. This resulted in a religious society with social customs that set the "liturgy of daily life."[8]

With the religious- and social-based society of Islam, the structured order begins with the family and works its way to the community at large. By contrast, Western society's structure starts with the governing body and works its way to the family. In the Arab world, the family head is the religious leader of his domestic community. This makes the physical "cell of the house virtually independent from any intermediate civic or religious institution."[9] In the end, there is no need for dominant civic institutions in the Arab world since governing typically takes place at the mosque.

The Islamic attitude toward religious and social organizations, combined with an appreciation of the tribal and family structure, determines the structure of sacred space. "On the one hand, the religious building of the mosque is fully integrated into the social life and the architectural fabric of the town and fulfills comprehensive civic functions. On the other hand, the private home has acquired a degree of sacredness, which is probably unique in comparison with other civilizations."[10] The religious structures are not located in one area, nor are they typically isolated monumental forms; they are integrated into the urban fabric (much like urban monasteries in the West).

In traditional Muslim cities, "the architectural fabric tends to be continuous, i.e. undisrupted by massive freestanding religious or public buildings or by major open spaces highlighting individual monuments. [I]t also shows a clear internal differentiation into a series of self-contained cellular compartments, which allow the private or sacred character of individual spaces to be protected where and when needed. As a rule, the public spaces lack the rigid layout, which is imposed by highly formalized institutions, allowing for a high degree of interaction between various social activities, including religious functions."[11] Markets usually flank the mosque complex, forming an urban core and making it easy to move back and forth for the daily prayer sessions.

In traditional Islamic cities, the residential quarters are typically located off the main public square. Each of the houses, commonly built wall to wall, has its own courtyard and is screened from the street or neighboring buildings. Access from the public areas to residential quarters is broken down into hierarchical segments that add to the level of residential privacy. The streets leading away from the markets and squares become less trafficked the further you move out of the public space. The residential areas are typically dense and void of much detail, and the streets are usually dead-ends, adding to a sense of privacy and safety for the residents.

In the Islamic urban setting, the religious culture concerning public versus private space results in cities that do not employ more Western plans that feature large avenues and public spaces. According to Bianca, "The prevailing attitude was to transform anonymous quantitative space into personalized qualitative space by defining and enclosing a multitude of self-contained individual volumes and developing them from within, in ways that made them virtually autonomous. The coordination between single units occurred implicitly through the inner affinity of their structuring principles, and not through outer geometric arrangements." And the interiors of residences reflected this attitude as well, featuring "a cellular

The Vástupurusamandala according to sixteenth-century Brihat Samhita.

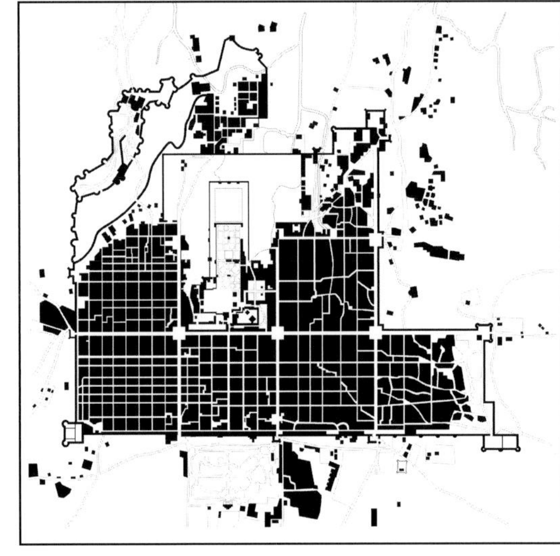

Jaipur, India, built ca. 1727 AD by Maharaja Sawai Jai Singh with Vidyadhar Bhattacharya, who formalized the city's plans in the grid system. The wide, straight streets and uniform rows of shops on either side of main bazaars were arranged in nine rectangular city sectors (*chokris*) in accordance with the principles of town planning set down in the *Shilpa Shastra,* an epochal treatise on Hindu architecture.

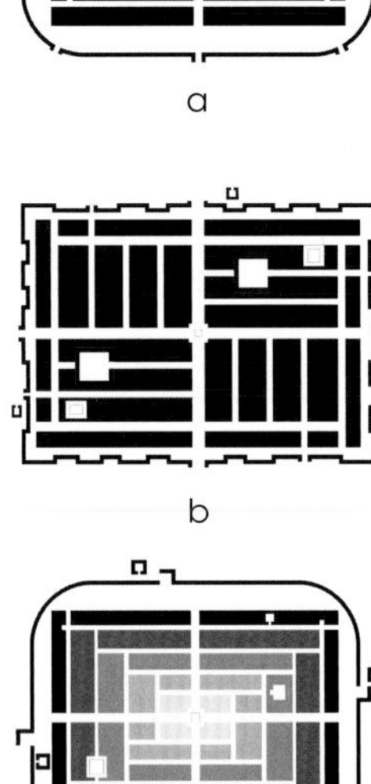

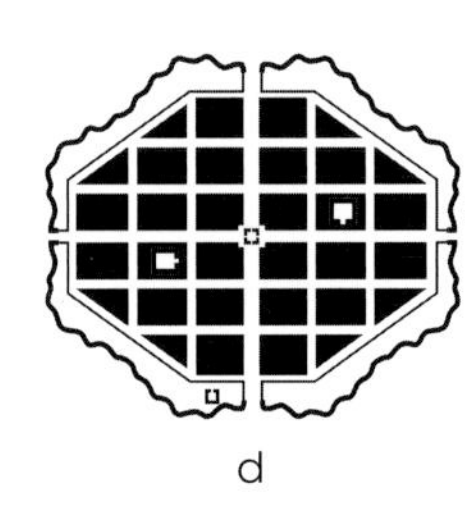

Above: Four of the eight village plan types specified by the Manasara Silpastra: (a) Dandaka; (b) Swasuka; (c) Padmaka; (d) Nandyavarta.

aggregation process [that] allowed the main reception rooms to become almost autonomous, self-centered shells and create 'houses' within the house." Both internally and externally, the Arab residential model is designed to restrict access and enhance privacy.[12]

India

In India the square symbolizes the Earth. The four corners represent either the cardinal directions—north, south, east, and west—or the sunrise and sunset and the two ends of the Earth's axis. The square is divided into nine equal parts and those nine are again subdivided into another nine, so that eighty-one parts exist in all. This diagram, the Vástupurusamandala, is one of the foundations for laying out a city plan in India and pays homage to Brahma, the Hindu god of creation.[13]

Urban Form and the Chinese Setting

In ancient China the *Hung fan,* or the Great Plan, specified the five elements and the five numbers that the (mythical) dynastic emperor Yü received from Heaven. Yü then measured and divided the Earth into nine regions. This diagram, one square divided into nine sections, underlies much of Chinese divination and remains a standard method of surveying Chinese town plans.[14]

Another form of divination, estimated to be more than 3,000 years old, is feng shui, or wind and water, the ancient practice of placement to achieve harmony with the environment and the forces of nature. Traditional feng shui is an ancient Chinese belief system that addresses the layout of cities, villages, dwellings, and buildings.[15] I. M. Pei grappled with feng shui when he designed a bank in Hong Kong in 1982. Many neighbors complained about Pei's bank, saying it looked like a cleaver ready to hack its banking competitors. One rival, the Hong Kong and Shanghai Bank, constructed two structures on top of its building, which looked like cannons pointed at Pei's bank, to counteract negative influences.[16] Even today there are architects in China who follow the feng shui principles in designing buildings.

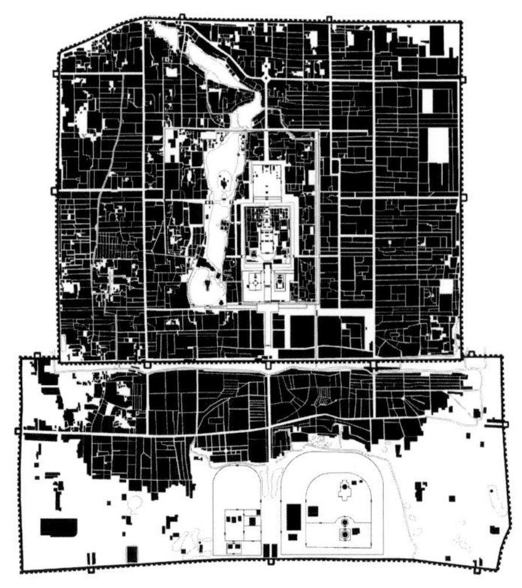

Right: Plan of Beijing, China, showing the use of the orthogonal grid in its makeup. At the plan's center is the Forbidden Palace.

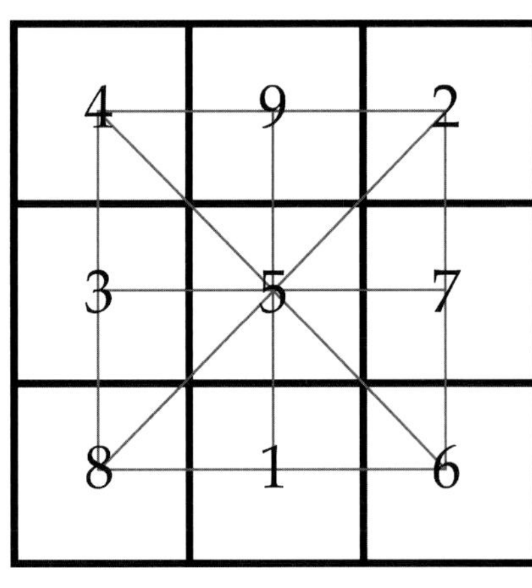

Far right: A nine-fold square is used in Chinese divination in the laying out of a city plan. Any line of three numbers adds up to 15.

Medieval Cities

No purely medieval cities survive today, but designers can study plans from the period to understand what they were like. Types of medieval cities included early cities built on the fabric of existing decaying Roman cities; settlements founded on existing strongholds or religious institutions; village settlements; and medieval new towns.

Existing Ancient Sites

A large number of early medieval towns grew out of the surviving physical organization of an existing town. The population was diminishing, mainly due to the lack of protection by the ruling Romans. Because of the risk of attacks, manufacture and trade shrank, and the urban settings transformed from places of production and exchange to places of consumption. These situations led to urban stagnation throughout Western Europe and to a diminishing population in various cities.[17] In Rome, for example, in the waning days of the empire, the aqueducts deteriorated so that by the end of the sixth century the city was in disrepair and ruin and people were forced to use water from the Tiber River. Also, without protection from a strong army, the diminished population moved out of vulnerable Rome and began to settle on the plain of Mars.

Other medieval settlements grew around an existing stronghold, such as a castle or citadel, or a religious site, such as a monastery. A good example is the monastery at Assisi, which served as the nucleus with the city growing out from it.[18]

The series of city edges as Florence, Italy, developed over time.

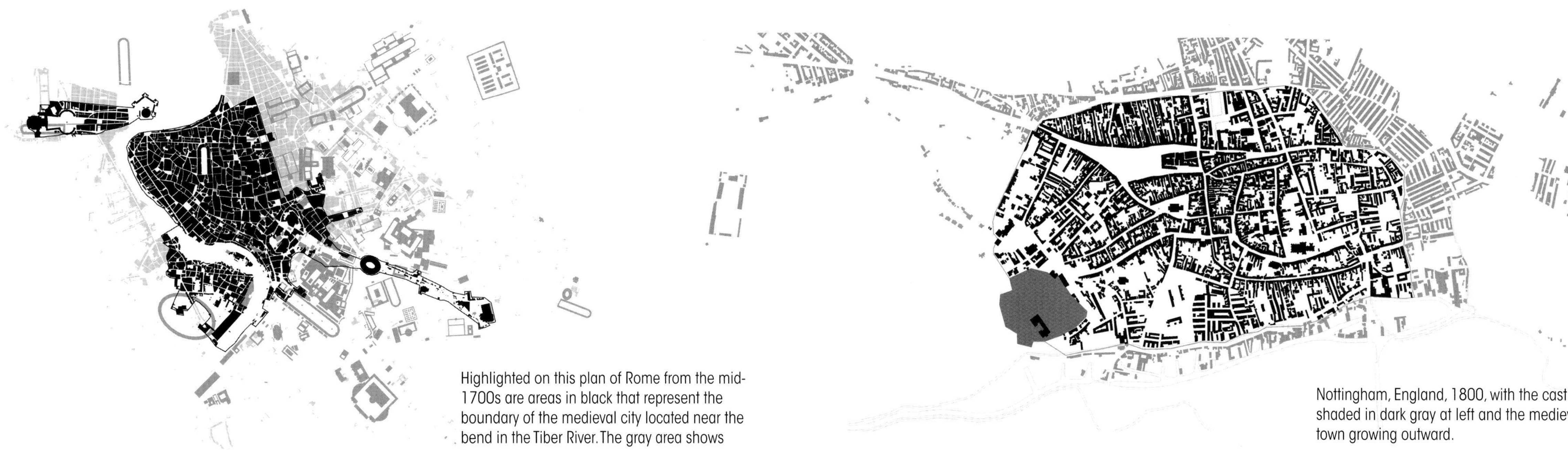

Highlighted on this plan of Rome from the mid-1700s are areas in black that represent the boundary of the medieval city located near the bend in the Tiber River. The gray area shows imperial Rome.

Nottingham, England, 1800, with the castle shaded in dark gray at left and the medieval town growing outward.

Example of an enclosed village, or a nucleated or squared village. Also depicted here is a medieval village with linear gardens located behind the dwellings, which surround the main square.

Example of a linear village, or street or roadside village.

Example of a dispersed or disintegrated village.

Village Settlements

A. E. J. Morris identifies three types of village settlements: enclosed villages, also known as nucleated or squared villages; linear villages, also known as street or roadside villages; and dispersed or disintegrated villages.[19]

Pure examples of these villages rarely exist. Typically, medieval settlements consisted of a combination of these three villages. A vital characteristic of the village type was the linear garden located behind each dwelling. These gardens frequently amounted to a small farm and in many instances were approached from the rear by an access lane.

New Towns

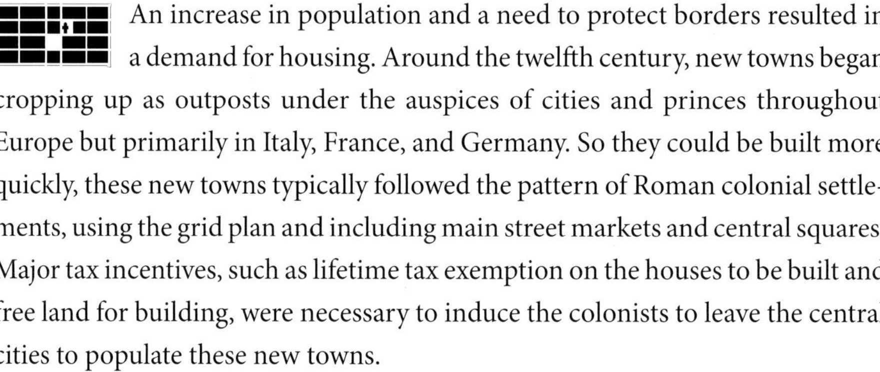

An increase in population and a need to protect borders resulted in a demand for housing. Around the twelfth century, new towns began cropping up as outposts under the auspices of cities and princes throughout Europe but primarily in Italy, France, and Germany. So they could be built more quickly, these new towns typically followed the pattern of Roman colonial settlements, using the grid plan and including main street markets and central squares. Major tax incentives, such as lifetime tax exemption on the houses to be built and free land for building, were necessary to induce the colonists to leave the central cities to populate these new towns.

The primary urban fabrics making up a medieval town included walls, gates and towers, faubourgs, bridgeheads, public and private space, institutions and urban scale public buildings, cathedrals, parishes, monasteries, hospices/hospitals, and universities. In some cases, monasteries, hospices/hospitals, and universities were in one complex and operated by one group, such as by monks.

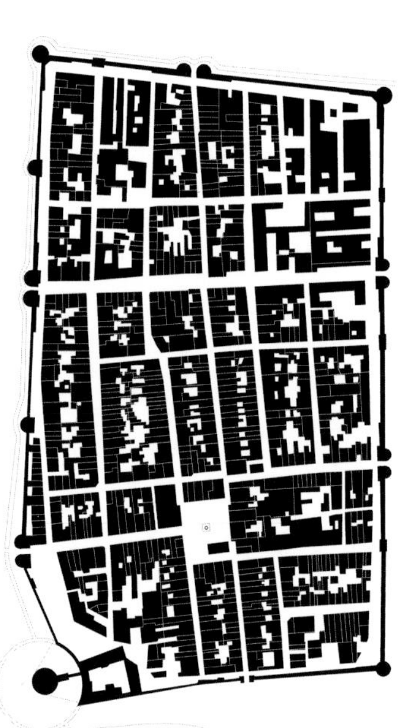

Aigues-Mortes, an example of a French medieval new town.

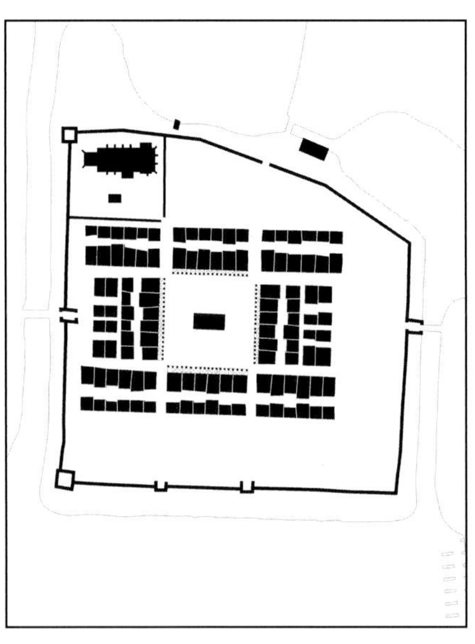

Friedland, an example of a German medieval new town.

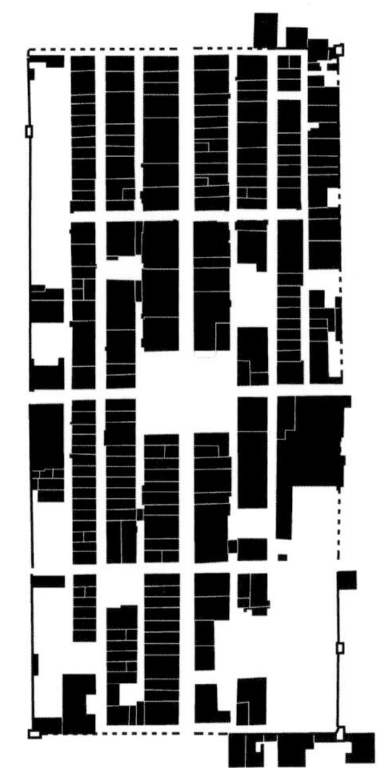

Terranuova Bracciolini, an example of an Italian medieval new town.

Renaissance

Six broad areas of urban planning were employed during the Renaissance: ideal city designs; fortification systems; new public spaces and streets; new main streets and artery systems that extended and connected on a regional level; new districts; and new towns.[20] Within these typologies are three main foundations for design: primary straight streets, gridiron-based districts, and enclosed urban spaces.[21]

One of the key tools that influenced the urban design of the Renaissance was the introduction of perspective. In the medieval period, the organization of the buildings, which bordered the street most typically, was haphazard and found the structures competing for space. The Renaissance street, in contrast, resembled a stage set, with buildings composed to enhance the perspectival view and designed as a whole architecture.

Early-twentieth-century photo of a medieval street common to Western Europe.

The set design for "Tragic Scene" by Sabastiano Serlio. From *Five Books of Architecture* (1537).

This copper engraving shows a perspective view of Strada Nuova in Genoa, ca. late 1700s. Begun in 1551, this avenue exemplifies the ideal Renaissance street.

Marsala, France, is an example of residential districts added to the existing urban fabric.

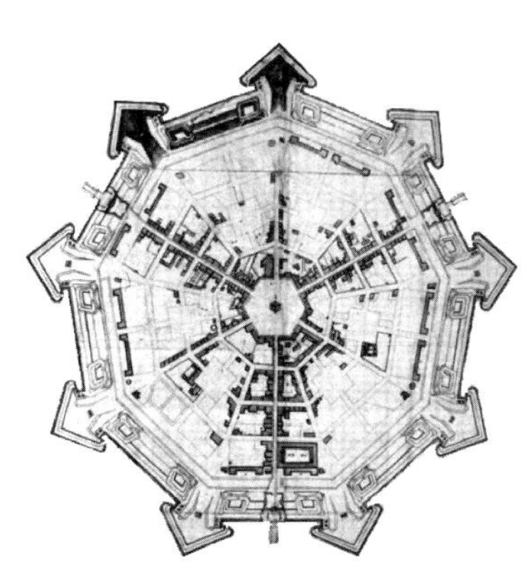

Palma Nova, Italy, is an example of an entire layout of a new Renaissance city.

Bari, Italy, is an example of an existing primary street system used to create a new urban area.

The gridiron, the most common form of urban design in the Renaissance, falls into three categories: the addition of residential districts to the existing urban fabric, the layout of a new Renaissance city, and the combination of an existing primary street system to create a new urban area.

A. E. J. Morris identifies three categories of enclosed urban spaces at that time: traffic space, residential space, and pedestrian traffic. Traffic space, which formed part of the urban route system for pedestrians and horse-drawn vehicles, was characteristically located at main intersections of primary streets. Residential space, intended for local traffic and foot traffic, often contained a monumental object and was usually restricted to the wealthy. Pedestrian traffic, which excluded wheeled traffic, generally served as public assembly areas for important civic, religious, or royal buildings.[22]

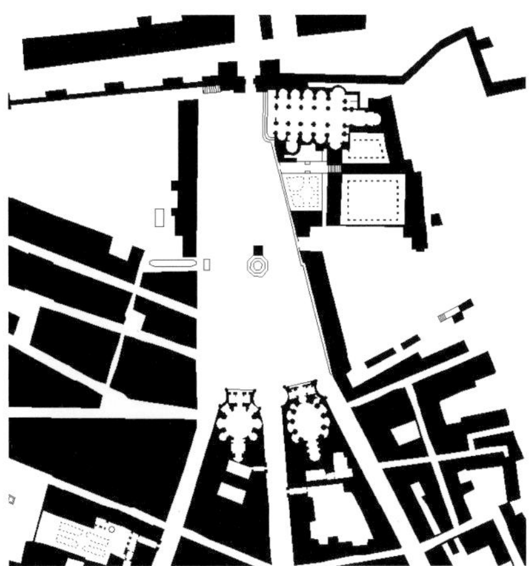

Piazza del Popolo, Rome, ca. 1585. The shape derived from placing the Egyptian obelisk where trident streets meet.

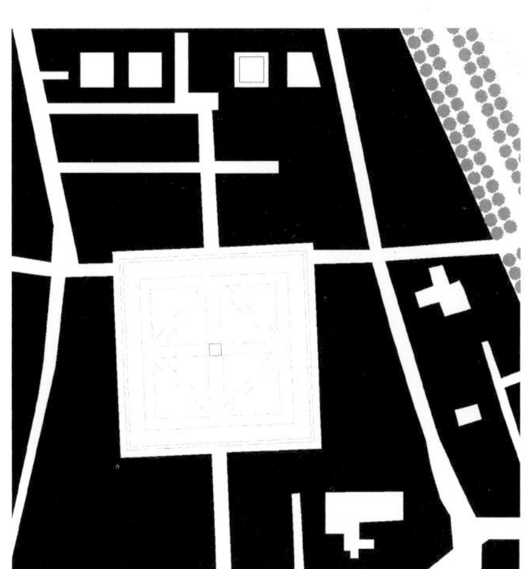

Place des Vosges, Paris, built by Henri IV, 1605–12, was a true square.

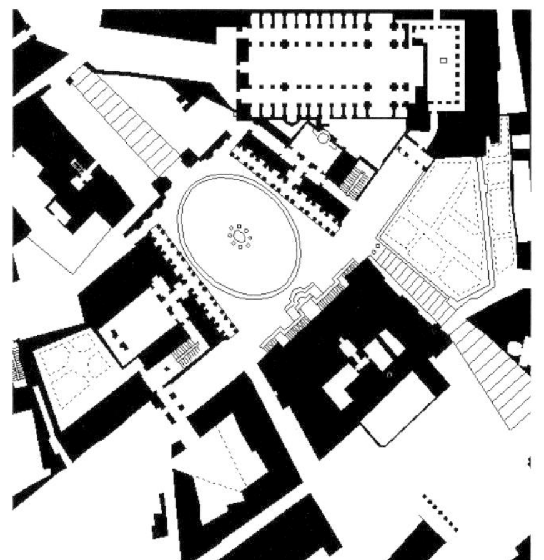

Michelangelo's Capitoline Piazza, Rome, designed in 1536.

Plan of Ferrara, Italy, ca. 1906. The area in gray is the original medieval city; the areas in black are the additions that were made during the Renaissance.

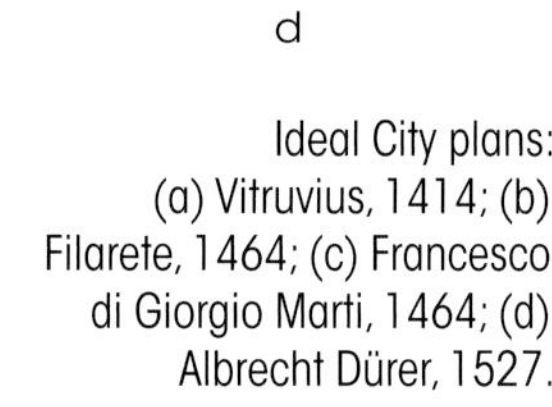

Ideal City plans: (a) Vitruvius, 1414; (b) Filarete, 1464; (c) Francesco di Giorgio Marti, 1464; (d) Albrecht Dürer, 1527.

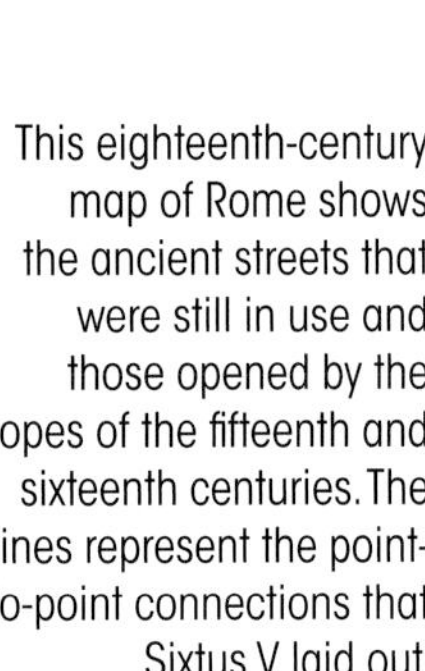

This eighteenth-century map of Rome shows the ancient streets that were still in use and those opened by the popes of the fifteenth and sixteenth centuries. The lines represent the point-to-point connections that Sixtus V laid out.

Sixtus V's plan (ca. 1588) for new streets in Rome, to be placed between monuments on the left bank of the Tiber.

The Ideal City

The common design of ideal cities was circular, starlike, or octagonal and was primarily laid out in a defensive shape. During the Renaissance, design values coincided with the advent of printing, allowing these new designs and theories of ideal city planning to be easily disseminated throughout the Western world. Vitruvius, an architect working during the time of Caesar Augustus, influenced the designs with his book *De Architectura*. Shown at left are four examples of ideal cities by different architects.

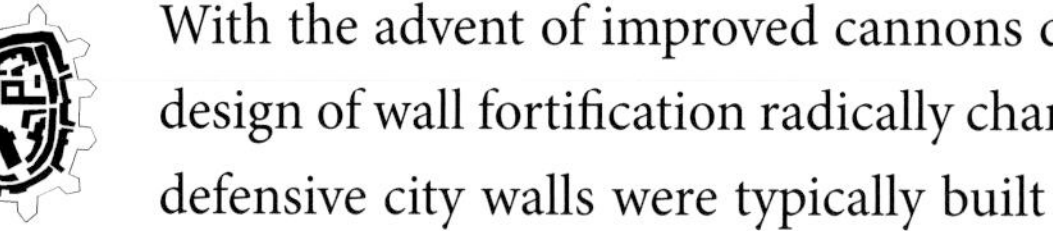

Fortification and the Design of Cities

With the advent of improved cannons during the Renaissance, the design of wall fortification radically changed.[23] Until this period, all defensive city walls were typically built at roughly a ninety-degree angle. The new defensive walls, however, were angled to resist the more powerful cannons. As a rule, these new walls were either built out of masonry and filled with earth or constructed solely out of tamped earth, or ramparts. Star-shaped bastions on the walls allowed for multiple angles of defense.

Extensive New Districts and Extensions

Ferrara, Italy, serves as an excellent example of the addition of new districts to earlier city fabric. Beginning in the mid-1400s, Ferrara ranked among Italy's premier cities—economically, politically, and culturally. In this period of growth, the original medieval city acquired two new quarters, planned using new architectural principles, and the result lent the city "a modern aspect that was unparalleled in Europe."[24] This form of extension is "stitched" alongside the existing medieval fabric and tended to be laid out in an orthagonal planned pattern.

The Renaissance approach to design differed from the "stitched" new district method by planning a comprehensive system of movement and circulation within the city. One example was the work initiated by Pope Sixtus V, who spent immense sums erecting public works in Rome. Among other things, he built the Lateran Palace, completed the Quirinal, restored the Church of Santa Sabina on the Aventine, rebuilt the church and hospice of San Girolamo dei Schiavoni, enlarged and improved the Sapienza, and completed the cupola of St. Peter's. From 1585 to 1590 he oversaw the building of a comprehensive circulation system on the existing city fabric and surrounding landscape. This system was the forerunner for later boulevard designs and one of the first major predesigned urban schemes. In many ways, the system was one of the leading precedents for urbanism's baroque period.

Baroque Period

As during the Renaissance, the early designs of the baroque period were typically restricted to redeveloping small parts of the city. Despite their small size,

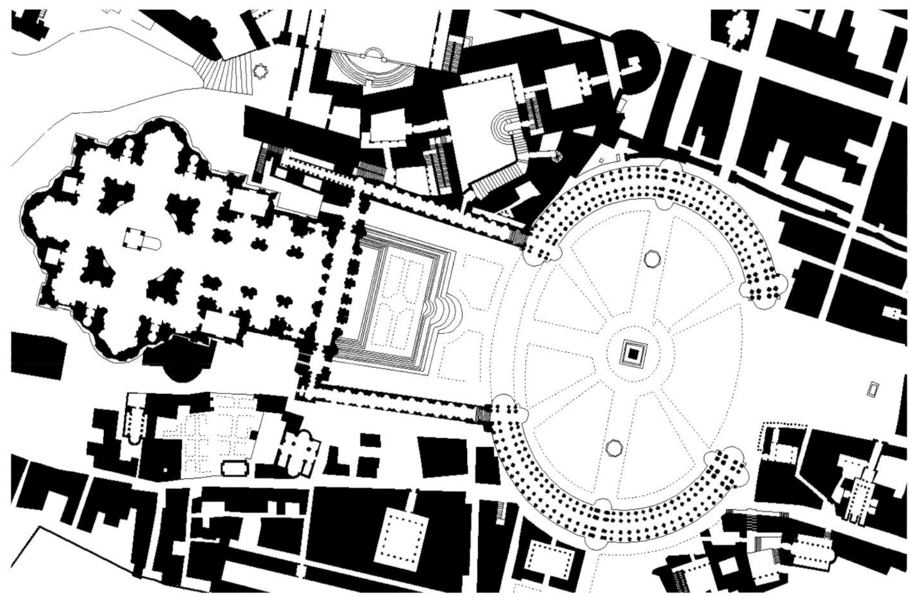

The piazza in front of St. Peter's Cathedral, Rome.

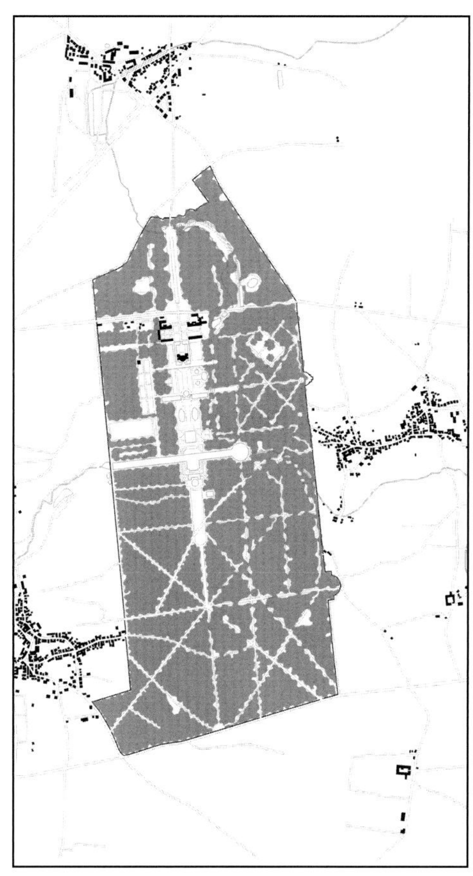

Plan of Vaux-le-Vicomte, France, designed by Ándré Le Nôtre, ca. 1661.

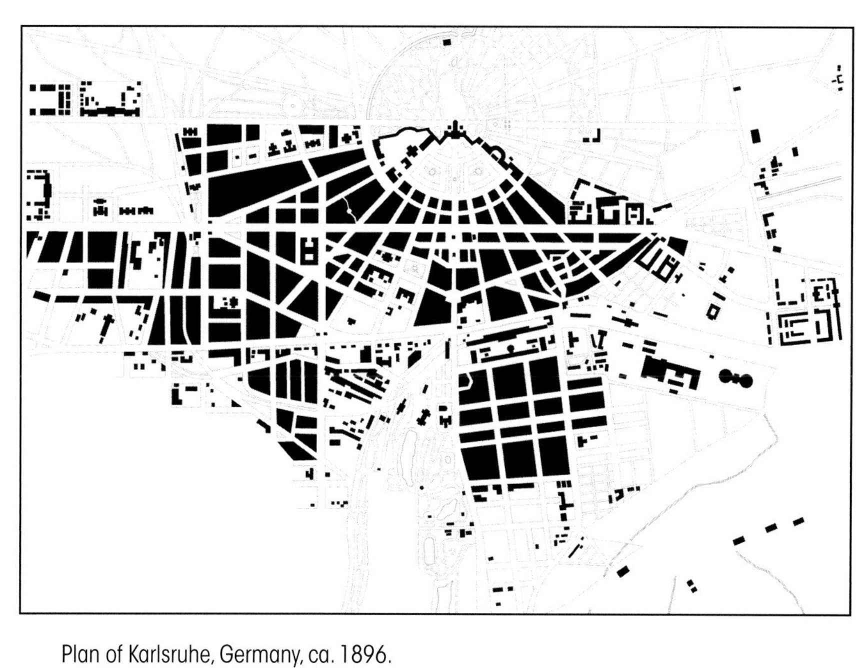

Plan of Karlsruhe, Germany, ca. 1896.

these works possessed a grandeur and theatricality that expressed movement and plasticity. The best example of design for the early baroque period is Rome, with its Piazza for St. Peter, Piazza Navona, the Spanish Steps, St. Ignazio, and the Trevi Fountain.

Urban designs from the baroque period were formal, planned, and featured large-scale extensions and additions to cities that had been laid out by autocratic rulers. The state of baroque urbanism is generally traced to the developments in design occurring mostly in Northern Europe at the time.

The Axis

One of the grand ideas of baroque urbanism is the axis, first introduced in Italy with garden design. The idea of the long perspectival axis (or *allé*) existed for some time in the form of linear hunting paths, usually contained within the grounds of a château. The baroque axis, or grand axial vista, first appeared in Paris with the design of the Luxembourg Gardens in 1620. It also appeared four decades later in the Château Vaux-le-Vicomte, built for Nicolas Fouquet, the finance minister of Louis XIV, and designed by André Le Nôtre. Shortly after the opening celebrations of the château, Fouquet was jailed, and Louis XIV then employed Le Nôtre for the expansion of his palace and grounds at Versailles.[25]

In 1666, shortly after the great fire of London, Christopher Wren submitted plans to Charles II for the complete rebuilding of the city. Similar to the long axes found in Vaux-le-Vicomte and Versailles, Wren's grand scheme called for cutting wide avenues through the former maze of alleys and narrow roads that had made

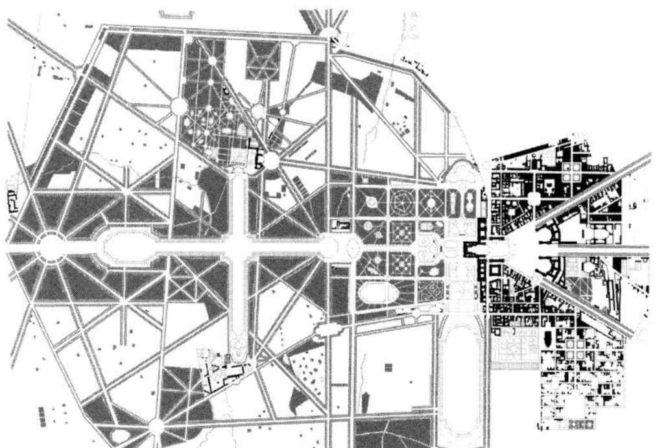

Plan of Versailles, ca. 1746.

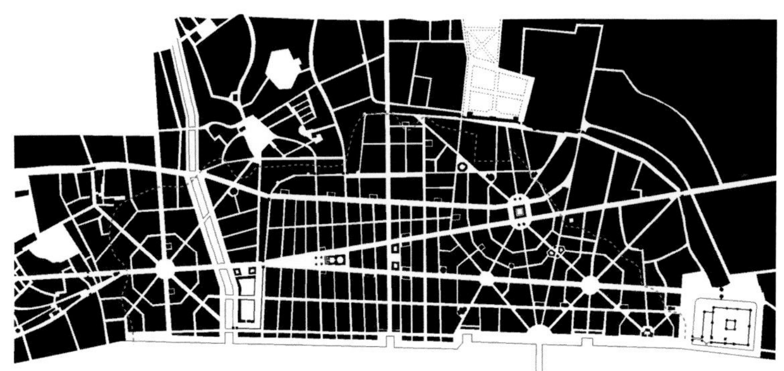

London after the Great Fire of 1666, from a plan drawn by Sir Christopher Wren.

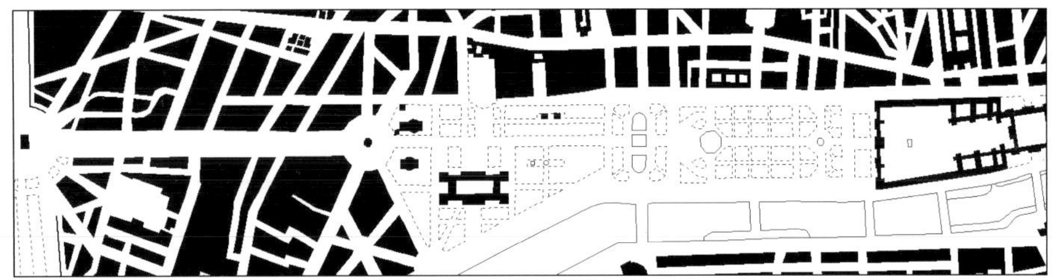

Unter den Linden Berlin (top) and Champ-Élysées, Paris (bottom).

Set design by Guiseppe Galli Bibiena, 1740.

Roman piazzas, ca. 1748: (a) Piazza del Popolo and (b) Piazza de Ponte.

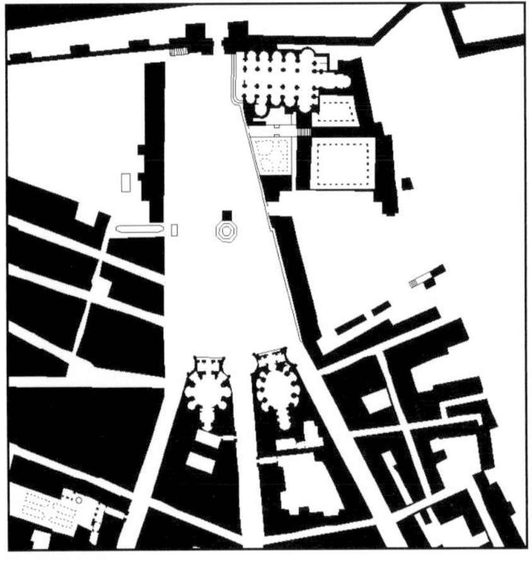

a

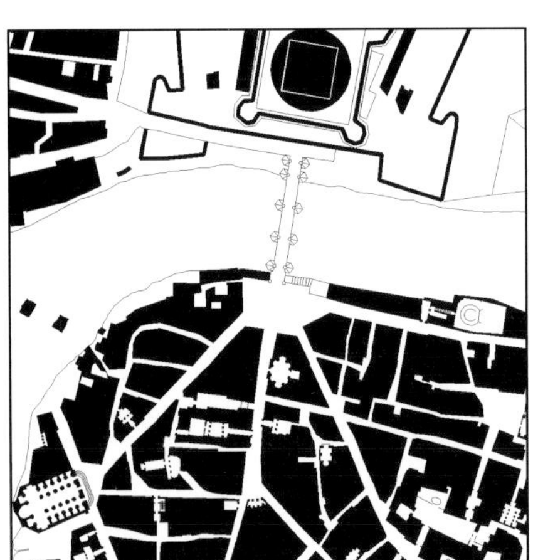

b

up old London. His proposal would open up the city to light and air. King Charles liked the scheme but believed the expense and the necessity of rebuilding as fast as possible made the plan unworkable. And so the plan was never implemented.

Karlsruhe, Germany, an example of baroque urban planning, was founded in 1715 and designed largely by the city's founding father, the margrave Karl Wilhelm, and by the architect and town planner, Friedrich Weinbrenner. After spending six years studying in Rome, Weinbrenner returned home in 1800 and was commissioned to expand his native city. The palace acts as the center for a series of fanned streets, which are fixed by a crossing grid.

The Square and Straight Streets

The early part of the Renaissance saw the controlled design of Italy's piazza. These piazzas, typically additions to existing urban spaces, differed from the baroque square, which was planned as a new space. As a result, the facades within the squares typically were designed as a continuous element, resulting in a more homogeneous space. The planned spaces most likely first appeared in the Veneto region of Italy and can be seen within the Renaissance new towns built by the Gonzaga family of Mantova between 1540 and 1600.[26]

The idea of the designed square with uniform facades within a large urban city first appeared in Paris. The main European prototype of a residential square, again with uniform facades, is usually attributed to Place des Vosges, which was completed around 1612.[27]

The baroque urban period also continued the Renaissance idea of the planned straight street as well as continuous facades (terraces/apartment blocks), tree-lined avenues (boulevards), and varied scale structures (residential to ceremonial). The two major boulevards begun during this period, the Champs-Élysées in Paris and the Unter den Linden in Berlin, have comparable scales and demonstrate the continuous facades and varied scale that typify the baroque urban straight street.

Formal Geometries

Baroque urban design used formal geometries that included the trivium, the circus, and the crescent.

A trivium (Latin for "three roads") is primarily distinguished as three streets converging at one focal point, often in the form of a piazza. A number of theater set designs, including one in 1740 by Giuseppe Galli Bibiena, portrayed a trivium. The baroque idea of a reaching toward the infinite perspectival is illustrated in some of Bibiena's works.

A circus, a circular area at a street intersection, occurs generally in the dense part of the urban fabric and is enclosed, while a crescent can be both imbedded and on the fringe of urban fabric. Due to its geometric form, the circle can have any number of streets intersecting it from any possible angle. In 1754 the circus in Bath, England, designed by John Woods, was completed. Twenty years later Woods's son, also John, added a crescent, as an extension, west of the circle.

Further Developments in Fortification

Sébastien Le Prestre de Vauban, one of the most important engineers of baroque fortification, acted as the commissary general of fortifications in France circa 1667. During this time he traveled frequently, and through letters and papers he wrote then and later, his technique of fortification became the focus of military studies in Europe for more than a century. During Vauban's military career, he

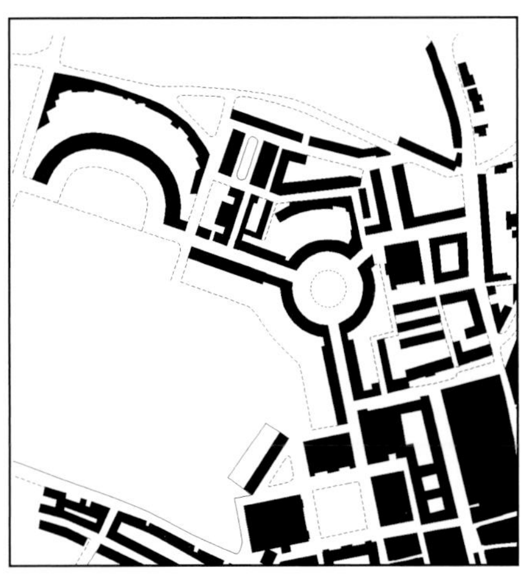

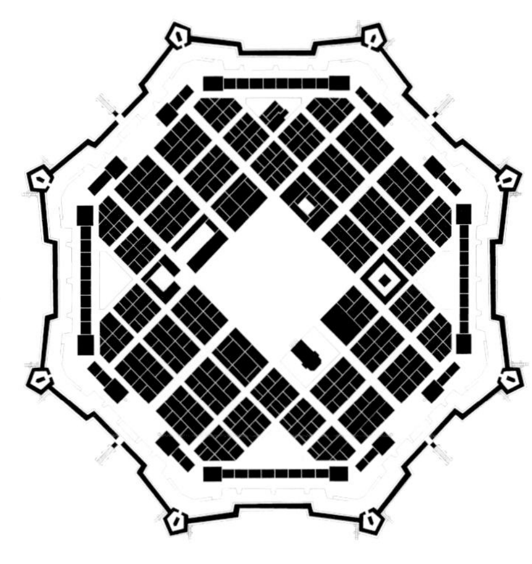

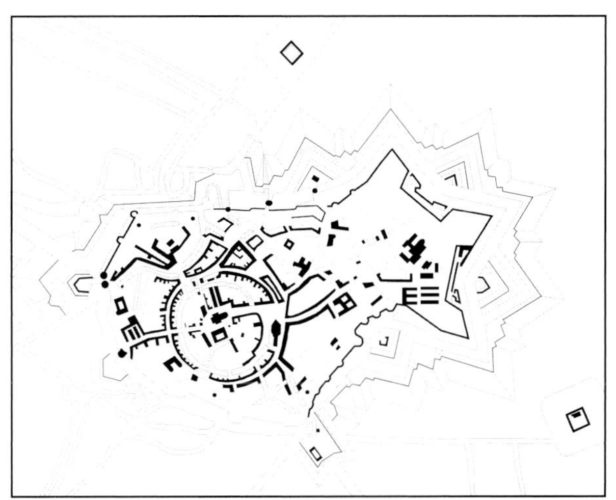

Left: The crescent and circus of Bath, England, ca. 1775.

Center: Complete new town design for Neuf-Brisach, France, by Marquis de Vauban, ca. 1696.

Right: Bergues, France, 1702, is an example of an encasement of existing medieval city.

built thirty-three forts, strengthened 300 walled towns, and fortified other walled towns, including Neuf-Brisach, Bergues, and the citadel of Lille.

In *Siege Warfare* Christopher Duffy says the new baroque method of constructing walls prevented cities from expanding since the walls could not be easily removed to accommodate growth. Previously, walls were removed and filled in, with new city fabric built as the population grew and expanded.[28] The normal path for expansion in the baroque period was outside what were once the Renaissance walls, now large open areas, or parks.

Prominence of Public or Civic Buildings Placed in Space

Also representative of late baroque urban expansion were the prominent, stand-alone building types that took advantage of the new, open spaces: palaces, hotels, mansions; churches and cathedrals; and civic halls, museums, theaters, and concert halls. The Vienna Ringstrasse, built after the baroque urban period, is still the best example of situating monumental buildings in existing parklike space. This space, obtained after the old walls were removed, had new urban fabric built outside the existing Renaissance walls. With the walls removed, the new urban fabric was designed to "weave" or "stitch" the old with the new.

St. Petersburg, Russia, founded in 1703 by Peter the Great, grew quickly following a well-planned design. The city's architectural monuments were created by Russian architects Ivan Korobov, Piotr Yeropkin, and Mikhail Zemtsov and by Western European architects Domenico Trezzini, Bartolomeo Francesco Rastrelli, and Alexandre Jean-Baptiste Le Blond, among others. In the early eighteenth century, architectural buildings were largely constructed in the style known as the Petrine baroque. The high baroque style in St. Petersburg found its full expression during the reign of Elizabeth, daughter of Peter the Great, and St. Petersburg became a beautiful European capital. St. Petersburg is a city that exemplified the

Lille, France, 1906, is an example of an encasement of an existing city with baroque interventions. The citadel is located in the northwest part of the city.

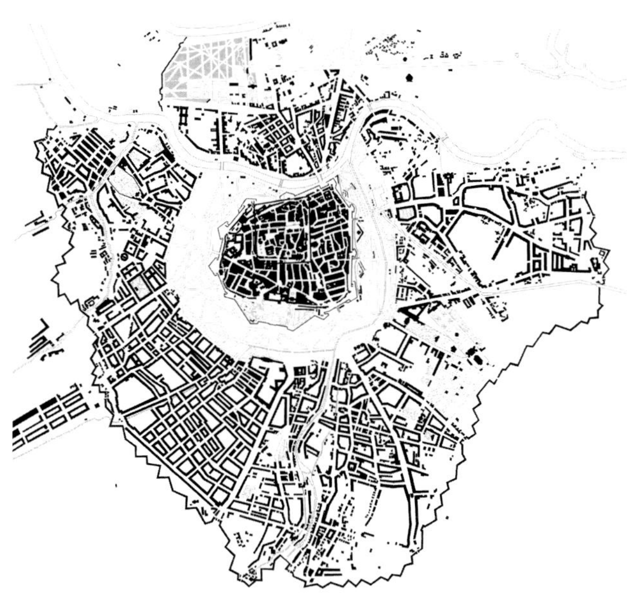

The plan of Vienna, ca. 1833, shows the outer wall of the city removed with the inner wall to the medieval city still in place.

Boston, Massachusetts, ca. 1640, with its layout following topography. Note that the dense area, where a number of streets come together, includes an open square

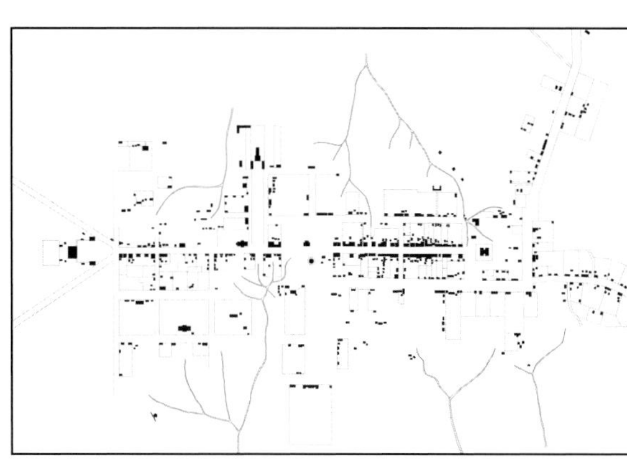

Williamsburg, Virginia, ca. 1762, with its layout based on a grid. Note that the main axial street runs east-west and terminates at a large building on each end; the streets and spaces are anchored onto this axis.

New Orleans, Louisiana, ca. 1720, follows a grid layout surrounded by fortification. The main square is located in the center and situated on the river. At the head of the square, and on the axis, is the cathedral.

Quebec, Canada, ca. 1762, follows the topography and thus appears haphazard. But a semblance of a grid structure is discernable in some of the street layout and in the rectilinear forms of the gardens. Enclosing all this is a fortified wall.

Vienna's Ringstrasse, ca. 1904.

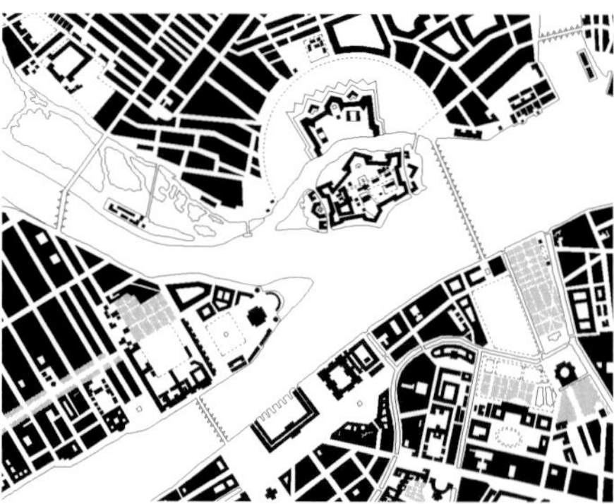

The center of St. Petersburg, Russia, ca. 1834.

period's placement of buildings within open space and is home to a trivium, focused on the isolated Admiralty building on the south side of the Neva River; a crescent, encompassing the Peter and Paul Fortress, located on the north shore of the Neva River; and a designed square, located in front of the Winter Palace near the Admiralty building.

Colonial North America

New Settlements

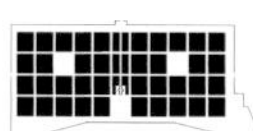

North America was settled in this early period by groups of immigrants from Spain, Britain, France, and Northern Europe. The location and structure of the settlements varied depending on the background of the founding communities. In all cases, the settlers brought with them knowledge of European design and architecture.

In the case of the British and French settlements, the towns either followed the topography of the land, resulting in town layouts having a haphazard-appearing structure, or were highly structured plans that commonly followed a grid.

But Spanish settlements followed the 1573 decree by King Philip II that established a broad set of rules for the layout of towns and cities in Spain's colonies in the Americas. The Law of the Indies, as it was known, dictated that all new towns must have a central plaza surrounded by key buildings, including arcades. From this plaza the principal streets, laid out in a grid pattern, would diverge. Smaller, secondary plazas were also planned, as well as narrow tree-lined streets, which, in hot climates, provided shade.

New and Separate Planned Communities

Ideal, Religious, and Worker Towns

Most religious settlers in North America, including the Puritans, Quakers, and Catholics, fled their home countries to escape persecution and follow their own beliefs. But a minority of religious groups, often called

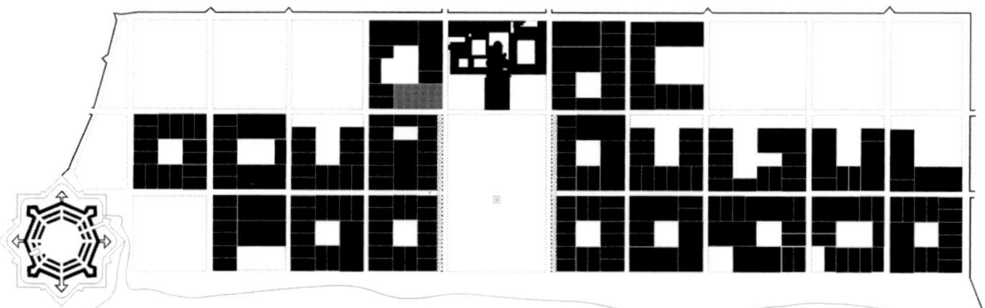

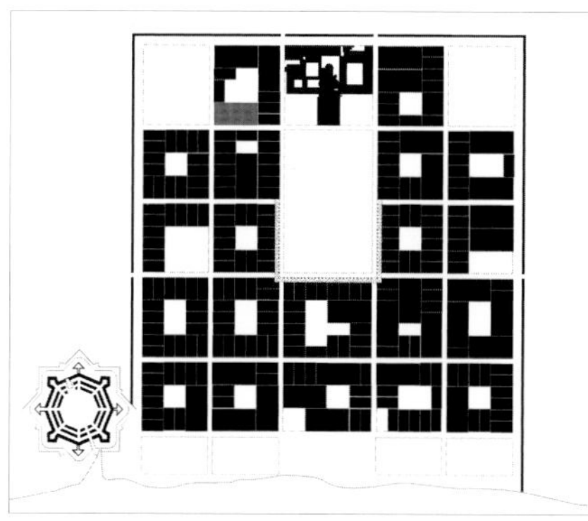

Examples of possible town layouts based on the Spanish Law of the Indies.

"utopians," preferred to create new communities rather than live in already-settled areas. The Huguenots and the Moravians were two examples. Some of the earliest Huguenot settlements in North America were New Amsterdam (later New York); Oxford, Massachusetts; and Manakin, Virginia.

With few exceptions, Huguenot settlements in North America were not closed communities; some Huguenots moved to other towns, while those remaining opened their communities to outsiders. By contrast, Moravian settlements typically did not welcome outsiders, but they did accept converts and Moravians from other communities. The Moravians had settlements in both North America and Europe, while the Huguenot settled primarily in North America. In 1722 the majority of Moravians emigrated to Saxony and founded the town of Herrnhut, but they were persecuted again. In 1734 a few Moravians migrated to North America and after a number of years established settlements in Bethlehem, Pennsylvania; Bethabara, North Carolina; Nazareth, Pennsylvania; and Bethania, North Carolina. While the Moravian towns varied in detail, the layouts had many common features: a central square, a grid plan, a concentration of buildings in close proximity to the town square, and a surrounding band of fields, orchards, and grazing lands farmed in common as a church venture.[29]

A new form of urban design, the "ideal town," emerged in France just prior to the revolution. The new design reflected society's growing interest in eliminating the class system and ensuring equality for all citizens. Ideal towns were meant to be self-sufficient, self-governing, free of child labor, and rich in educational and recreational facilities. One example, Claude Nicholas Ledoux's design of the royal salt works of Chaux-de-Fonds, was commissioned by the court and built between 1775 and 1779. It was located in open French countryside between two small villages. Ledoux actually conceived three designs for Chaux-de-Fonds before settling on the semi-oval plan. The first design was rectangular and the second, oval.

In 1799 English social reformer Robert Owen purchased the New Lanark industrial mills from his father-in-law, David Dale. Located approximately thirty-

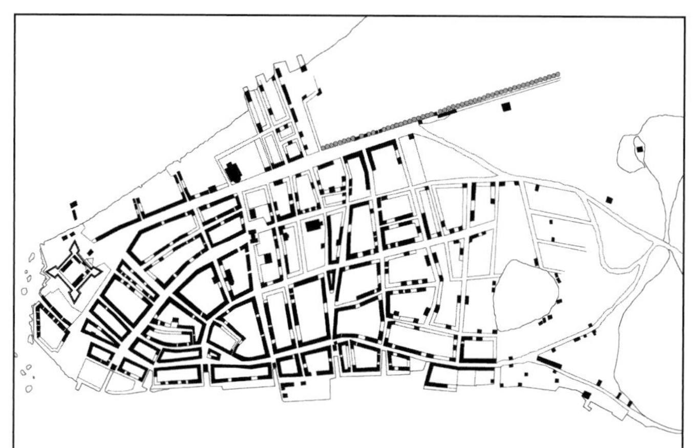

Plan of the religious settlement Herrnhut in Saxony, ca. 1782.

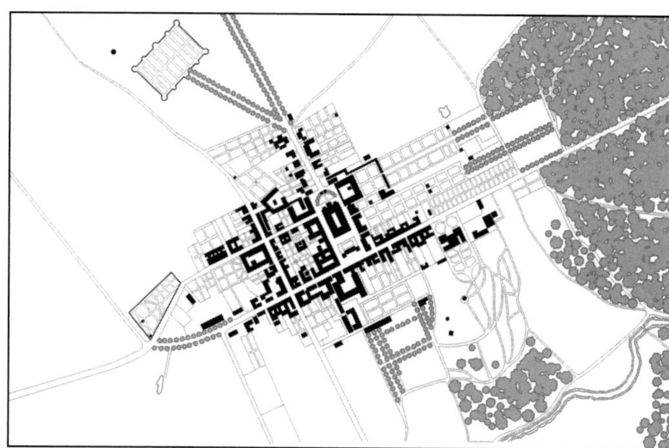

A plan of New York City, ca. 1731, roughly thirty years after the British took control of the settlement from the Netherlands.

six miles southeast of Glasgow, the mills housed 800 to 1,200 people on 600 to 1,800 acres of land.[30] Like Chaux-de-Fonds, New Lanark was intended to be self-sufficient and free of child labor. Following New Lanark, several "Owenite" communities were built in both England and North America, following a grid pattern that situated housing radiated away from the primary industry or company buildings.

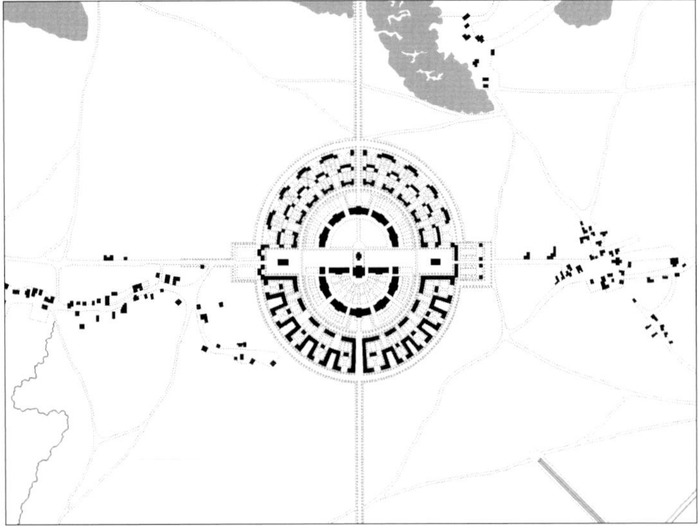

The later design for Saline Royal at Arc-et-Senans, France, ca. 1800.

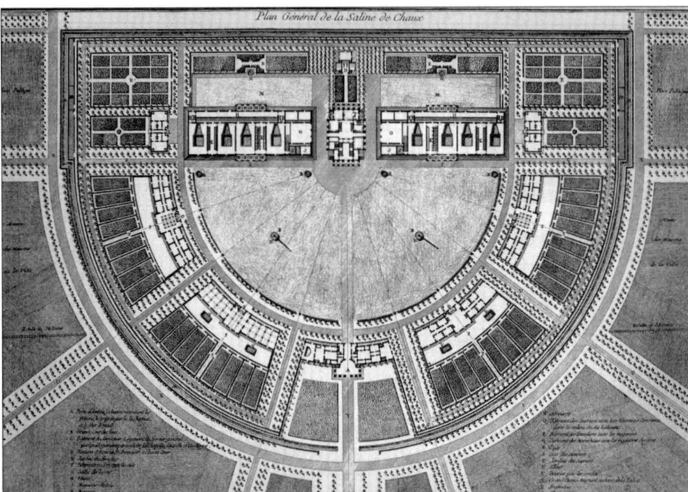

The built plan of Saline Royal, ca. 1775.

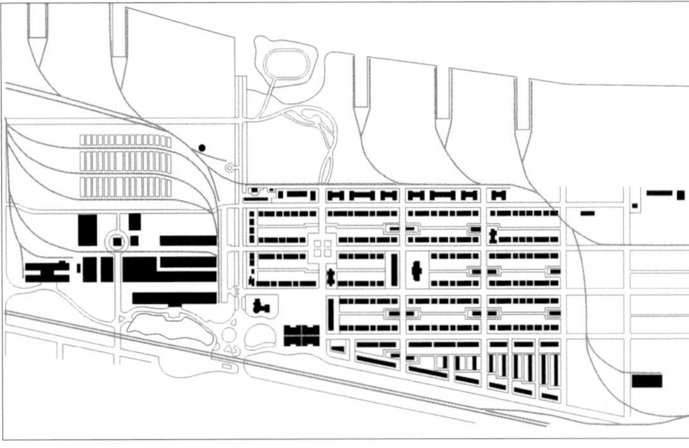

The company town of Pullman, Illinois, 1885.

Company Towns

With the advent of the industrial age, large-scale manufacturing buildings were constructed most typically in already-existing and populated cities. To accommodate the swells in population of workers and immigrants to these job centers, some manufacturers moved production facilities outside the already-filled urban fabric and built whole towns to house their workers. The owners of these company towns provided all the amenities, including houses, schools, shops, and recreational areas.

Some manufacturers-owners provided the "town" but turned governance over to the locals, their workers. Others, however, exercised full control of the town and government, leasing houses to the workers and mandating that they purchase all goods and services from the company's stores. And when a worker lost his job, he had to leave the town. One company town, Pullman, Illinois, was built by train car manufacturer George Pullman, who, in an unusual move, hired architect Solon S. Beman and landscape architect Nathan F. Barrett to design the town rather than use his own company engineers. Not exerting a tight control, Pullman appears to have given the architects free reign. Beman and Barrett followed the most up-to-date theories and practices of design for the time.[31]

The Park Movements

The first landscaped public park in the United States was New York City's Central Park. Manhattanites who had traveled to the public grounds of London and Paris wanted a comparable setting, and the working class needed relief from their cramped, unhealthy quarters. So in 1853 the state authorized the city of New York to acquire more than 700 acres of land in the center of Manhattan, inside the boundary of the original grid as laid out by early developers. The geography of the land included swamps, rock outcroppings, and bluffs. To occupy this site, the city had to displace approximately 1,600 poor residents, including German gardeners and Irish pig farmers. The city also had to supplant the village of Seneca, a stable African American settlement that had three churches and one school. In 1857 the Central Park Commission held the United States's first landscape design contest and selected the Greensward

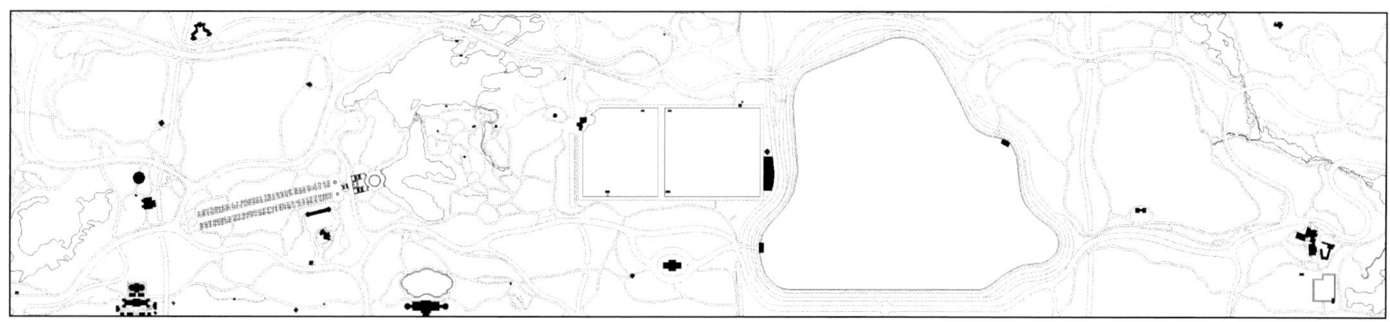

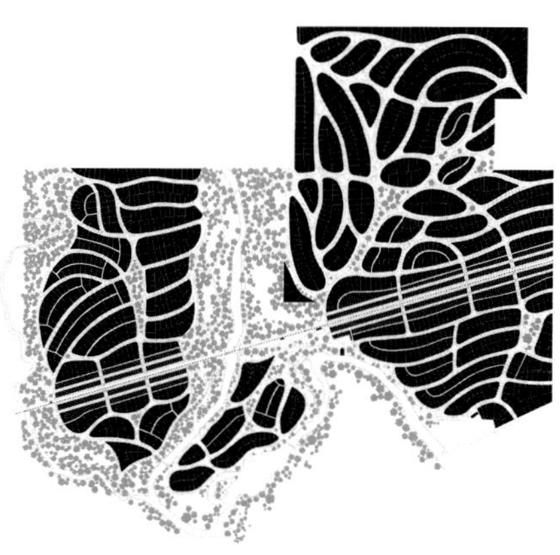

Far left: Central Park, New York City, as designed by Frederick Law Olmsted and Calvert Vaux, 1871.

Left: An example of the romantic garden movement was Riverside, Illinois, designed by Olmsted, Vaux & Co. in 1869.

Plan submitted by Frederick Law Olmsted and Calvert Vaux, which was a pastoral landscape in the English romantic tradition. Central Park ended up encompassing 843 acres.

Garden City Movement

One of the founders of the Garden City movement was Ebenezer Howard, author of *To-Morrow: A Peaceful Path to Real Reform* (1898; reprinted in 1902 as *Garden Cities of To-Morrow*). Howard, possibly influenced by Edward Bellamy's utopian novel *Looking Backward,* wrote of towns with job opportunities, high wages, entertainment, low rent, fresh air, and no slums. Viewed as one of the pioneers of town planning, Howard and his work in the early 1920s helped establish the new towns of Letchworth, England (designed by Raymond Unwin and Barry Parker in 1903), Welwyn Garden City, England, and new towns outside Moscow (1923) and Paris (1912–30s).[32]

Plan of Letchworth, England, ca. 1903.

Early plan of Welwyn Garden City, ca. 1920.

The City Beautiful Movement

As the nineteenth century drew to a close, the large urban areas in the United States struggled with social unrest, violence, economic downturn, government corruption, and overcrowding. With the advent of improved rail and roadways, the wealthy upper-middle class, and eventually even the middle class, could withdraw from the cities into the suburbs, leaving the poor in the decaying city neighborhoods.

The City Beautiful movement originated with the middle and upper-middle classes, who, out of their own fears, sought to reform the squalor and decay of the city. They believed they could solve urban problems by introducing moral and civic virtue to the city population. The premise of the movement was that beauty could be an effective social control device.

The City Beautiful leaders adhered to the beaux arts style, which instructed designers in the prerequisites of order, formality, and harmony. The footholds

Right: Chicago's World Columbian Exposition of 1863.

Far right: Daniel H. Burnham's design for Chicago, 1909.

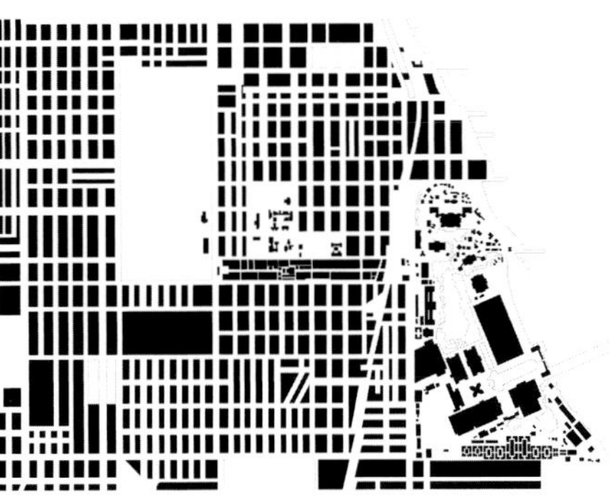

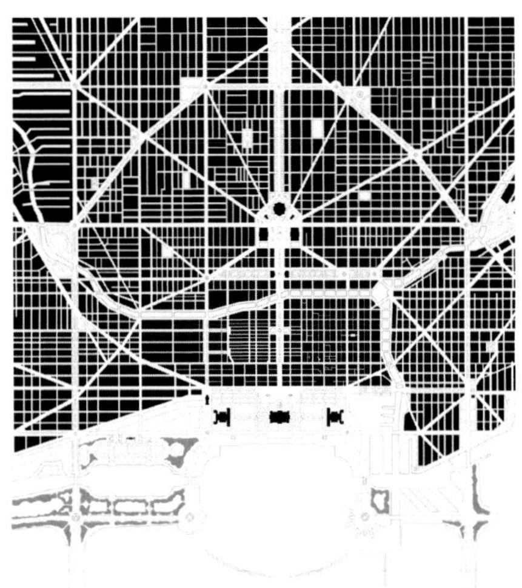

Plan of the fascist new town Latinia, Italy. Note the similarities between this plan and that of Parc de la Villette later in this chapter.

of this movement can be found in the World's Columbian Exposition of 1893 in Chicago. The director of construction, Daniel H. Burnham of Chicago (who would later become one of history's best-known urban planners, thanks largely to his redesign of Chicago in 1909), brought in American architect Louis Sullivan, who designed Chicago's Transportation Building. Civic centers, a basic idea of the City Beautiful movement, typically had radiating axial tree-lined boulevards, open spaces, and water elements moving out from the city center. This resulted at times in a shifted grid pattern.

Fascist New Towns

In the early 1930s, increasing unemployment in Italy led to a large migration of people to cities in hopes of a better life. Italy, though, was not as industrialized as other European countries, so there were no jobs available in major urban centers. Benito Mussolini and his fascist government strongly disliked urban areas; they feared the consequences of large metropolitan cities, where masses of unemployed workers would be crowded together. The fascist government's solution was to build several new towns in areas that before were uninhabitable, such as malaria-infested marshlands near coastlines. The towns were laid out on somewhat classical urban methods and were quickly and efficiently constructed, with the town center built first and the housing units next.[33] A number of these towns still exist between Rome and Naples, including Sabaudia, Littoria (now known as Latinia), Pontinia, Aprilia, and Pomezia.[34]

Modern City Planning

In 1928 the Congrès International d'Architecture Moderne (CIAM) was formed and became the major think tank of the modern movement, or international style, in architecture and urbanism. At the fourth congress, held in 1933, the CIAM conceived of the "Athens Charter," a document that adopted a functional conception of modern architecture and urban planning and included ideas that were unique and provocative. The charter, based on discussions held ten years earlier, claimed that the problems facing cities could be resolved by strict functional segregation of city functions and the distribution of the population into tall apartment blocks at widely spaced intervals. Le Corbusier was one of the founding members of the CIAM, and it was his urban proposals that were the most influential of this period.[35]

Le Corbusier's answer to urban crowding, filth, and a lack of a moral landscape was to create, in conjunction with the modern industrial age, a new theory of capitalist authority and to recognize workers' individual freedom of choice. His plans proposed razing the "infected" historic city fabric and replacing it with his so-called "vertical garden city," or modern self-standing high-rises. One fifty-meter apartment building would accommodate 2,700 inhabitants with fourteen square meters of space per person. The buildings would be placed on *pilotus* standing five meters off the ground, with the intent of turning leftover space into a large park that would weave between buildings. There would also be elevated traffic roads and raised pedestrian interior streets connecting one building to another. All shopping centers would be placed along the outside edge of the living center, allowing for the ground floor of the living area to be open to pedestrians. Also along the edges would be skyscrapers that would provide office space for about 3,200 workers per building.

Each apartment block would be equipped with laundry services and a cafeteria in the basement, where families could eat daily meals, if desired. The time saved with these services would enable residents to think, write, or use the recreation and sports facilities that covered much of the open parkland. Supplied with the apartment houses were rooftop gardens and sunbathing areas.

By the close of the twentieth century, Le Corbusier's idea of modern urban design had been implemented throughout the world. Some designs have succeeded and some have failed; regardless, Le Corbusier radically changed the modern urban fabric.

The Traditionalists and the Spin-Offs

In the 1950s and 1960s, theorist and teacher Colin Rowe began to speak out against the modern urban movement proposed by Le Corbusier. Rowe's counterproposal was an urban design approach that studied the context of a site, both past and present, to establish a foundation that recalled similar historical urban designs for the locale.[36] *College City* (1978) and *Roma Interrotta* (1979) helped establish Rowe's traditionalist ideas of urbanism. *Roma Interrotta* was an invitation by Michael Graves to a select number of prominent architects of that time.[37] Graves gave each architect one of twelve sections of Nolli's 1748 plan of Rome. Rowe and his team of designers produced a plan that wove the existing fabric into their new design so that it was difficult to tell the new from the old.

Although Colin Rowe never built any of his urban designs, he produced a large number of acolytes who studied with him throughout the years and went on either to build in the traditionalist style or to move in their own direction. A group that investigates traditionalist urbanism calls its approach new urbanism.

New urbanism, loosely defined as the return to the neotraditional town, attempts to reign in urban sprawl and put people and community back into cities. The movement, most evident in upscale "gated" communities, promotes a sort of antisuburbanism with dense, small, manageable "villages" with a town center, public green spaces, and narrow, tree-lined streets. New urbanists typically use the grid as a design tool, which allows for the growth of a city, thereby creating

Paris in 1924.

The area Le Corbusier proposed to demolish.

Le Corbusier's design proposal for the center of Paris, 1924.

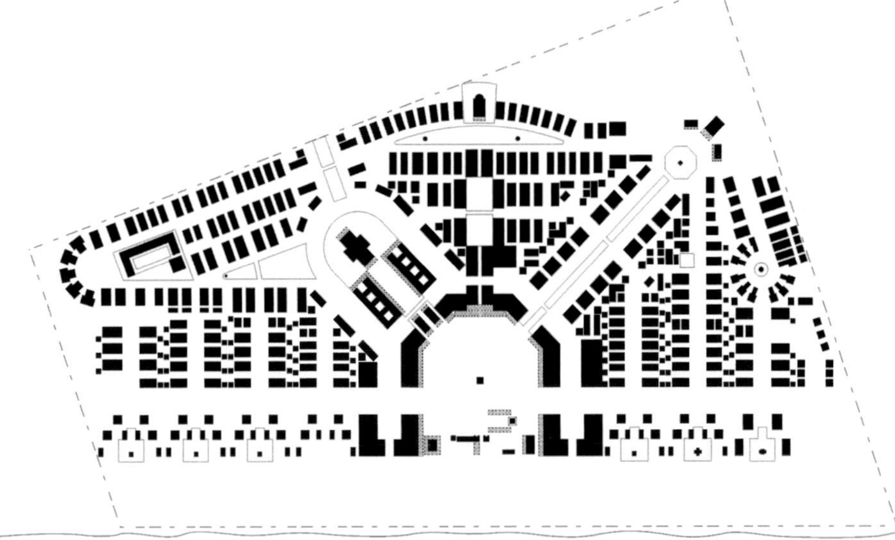

A plan of Seaside, Florida, designed in the early 1980s by architects and new urbanists Andrés Duany and Elizabeth Plater-Zybeck. Seaside is a prime example of new urbanism and neo-vernacular architecture.

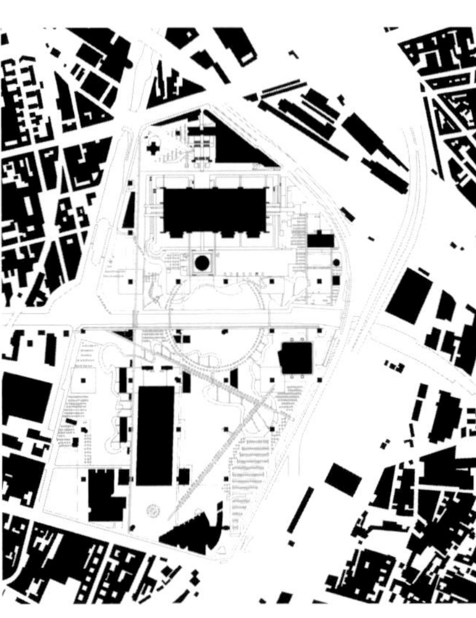

a b

(a) Bernard Tschumi's winning design proposal for Parc de la Villette, which was eventually constructed, and (b) Leon Krier's design for the same competition. Tschumi's design is the epitome of deconstructivism, and Krier's represents the school of urban traditionalism.

continuity as the town expands. The grid sets limitations by discouraging growth outside of the set boundaries.

The New Modernist

In 1982 Bernard Tschumi won the competition in Paris for the Parc de la Villette which may be the first deconstructionist urban scheme ever built. Deconstructionism occurred in response to the traditionalist, or postmodern, movement. It draws its philosophical source from deconstructionism, a literary movement, and from the Russian constructivism movement of the 1920s.

Deconstructionism counters the ordered, rational formalism of the modern movement and the contextual moves of the postmodern practitioners and employs fragmentation, non-Euclidean geometry, nonlinear design processes, and negating polarizations, such as structure and envelope. The finished appearance of this style is characterized by a stimulated unpredictability and a controlled disorder.

Today, urban design styles are no longer always regional; a design originating in one country may also appear halfway around the globe. But it is possible to identify individual examples that arise and become the dominant urban design model for that period. After the 2001 terrorist attack on the World Trade Center, an invitational competition was held to commemorate and build anew on the existing site. With the final submissions, it was possible to see a wide range of existing styles and of styles possibly to come.

It may be too early to identify today's urban design style. After all, it is easier to review history and identify the predominant urban design movements than to try to analyze the present styles and assign a label. It is, though, possible even now to see the countries that could lead urban design movements, among them China, India, and Dubai. And, if indicators are correct and we are seeing urban sprawl reaching its peak, the only places left to build in the Western world are the urban centers we abandoned in the 1960s.

Notes

1. Douglas Fraser, *Village Planning in the Primitive World* (New York: George Braziller, 1968), 8. Fraser follows this comment with, "This essentially authoritarian outlook has nowadays been largely supplanted in industrialized societies by an insistence on sanitary, economic, and aesthetic reasons for planning; but the willingness to subordinate the rights of private owners to the commonweal remains as a heritage from earlier aristocratic era."

2. Ibid.

3. For further information on the history of early settlements, see A. E. J. Morris, *History of Urban Form: Before the Industrial Revolutions* (Harlow, Essex, England: Longman Scientific and Technical, 1994).

4. In some cultures the shape of a circle symbolizes many forms, such as Mother Moon and Father Sun.

5. Cecil Stewart, *A Prospect of Cities: Being Studies Towards a History of Town Planning* (London: Longmans, Green, 1952), 5.

6. E. A. Gutkind, *Urban Development in Southern Europe: Italy and Greece,* vol. 4 (New York: Free Press, 1969), 16–18.

7. Stefano Bianca, *Urban Form in the Arab World: Past and Present* (London: Thames Hudson, 2000).

8. Ibid., 25–27.

9. Ibid., 34–36.

10. Ibid., 36.

11. Ibid., 37.

12. Ibid., 39–40.

13. Joseph Rykwert, *The Idea of a Town: The Anthropology of Urban Form in Rome, Italy and the Ancient World* (Cambridge, Mass.: MIT Press, 1988). Rykwert writes that the process of laying out the boundaries for an Indian city, found in the Verdic and Hindu religions and in the *Vástupurusamandala,* is similar to that of the Romans and Etruscans. In all three observances an oxen is used to dig a furrow for the city boundaries or walls, and when the oxen approached the area to house the gates the plow was raised. For more information, read Rykwert's chapter "The Parallels."

14. Ibid., 180.

15. Hong-Key Yoon, *Culture of Feng Shui in Korea: An Exploration of East Asia Geomancy* (New York: Lexington Books, 2006); Baolin Wu, *Lighting the Eye of the Dragon: Inner Secrets of Taoist Feng Shui* (New York: St. Martin's Press, 2000).

16. Mike Pramik, "Hong Kong Blends Myths, Reality," *Columbus (Ohio) Dispatch*, June 10, 1997.

17. For information on the urban history of Florence, see Giovanni Fanelli, *Firenze* (Laterza, Italy: Roma-Bari, 1981).

18. Morris, *History of Urban Form.*

19. Ibid.

20. Ibid., 59. The author added the first broad area, and the rest are from Morris.

21. Ibid.

22. Ibid., 163–64.

23. The Turks used this new form of firepower in conquering Constantinople in 1453.

24. Leonardo Benevolo, *The History of the City* (Cambridge, Mass.: MIT Press, 1980).

25. Clemens Steenbergen, *Architecture and Landscape: The Design Experiment of the Great European Gardens and Landscapes* (New York: Prestel, 1996).

26. Mario Gallarati, *Urban Scale Architecture: L'Architettura A Scala Urbana* (Florence: Alinea, 1994).

27. Place des Vosges, originally called Place Royale, received its present name after the French Revolution. In *History of Urban Form,* Morris attributes the idea that Place des Vosges was Europe's prototype of a residential square to a number of authors (196n.17).

28. Christopher Duffy, *Siege Warfare,* (London: Routledge, 1979).

29. John W. Reps, *The Making of Urban America: A History of City Planning in the United States* (Princeton, N.J.: Princeton Univ. Press, 1965).

30. Paul D. Spreiregen, *Urban Design: The Architecture of Towns and Cities,* written and illustrated by Paul D. Spreiregen (New York: McGraw Hill, 1965).

31. For further information on Pullman, see Richard T. Ely, "Pullman: A Social Study," *Harper's Magazine* 70 (Feb. 1885): 452–66, available at www.library.cornell.edu/Reps/DOCS/pullman.htm (accessed Nov. 19, 2007).

32. For further information on garden cities, see "Urban Planning, 1794-1918: An International Anthology of Articles, Conference Papers," comp. John W. Reps, available at www.library.cornell.edu/Reps/DOCS/howard.htm (accessed Nov. 19, 2007).

33. In some ways, the scale, layout, and building process of these fascist new towns resemble those of today's new urbanism.

34. For further information on fascist new towns, see http://welcome.to/Sabaudia (accessed Nov. 17, 2007).

35. Le Corbusier, *Concerning Town Planning,* trans. Clive Entwistle (New Haven, Conn.: Yale Univ. Press, 1948).

36. In their study of context, traditionalists are sometimes called "contextualists."

37. Michael Graves, *AD Profile 20: Roma Interrotta* (London: Architectural Design, 1979).

Plans of Cities and Places

The following section represents the historical city types written in the previous chapter. The icons for these periods are arranged at the bottom of the page and chronologically arrange to move up in time from prehistory to today's cities. Note that this occurs from right to left on the left-hand page and from left to right on the right-hand page. Plans change in scale but can be compared in the same scale by referring to the smaller plan in red.

Even though I've identified various periods of city types throughout history, by no means do these historical types always have to be created within a given time frame, and the time frames can overlap. A good example is the Ringstrasse in Vienna, which is completed after what I'm describing as Baroque Urban Expansion. Design styles overlap, and it is rare to find change from one style to the next occurring globally.

The plans are listed in alphabetical order by city on the plan pages, using modern spellings throughout. All elements on the plans correspond to the appendixed material.

The *Scale Bar* is divided into a centimeter, and 1 tenth divisions. The total equals 100 Meters.
100M
City
Country
Date
city / country / date
Parma, Italy 1840
City Plan
scale comparison
Letter bar slides up for each letter
Each city plan is outlined and filled in red, set at a constant for scale comparison, and always oriented north.
The spacing between the lines represents 425 meters.
Alphabetical listing
P
North arrow for city plan.
Historical Typology highlighted and indicated in white.

100M
Aarau, Switzerland [1974]
city / country / date
scale comparison

100M

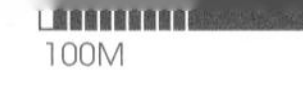

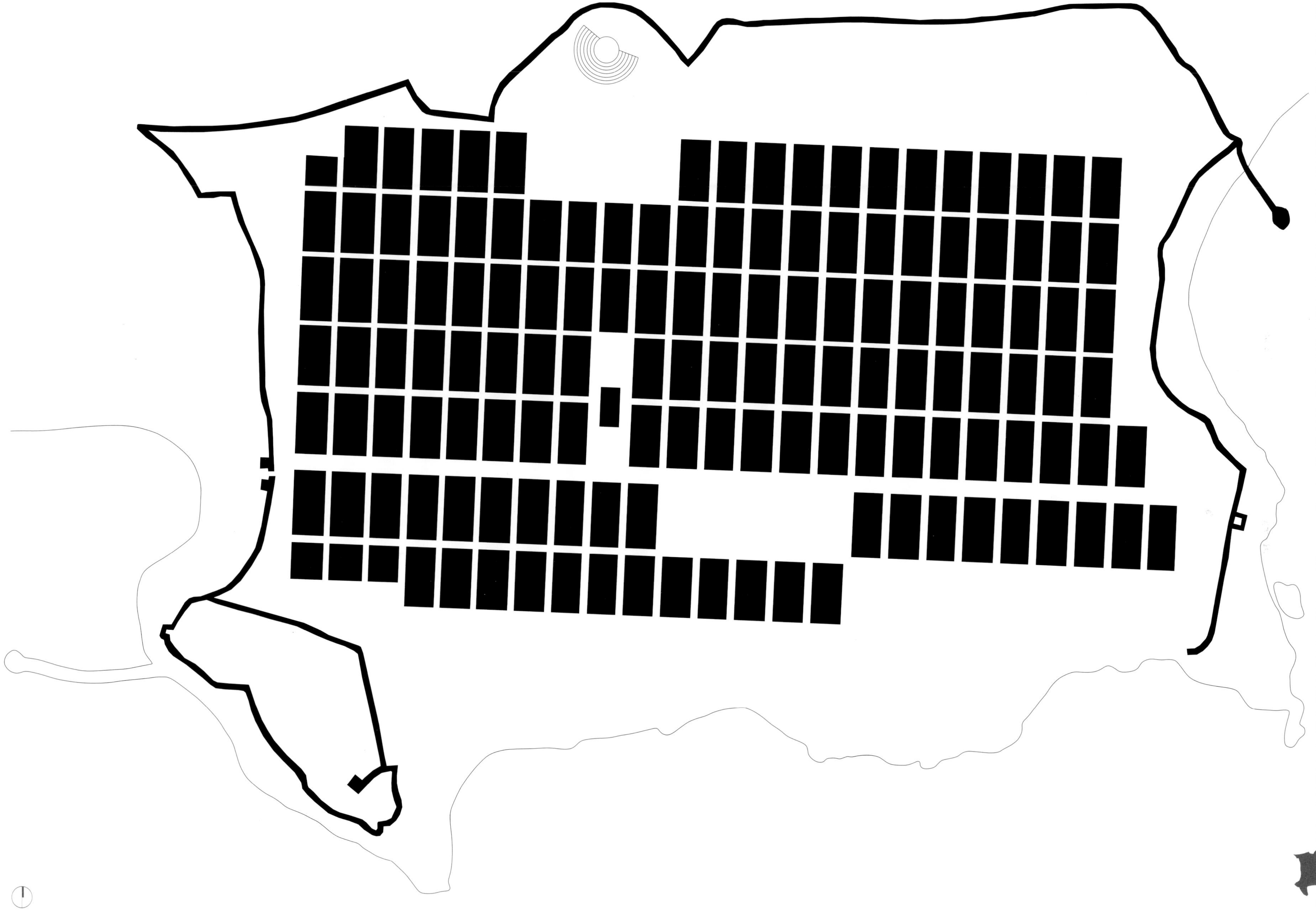

Abdera, Greece 545 BC

city / country / date

scale comparison

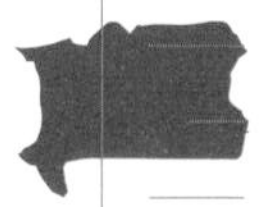

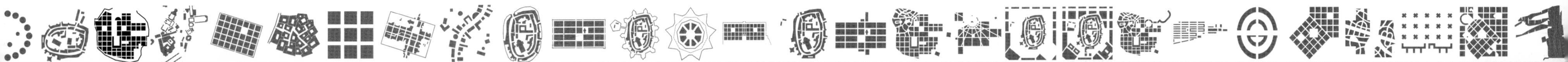

100M

Aigues Mortes, France 1246

city / country / date

scale comparison

100M

Aix, France 1906

city /country / date

scale comparison

A

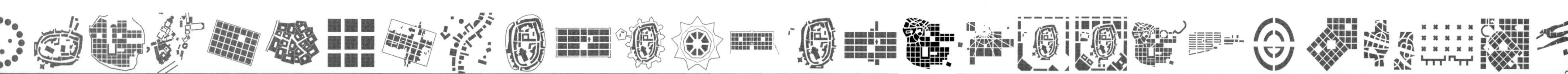

100M

city / country / date

Alatri, Italy 1984

scale comparison

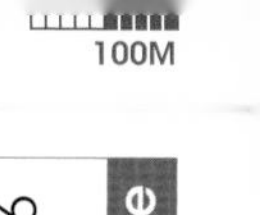

Alexandria, Egypt 1906

city /country / date

scale comparison

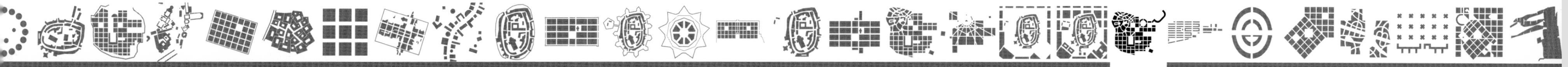

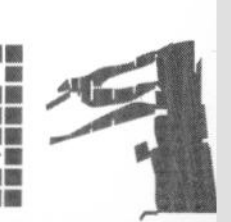

Algeri, Algeria 1837

city / country / date

scale comparison

100M

100M

Alghero, Italy 1550 & 1984

city /country / date

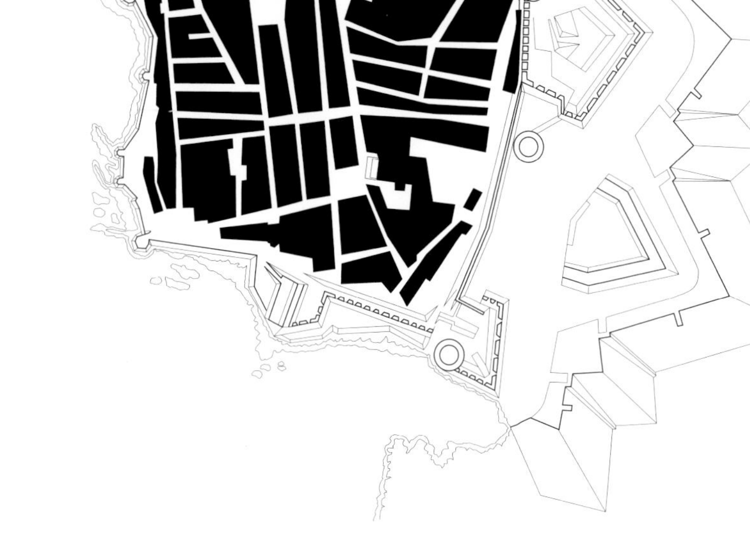

scale comparison

100M

city / country / date

Alkmaar, Netherlands 1865

scale comparison

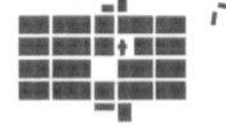

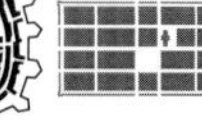

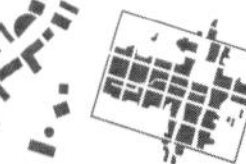

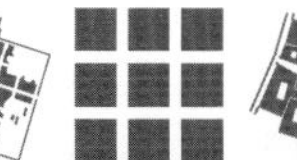

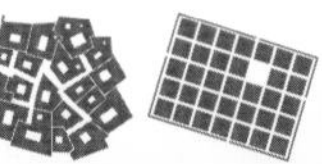

100M

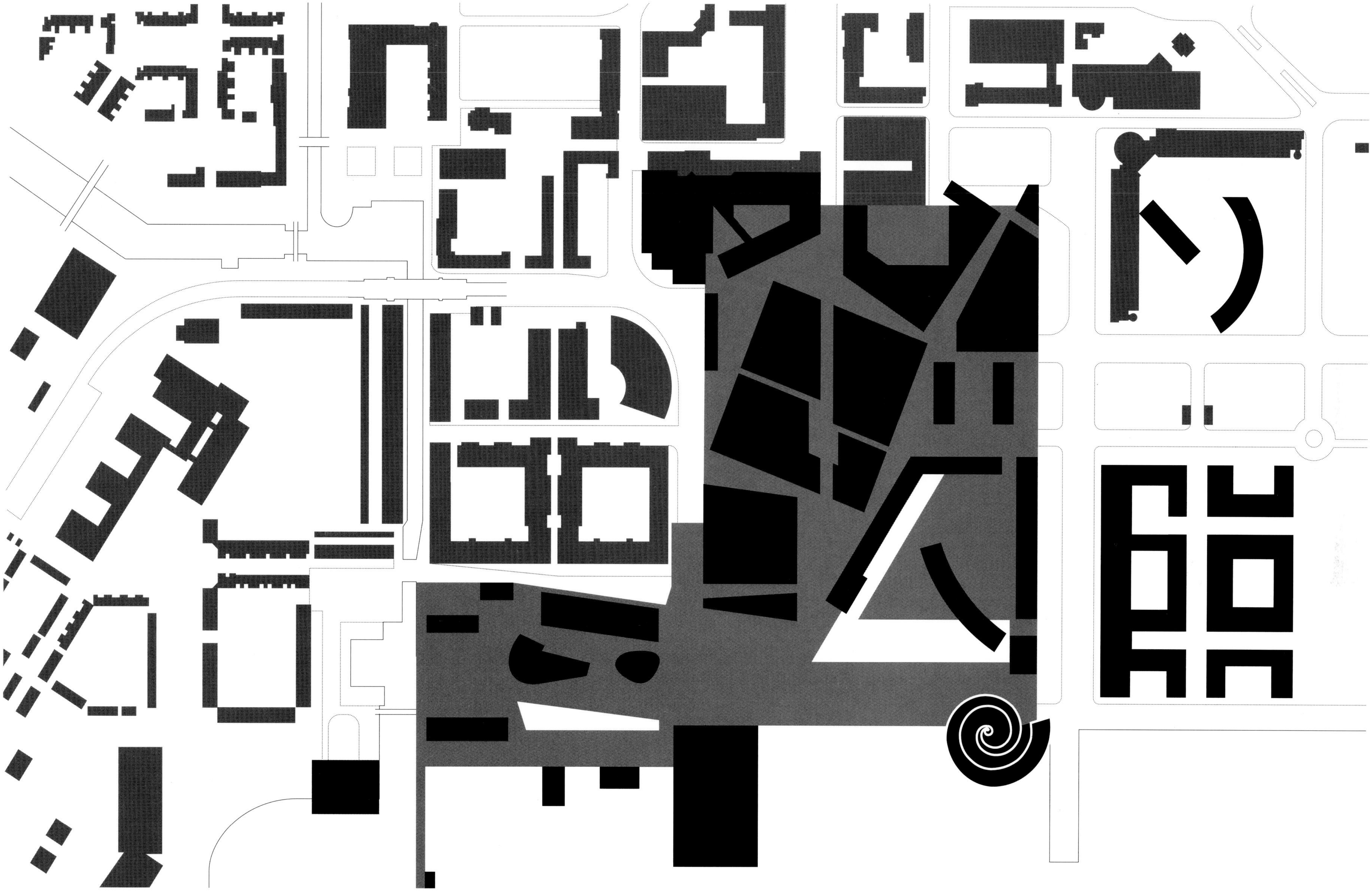

city / country / date

Almere, Netherlands (proposal by Rem Koolhaus) 1994

scale comparison

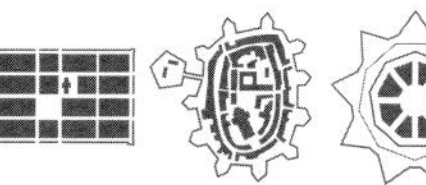
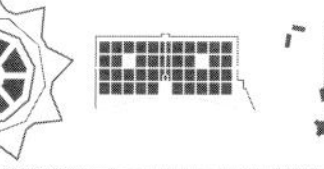

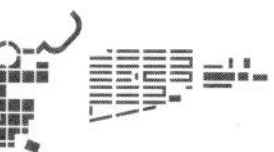

100M

city / country / date

Amarna, Egypt 1350 BC

scale comparison

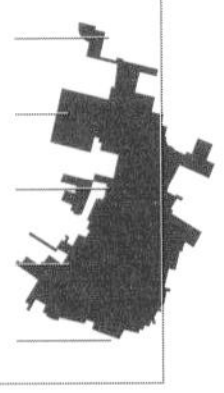

A

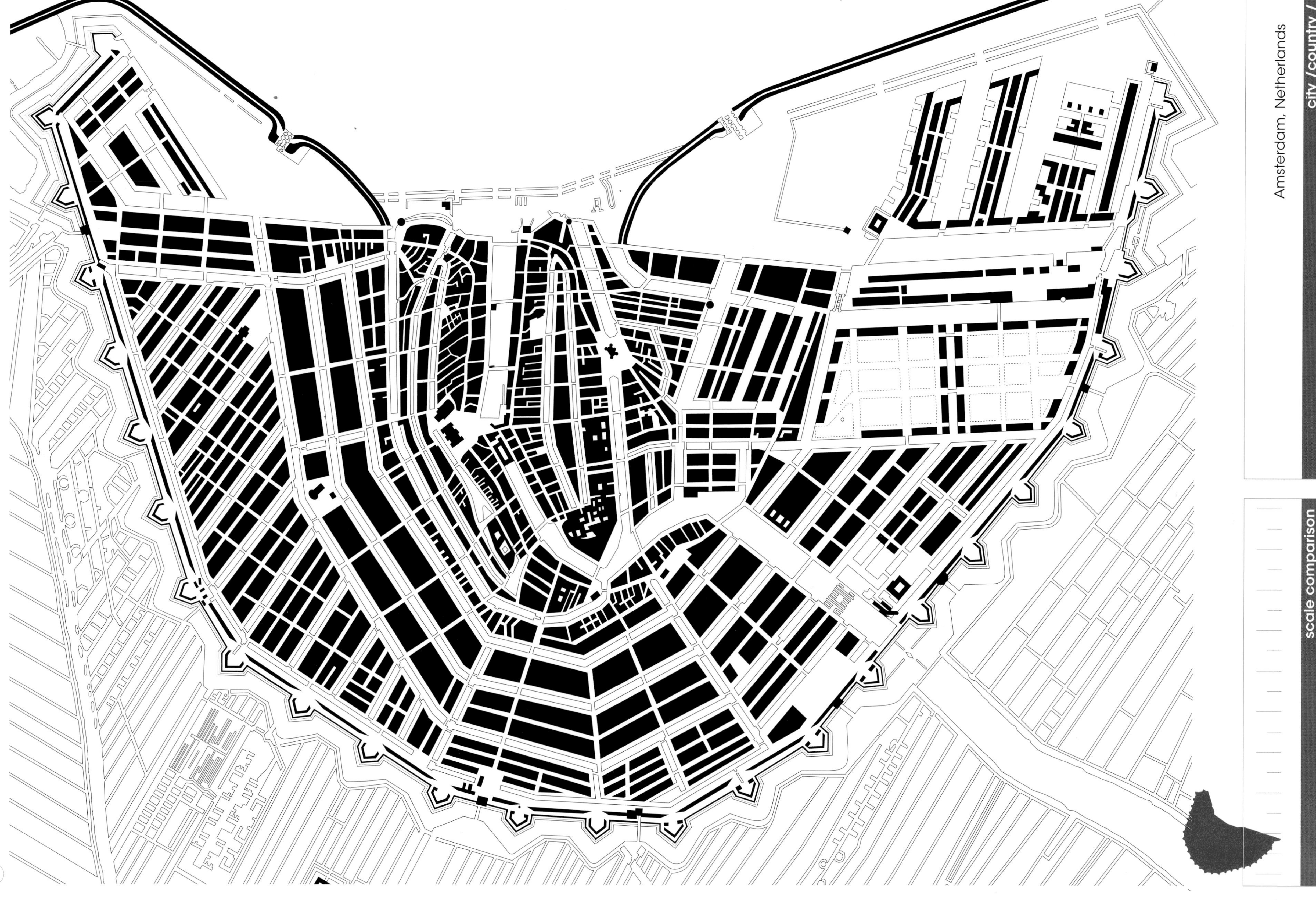
100M
Amsterdam, Netherlands
1835
city / country / date
scale comparison

100M
Ancona, Italy 1909
city / country / date
scale comparison

100M

Anguillara Sabazia, Italy 1982

city /country / date

scale comparison

Antwerp, Belgium 1832 & 1933 (proposal by Le Corbusier)
city /country / date
scale comparison
100M

100M

Aosta, Italy 1950

city /country / date

scale comparison

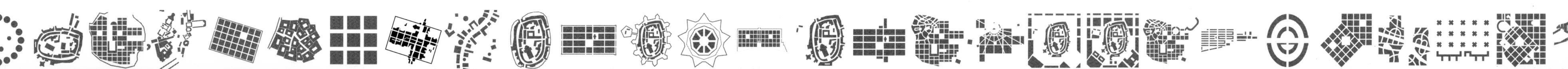

100M
Arezzo, Italy 1909
city / country / date
scale comparison

100M

city / country / date

Asbury Park, NJ, USA (proposal by Koetter/Kim Architects) 1990

scale comparison

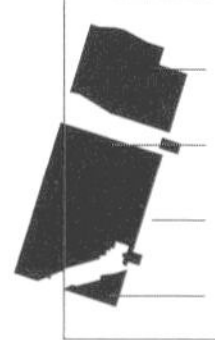

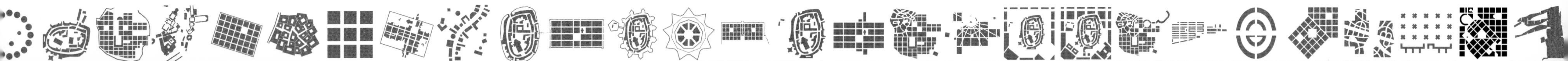

city / country / date

Asmara, Libya 1932

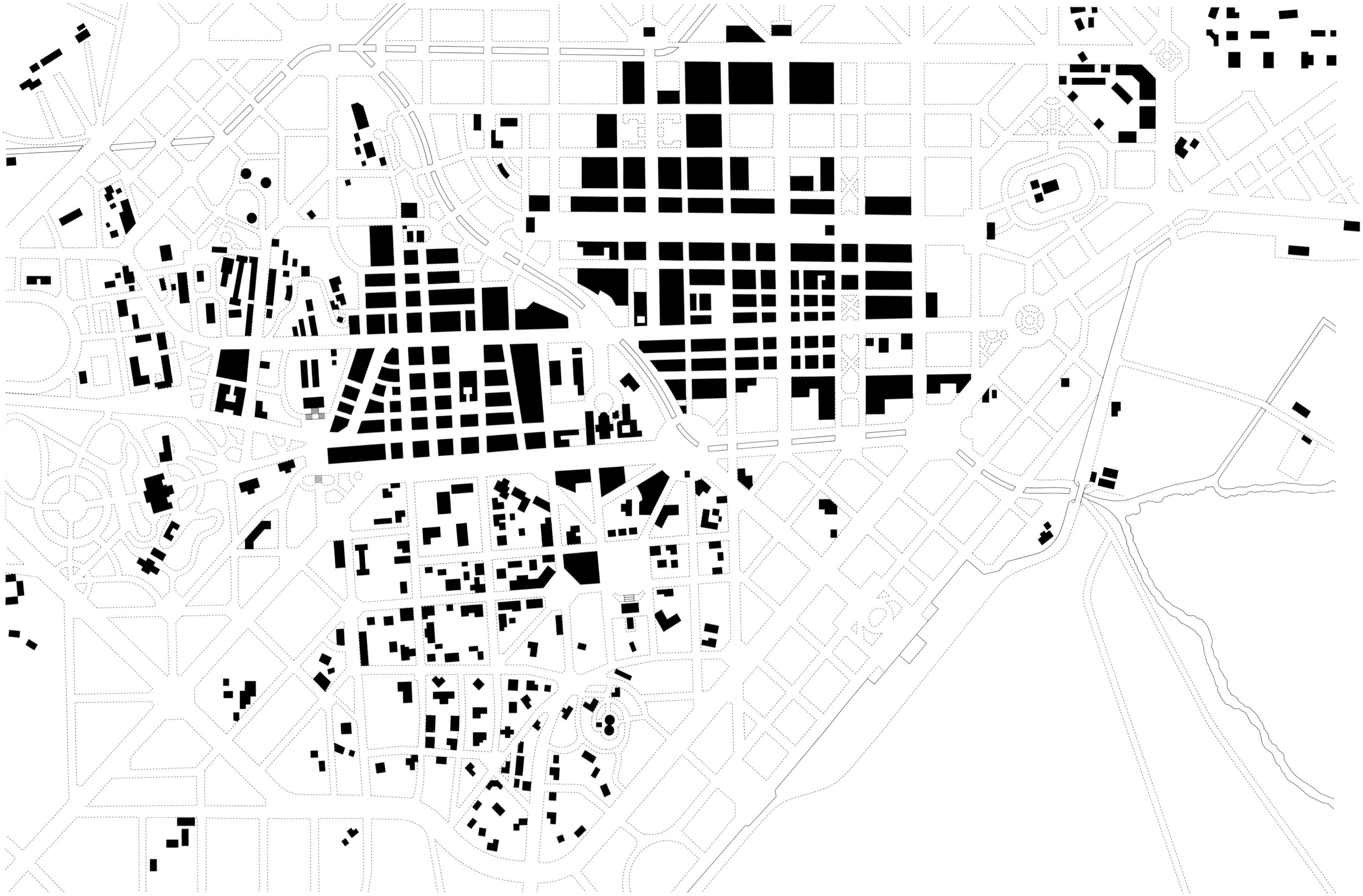

scale comparison

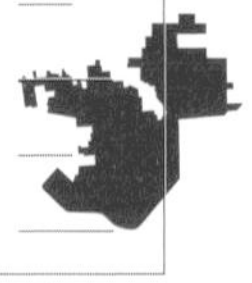

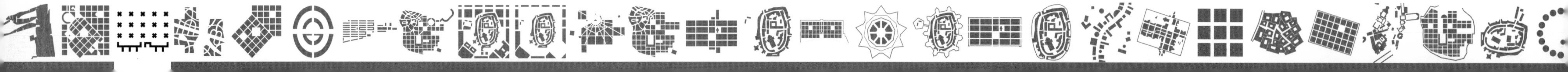

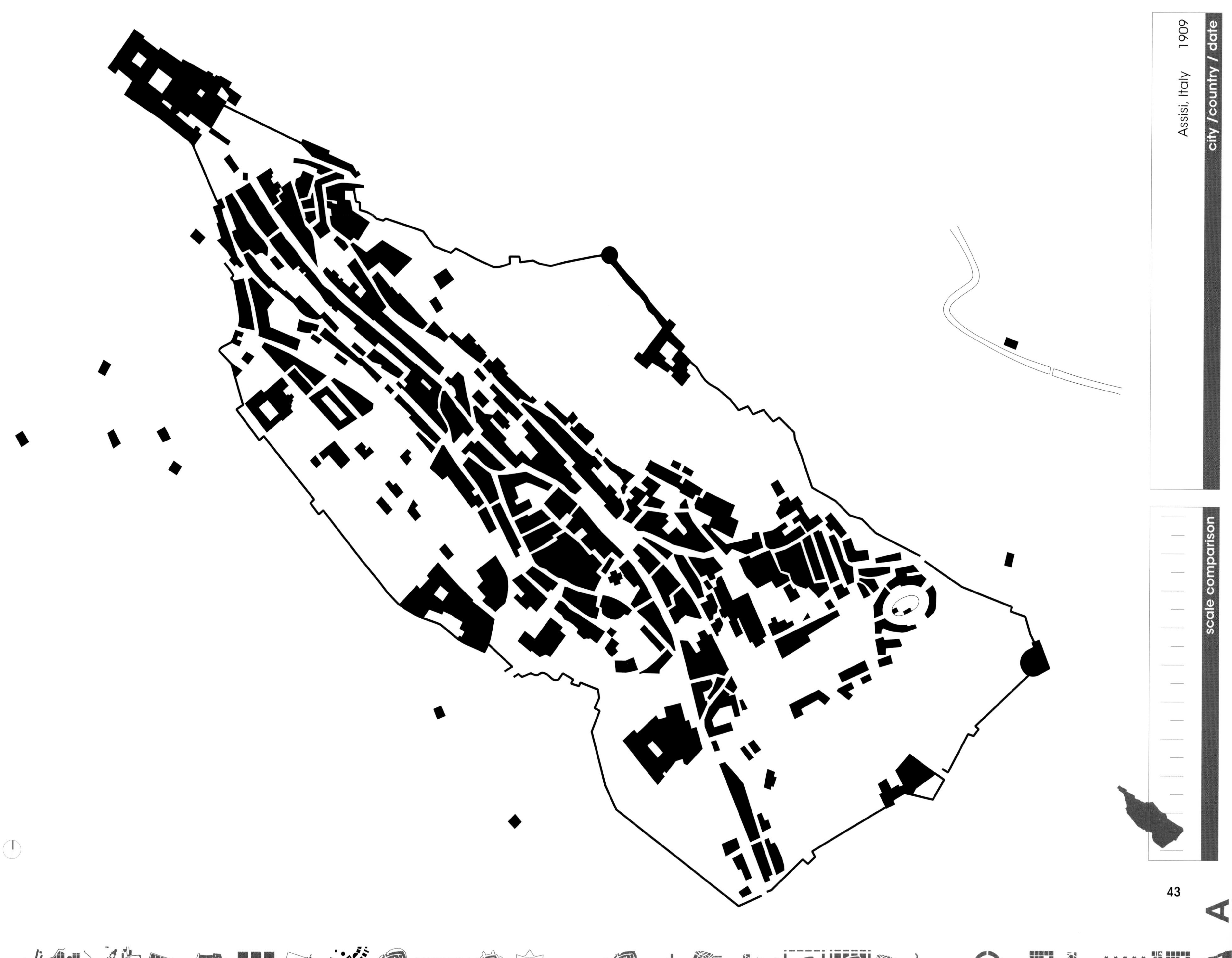
100M
Assisi, Italy
1909
city /country / date
scale comparison

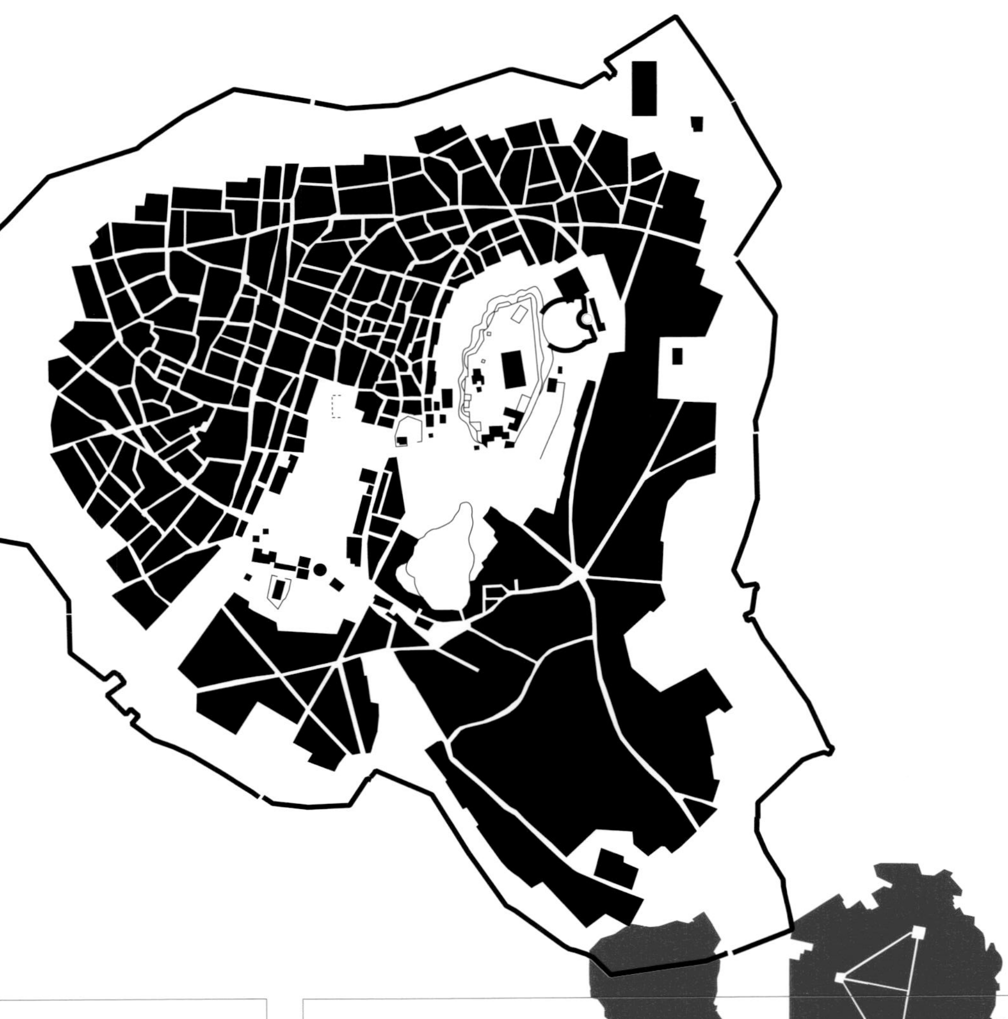

Athens, Greece 450 BC & 1909

city / country / date

scale comparison

100M

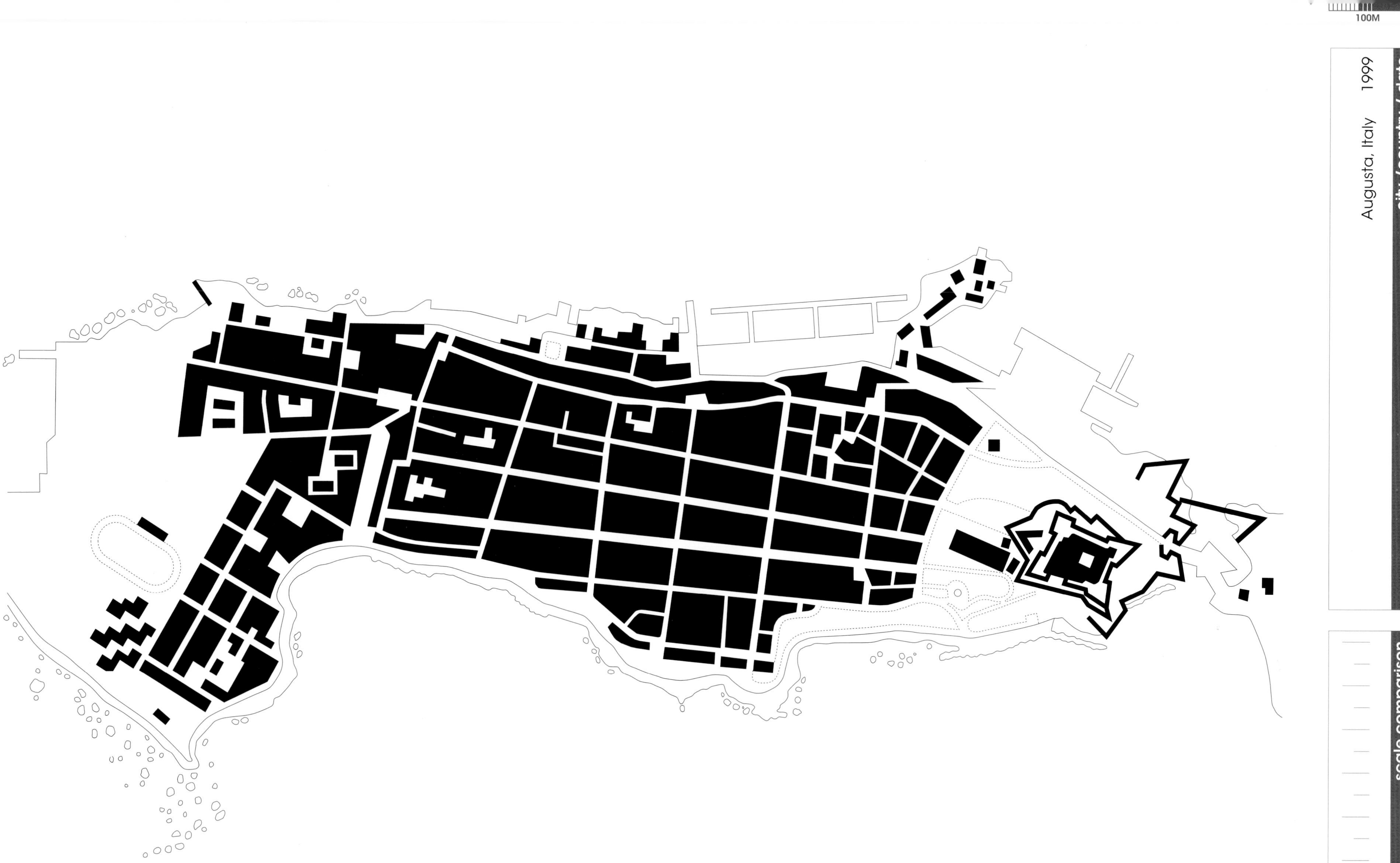

100M

city / country / date

Augusta, Italy 1999

scale comparison

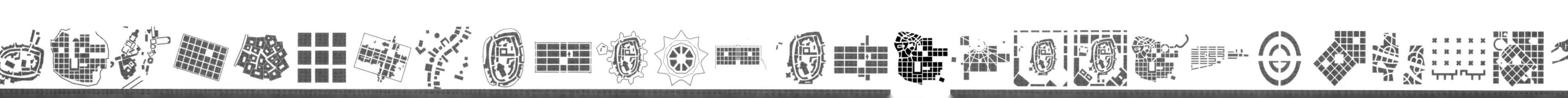

Bagnaia, Italy (w/ Villa Lante) 1950

city / country / date

scale comparison

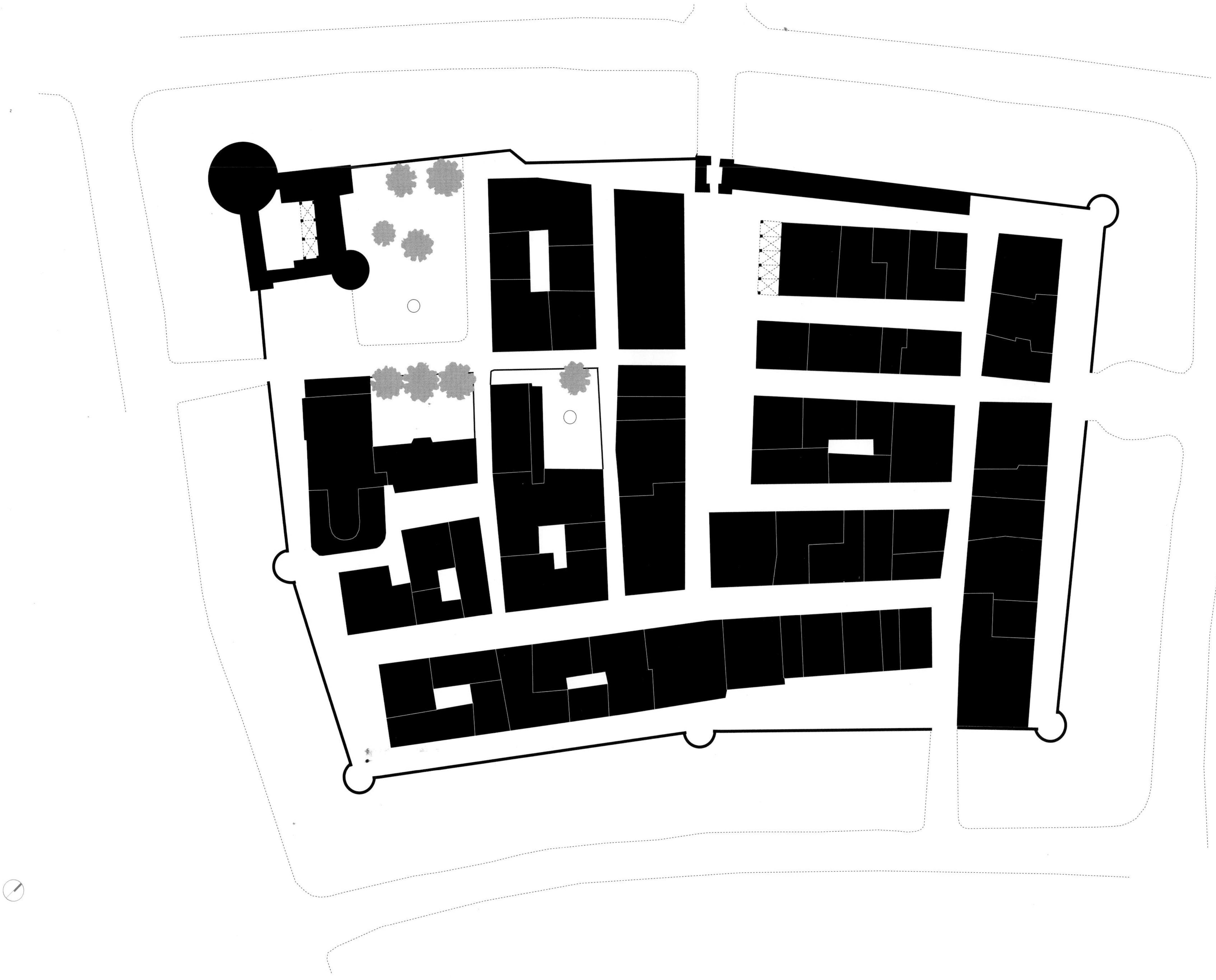

100M

Bagnara di Romagna, Italy [1963]

city / country / date

scale comparison

100M

city / country / date

Baltimore, MD, USA 1869

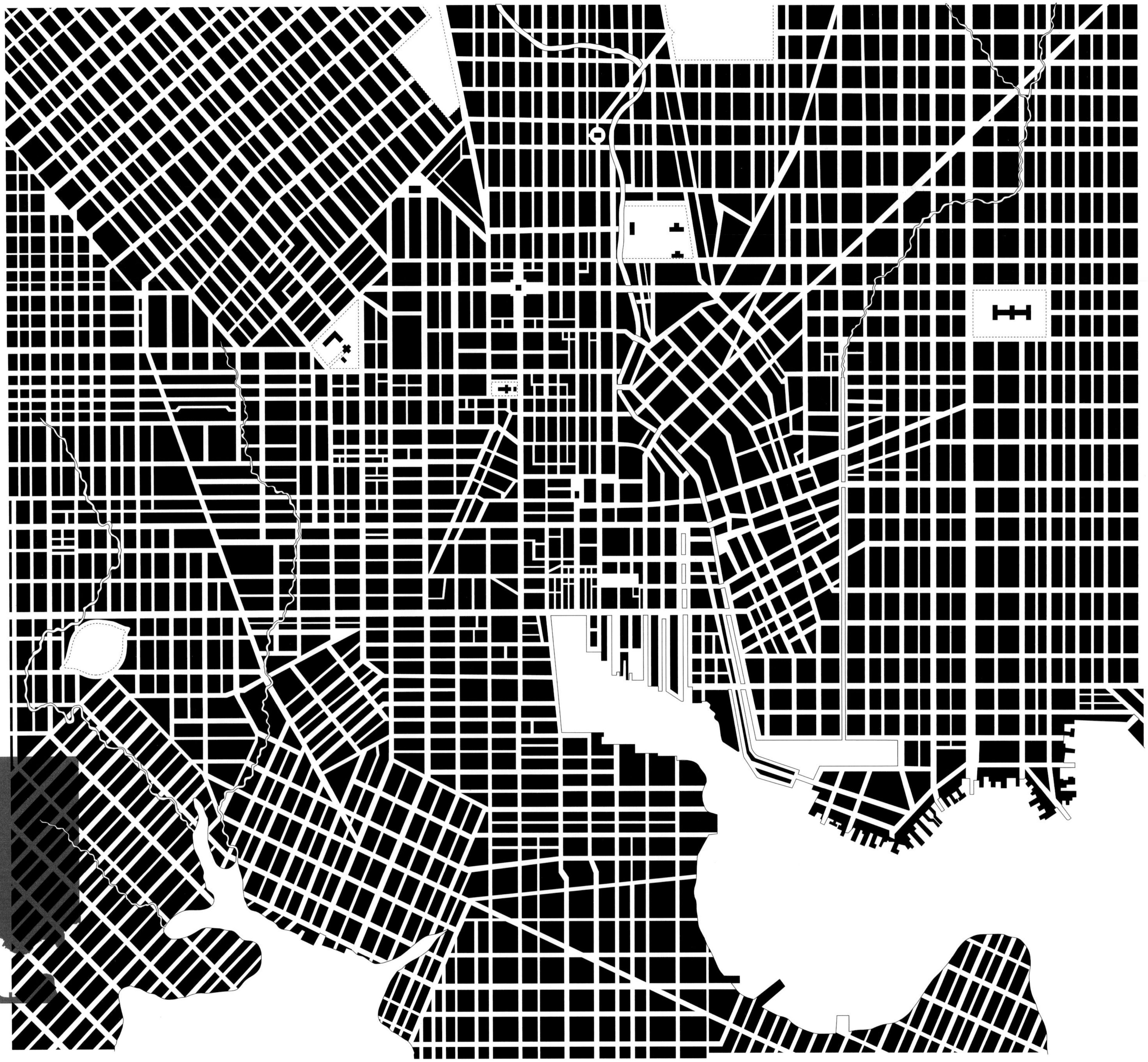

scale comparison

100M

Barbarano Romano, Italy 1980

city / country / date

scale comparison

100M

city / country / date

Barcelona, Spain 1492, 1687, & 1715

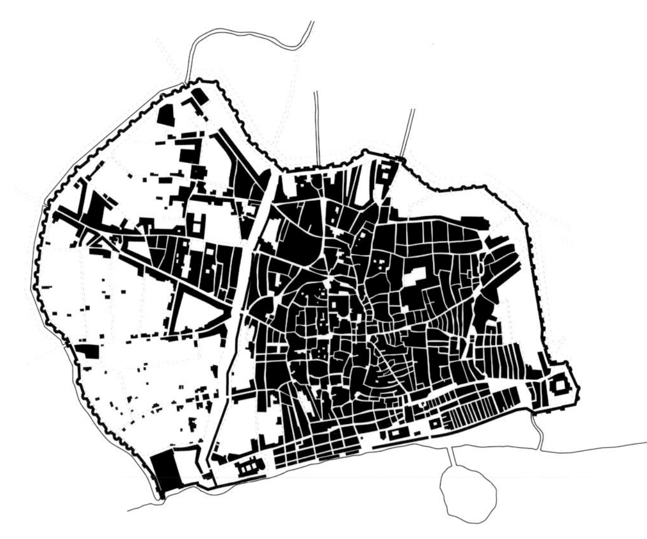

scale comparison

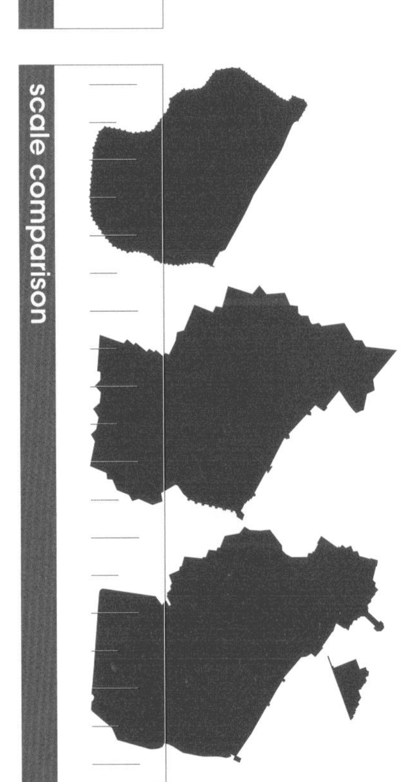

100M

Barcelona, Spain 1906

city /country / date

scale comparison

100M

city /country / date

Bath, England 1300, 1720, & 1740

scale comparison

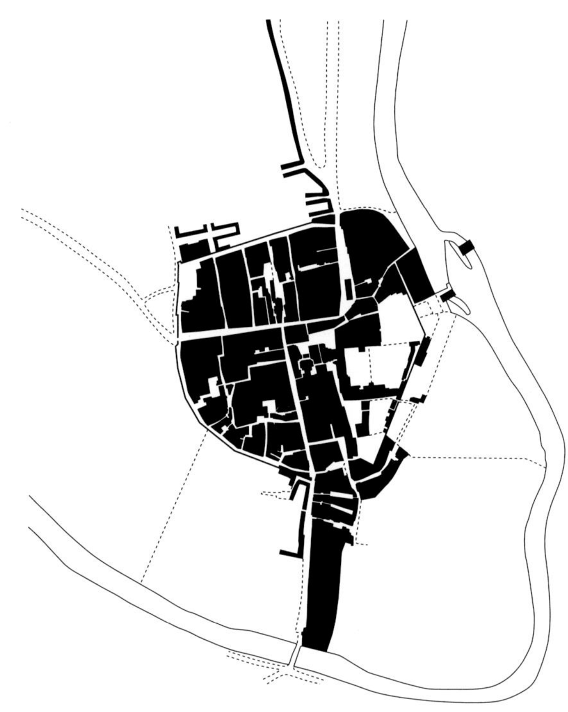

city / country / date

Bath, England 1775 & 1790

scale comparison

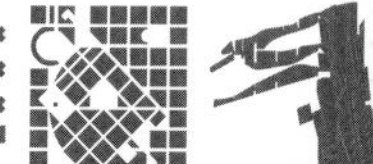

100M

city / country / date

Beaumont de Lomagne & Beaumont en Argonne France [1974]

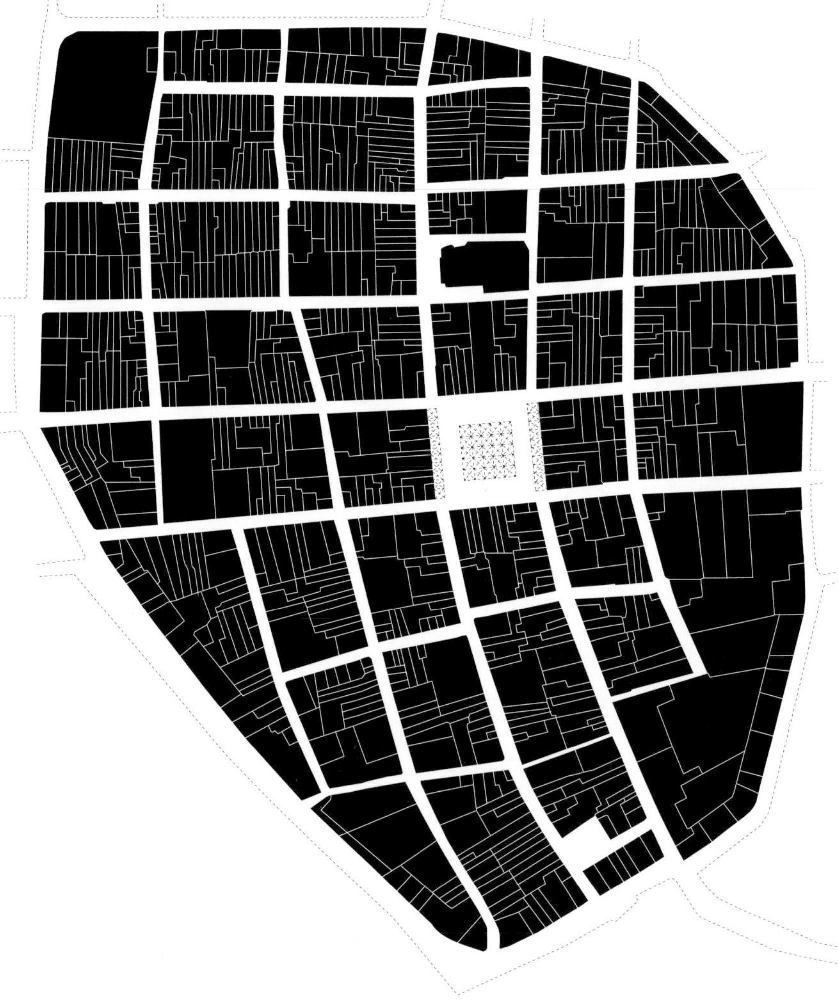

scale comparison

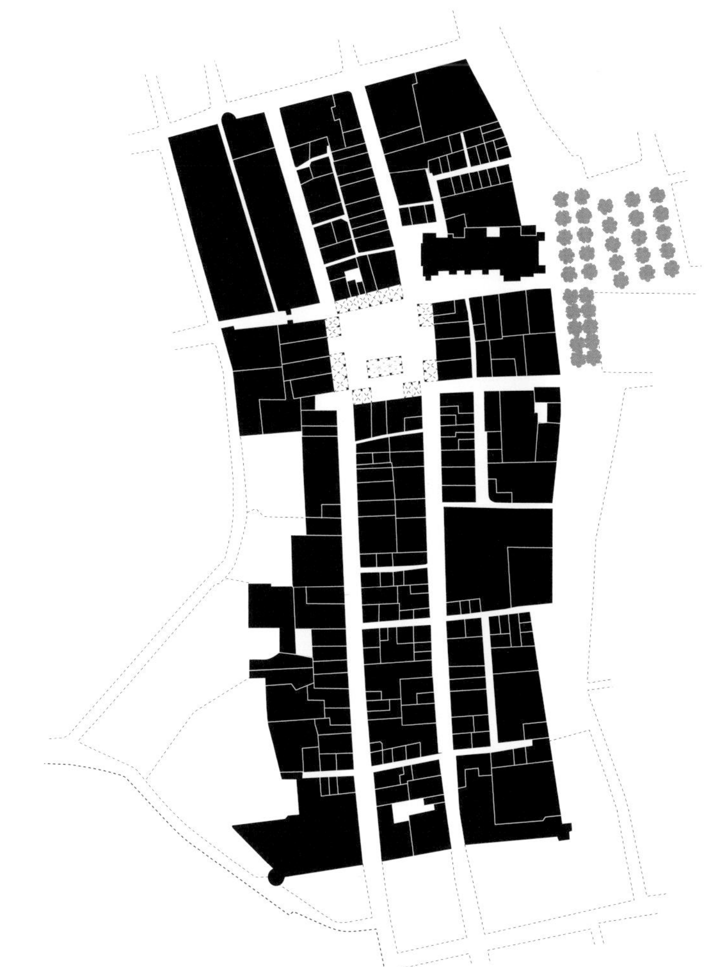

city /country / date

Beaumont-en-Périgord & Beaune, France [1974]

scale comparison

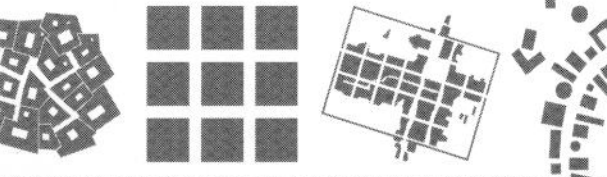

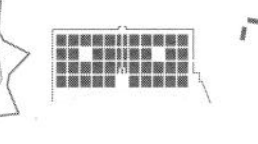
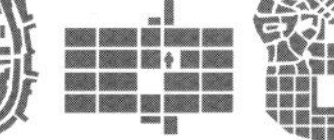

100M

city / country / date

Beijing, China 1950

scale comparison

B

Berlin, Germany 1688

city / country / date

scale comparison

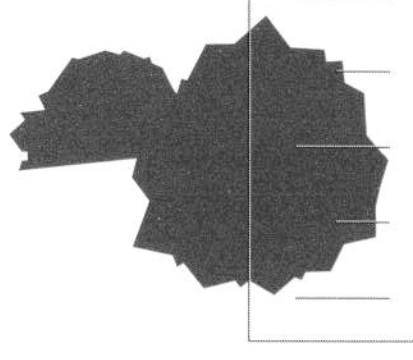

100M
Berlin, Germany 1863
city / country / date
scale comparison

100M

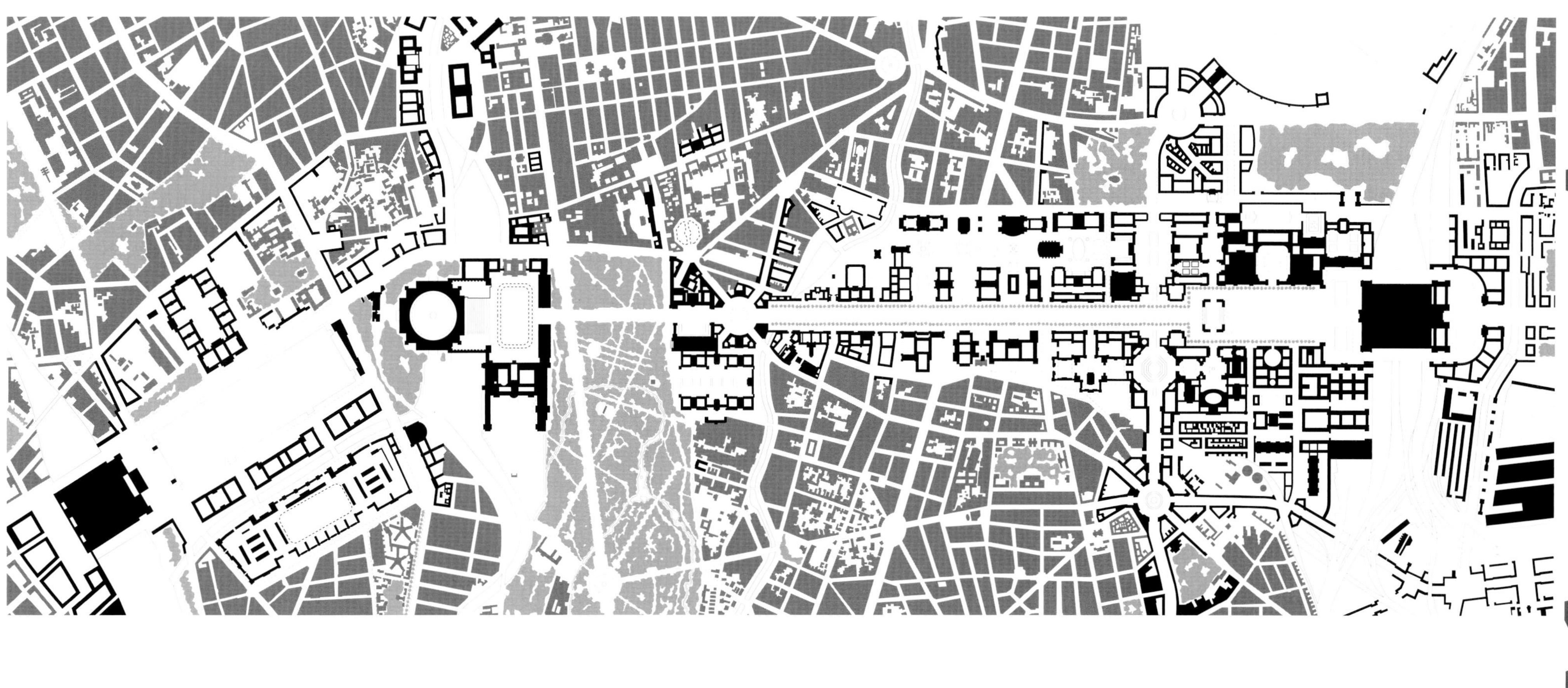

Berlin, Germany (Lower image -Design proposal by Albert Speer) 1688 & 1940

city /country / date

scale comparison

100M

city / country / date

Berlin, Germany (proposal by Le Corbusier) 1961

scale comparison

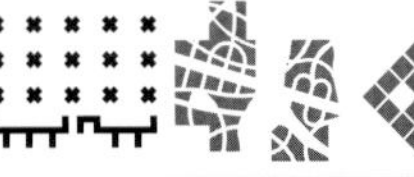

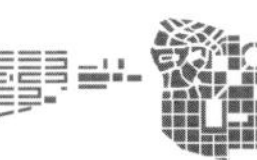

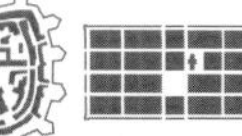

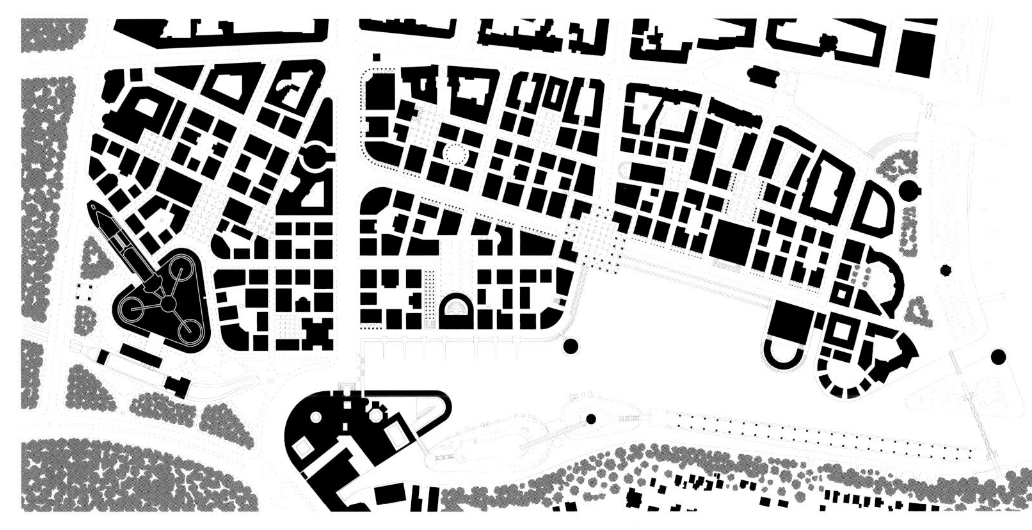

Berlin-Tegel Competition Proposal, Léon Krier

Berlin-Tegel Competition Proposal, Charles Moore

Berlin-Tegel Competition Proposal, Arata Isozaki

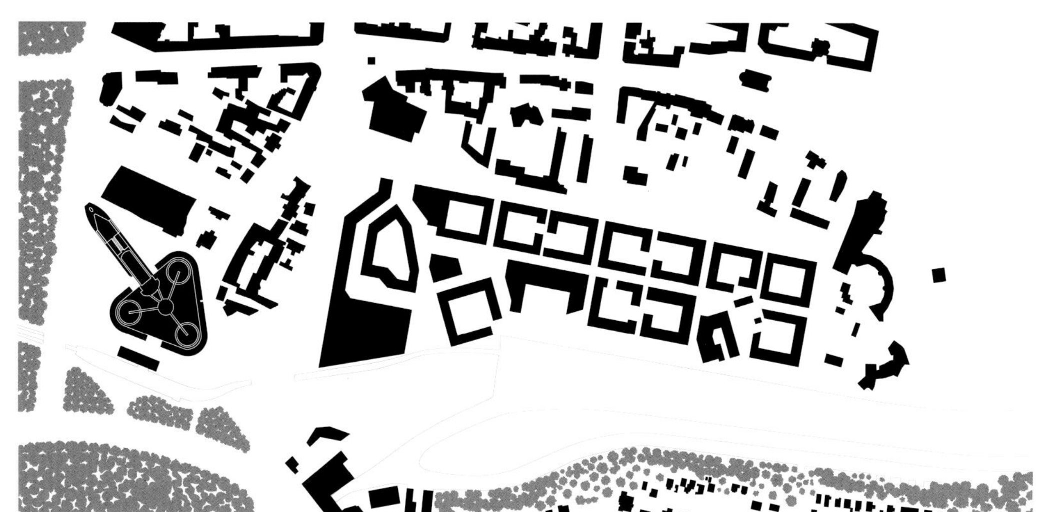

Berlin-Tegel Competition Proposal, Arata Isozaki

Berlin-Tegel Competition Proposal, Behnisch & Partners

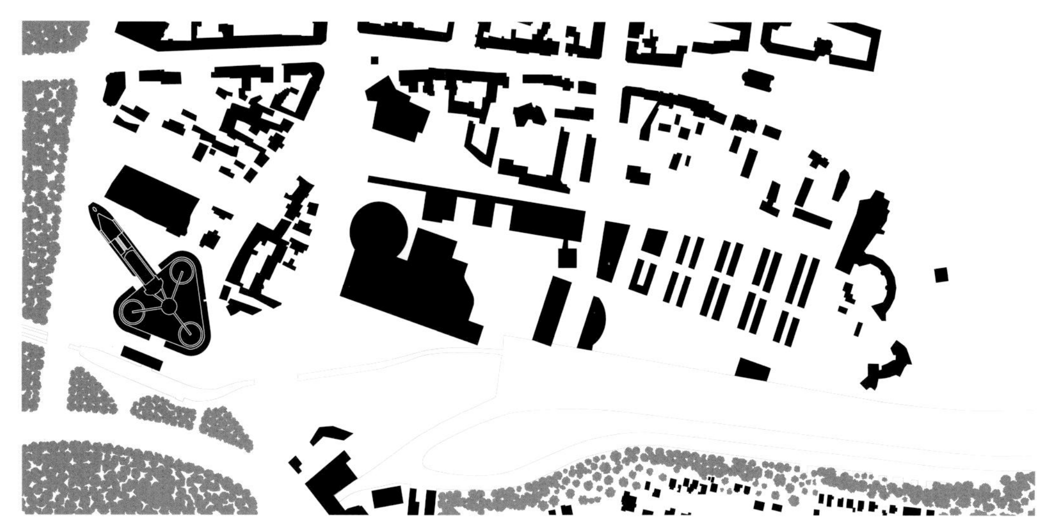

Berlin-Tegel Competition Proposal, Stavro project

Berlin-Tegel, Germany (proposals) 1982

city / country / date

scale comparison

100M

city / country / date

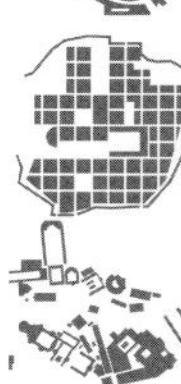

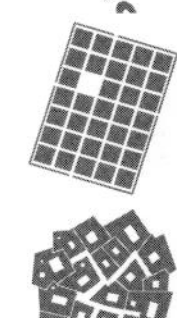

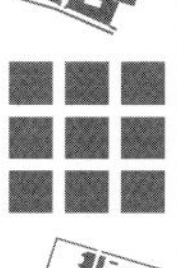

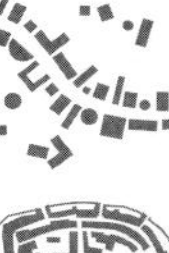

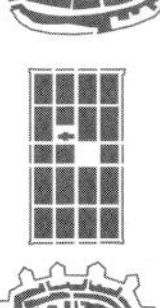

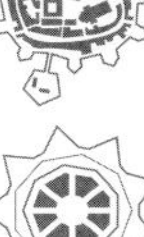

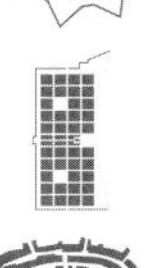

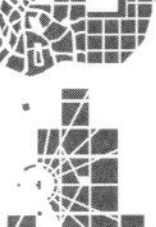

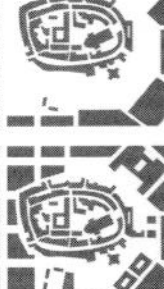

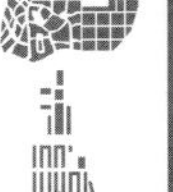

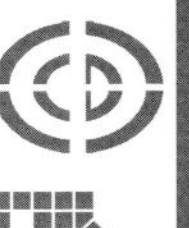

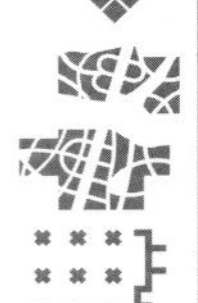

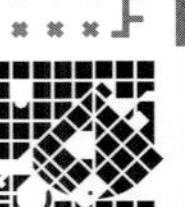

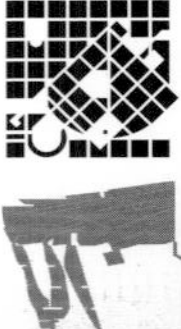

Berlin-Potsdam Platz, Germany (proposal by Augusto Romanano Burelli) 1991

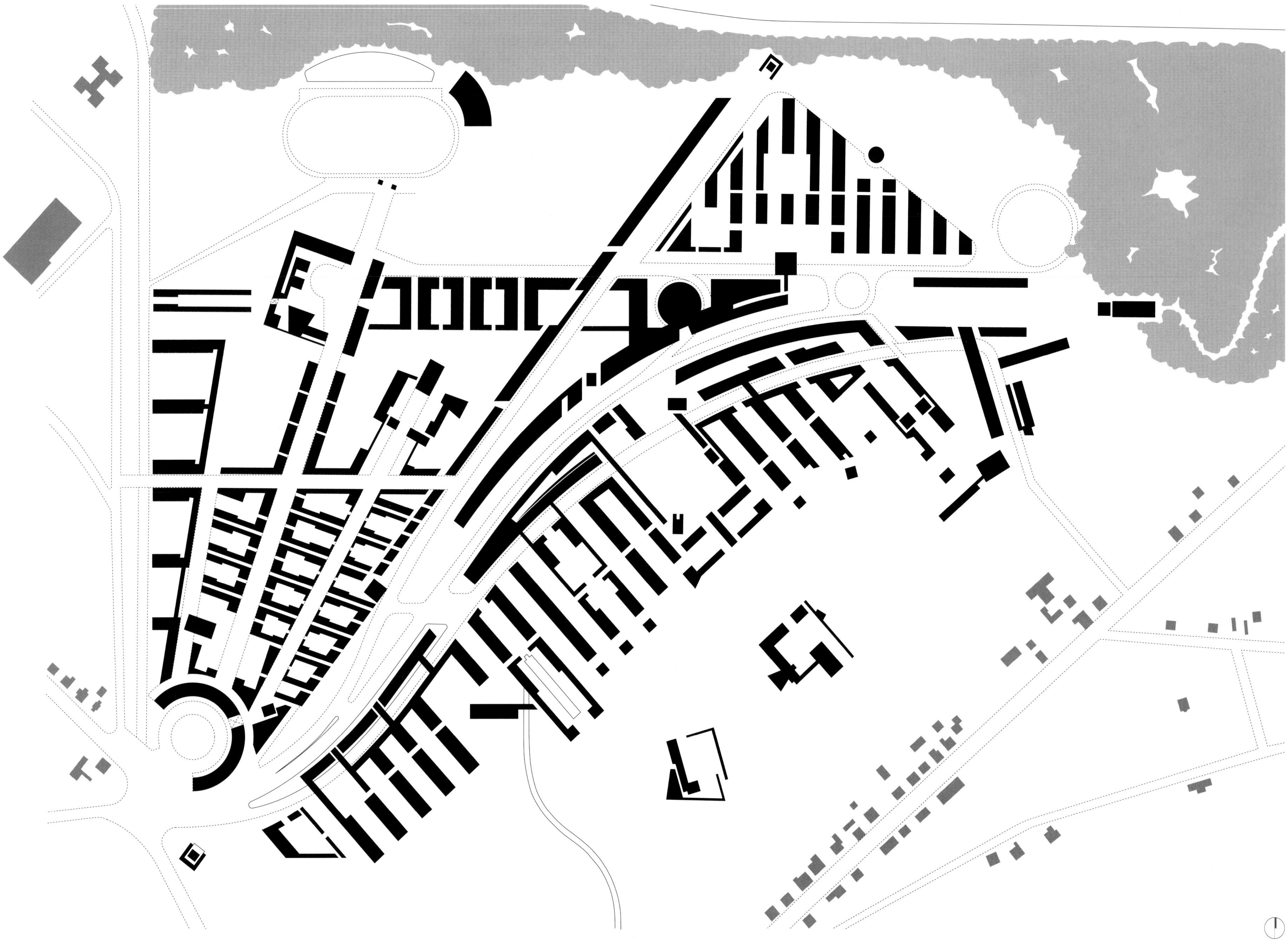

scale comparison

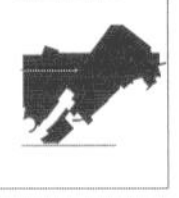

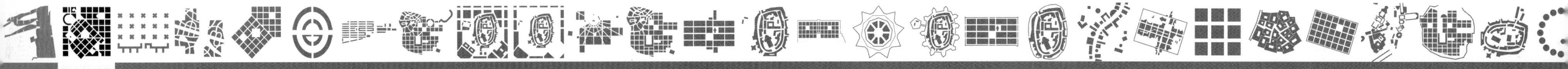

100M

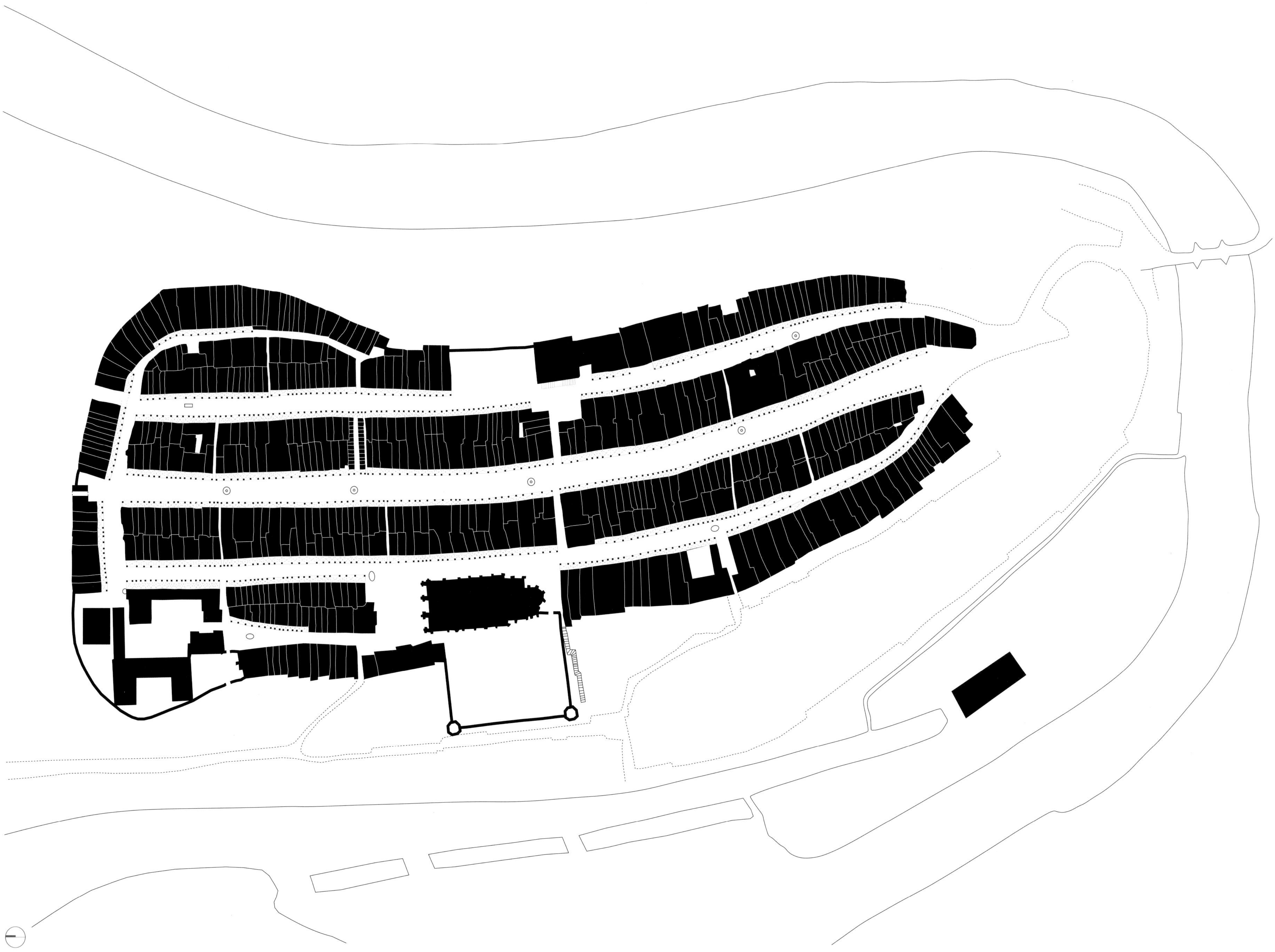

Bern, Switzerland 1191

city / country / date

scale comparison

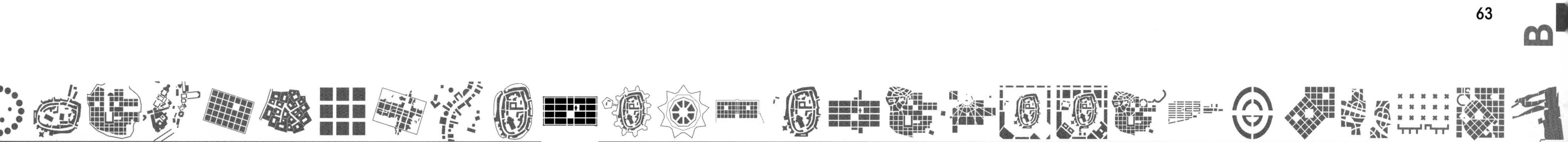

B

100M

city /country / date

Bern, Switzerland 1191& 1800

scale comparison

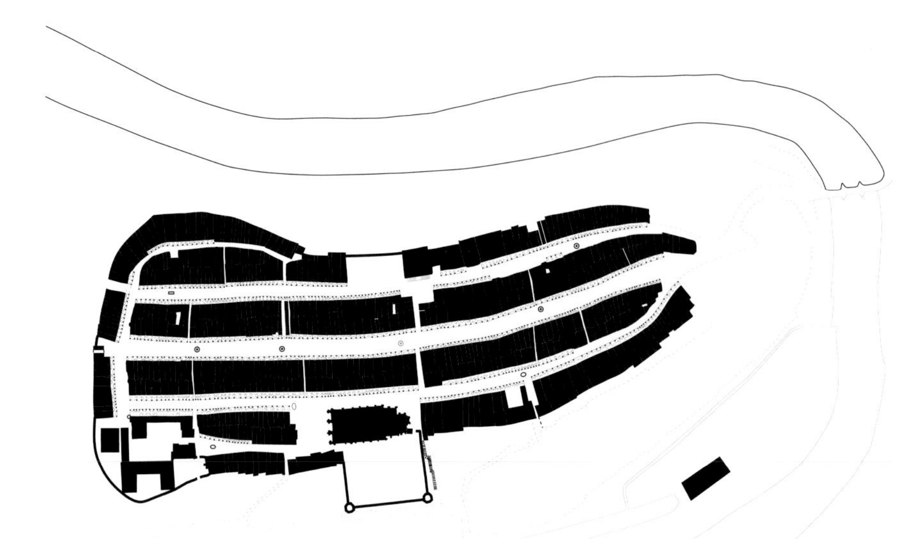

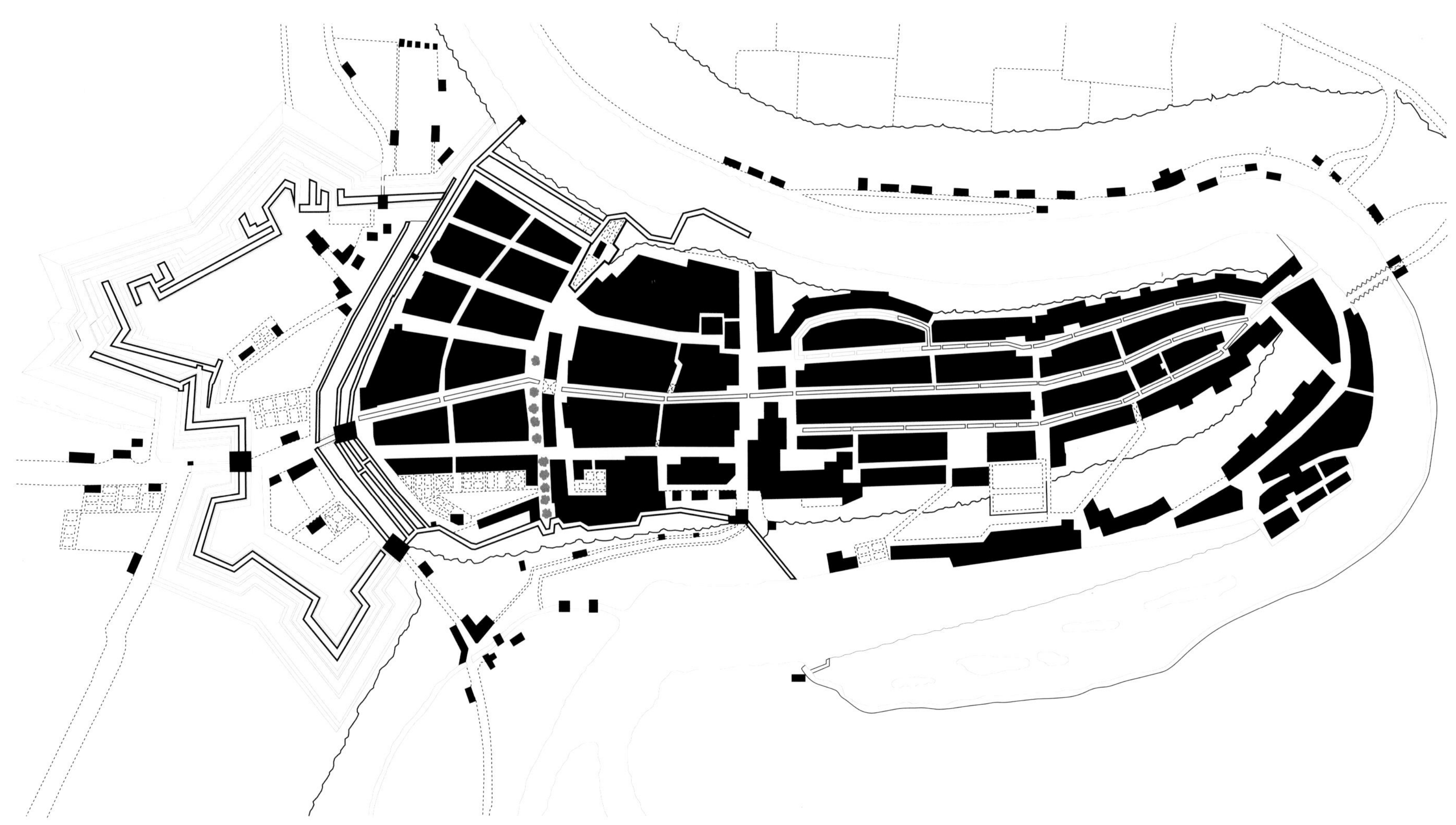

B

100M

city / country / date

Bern, Switzerland 1888

scale comparison

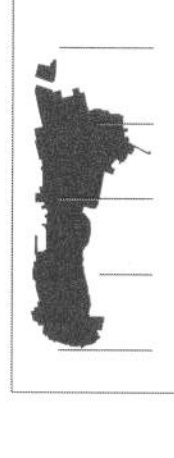

Birmingham, England 1839
city / country / date
scale comparison
100M
B

100M

Blanchland, England 1946

city / country / date

scale comparison

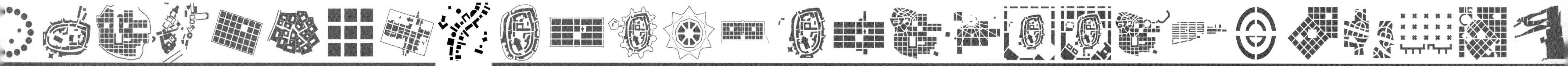

100M

city / country / date

Bologna, Italy 1913

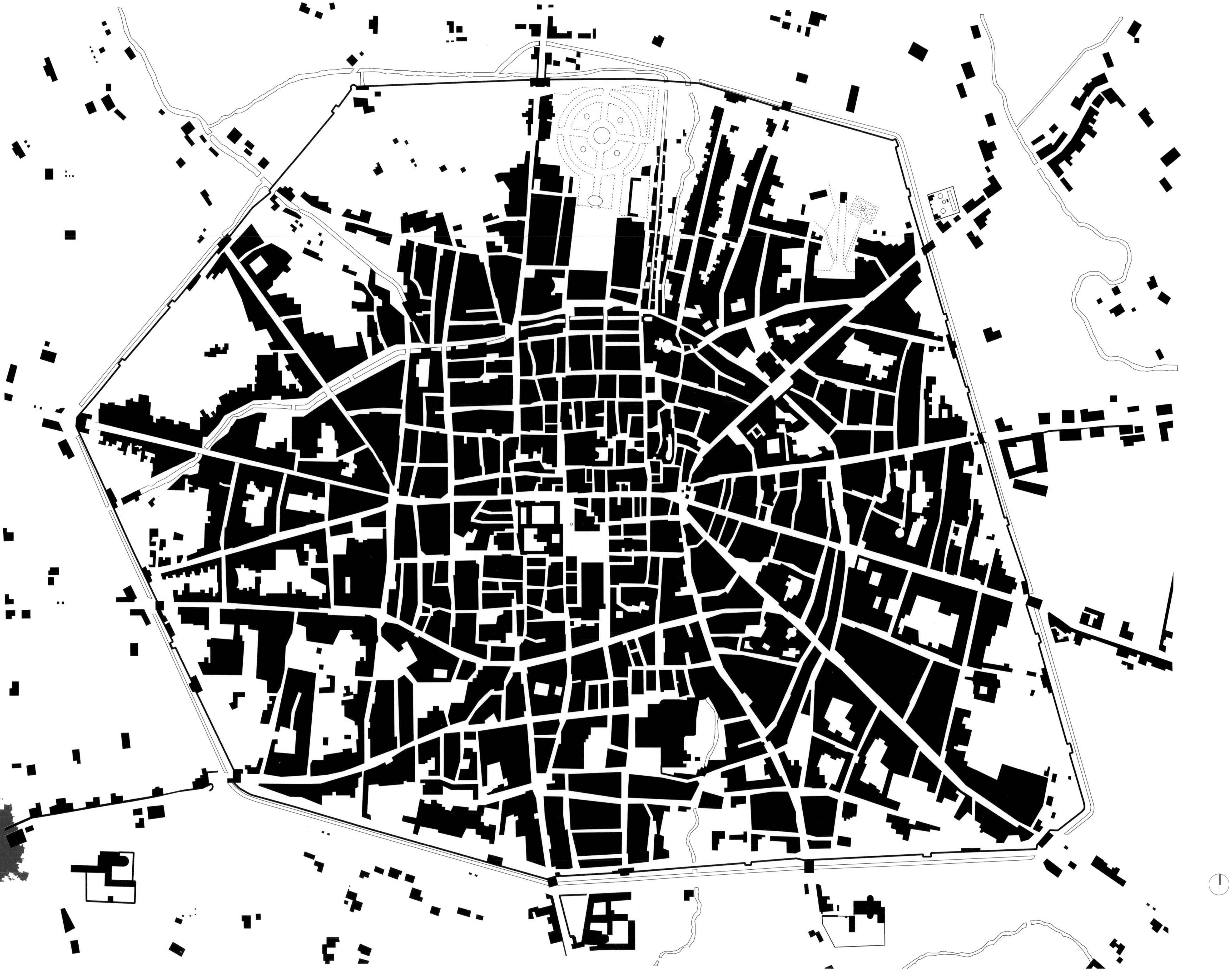

scale comparison

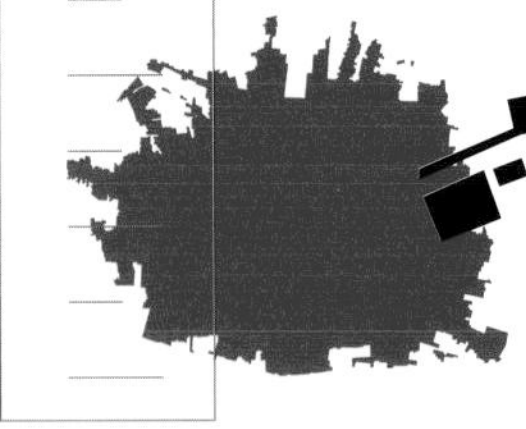

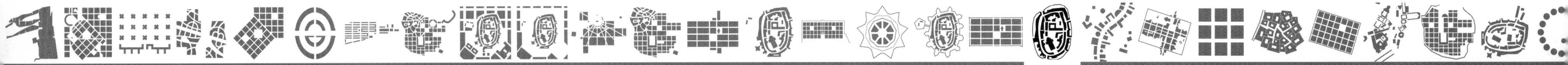

100M

Bonne & Bonneville, France [1974]

city / country / date

scale comparison

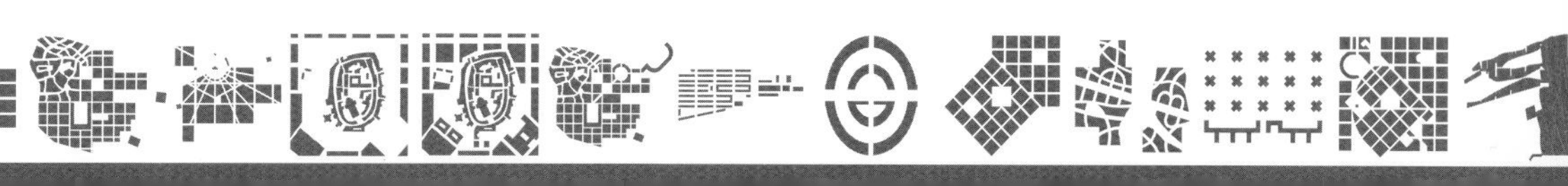

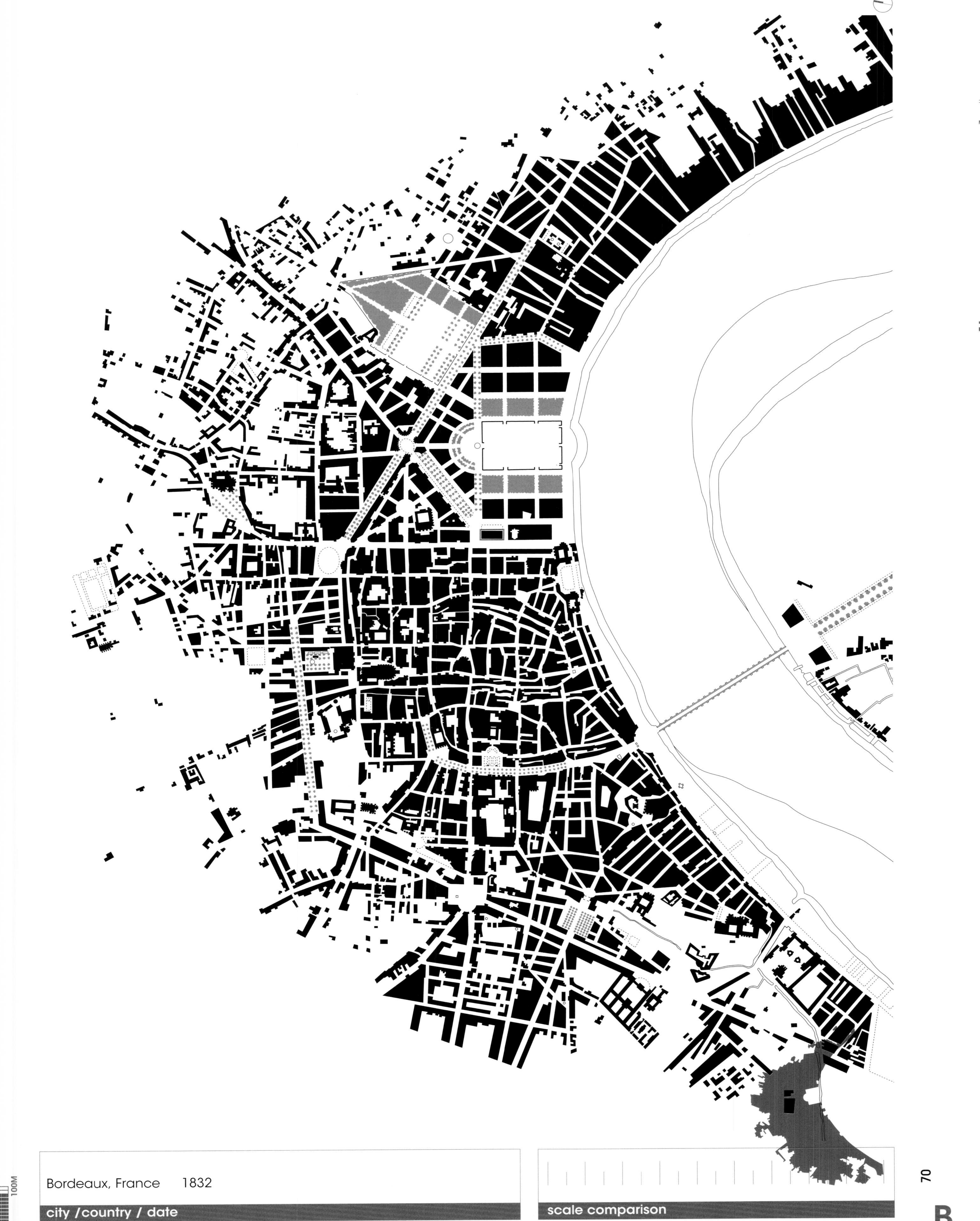
100M
Bordeaux, France 1832
city / country / date
scale comparison
B

100M

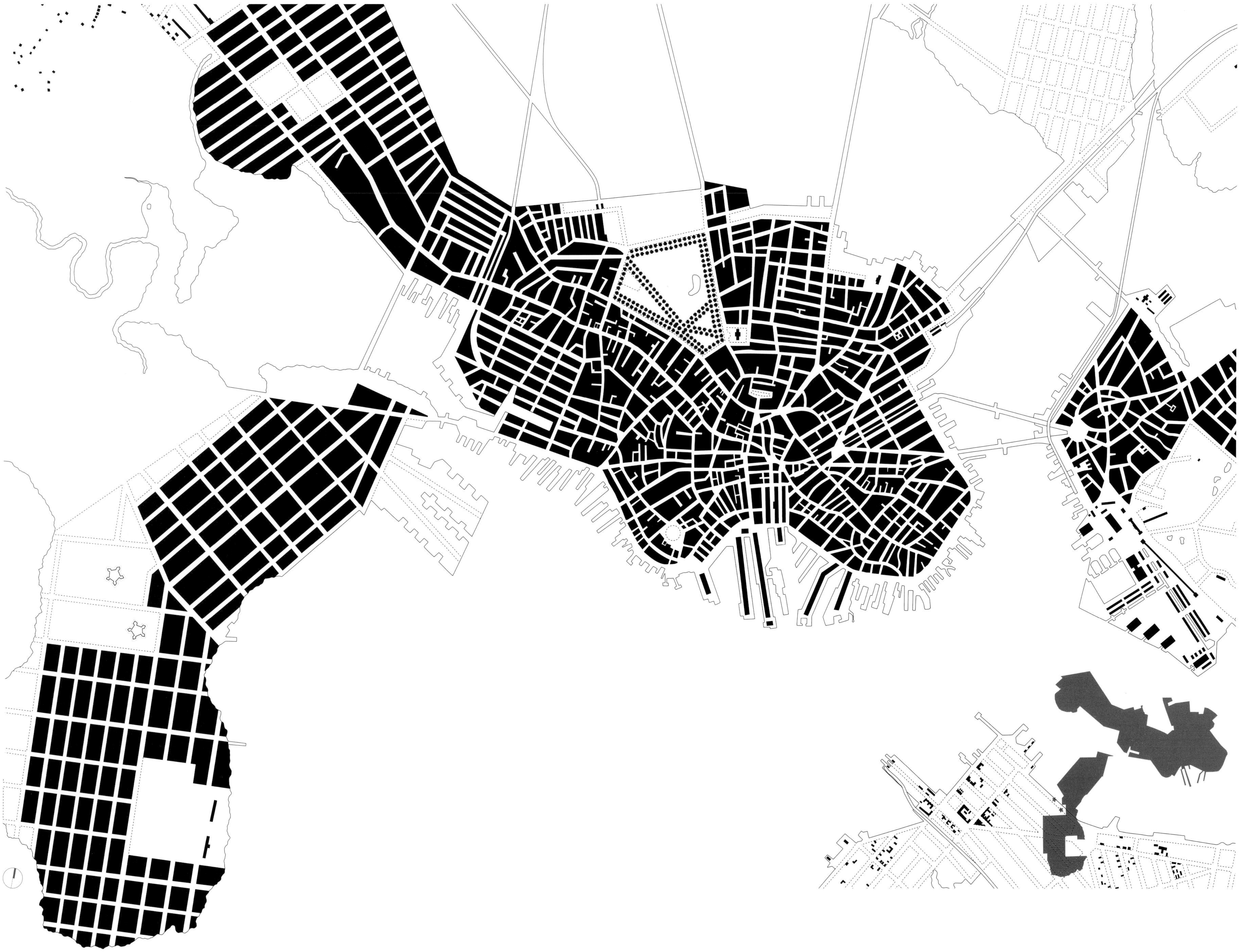

Boston, MA, USA 1852

city /country / date

scale comparison

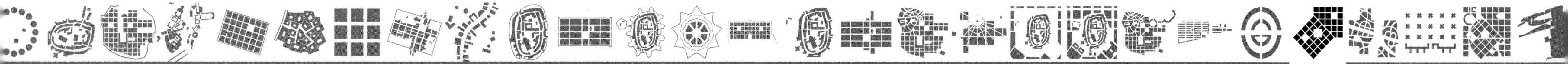

B

100M

city / country / date

Boulogne-sur-Gesse, France [1974]

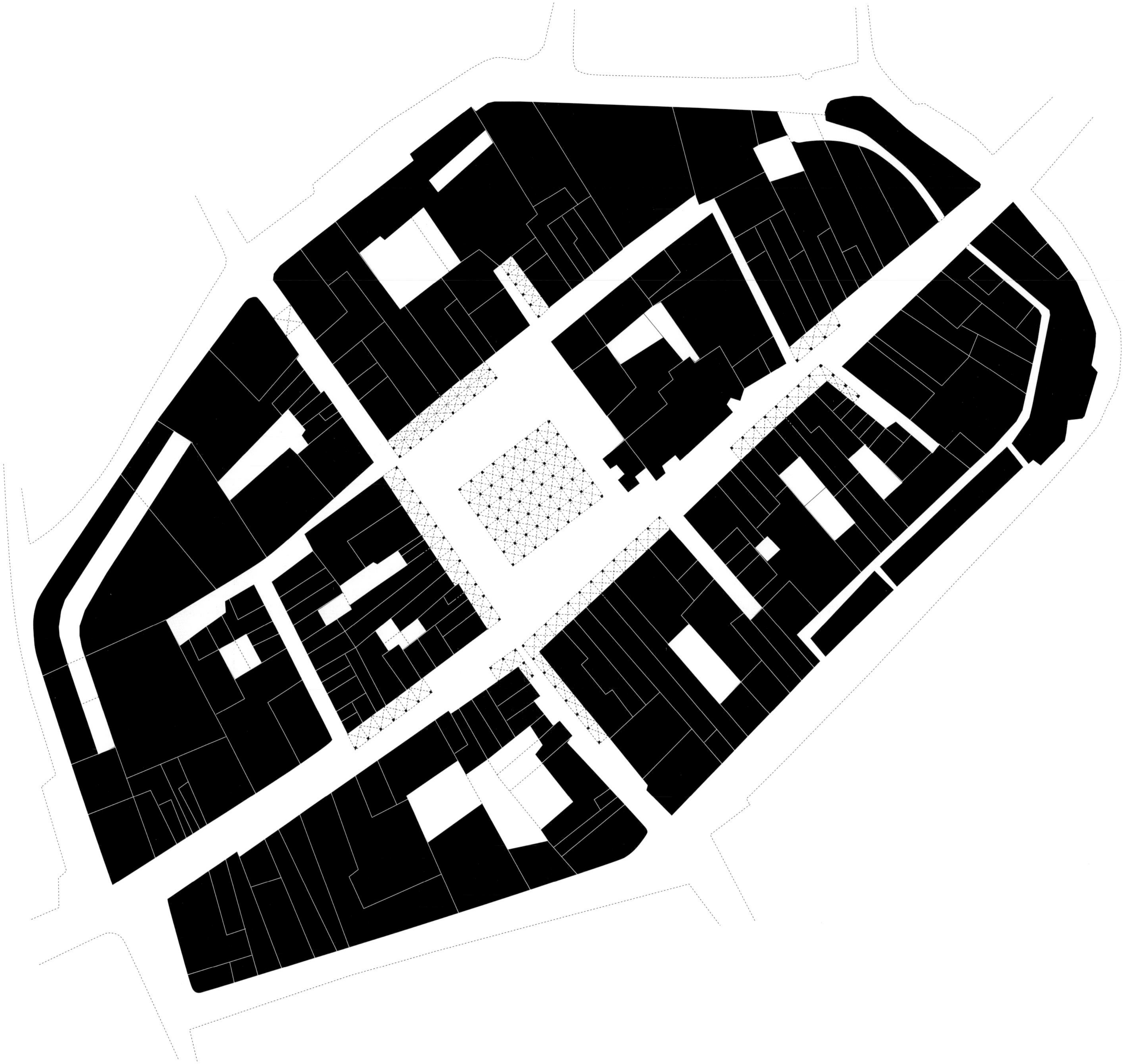

scale comparison

B

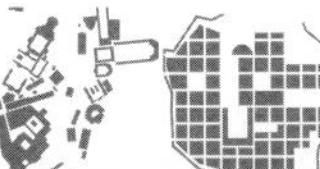

100M
city / country / date
Bournville, England (Cadbury Chocolate Works)
1879
scale comparison
73
B

100M

city /country / date

Brasilia, Bazil 1956

scale comparison

100M

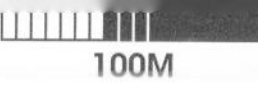

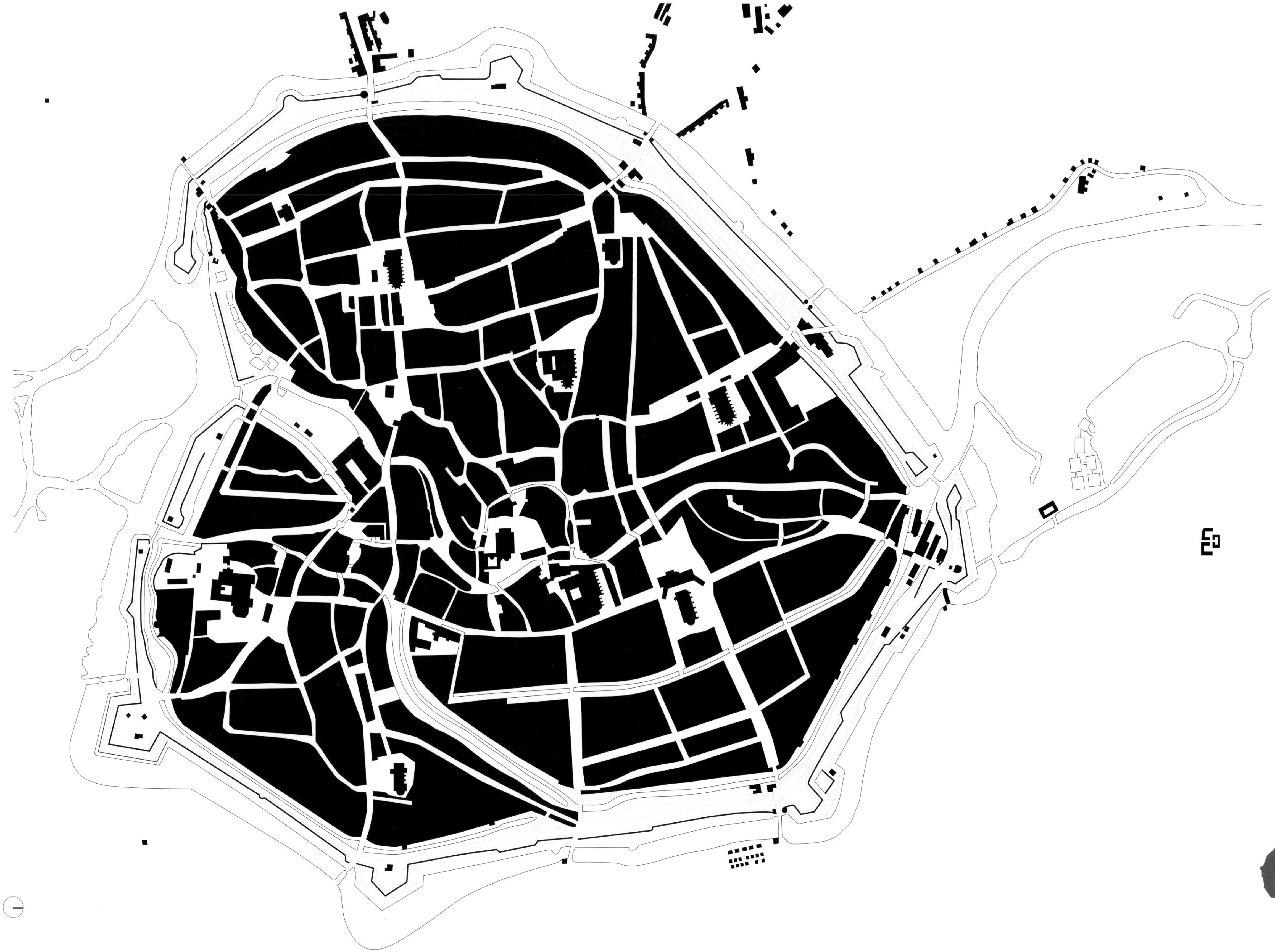

Braunschweig, Germany 1671

city /country / date

scale comparison

B

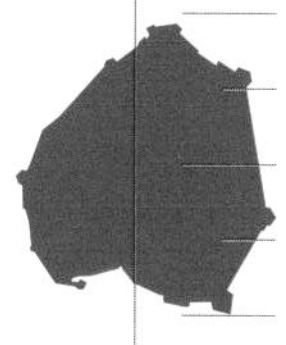

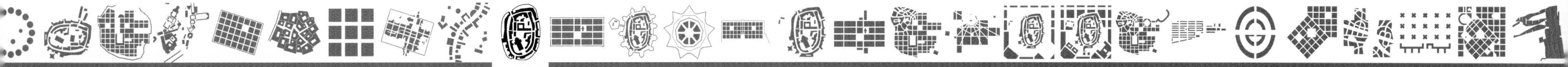

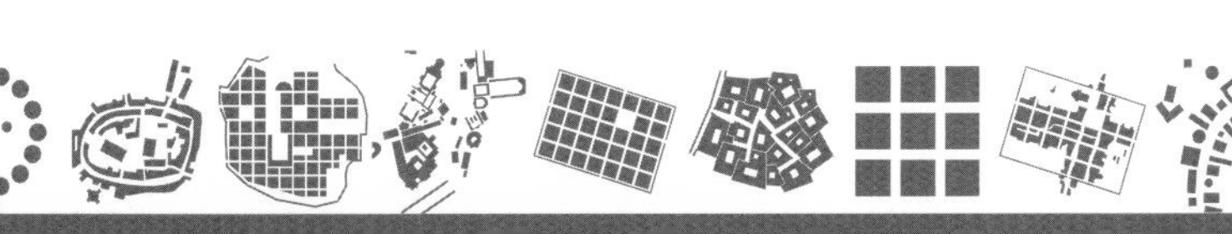

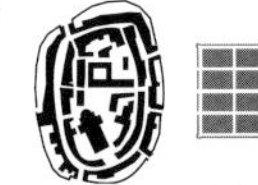

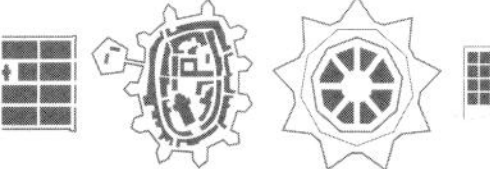

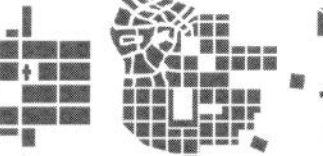

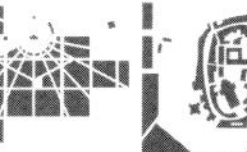

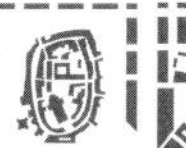

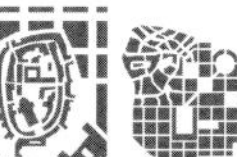

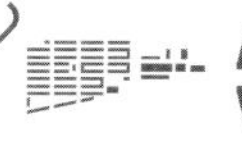

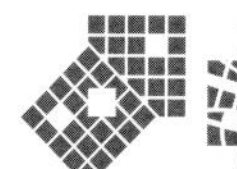

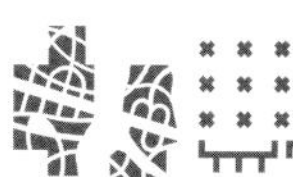

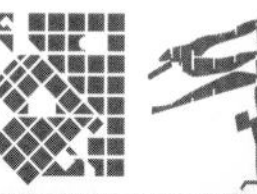

100M

city / country / date

Breda, Netherlands 1865

scale comparison

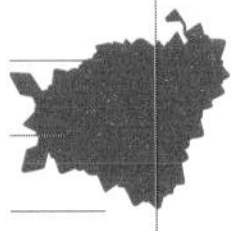

B

100M

Bremen, Germany 1893

city /country / date

scale comparison

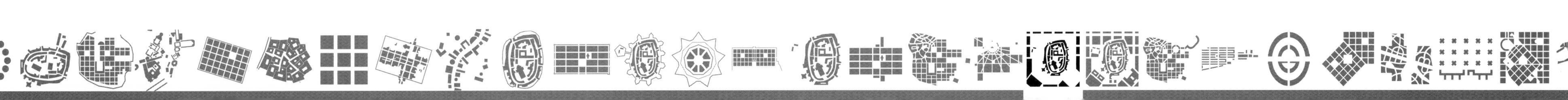

city / country / date

Brescia, Italy 1937

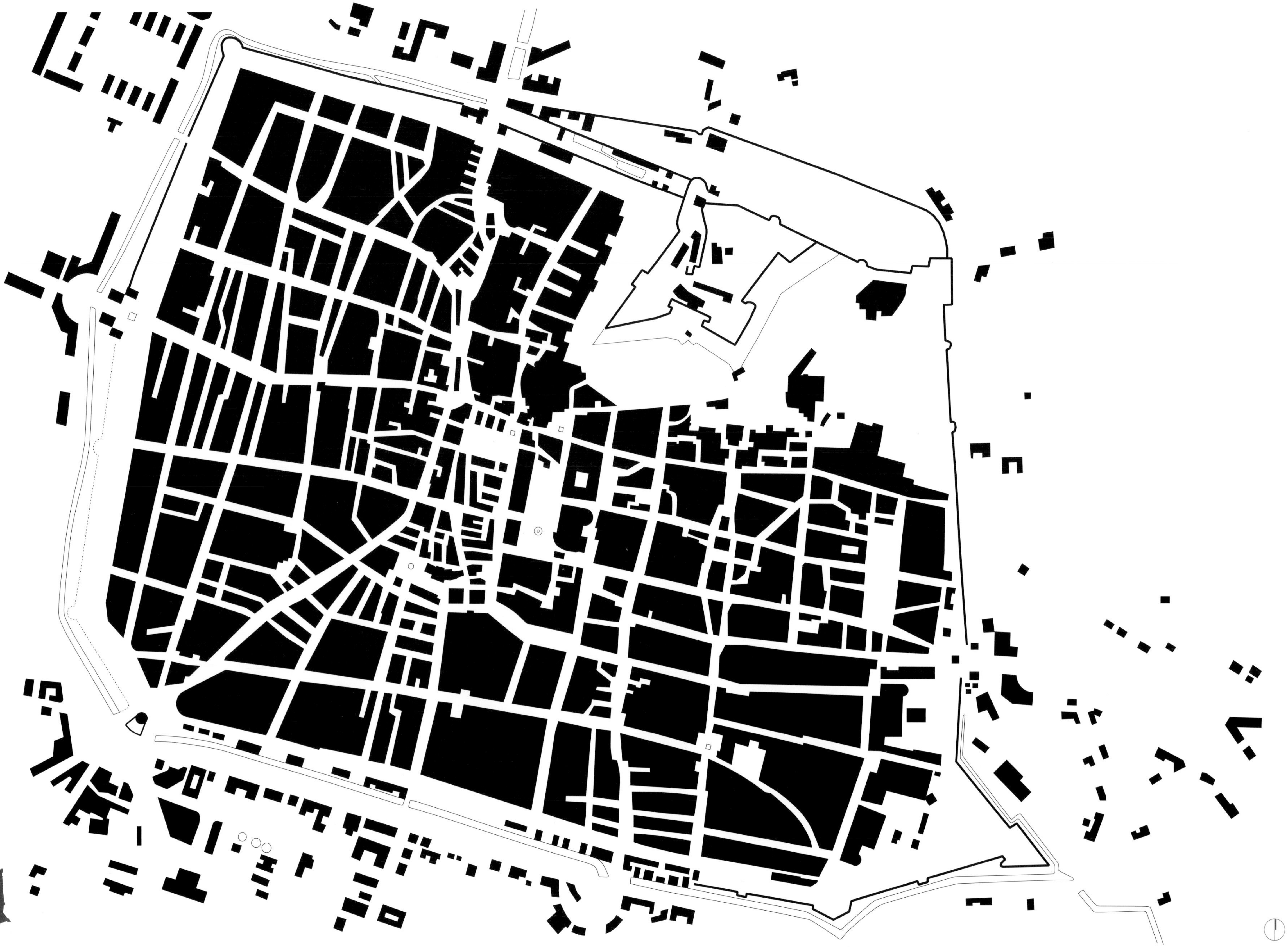

scale comparison

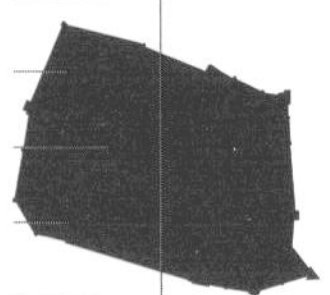

100M

Breslau, Poland 1893

city / country / date

scale comparison

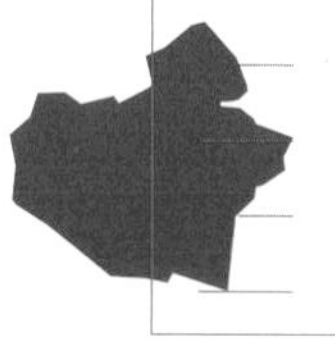

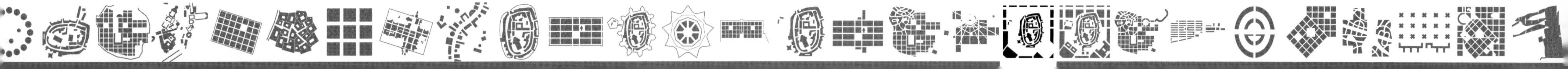

B

100M

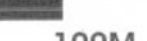

city / country / date

Brest, France 1909

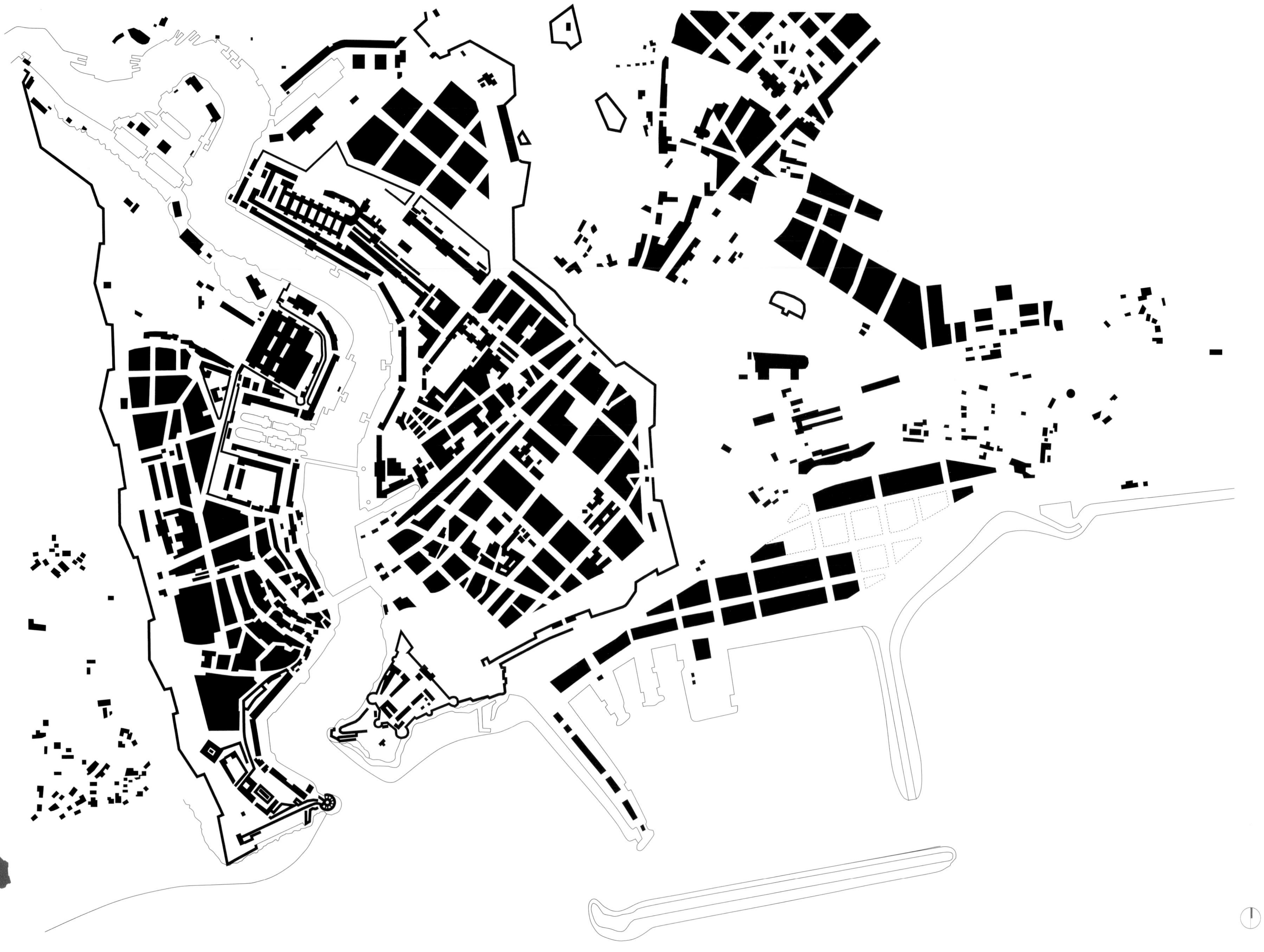

scale comparison

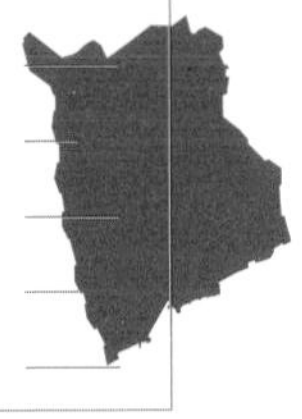

B

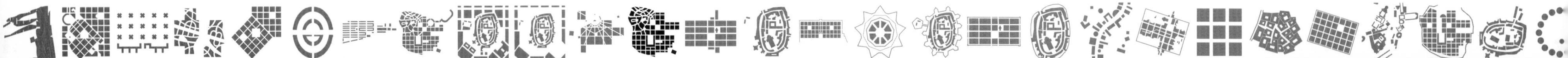

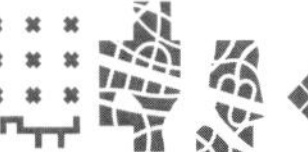

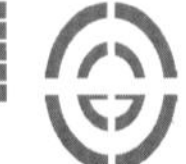

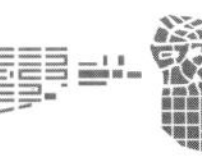

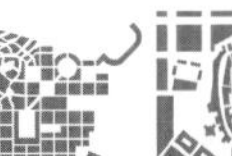

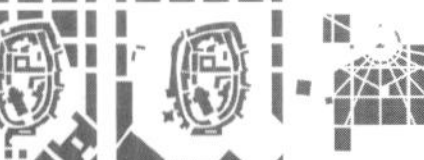

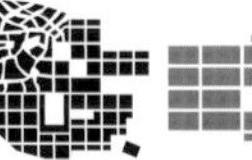

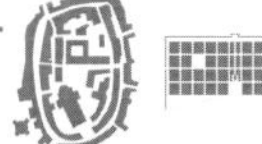

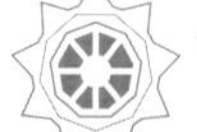

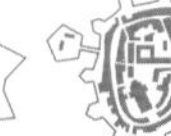

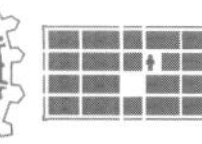

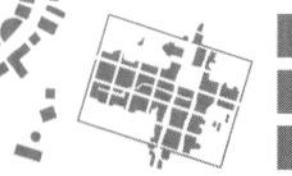

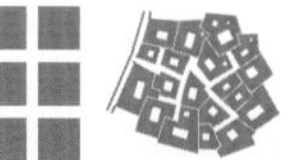

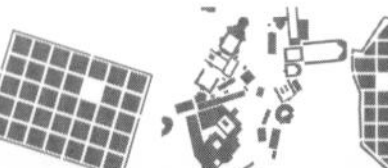

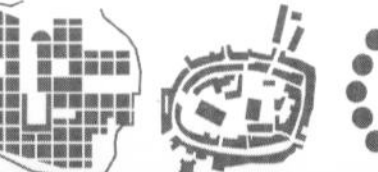

100M

Brighton, England 1840

city / country / date

scale comparison

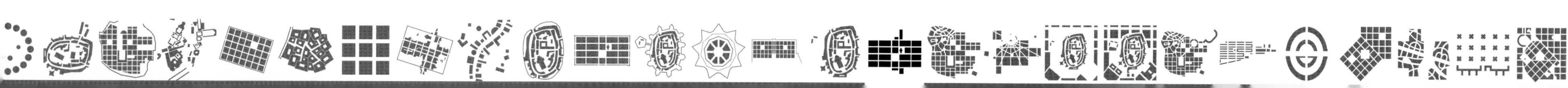

100M

city / country / date

Brive, France [1974]

scale comparison

100M

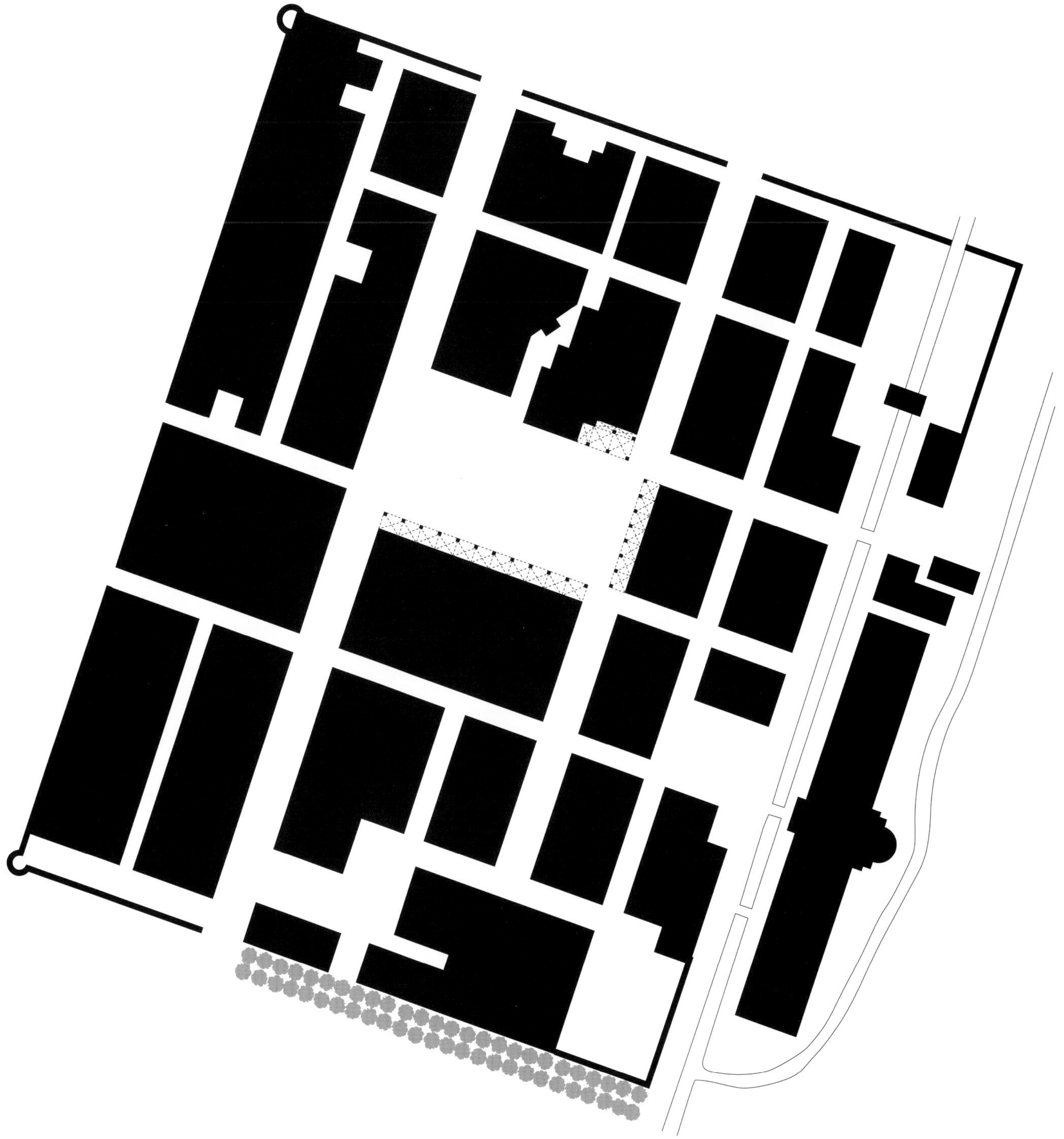

Briviesca, Spain [1974]

city /country / date

scale comparison

100M

city / country / date

Bruck an der Mur, Austria [1974]

scale comparison

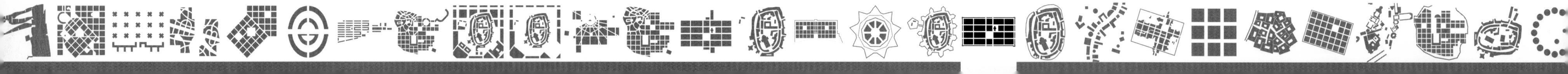

B

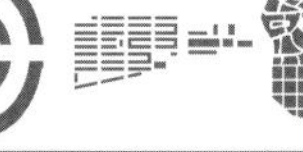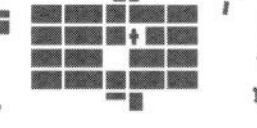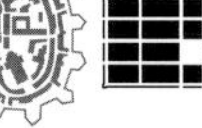

100M

Bruges, Belgium [1974]

city / country / date

scale comparison

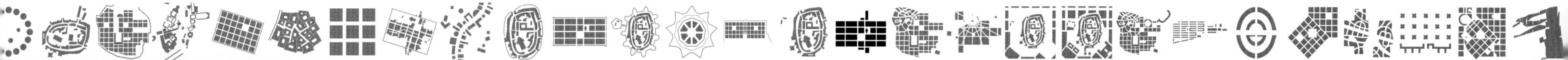

100M

city / country / date

Brussels, Belgium 1837

scale comparison

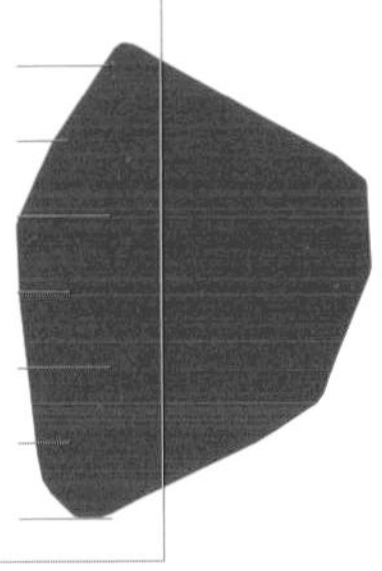

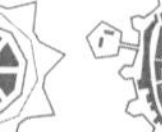
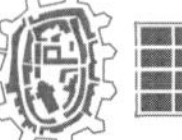

100M

Cairo, Egypt 1914

city /country / date

scale comparison

100M

city / country / date

Calais, France 1909

scale comparison

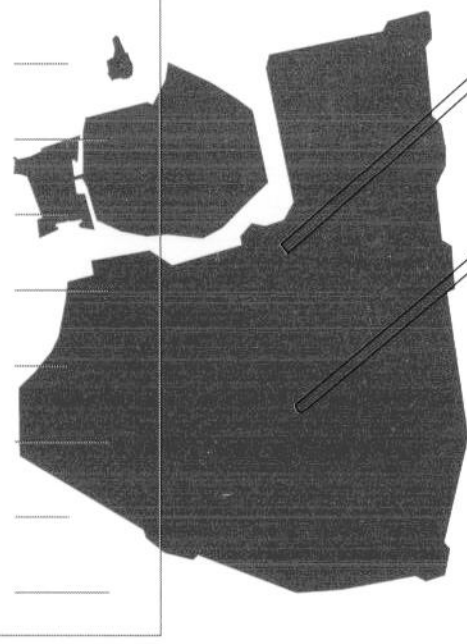

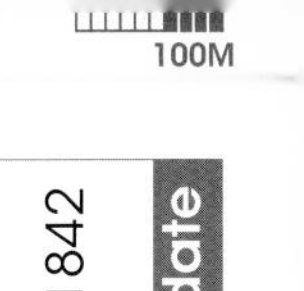

Calcutta, India 1842

city /country / date

scale comparison

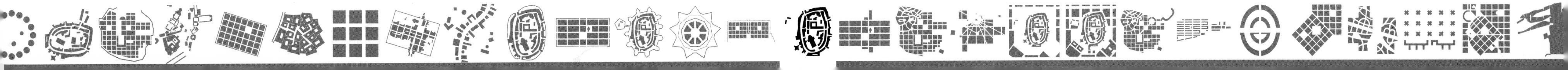

100M

city /country / date

Camaiore, Italy 1255

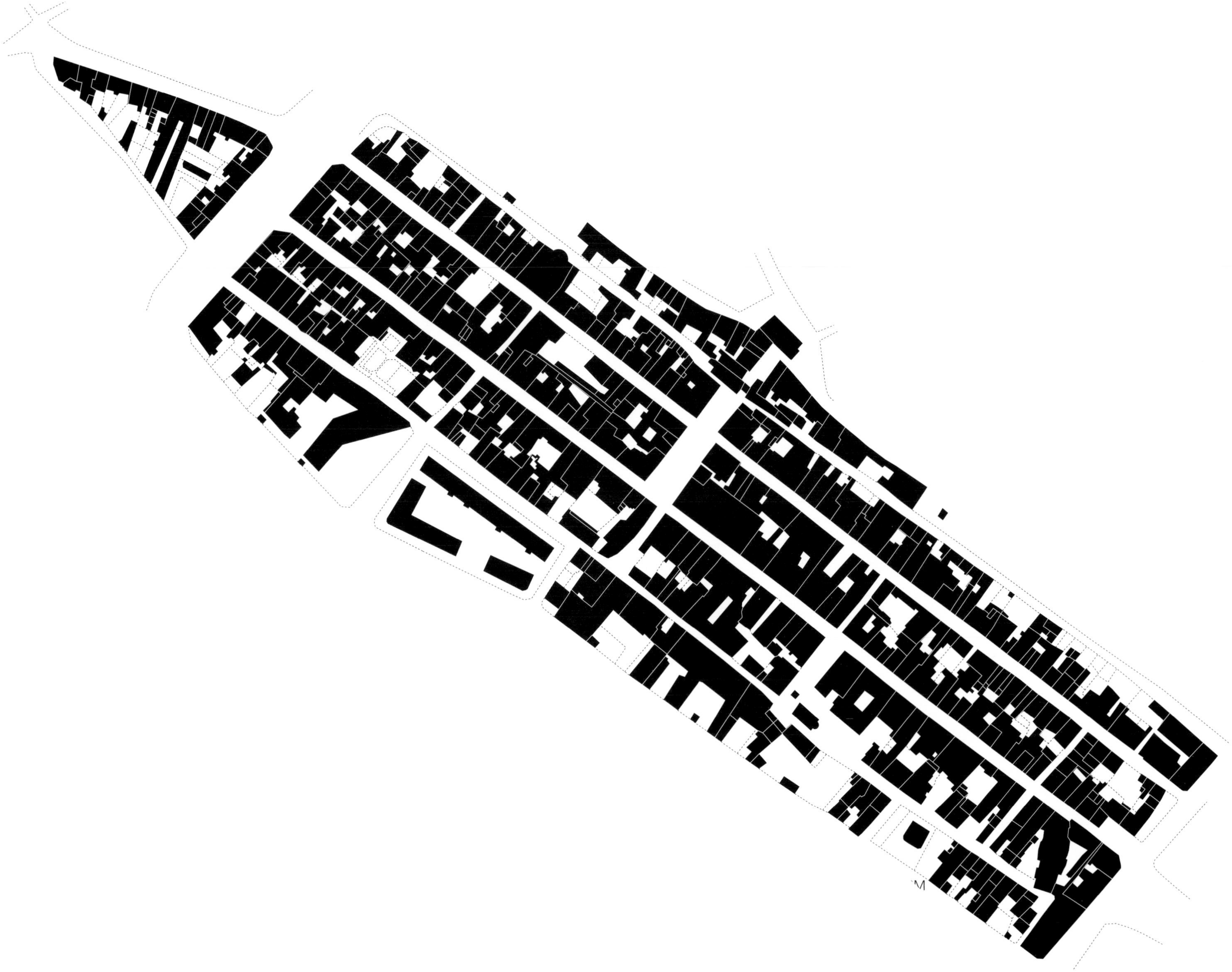

scale comparison

M

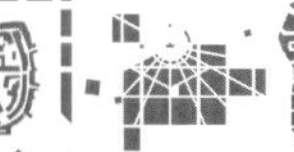

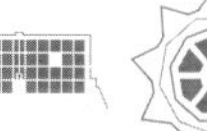

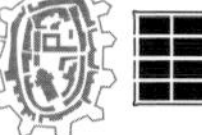

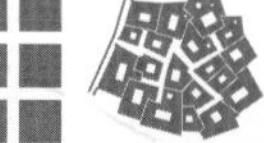
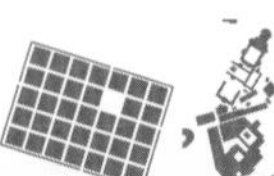

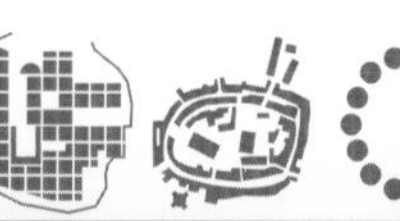

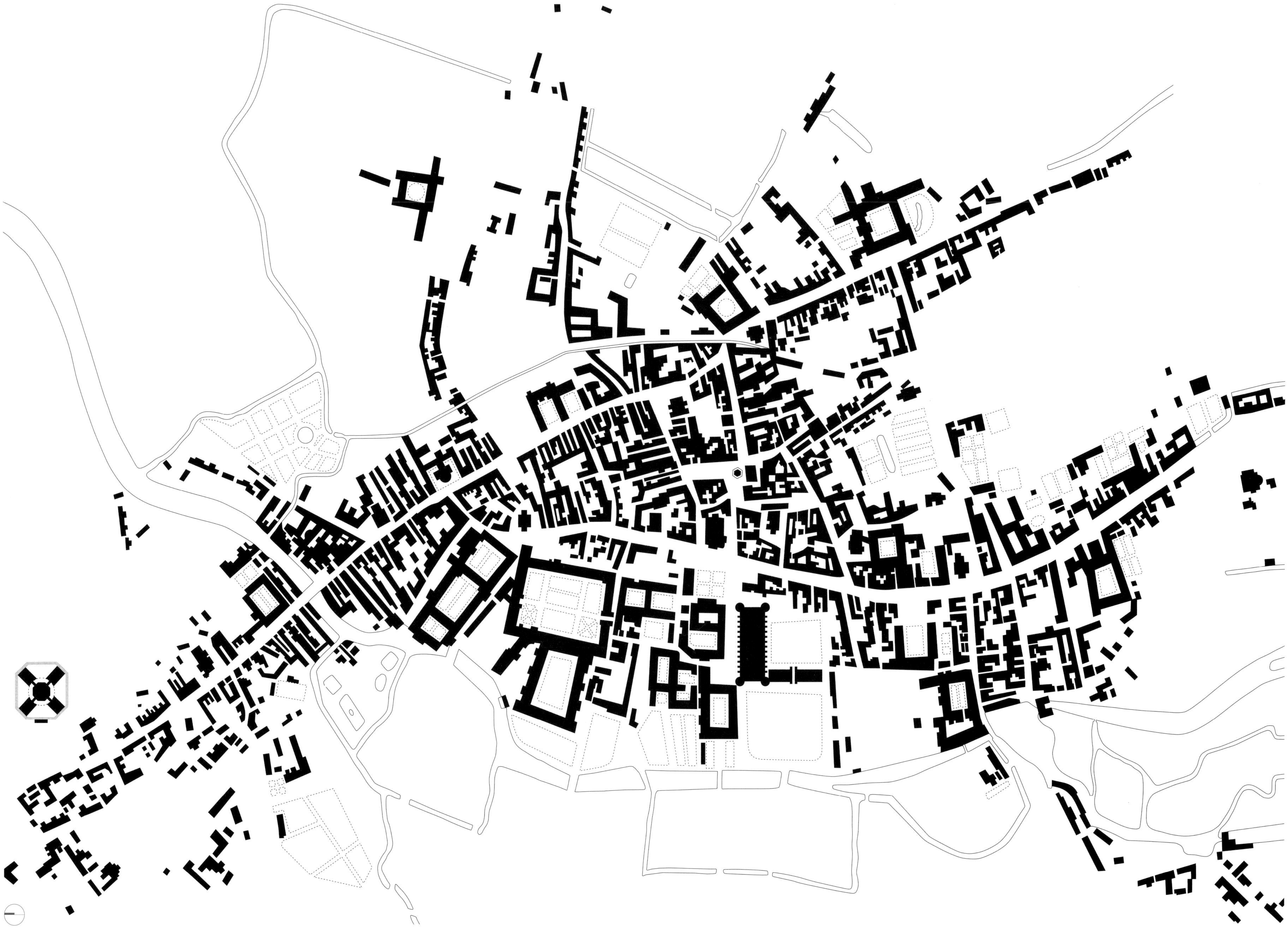

Cambridge, England 1800

city /country / date

scale comparison

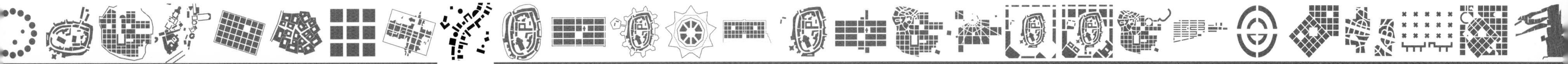

100M

city /country / date

Cambridge, MA, USA (proposal by Charles Graves) 1977

scale comparison

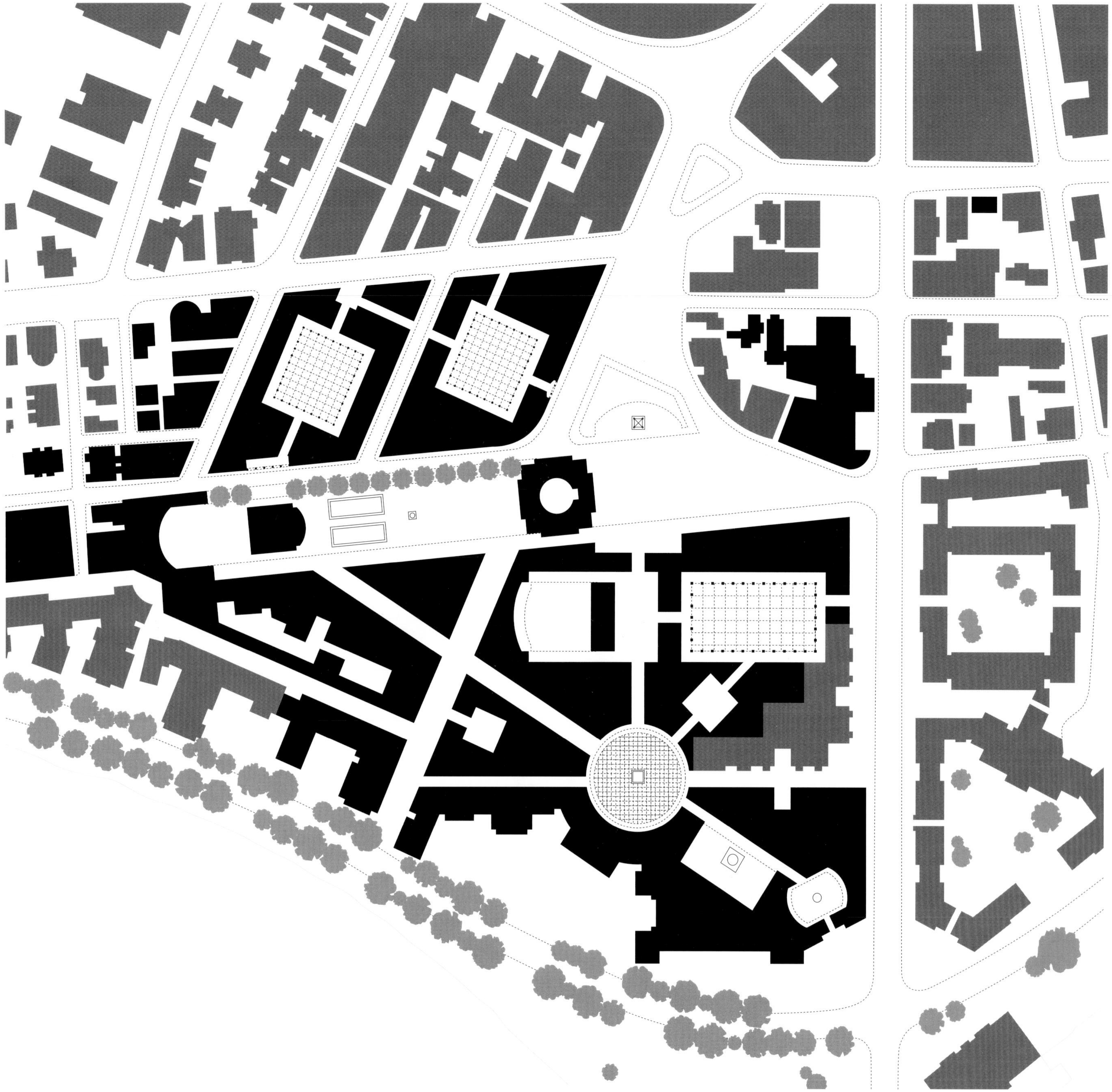

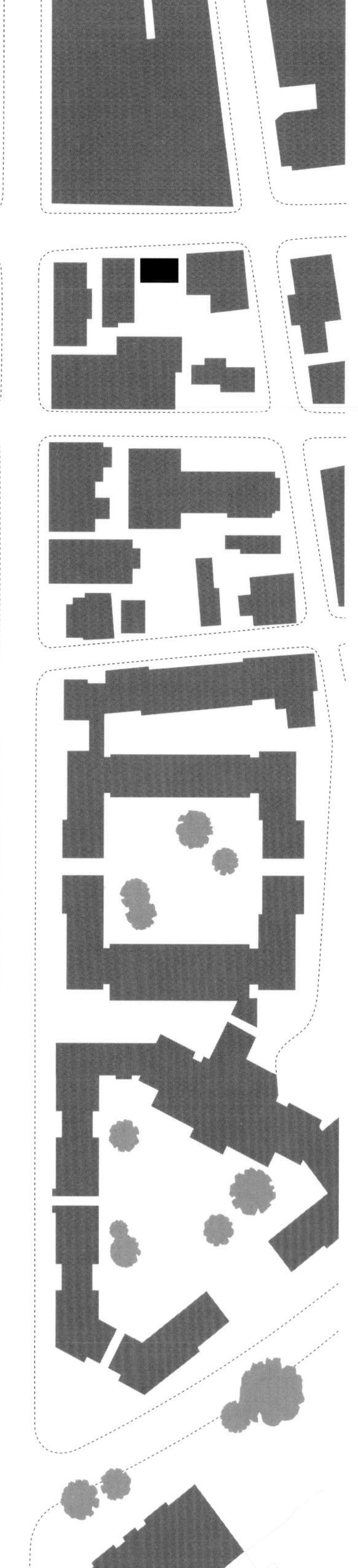

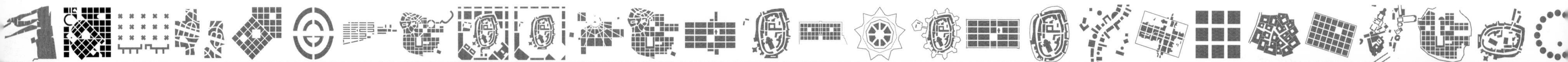

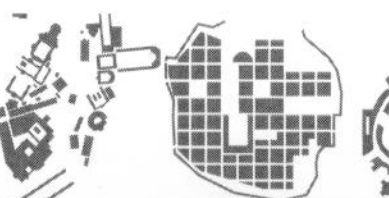

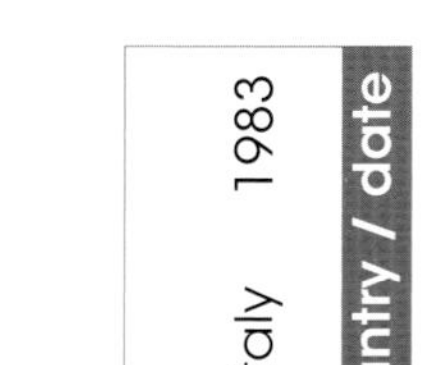

Campagnano, Italy 1983

city /country / date

scale comparison

100M

city / country / date

Canberra, Australia (design by Walter Burley Griffin) 1911

scale comparison

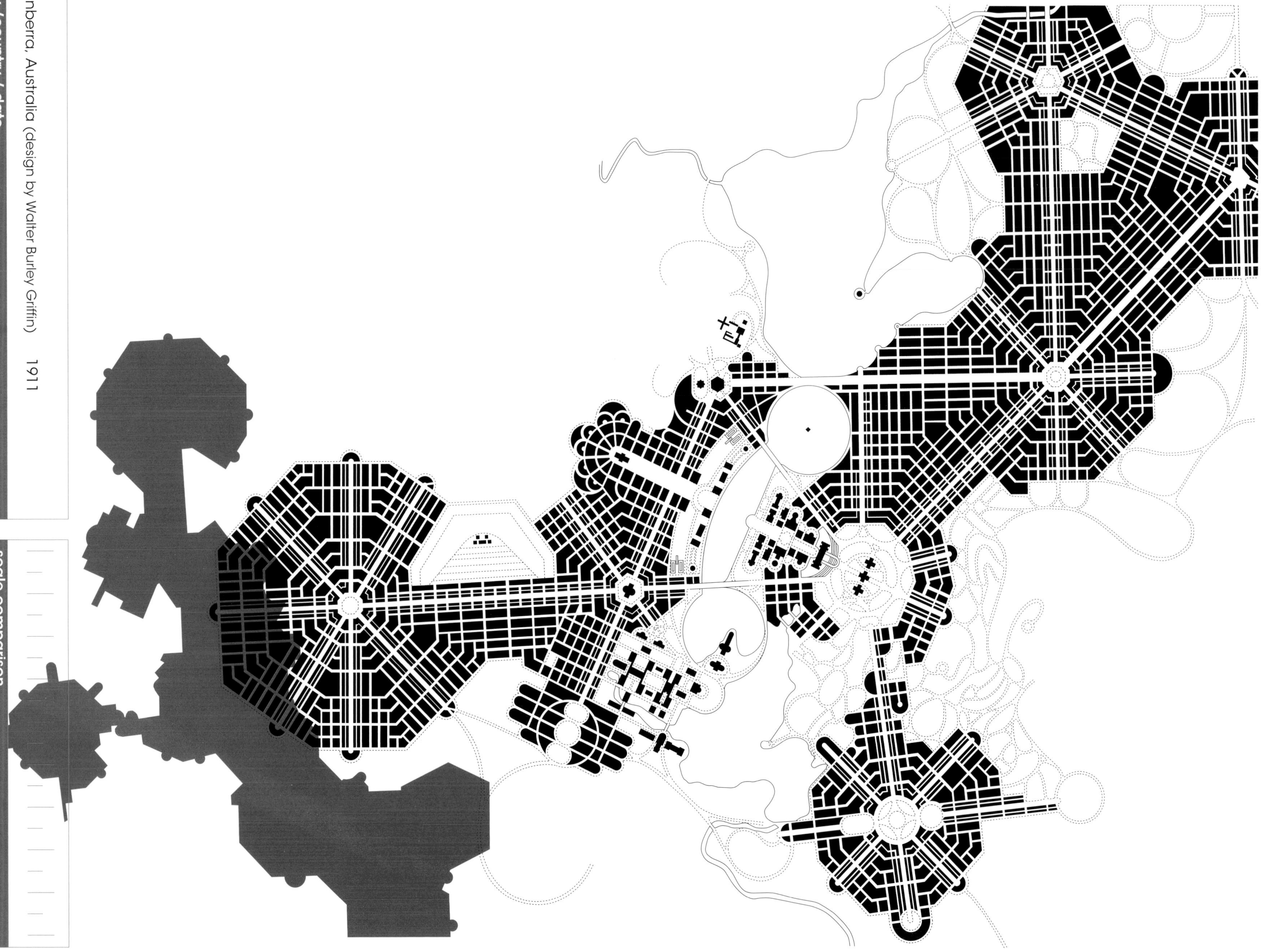

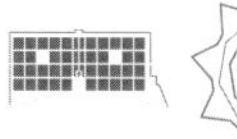

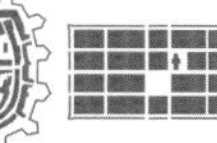

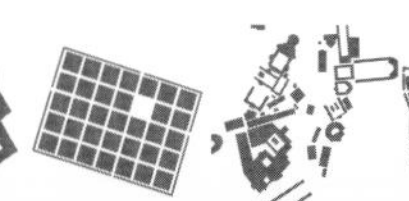

100M

Canino, Italy 1982

city /country / date

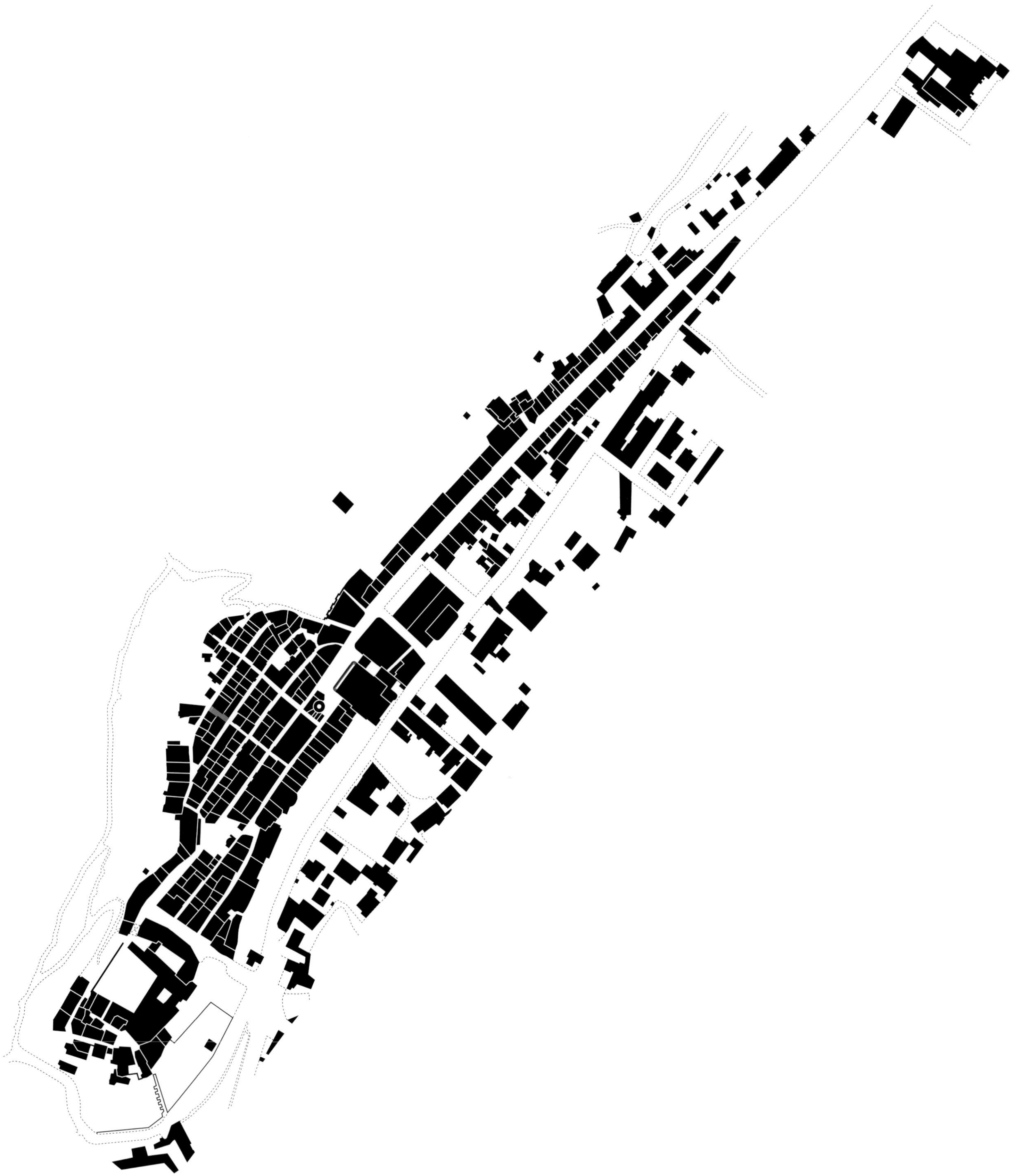

scale comparison

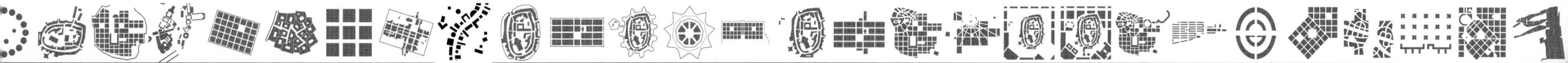

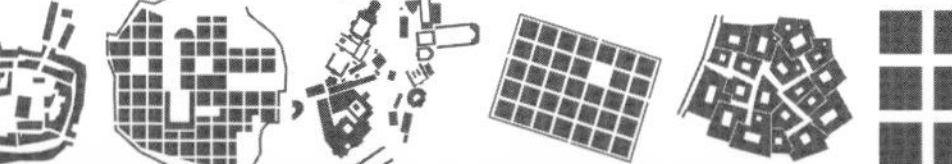
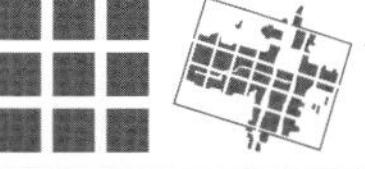

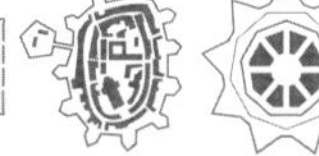
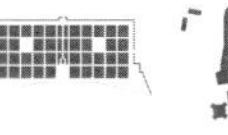

100M

city / country / date

Caparola, Italy (with Villa Farnese) 1983

scale comparison

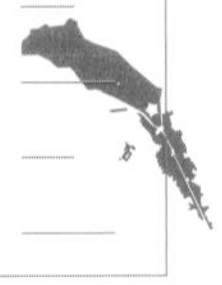

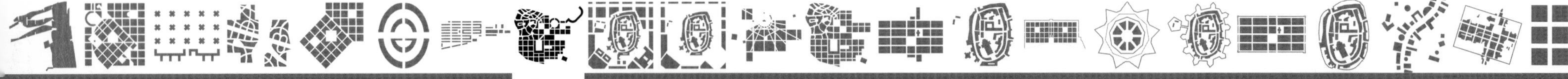

100M

Cape Town, South Africa 1764

city / country / date

scale comparison

100M

city / country / date

Carcassonne, France [1974]

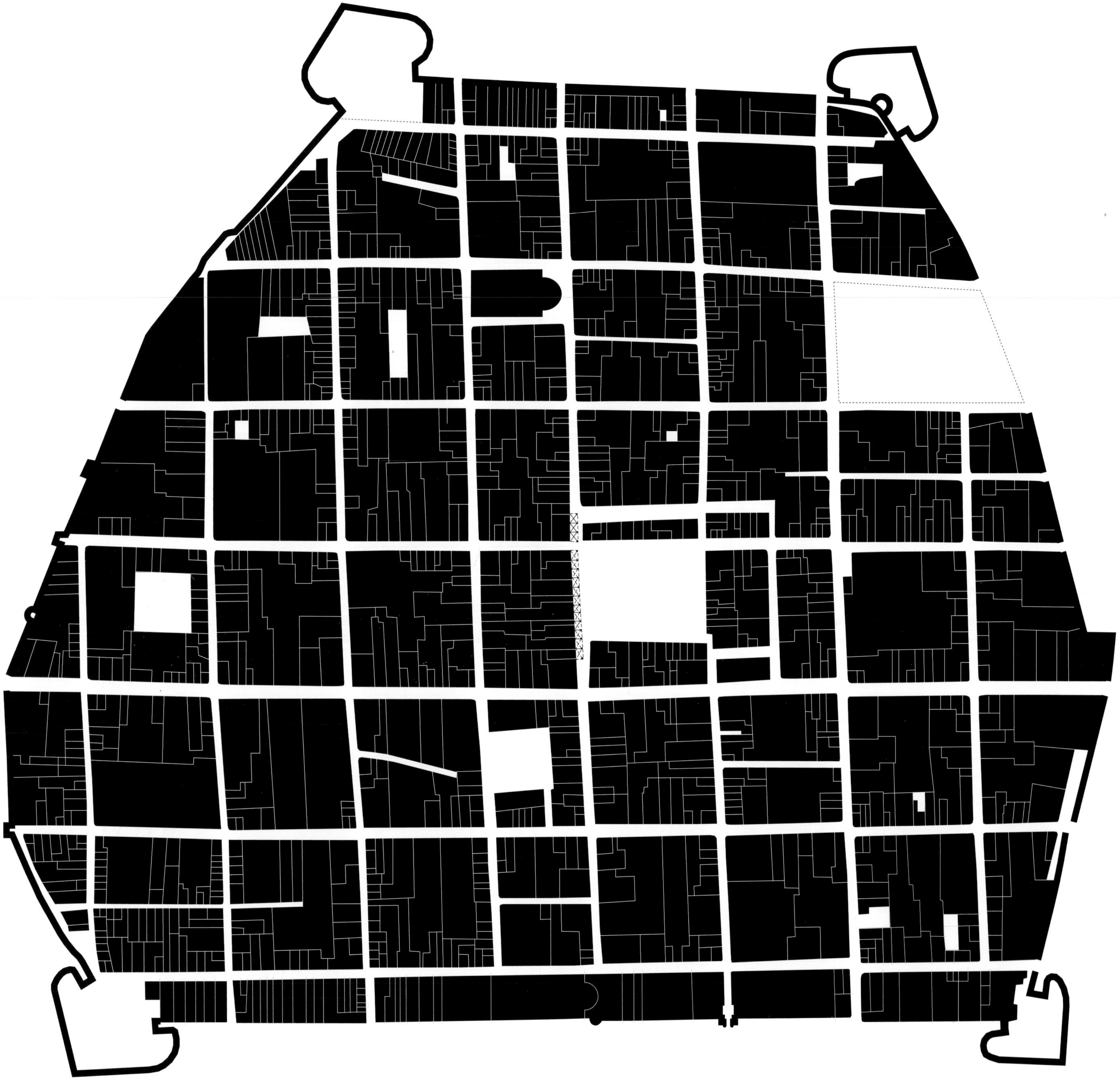

scale comparison

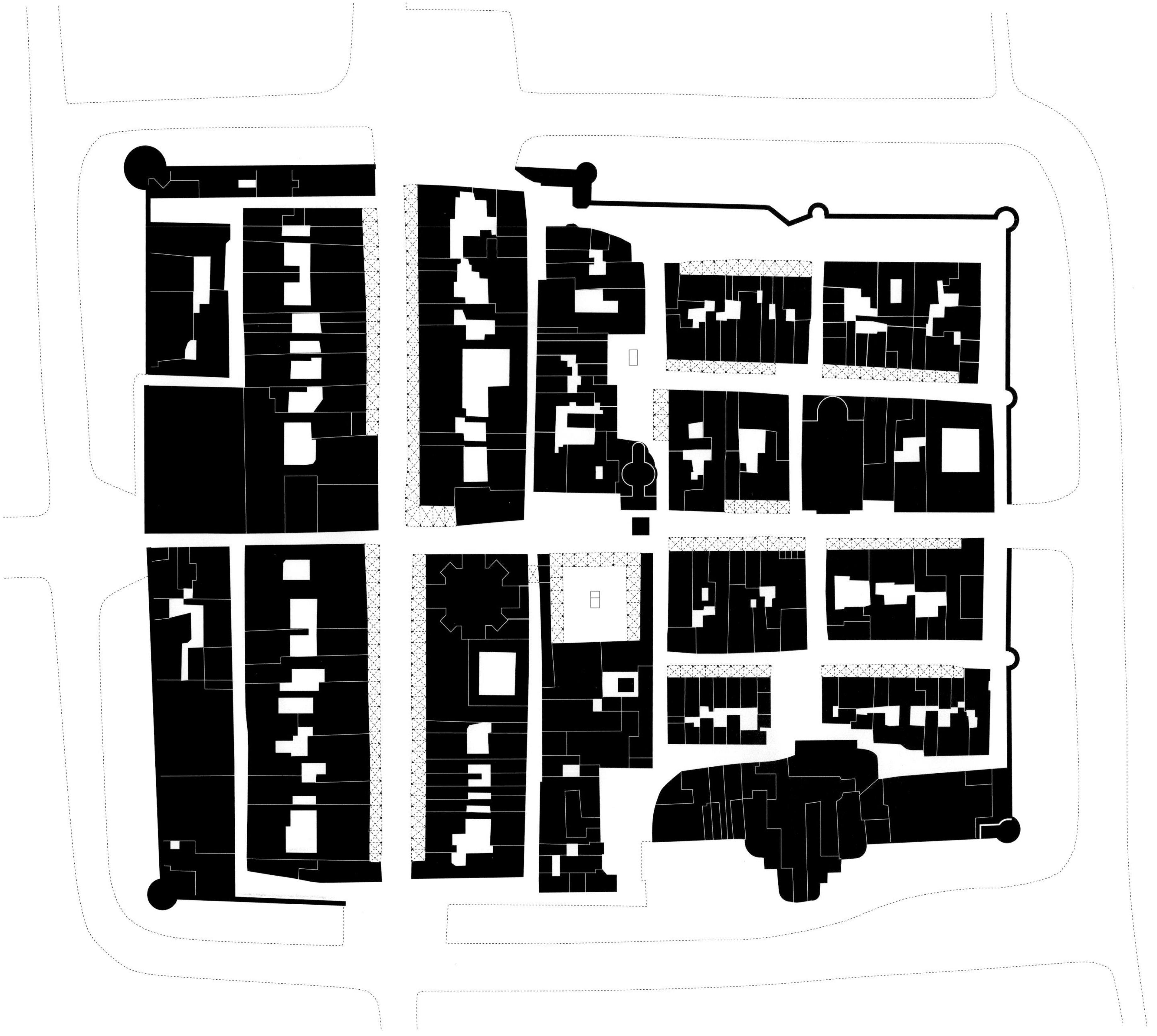

100M

Castel Bolognese, Italy [1974]

city / country / date

scale comparison

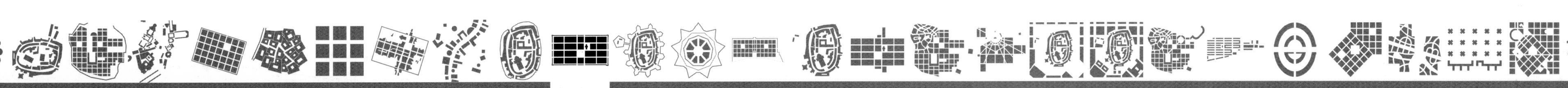

100M

city / country / date

Castelsarrasin, France [1974]

scale comparison

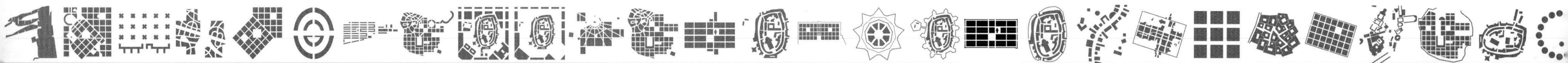

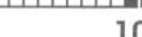

Castillonnés, France [1974]

city /country / date

scale comparison

city / country / date

Castle Acre, England 1946

scale comparison

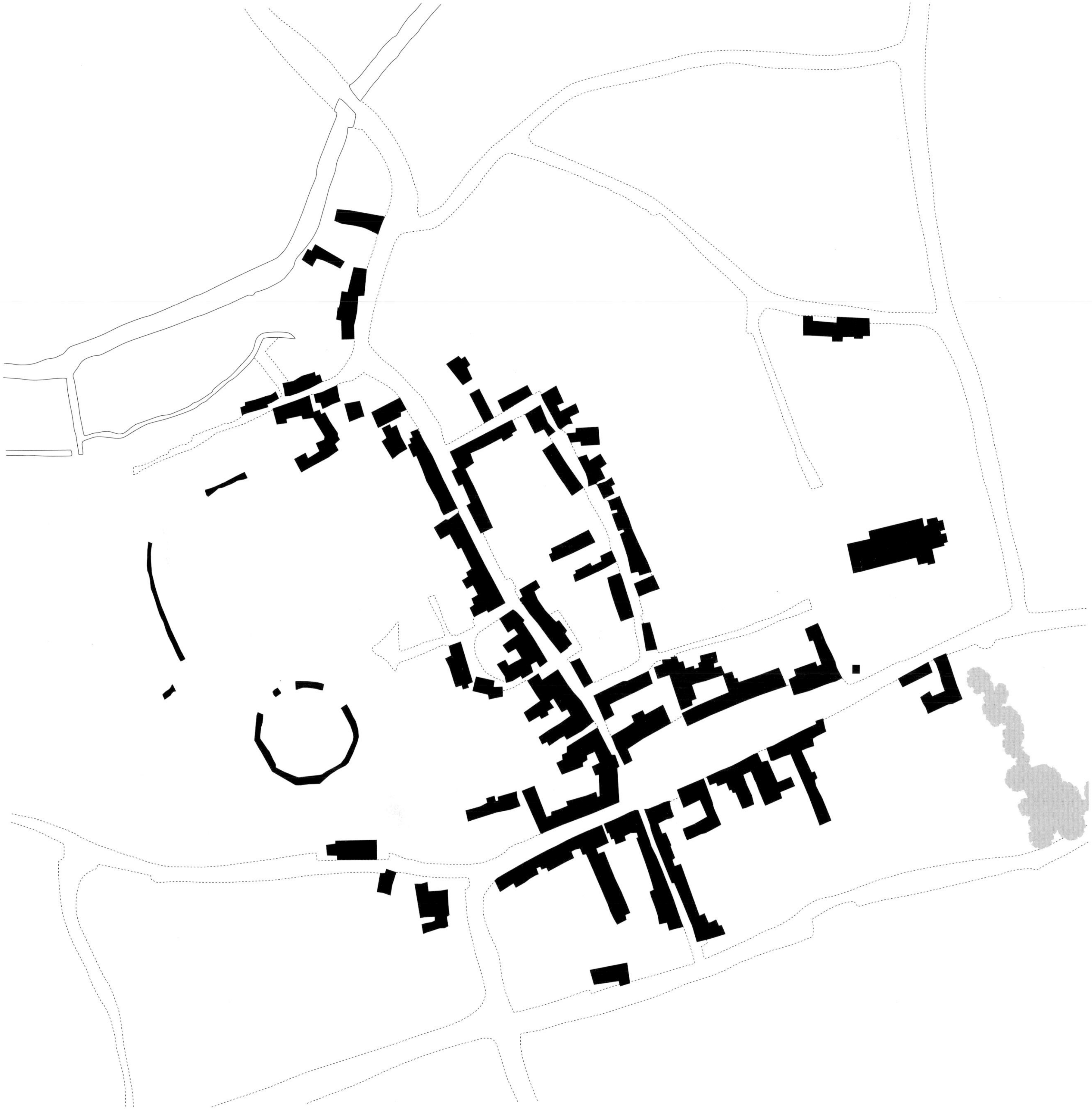

city /country / date

Central Park, Manhattan, NY, USA 1871

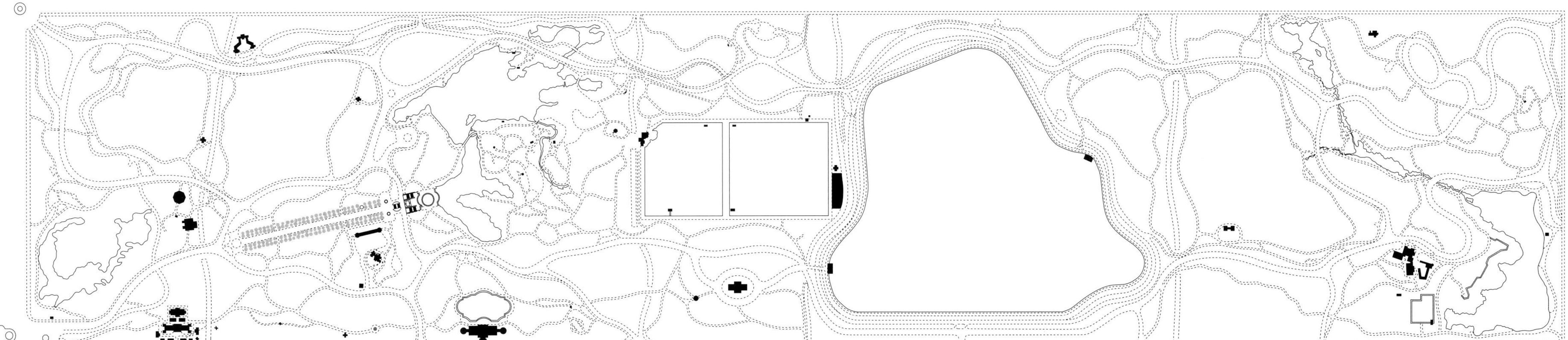

scale comparison

100M
city / country / date
Chandigarh, India, (proposal by Le Corbusier)
1956
scale comparison

100M

Chandigarh Capitol, India (proposal by Le Corbusier) 1956

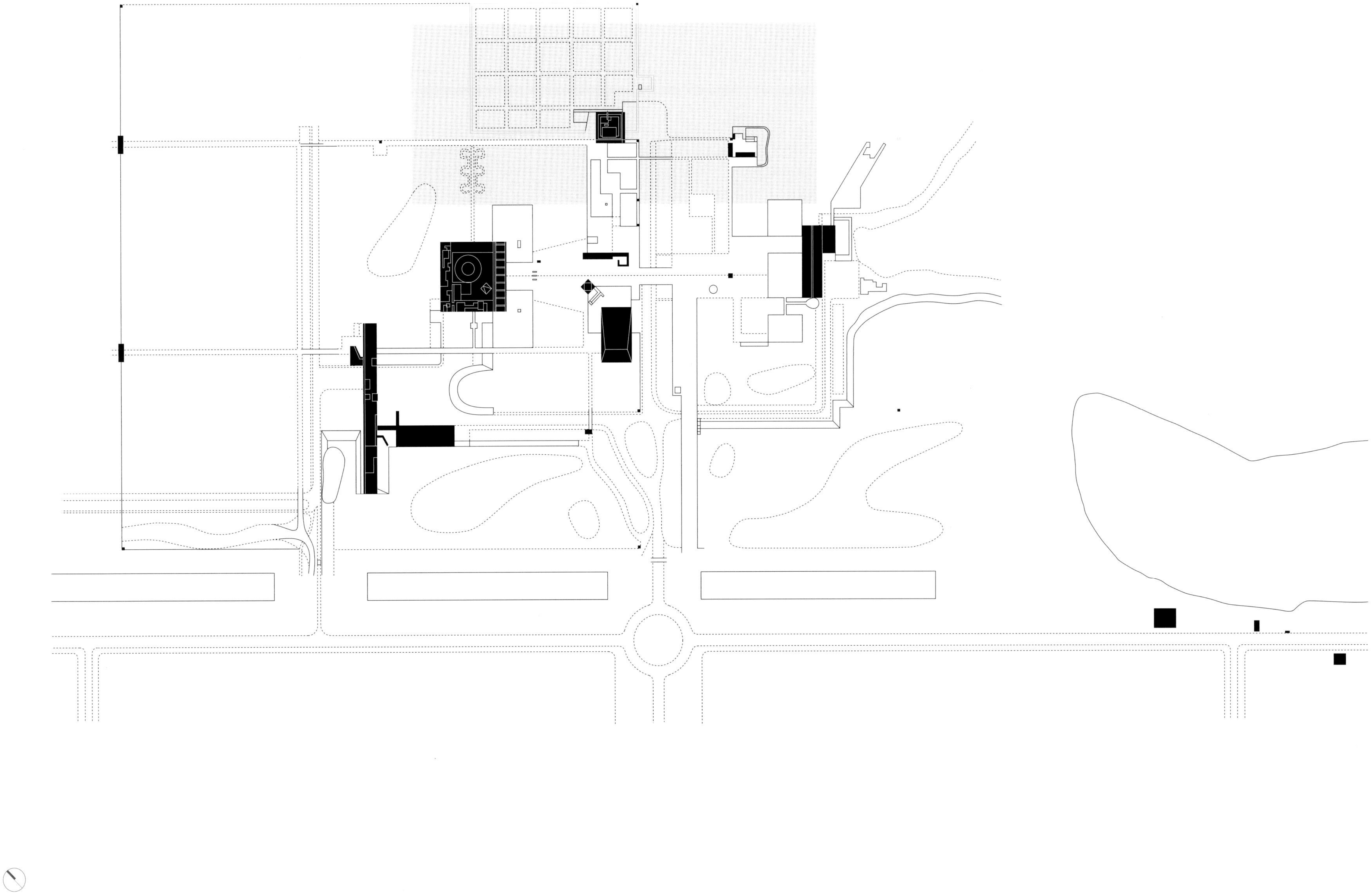

city /country / date

scale comparison

C

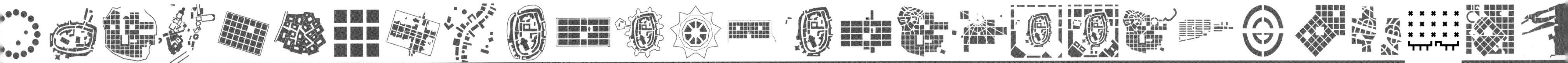

city / country / date

Charlestown, SC, USA 1704

scale comparison

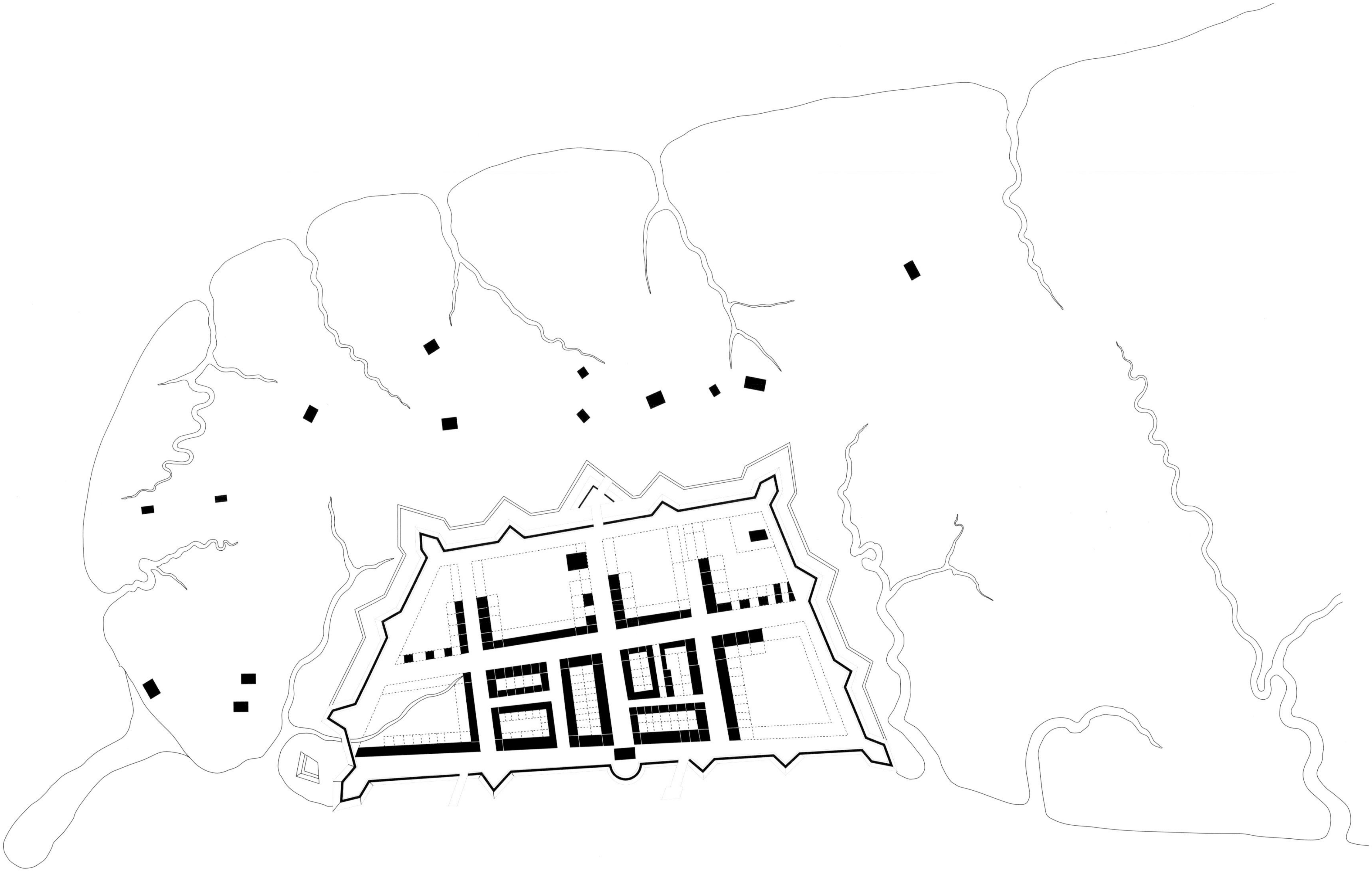

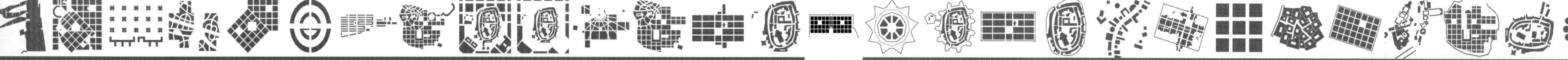

100M

Charlestown, SC, USA 1739

city /country / date

scale comparison

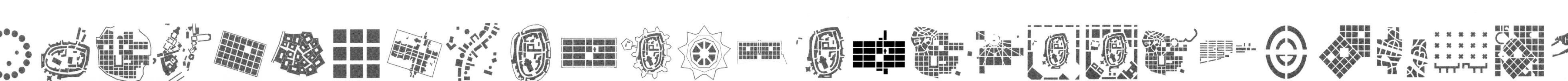

city / country / date

Charleville, France 1909

scale comparison

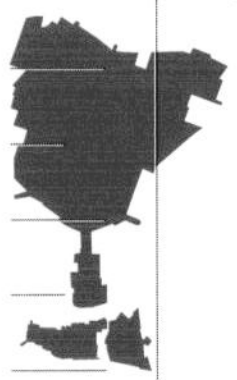

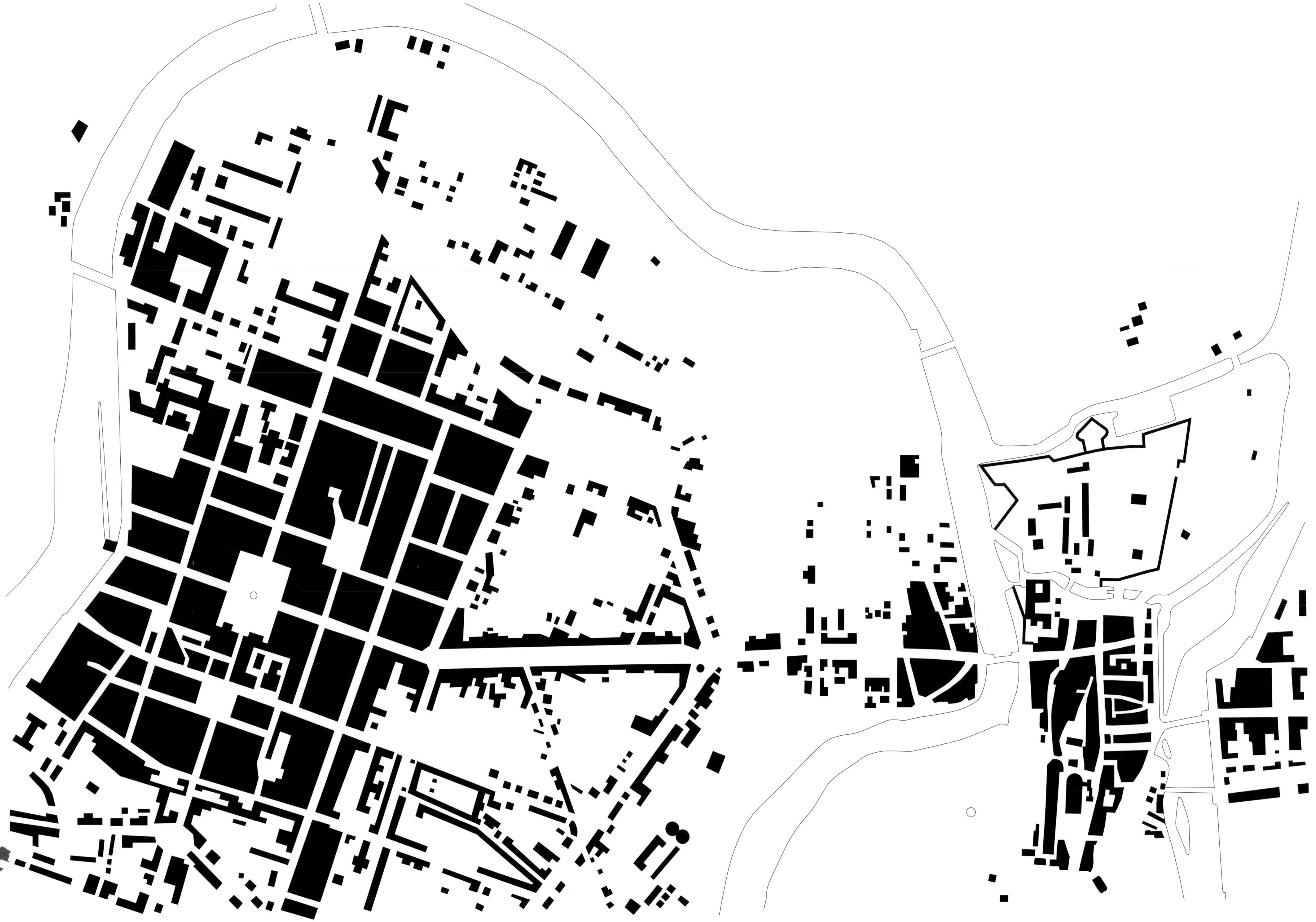

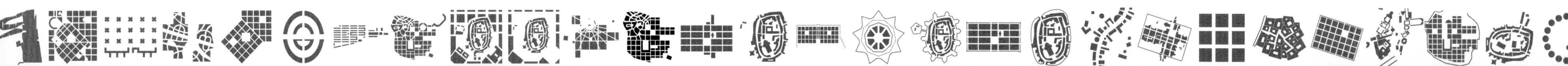

100M

Charlieu, France [1974]

city /country / date

scale comparison

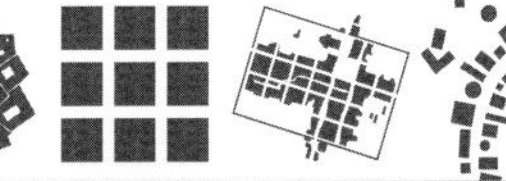
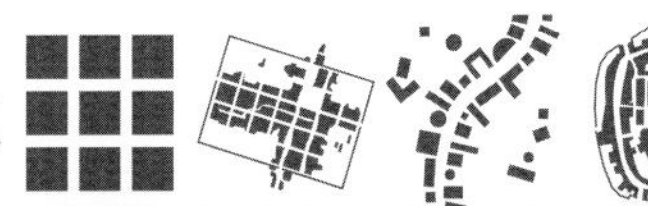
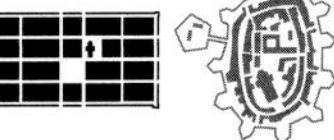

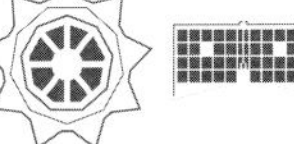

100M

city / country / date

Chateaux Meudon, France 1708

scale comparison

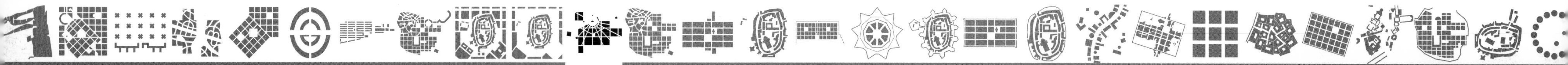

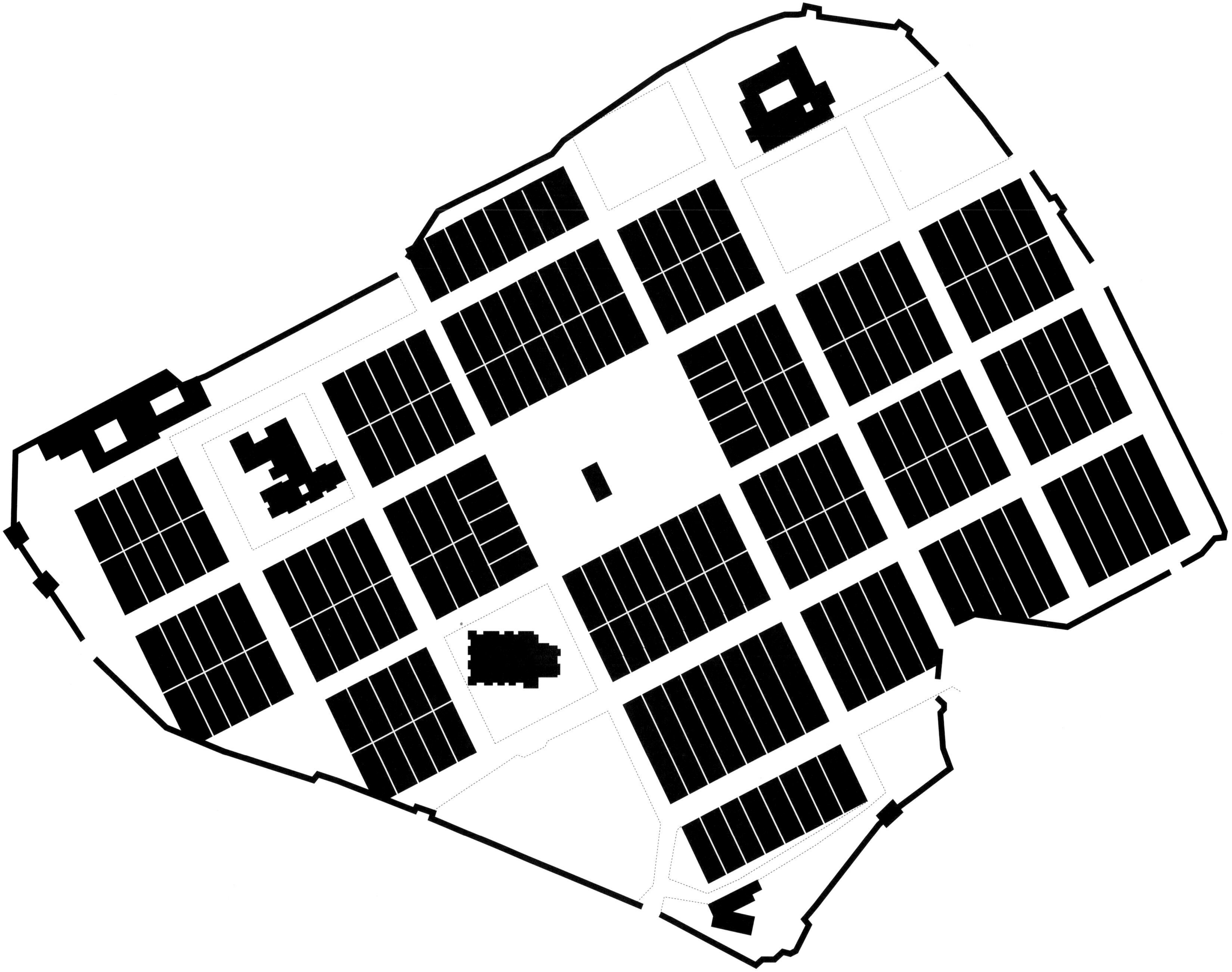

Chelmno (Kulm), Poland [1974]

city /country / date

scale comparison

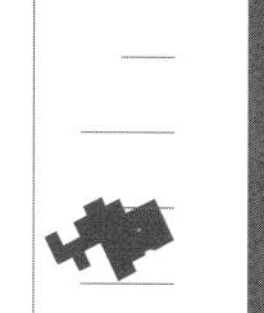

100M
Cherbourg, France 1909
city /country / date
scale comparison

100M

Chester, England 1800

city / country / date

scale comparison

100M

city / country / date

Chiari, Italy 1963

scale comparison

Chicago, IL, USA (proposal by Daniel H. Burnham) 1909

city / country / date

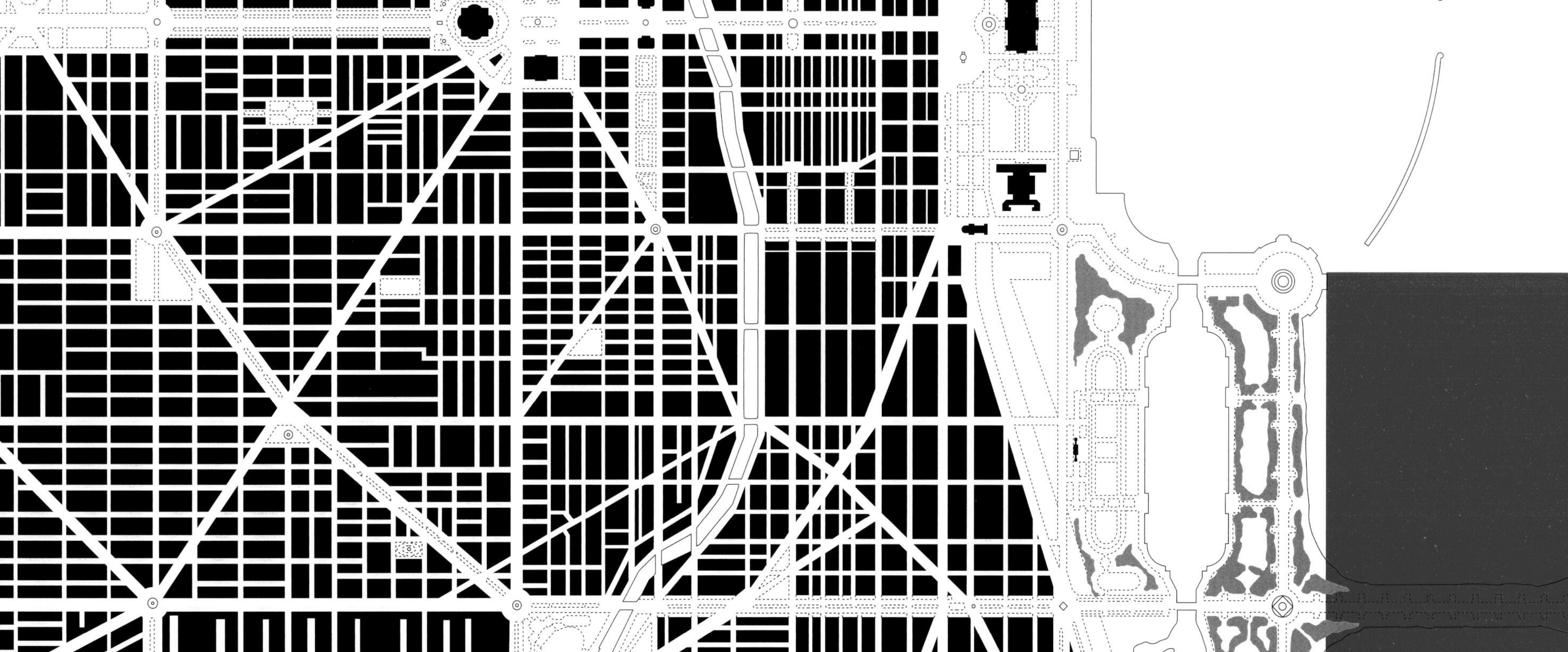

scale comparison

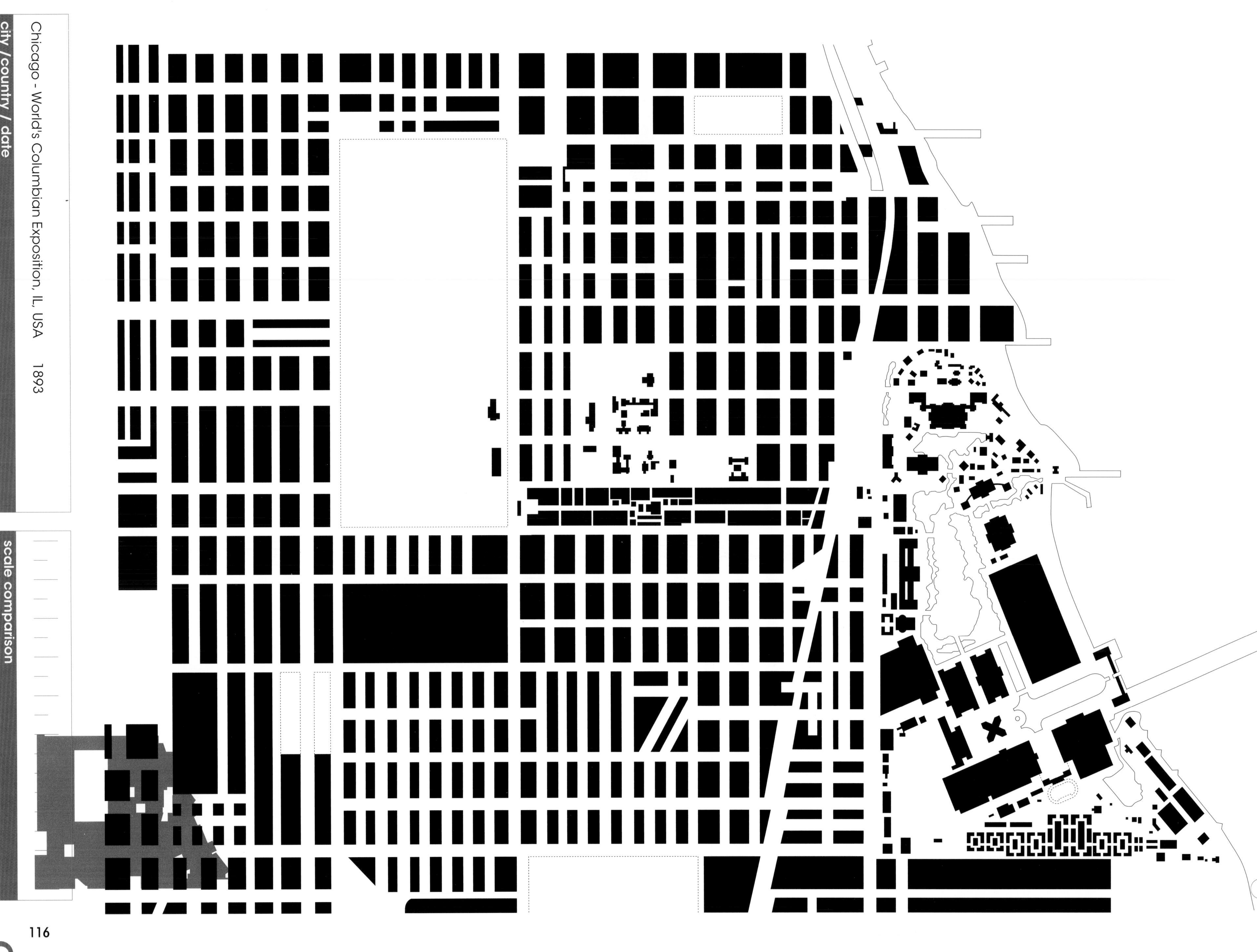

100M
city / country / date
Chicago - World's Columbian Exposition, IL, USA 1893
scale comparison

100M

Chioggia, Italy 1984

city / country / date

scale comparison

100M

city / country / date

Cittadella, Italy 1984

scale comparison

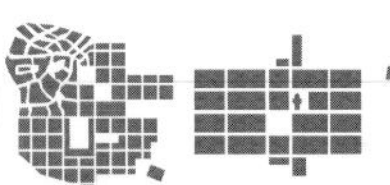
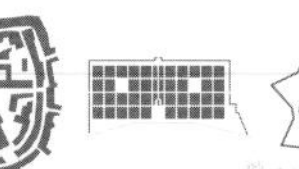

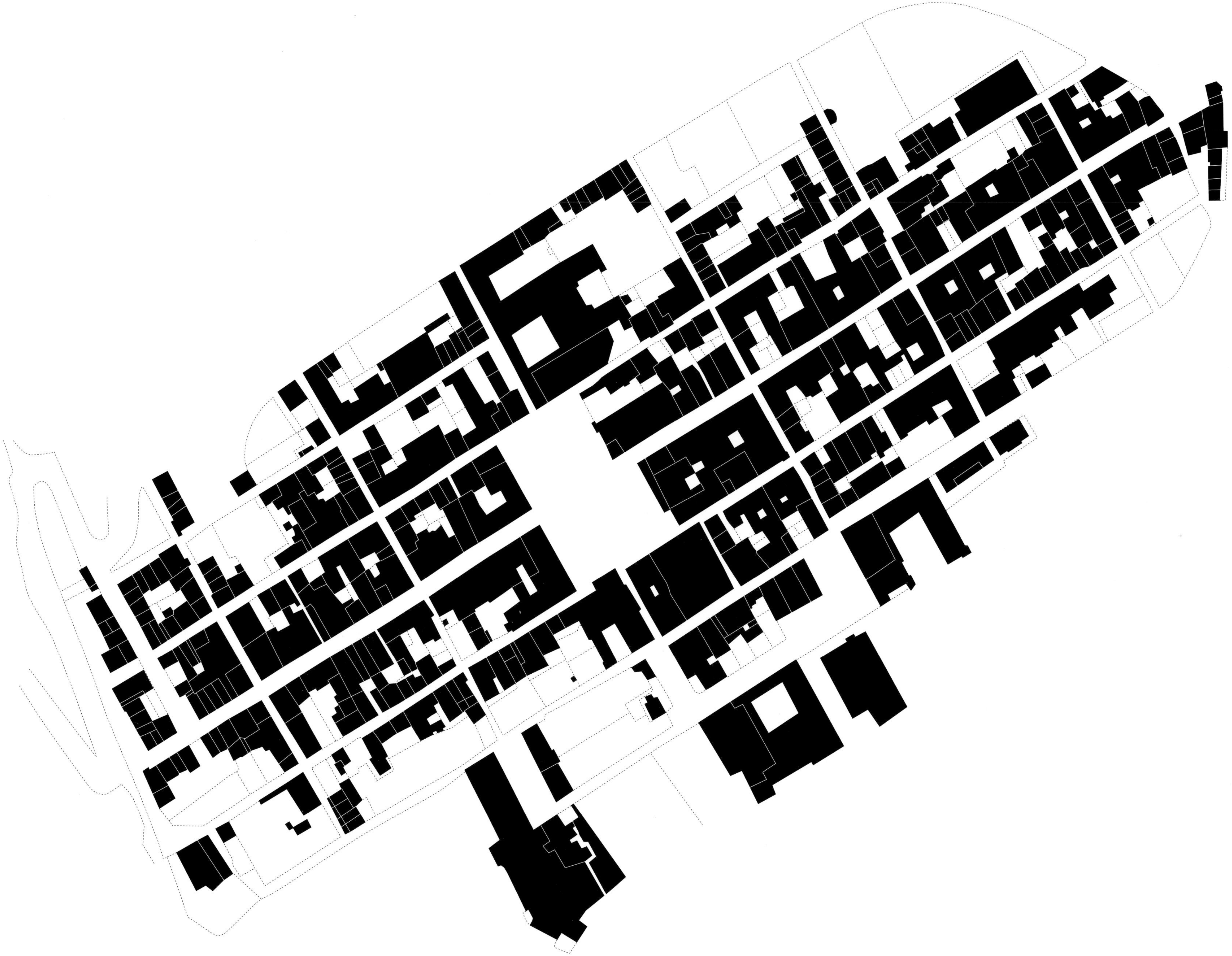

Cittaducale, Italy 1309

scale comparison

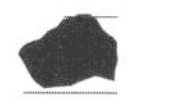

100M

city / country / date

City for Three Million (proposal by Le Corbusier) 1924

scale comparison

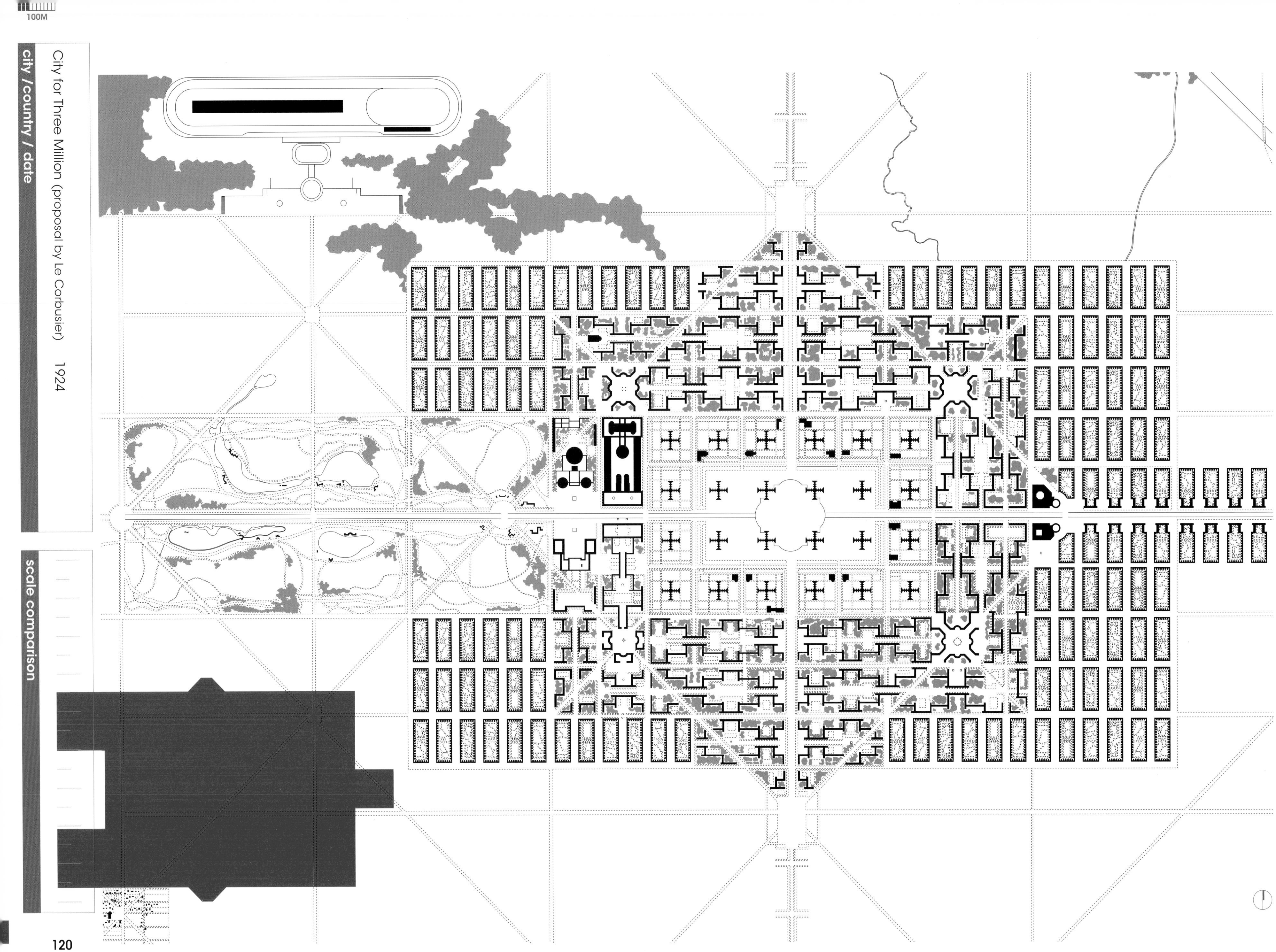

100M

Clare, England 1946

city /country / date

scale comparison

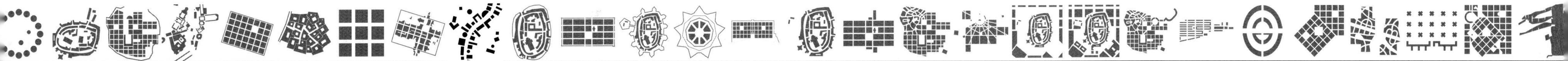

100M

city /country / date

Cleveland, OH, USA 1835

scale comparison

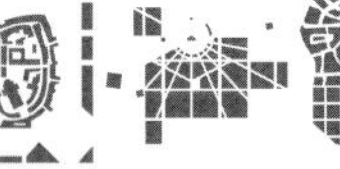

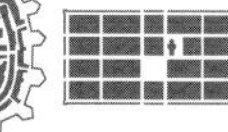

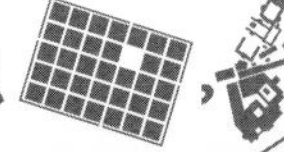
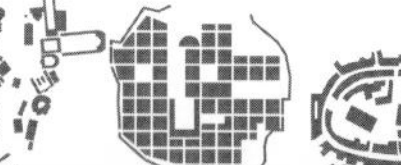

100M
Cleveland, OH, USA
1990
city / country / date
scale comparison
C

city / country / date

Cluny, France 1650

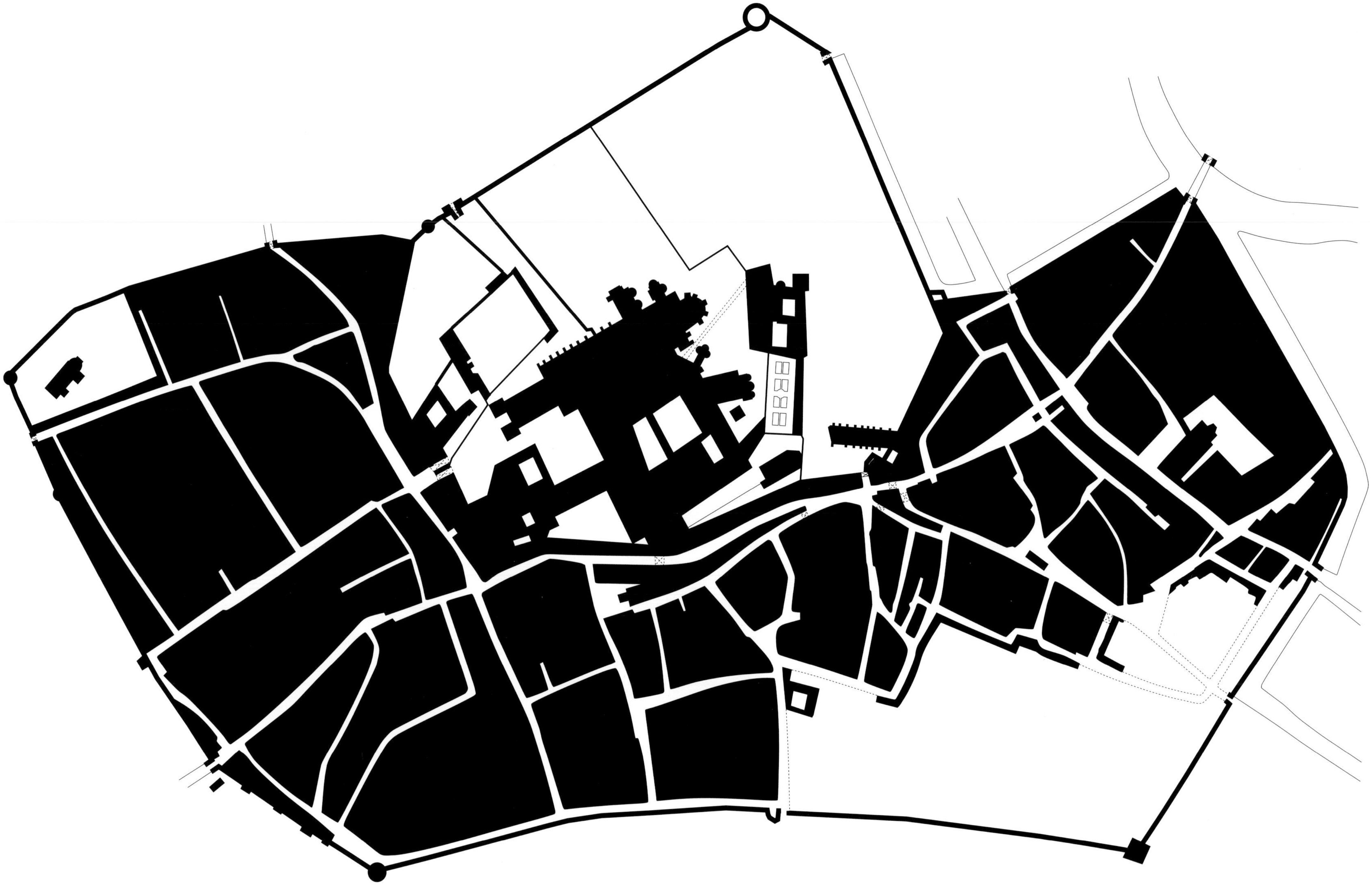

scale comparison

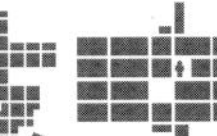
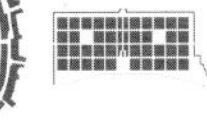

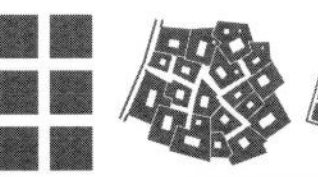

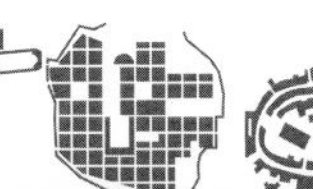

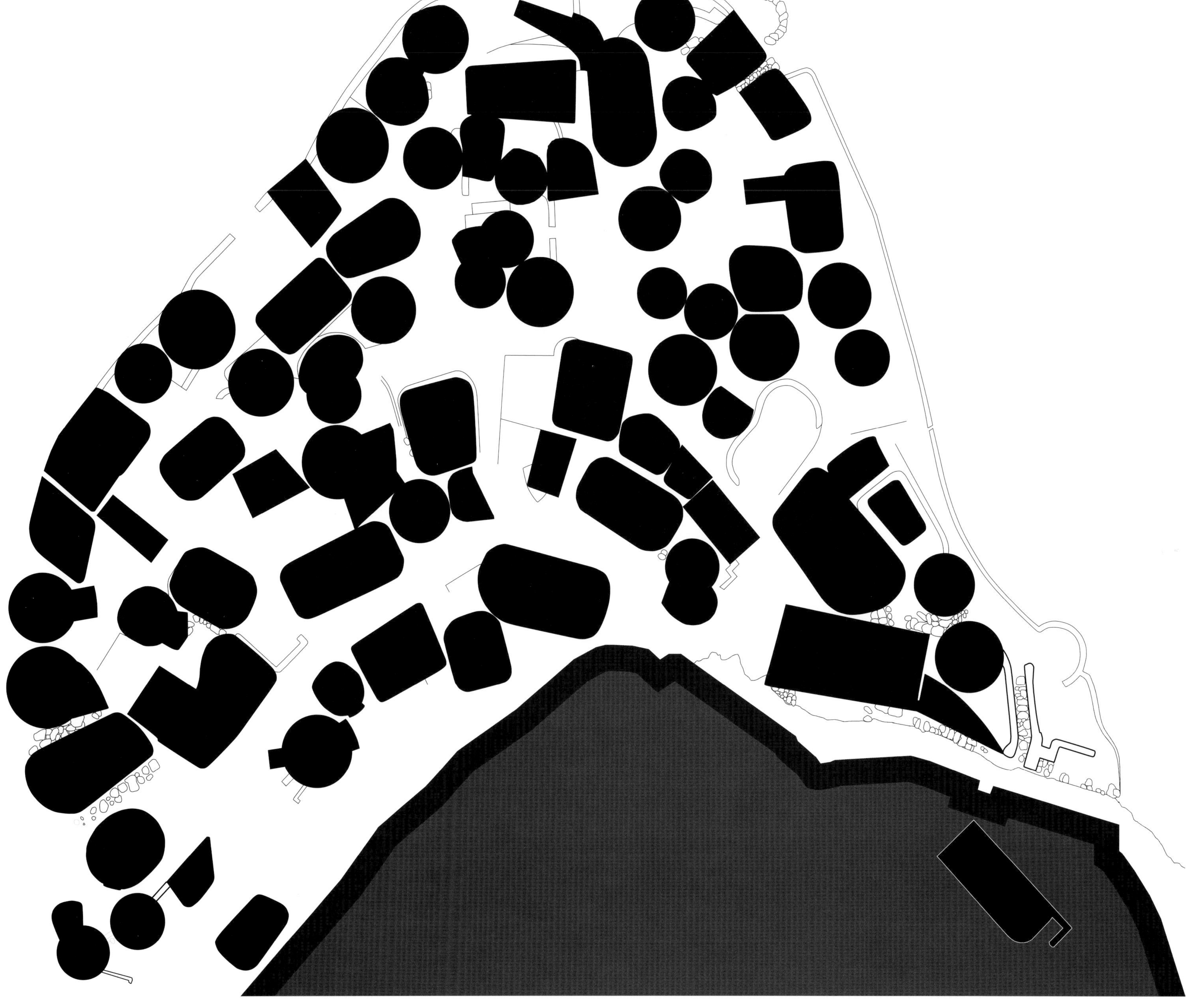

Coaña, (Castro del), Spain 1100 BC

city /country / date

scale comparison

city / country / date

Coblenz (Koblenz), Germany 1907

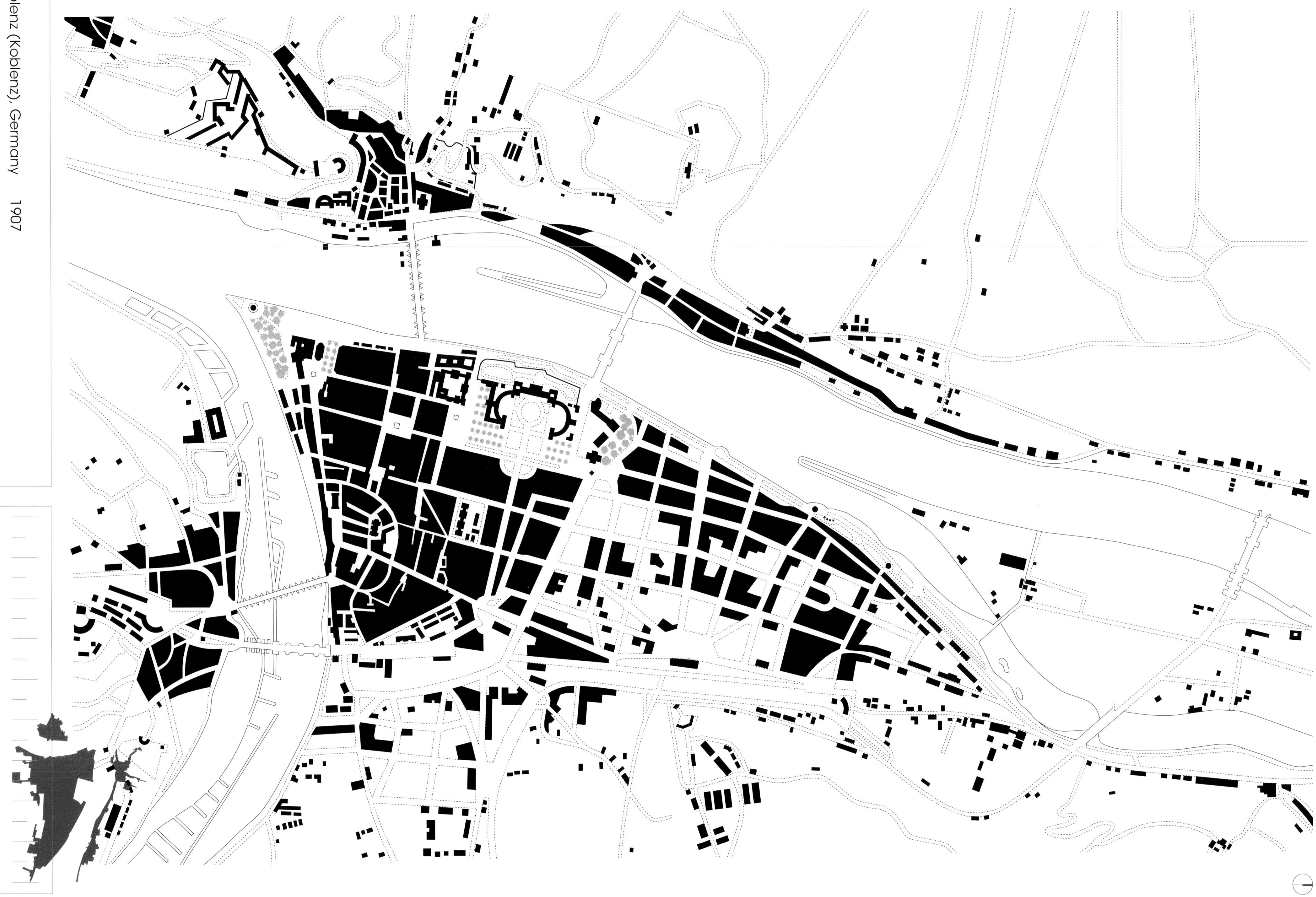

scale comparison

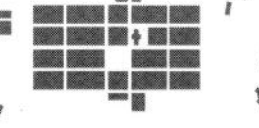

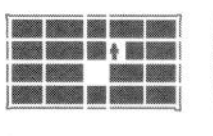

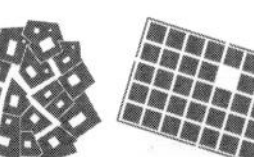

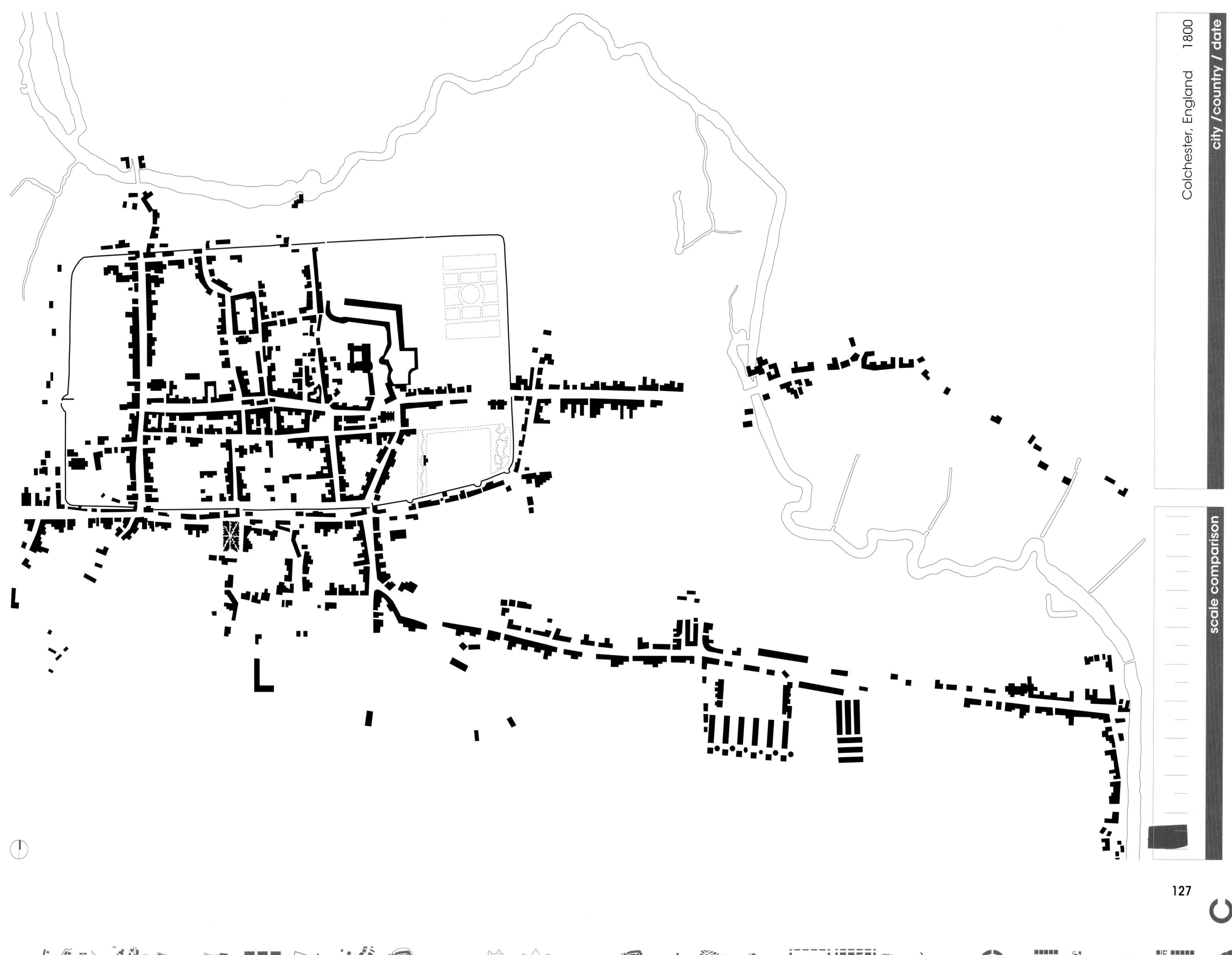
100M
Colchester, England 1800
city /country / date
scale comparison

100M

city / country / date

Como, Italy 1958

scale comparison

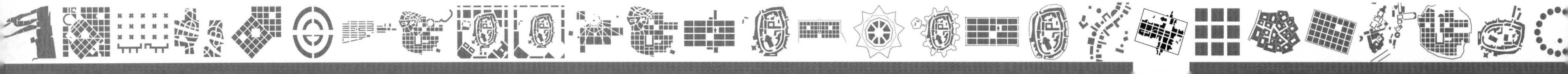

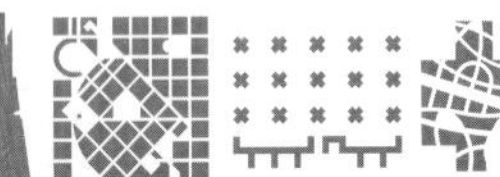

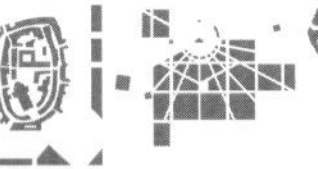

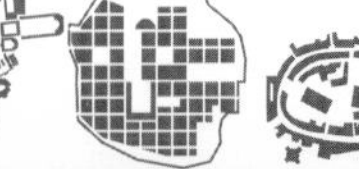

100M

Compiegne, France 1974

city / country / date

C

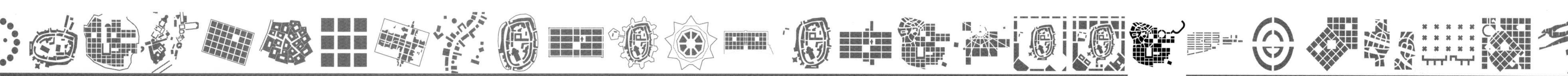

100M
Coneysthorpe, England 1946
city /country / date
scale comparison

Constantinople (Istanbul), Turkey 1841

city /country / date

scale comparison

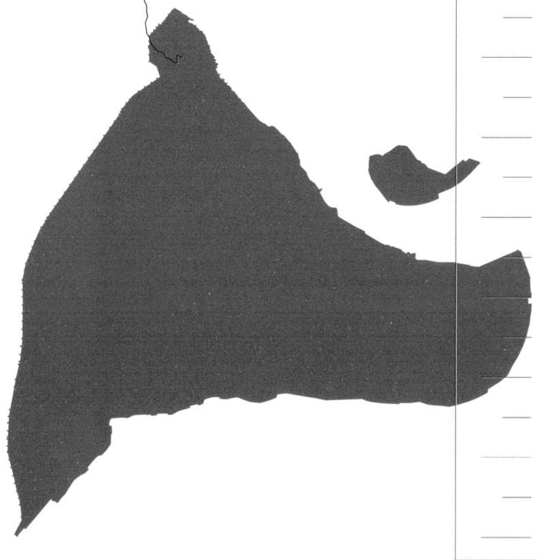

100M
Copenhagen, Denmark 1535 & 1650
city / country / date
scale comparison

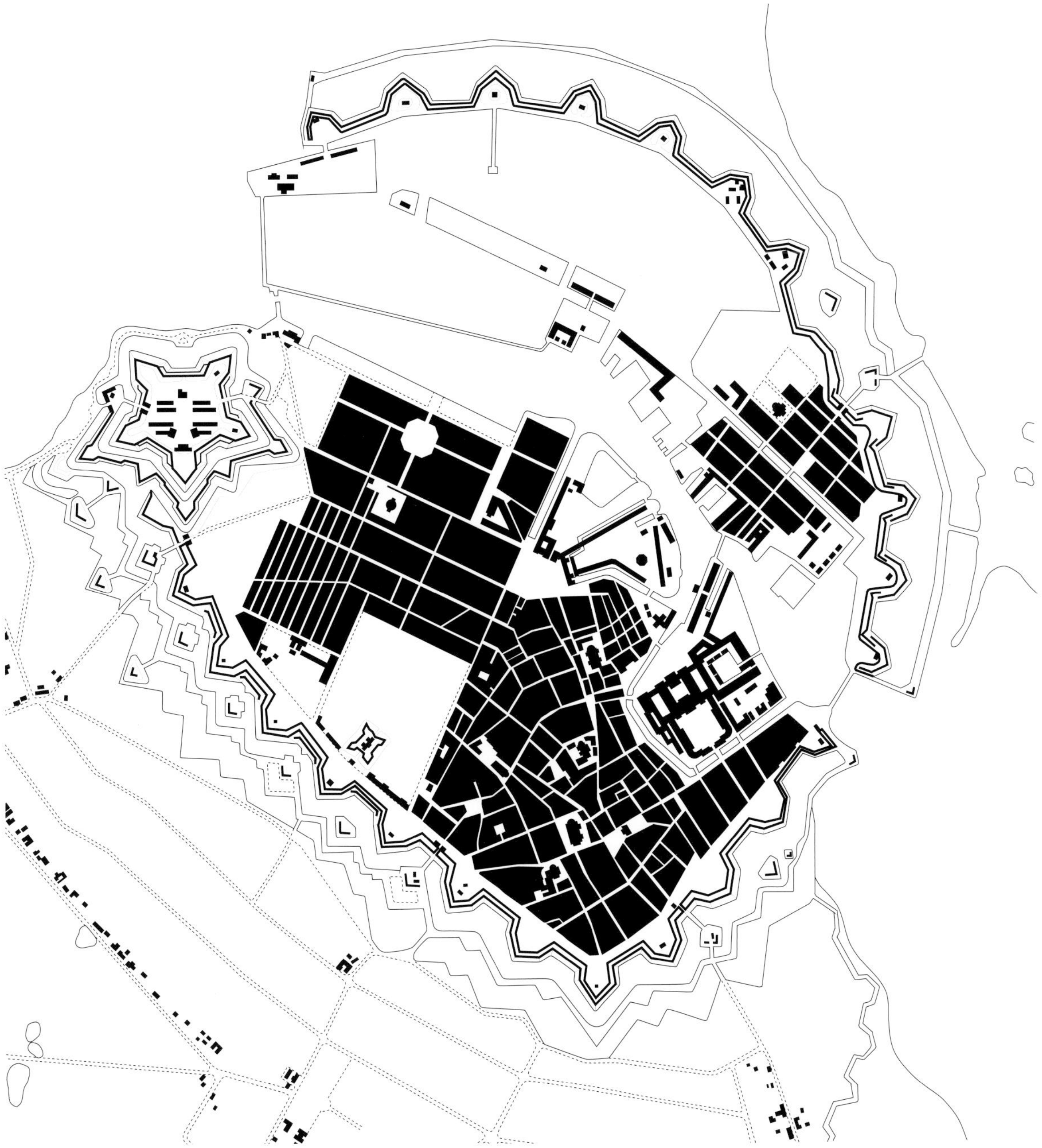

city /country / date

Copenhagen, Denmark 1750 & 1850

scale comparison

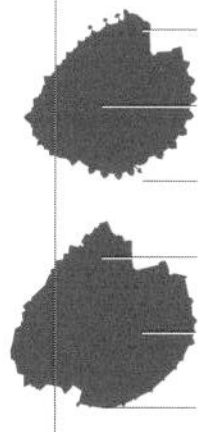

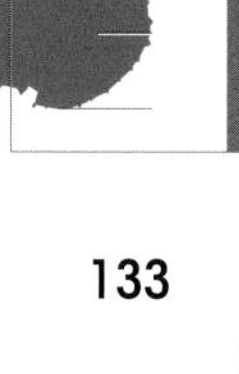

city / country / date

Cordova, Spain 1906

scale comparison

C

100M

Coventry, England 1800

city / country / date

scale comparison

C

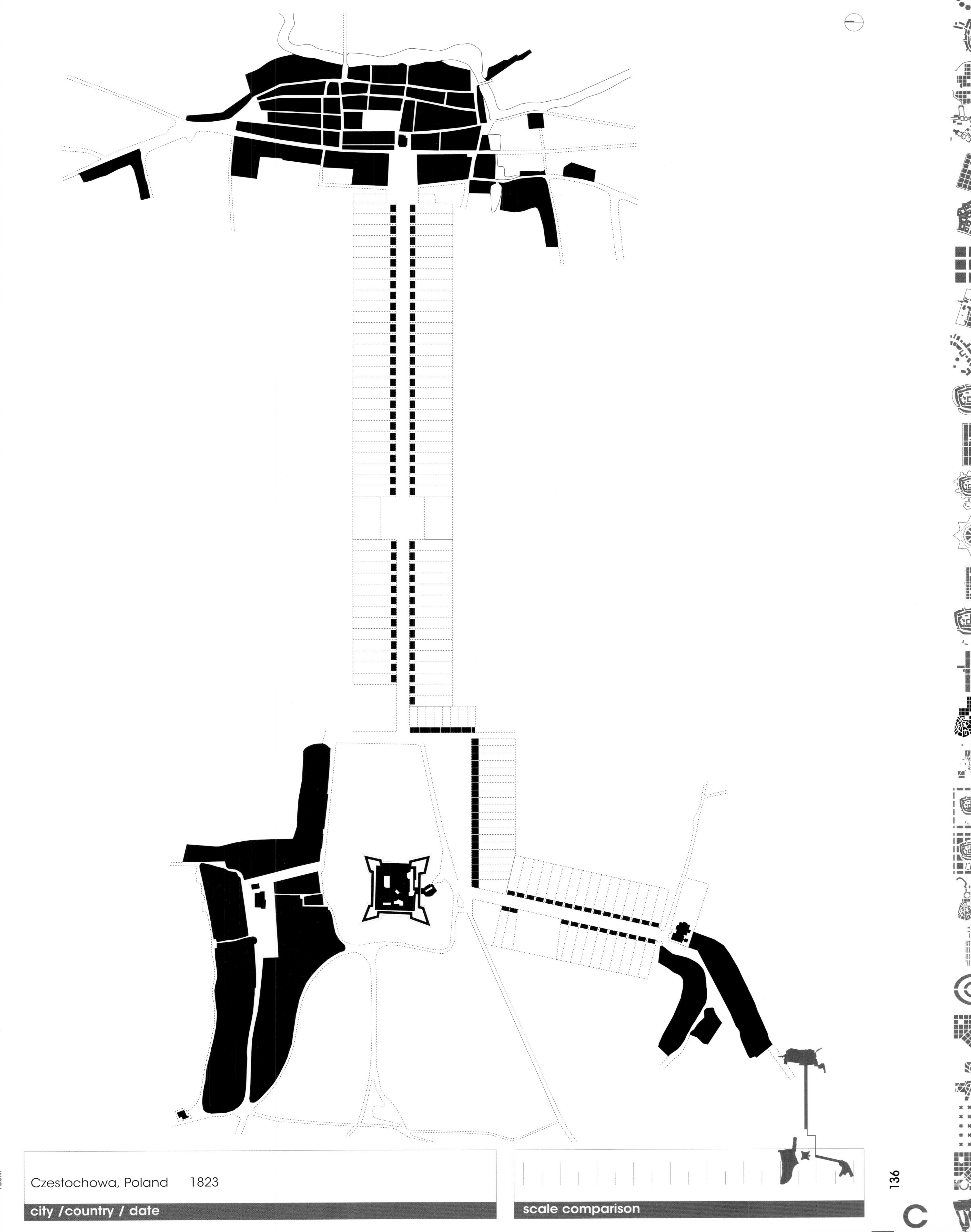
100M
Czestochowa, Poland 1823
city /country / date
scale comparison

100M

Detroit, MI, USA 1830

city /country / date

scale comparison

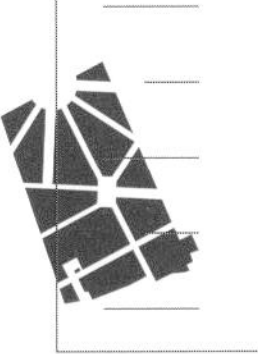

100M
Dijon, France 1909
city / country / date
scale comparison

Domazlice, Czech Republic 1838

city / country / date

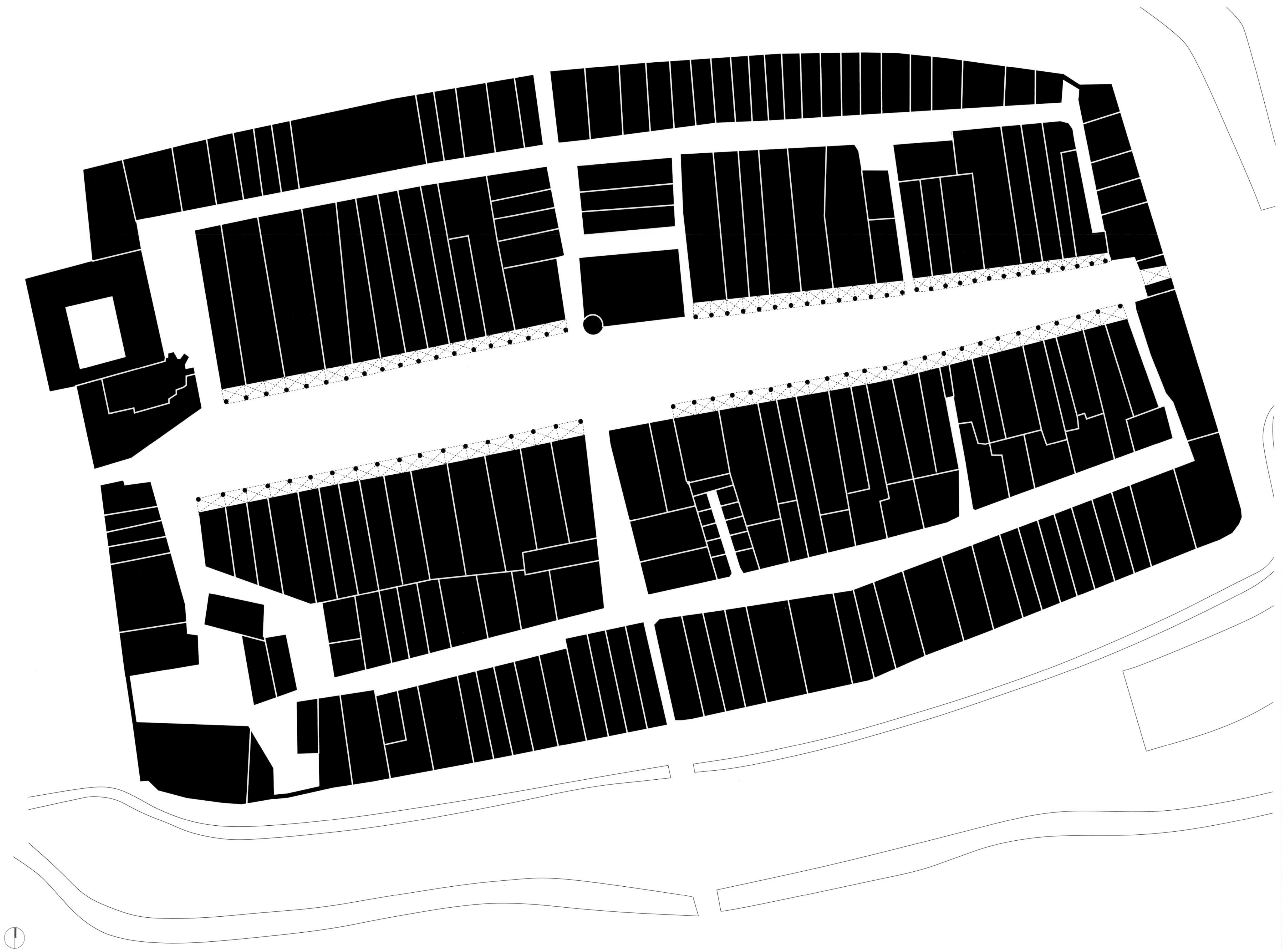

scale comparison

100M
city / country / date
Dordrecht, Netherland 1867
scale comparison

Dresden, Germany 1833

city / country / date

scale comparison

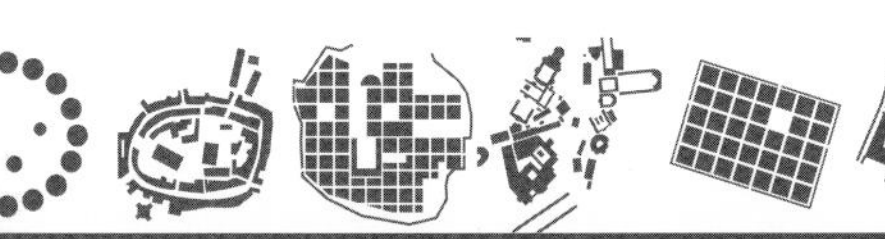

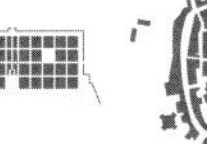

100M
Dublin, Ireland 1836
city / country / date
scale comparison

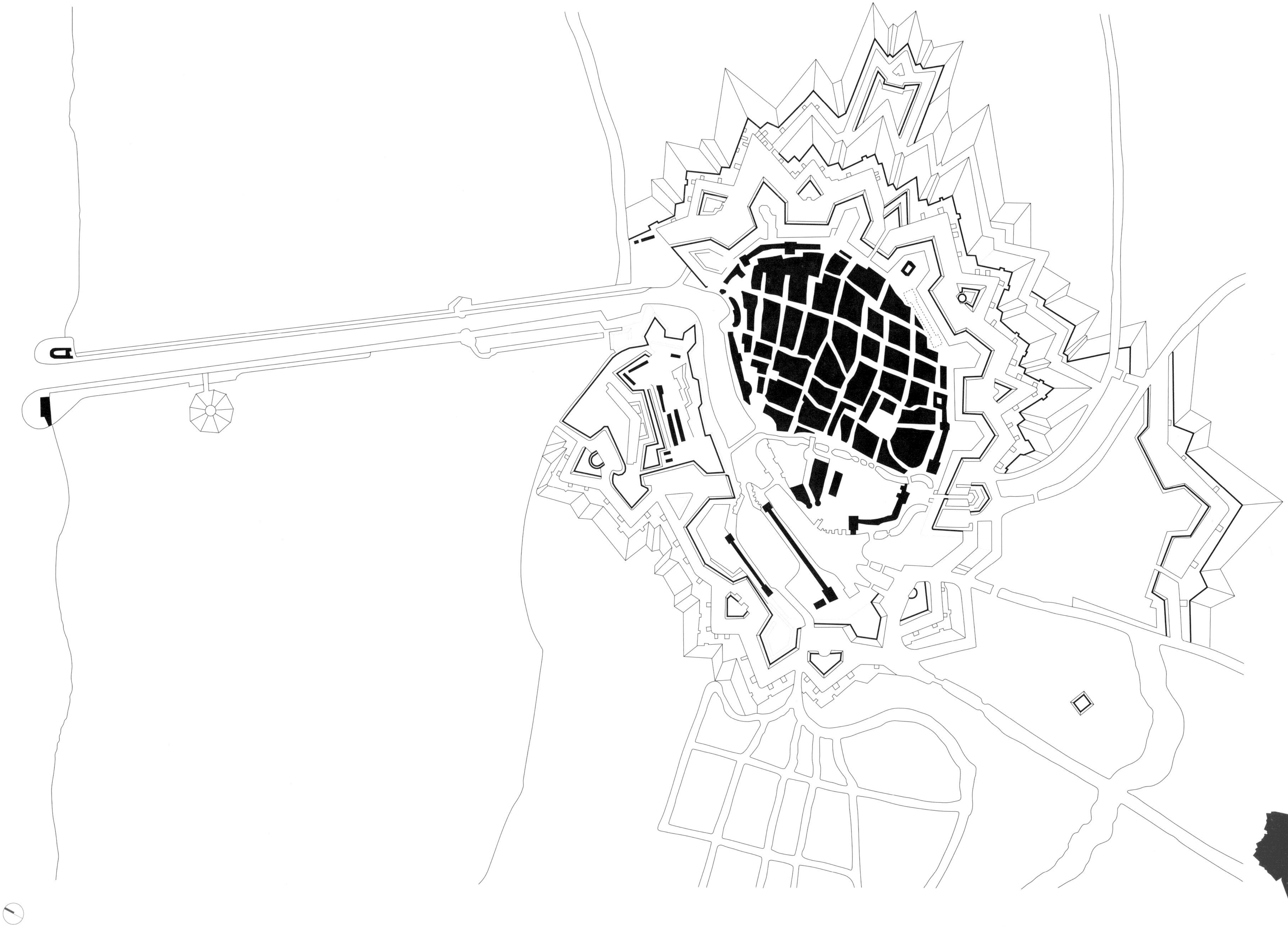

city /country / date

Dunkerque, France 1690

scale comparison

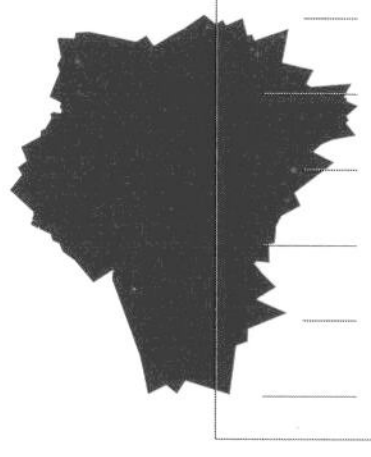

city / country / date

Düsseldorf, Germany 1896

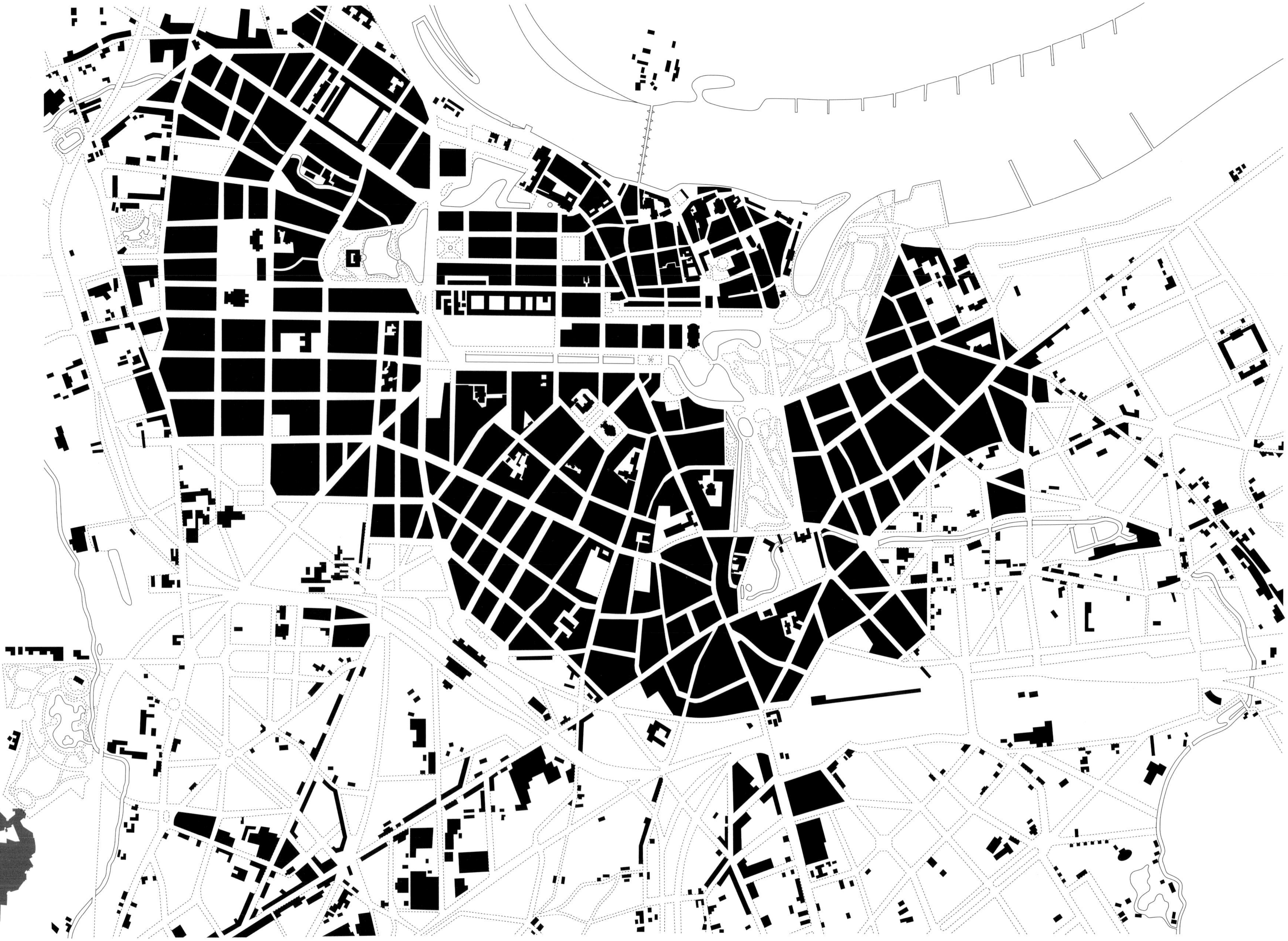

scale comparison

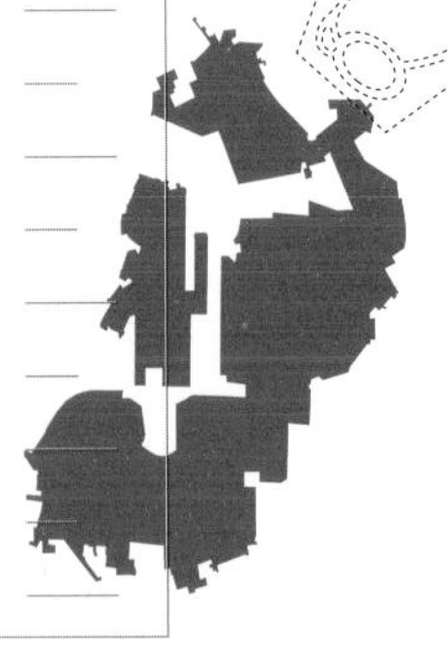

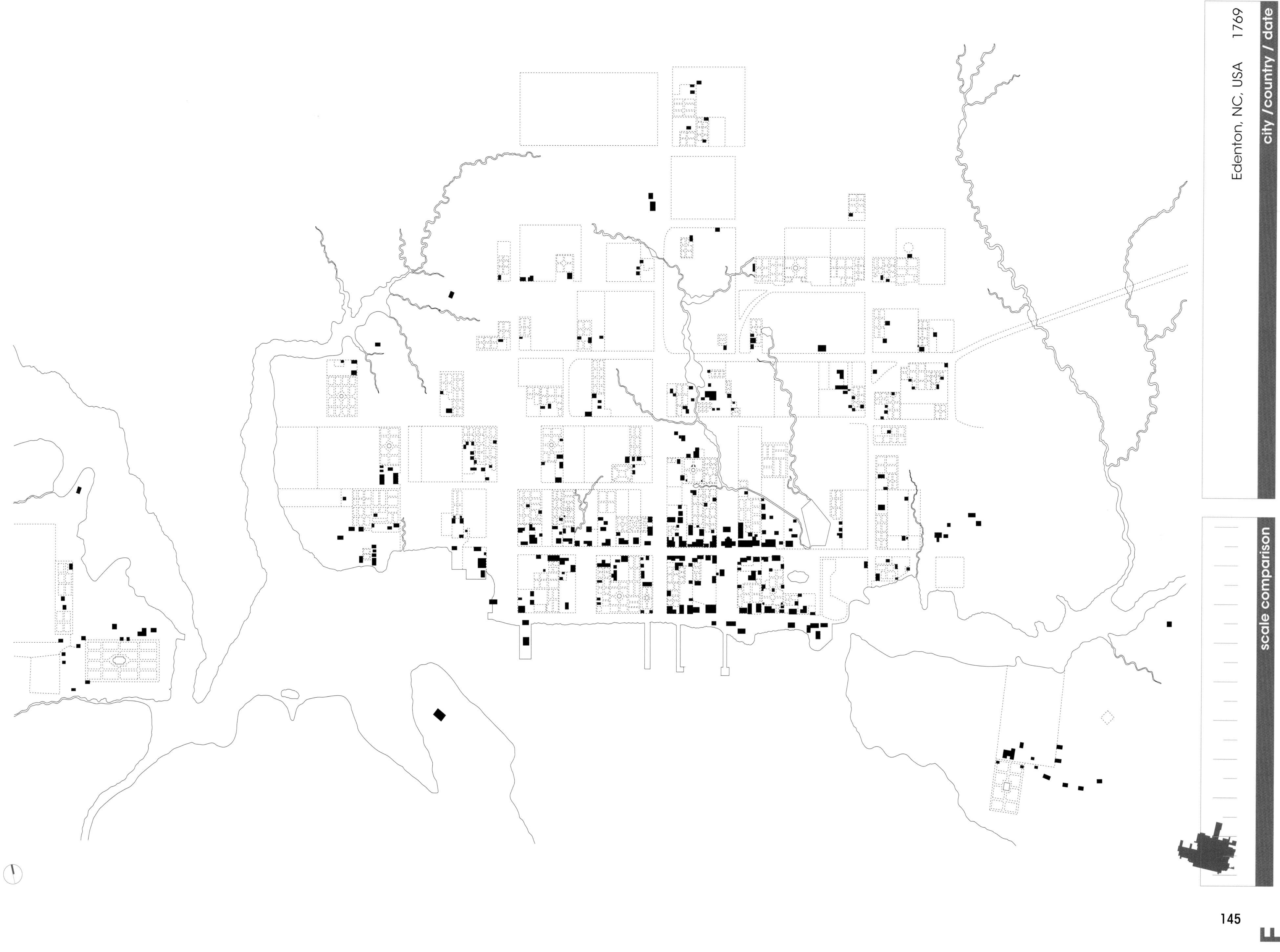
100M
city /country / date
Edenton, NC, USA 1769
scale comparison

100M

city /country / date

Edinburgh, Scotland 1750

scale comparison

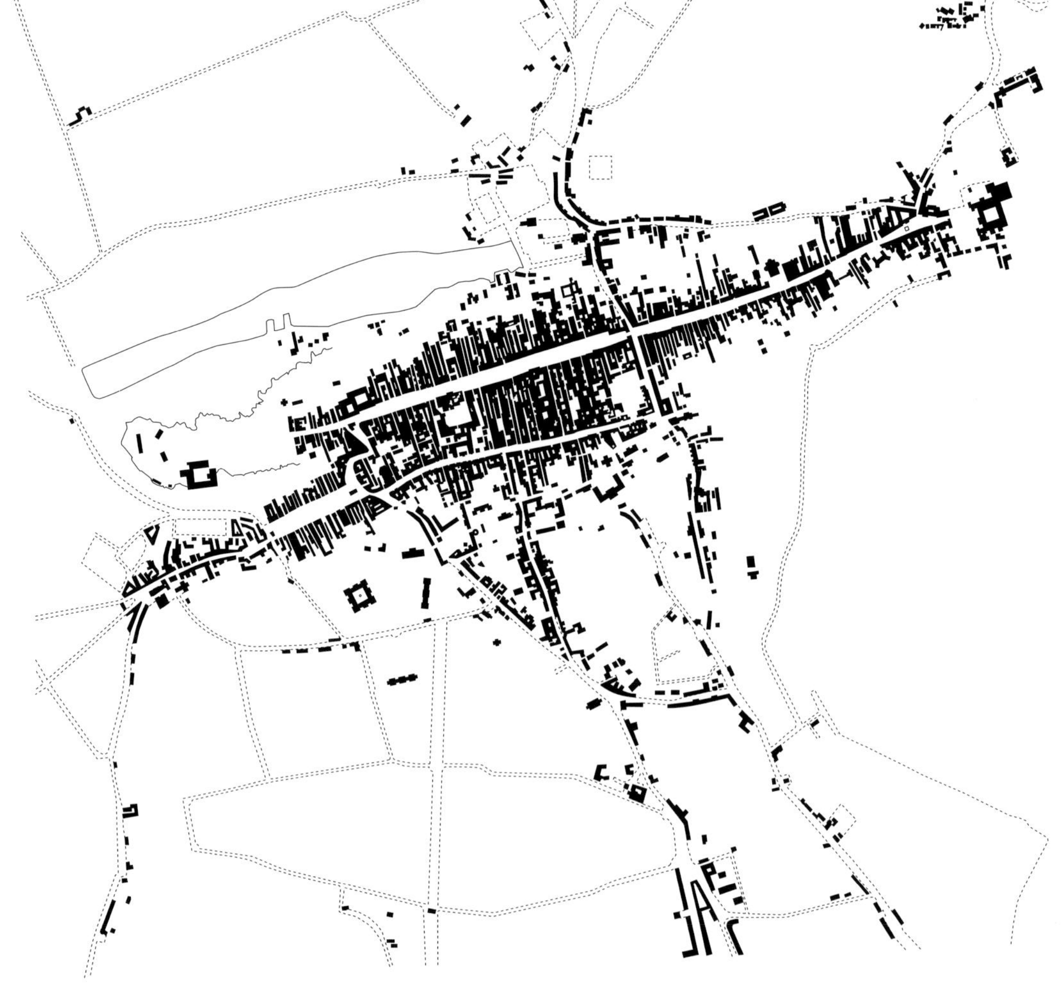

100M

Edinburgh, Scotland 1860

city / country / date

scale comparison

100M

city / country / date

Elblag, Poland [1974]

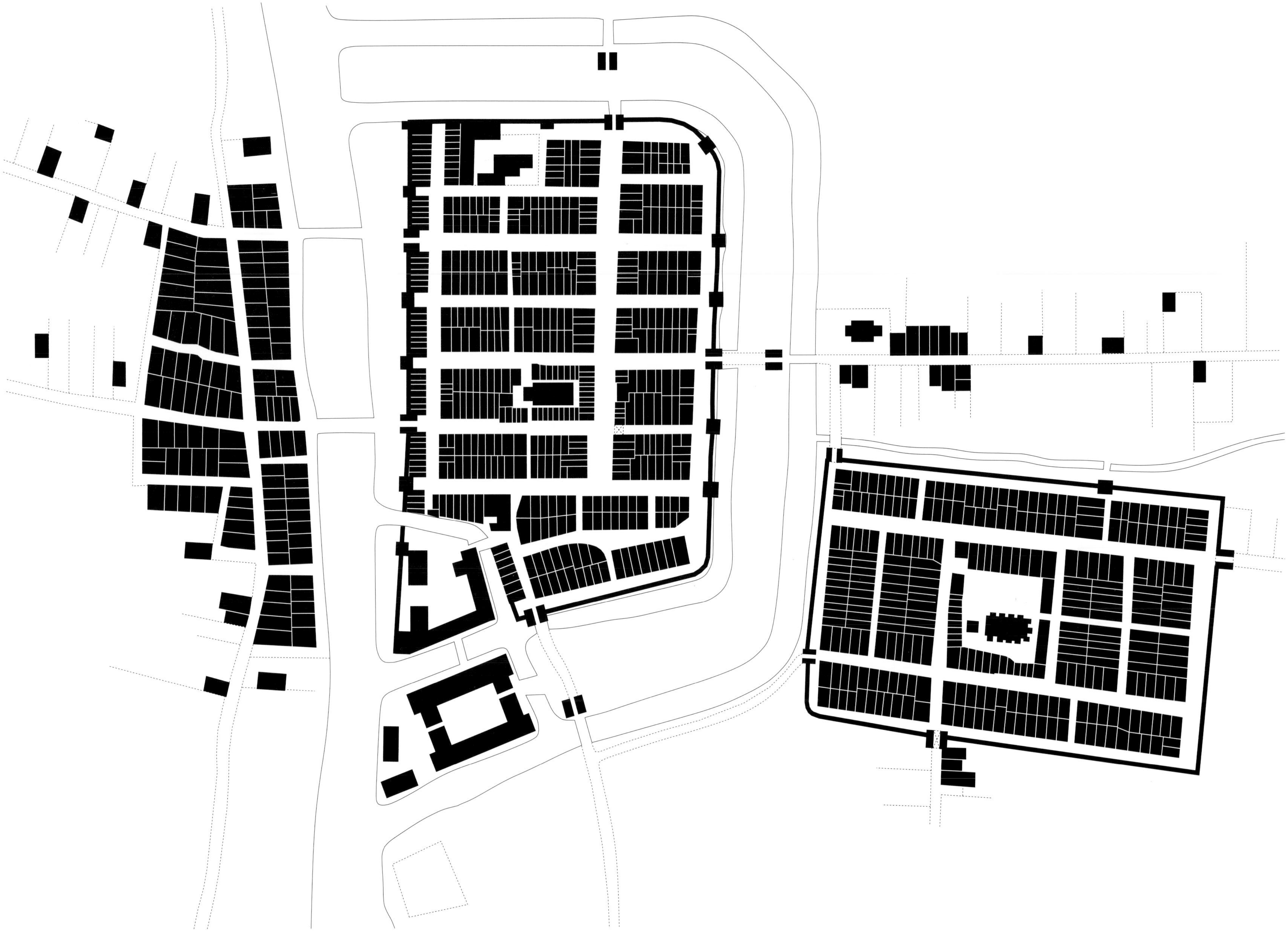

scale comparison

E

100M

Ellwanger, Germany [1974]

city / country / date

scale comparison

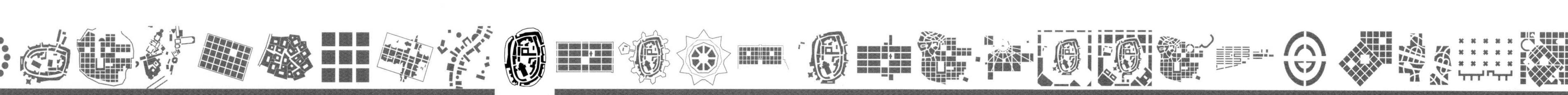

100M

city / country / date

E.U.R., Italy (design by architects Pagano, Piacentini, Piccinato, Rossi, & Vietti)

1937

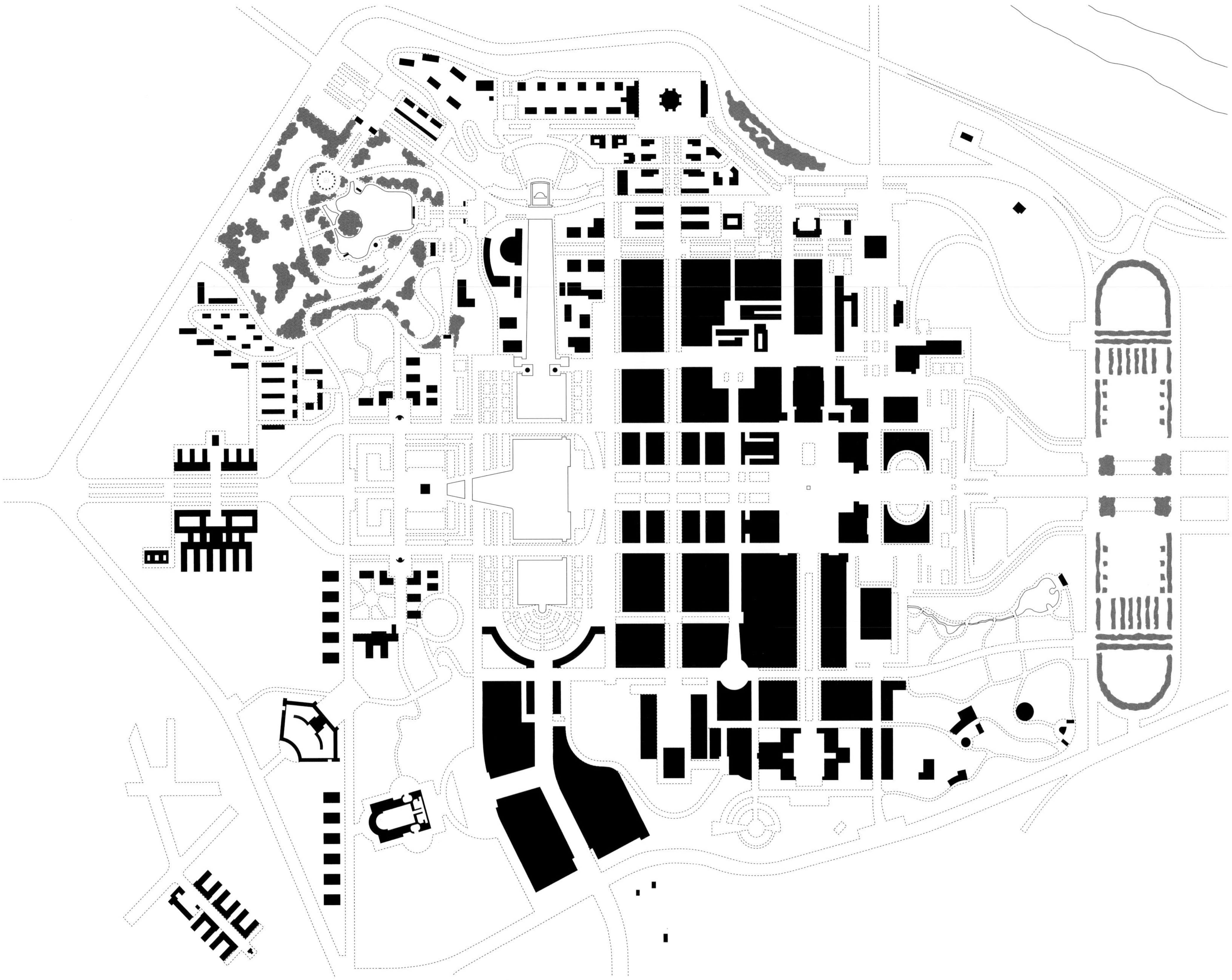

scale comparison

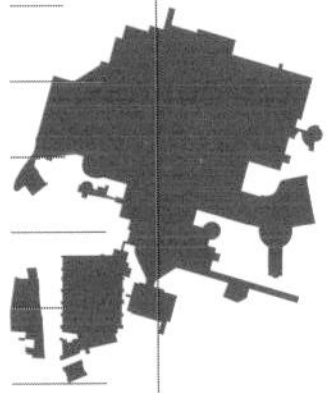

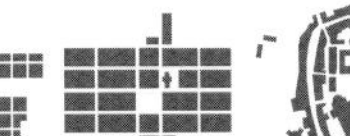
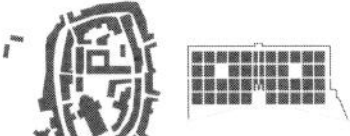

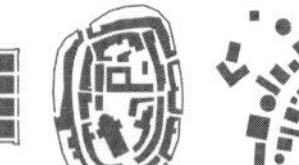
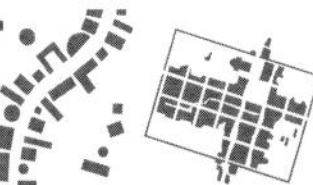

100M

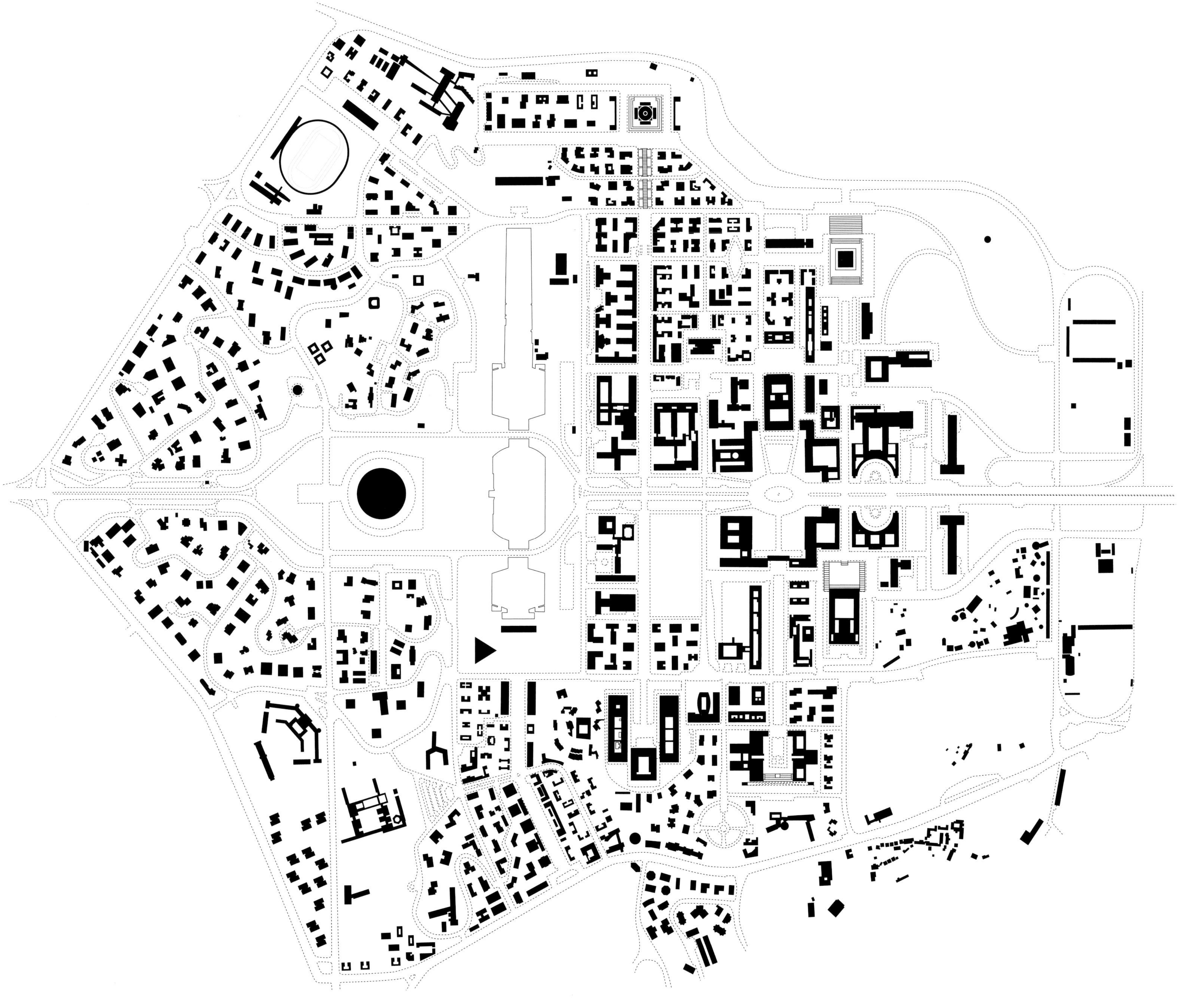

E.U.R., Rome, Italy 1995

city /country / date

scale comparison

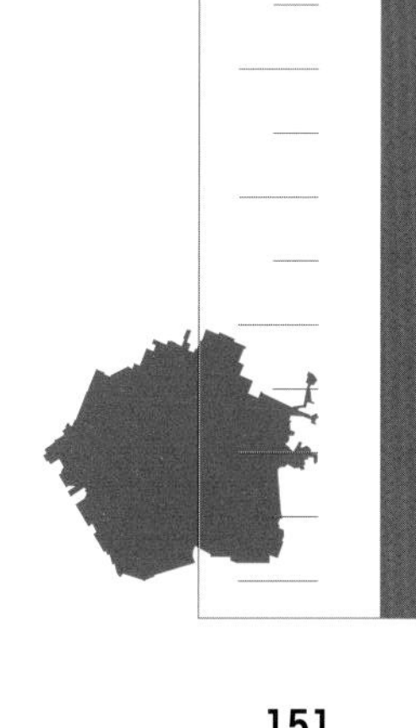

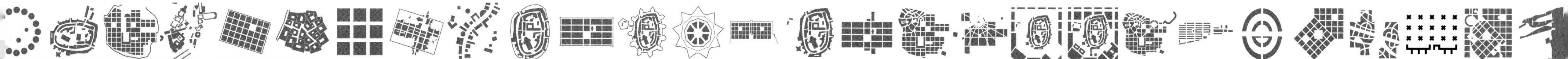

100M

city / country / date

Fair Haven, VT, USA 1869

scale comparison

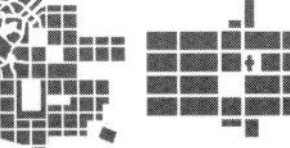

100M

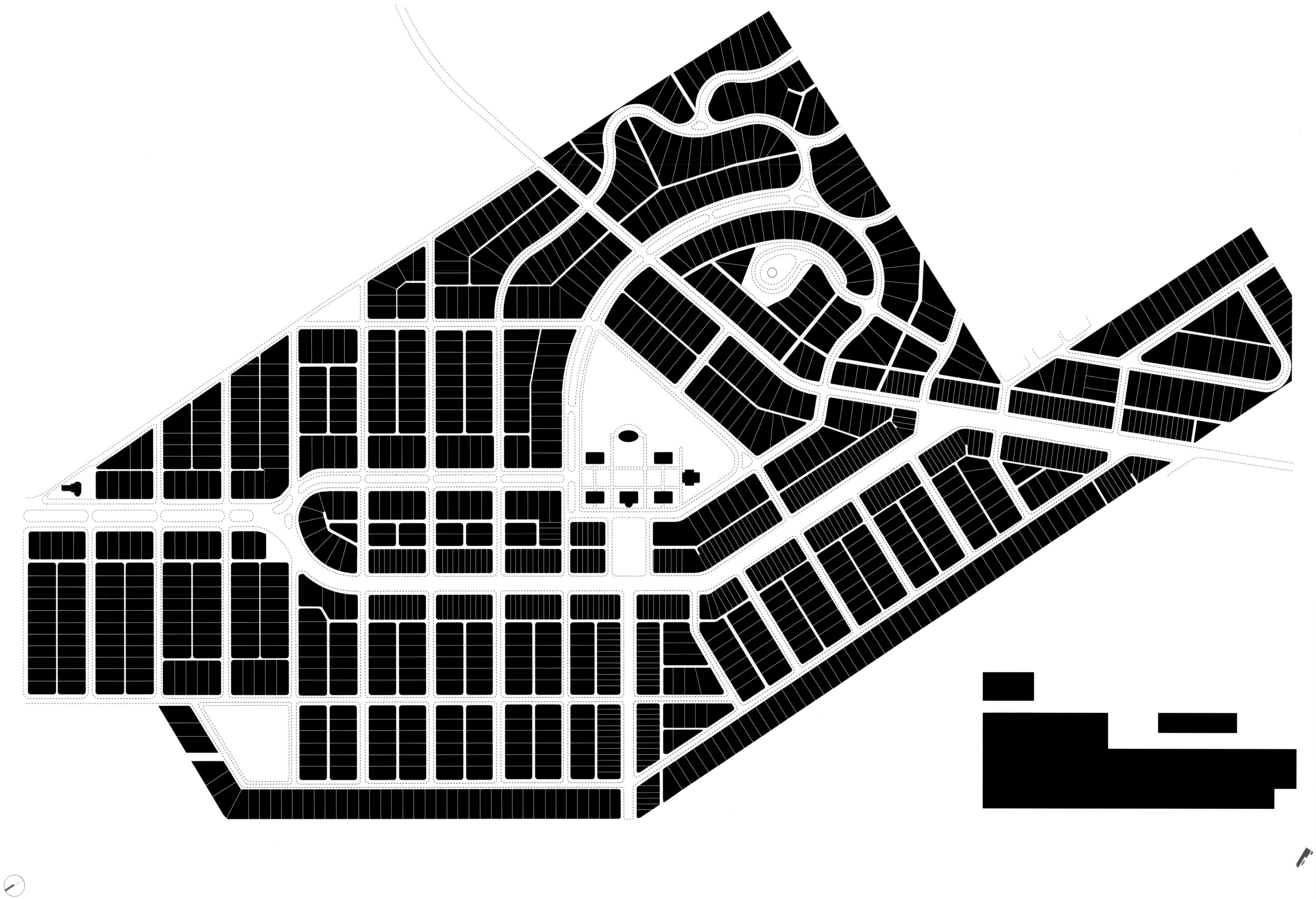

Fairfield, AL, USA 1910

city /country / date

scale comparison

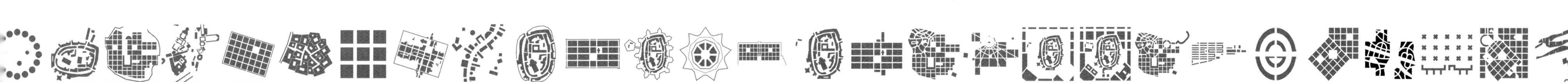

100M

city / country / date

Faleria, Italy 1983

scale comparison

city /country / date

Ferrara, Italy [1963]

scale comparison

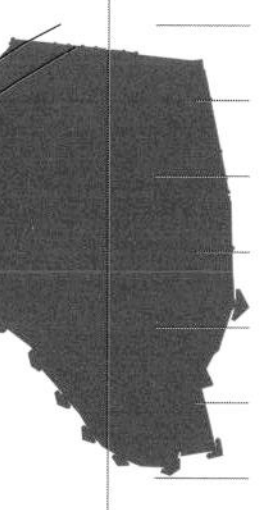

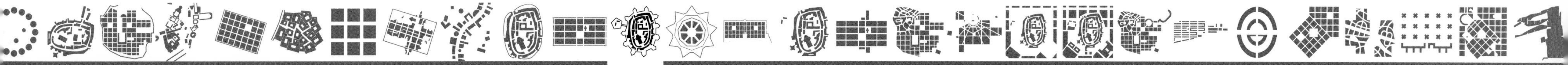

100M

city /country / date

Firenzuola, Italy 1850

scale comparison

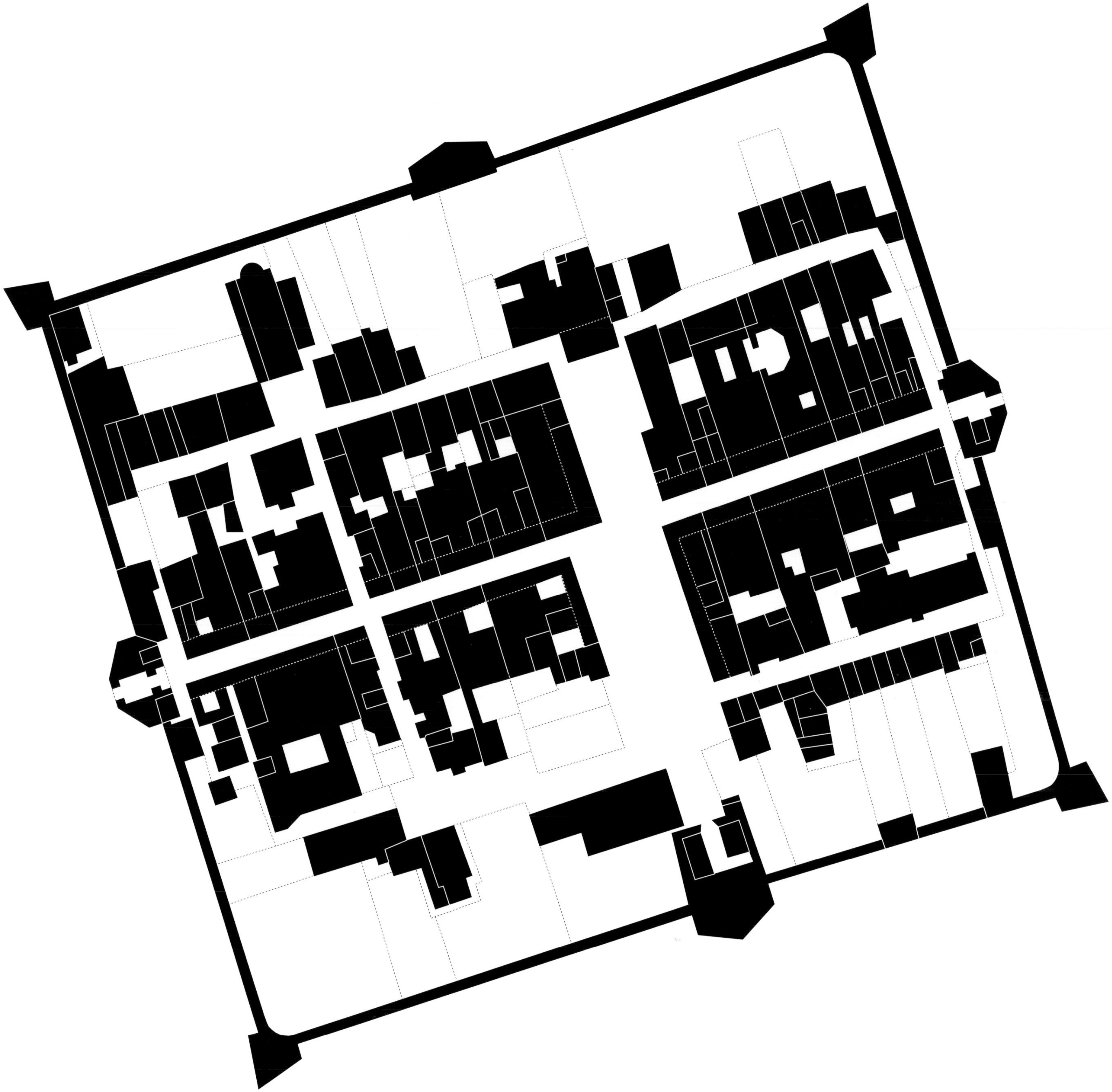

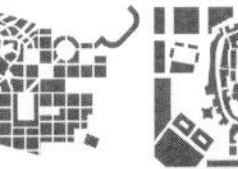

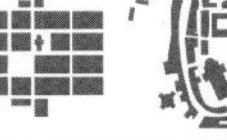

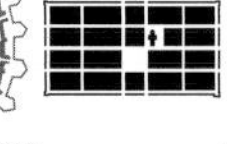

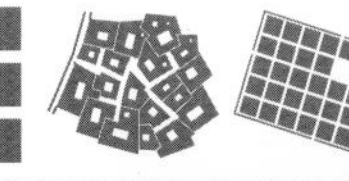
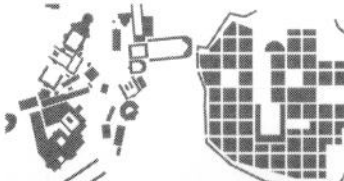
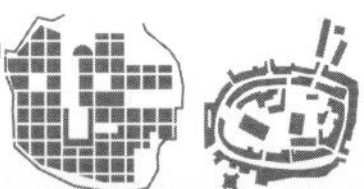

100M

Florence, Italy 1843

city / country / date

scale comparison

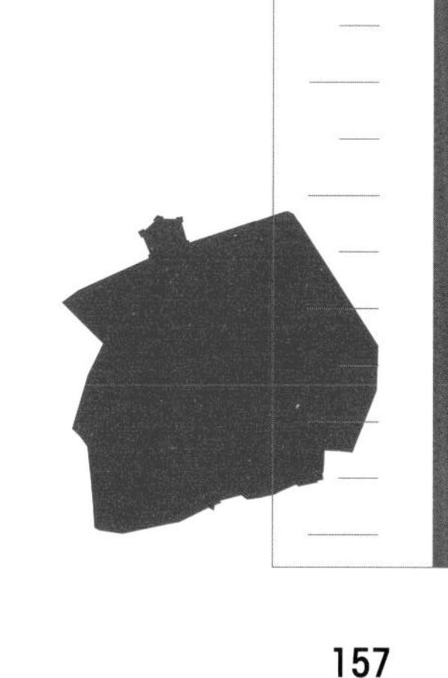

F

city / country / date

Fondi, Italy 1990

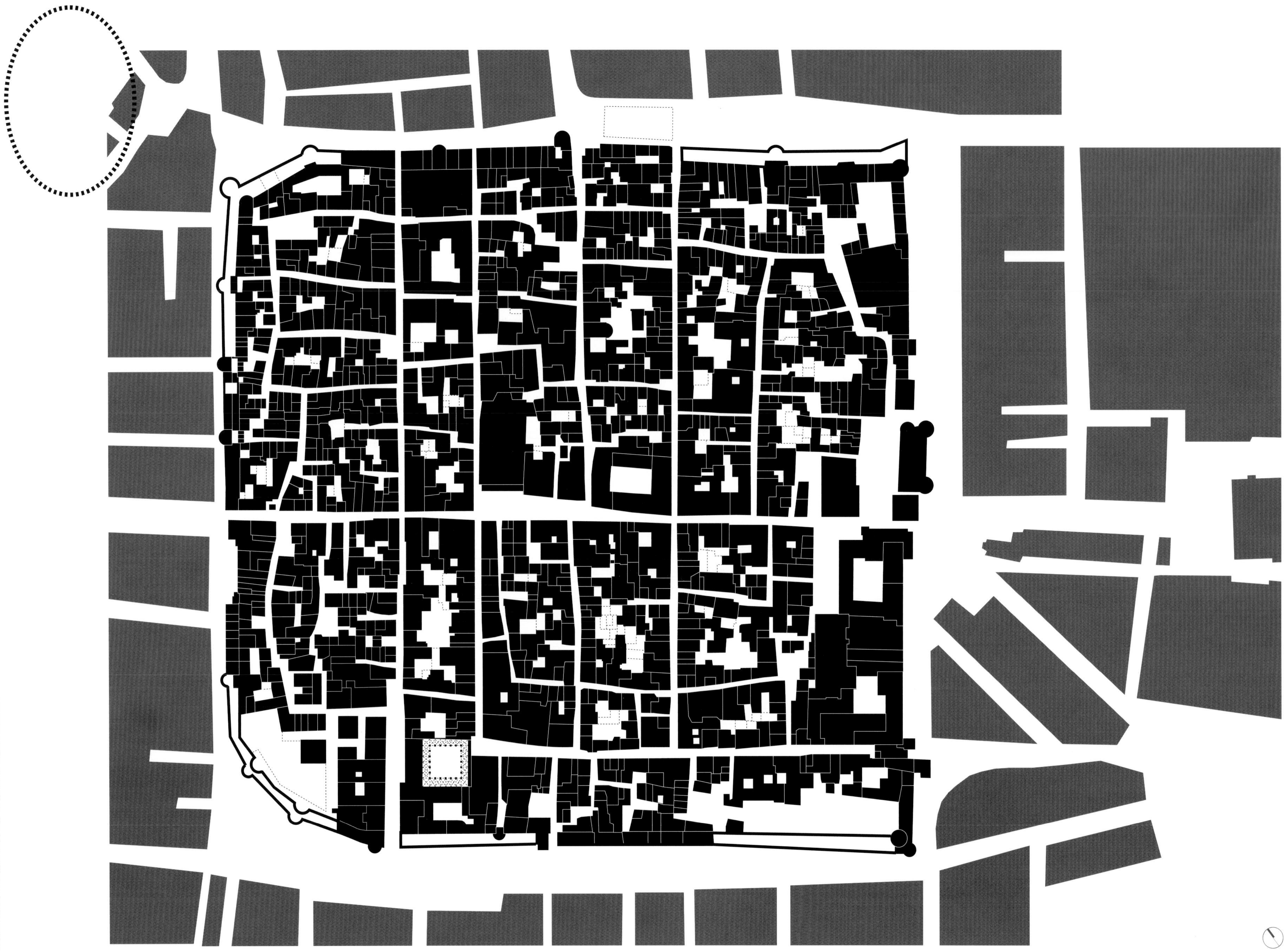

scale comparison

100M

Fontainebleau, France 1974

city /country / date

scale comparison

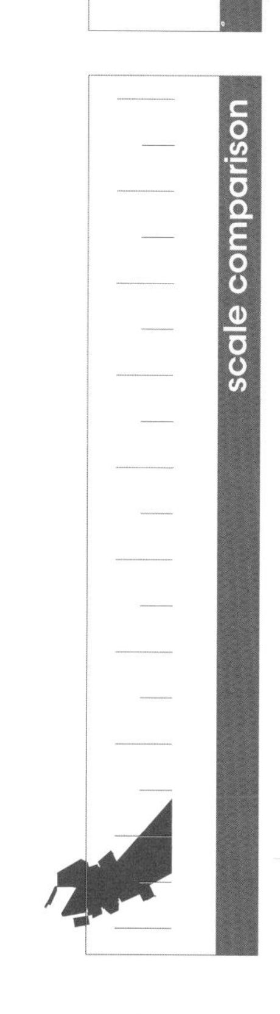

Frankfurt, Germany 1837
city / country / date
scale comparison
100M
F

100M

Frankfurt, Germany (proposal by David Chipperfield) 1994

city / country / date

scale comparison

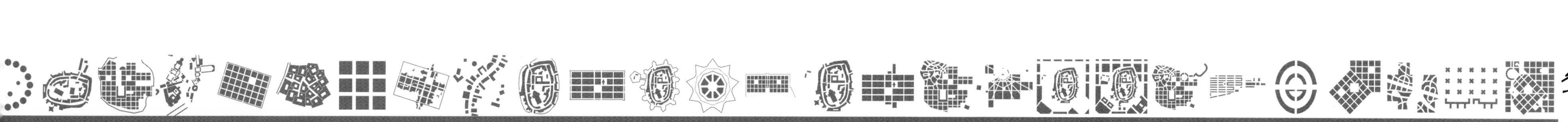

city / country / date

Friedberg, Germany 1200

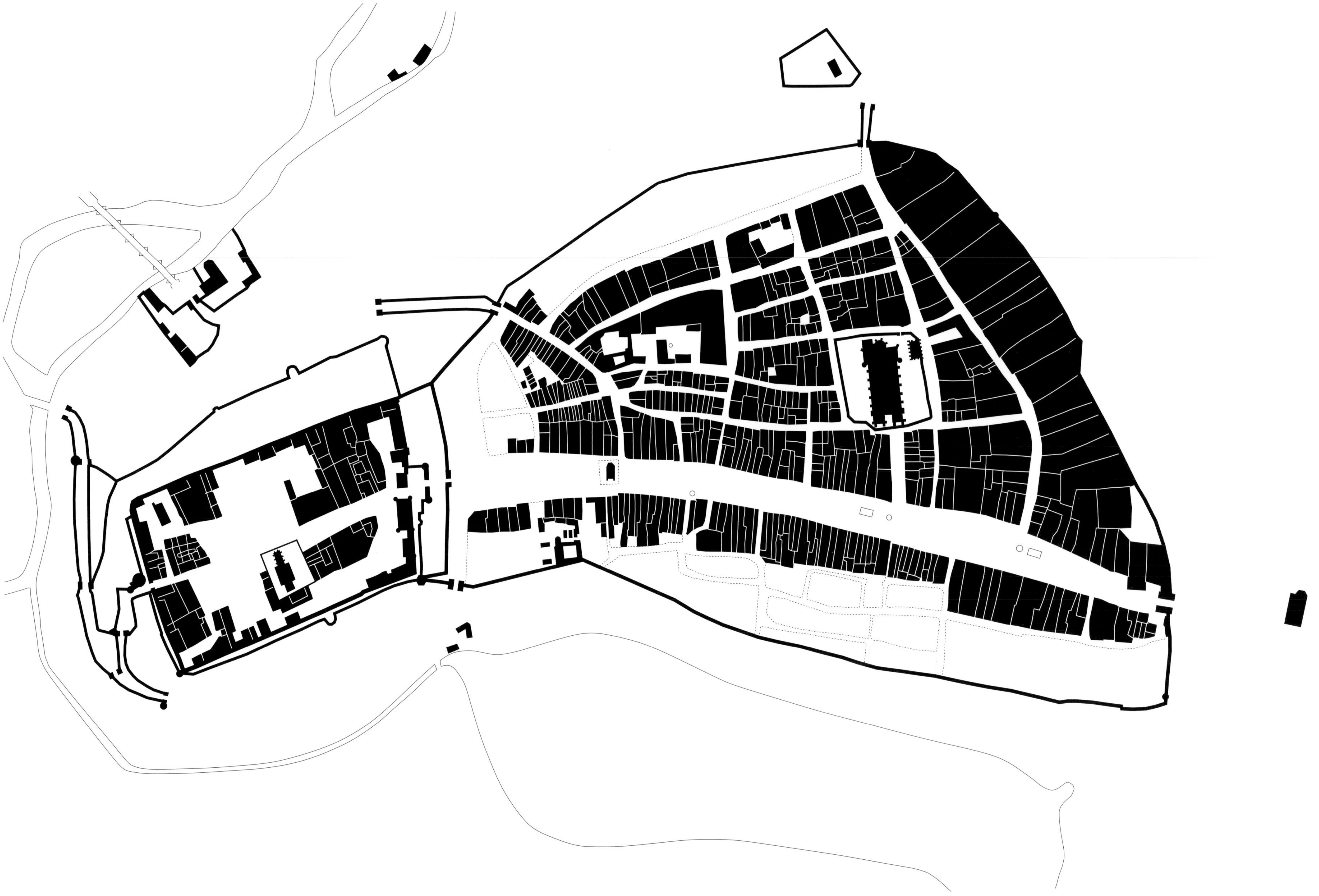

scale comparison

Geneva, Switzerland 1841

city /country / date

scale comparison

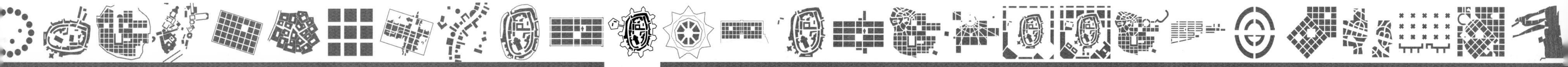

100M

city / country / date

Genzano, Italy 1979

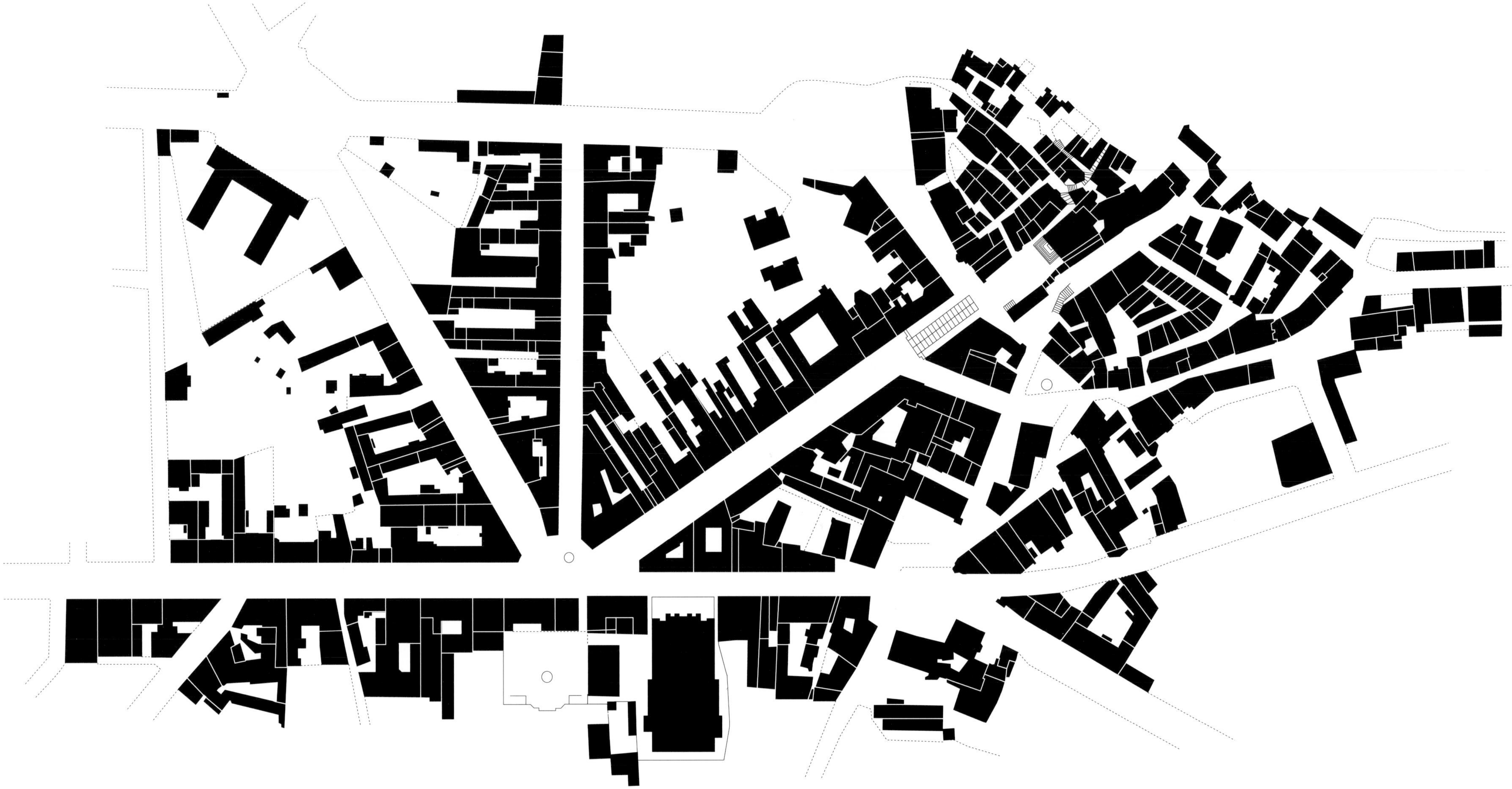

scale comparison

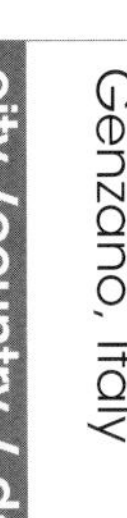

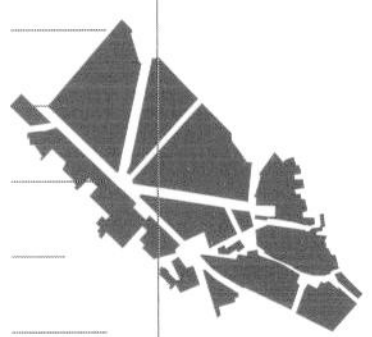

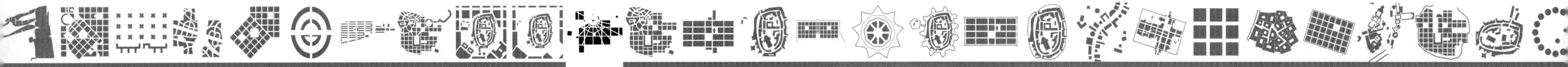

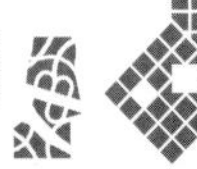

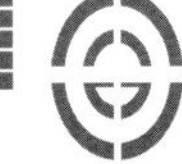

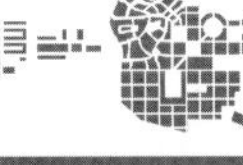

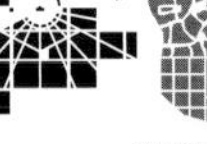

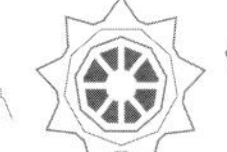

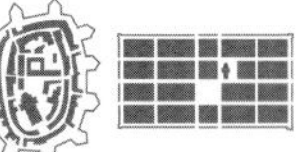

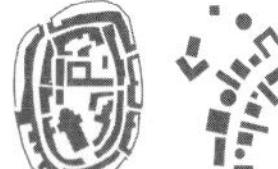

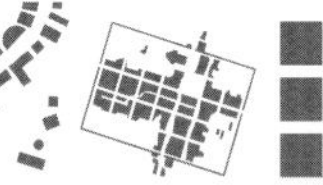

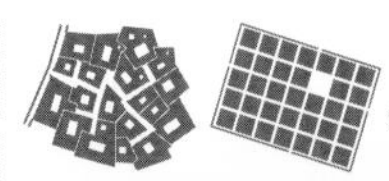

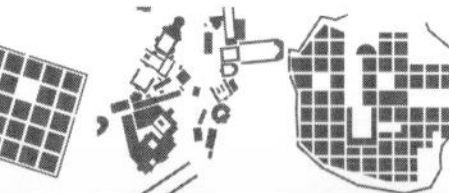

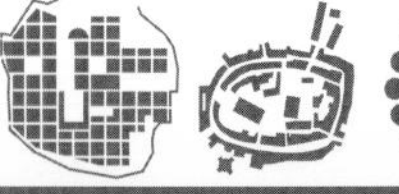

100M

Glasgow, Scotland 1860

city /country / date

scale comparison

100M

city / country / date

Grammichele , Italy 1693

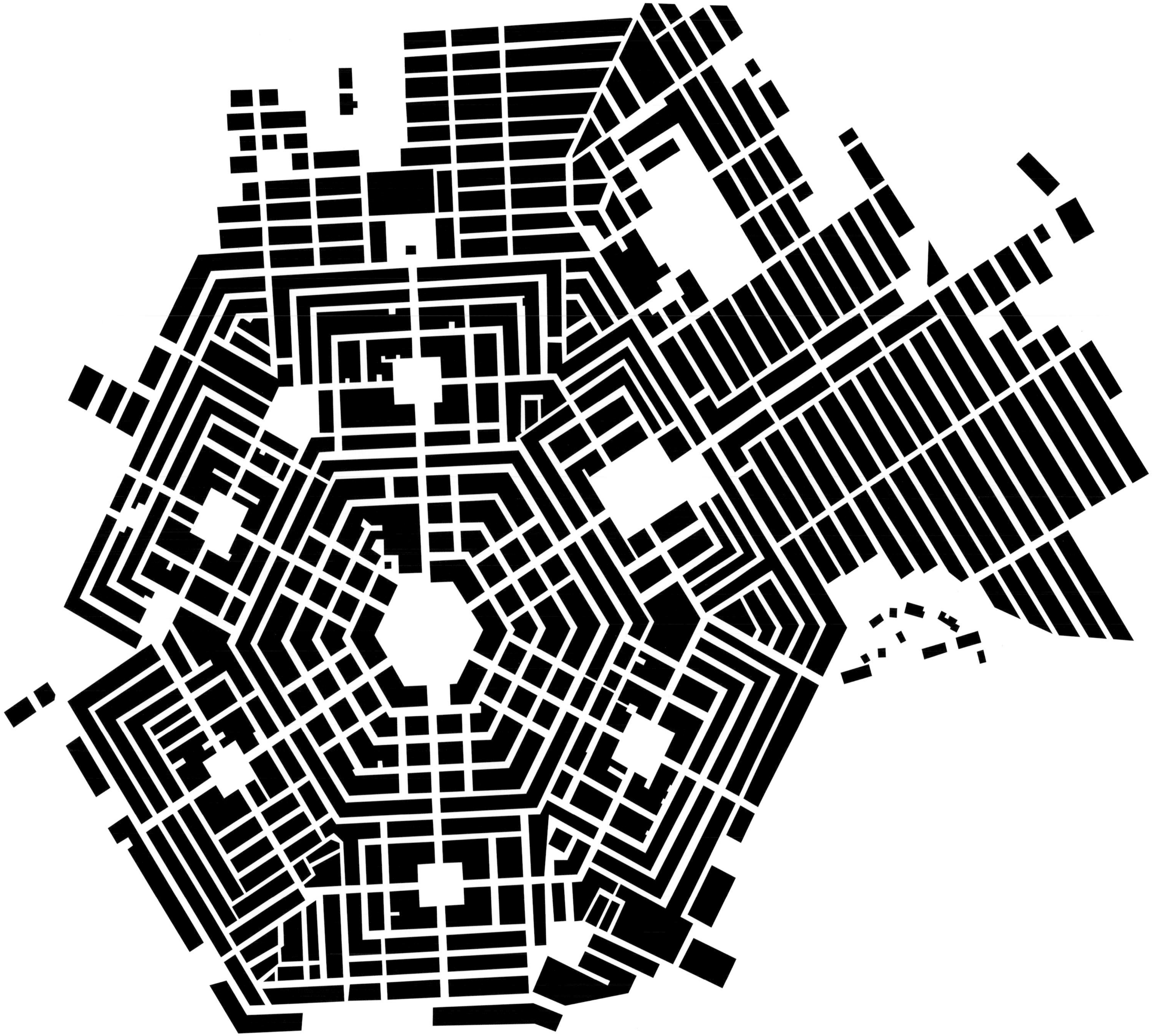

scale comparison

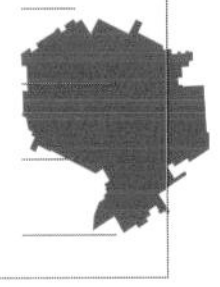

100M

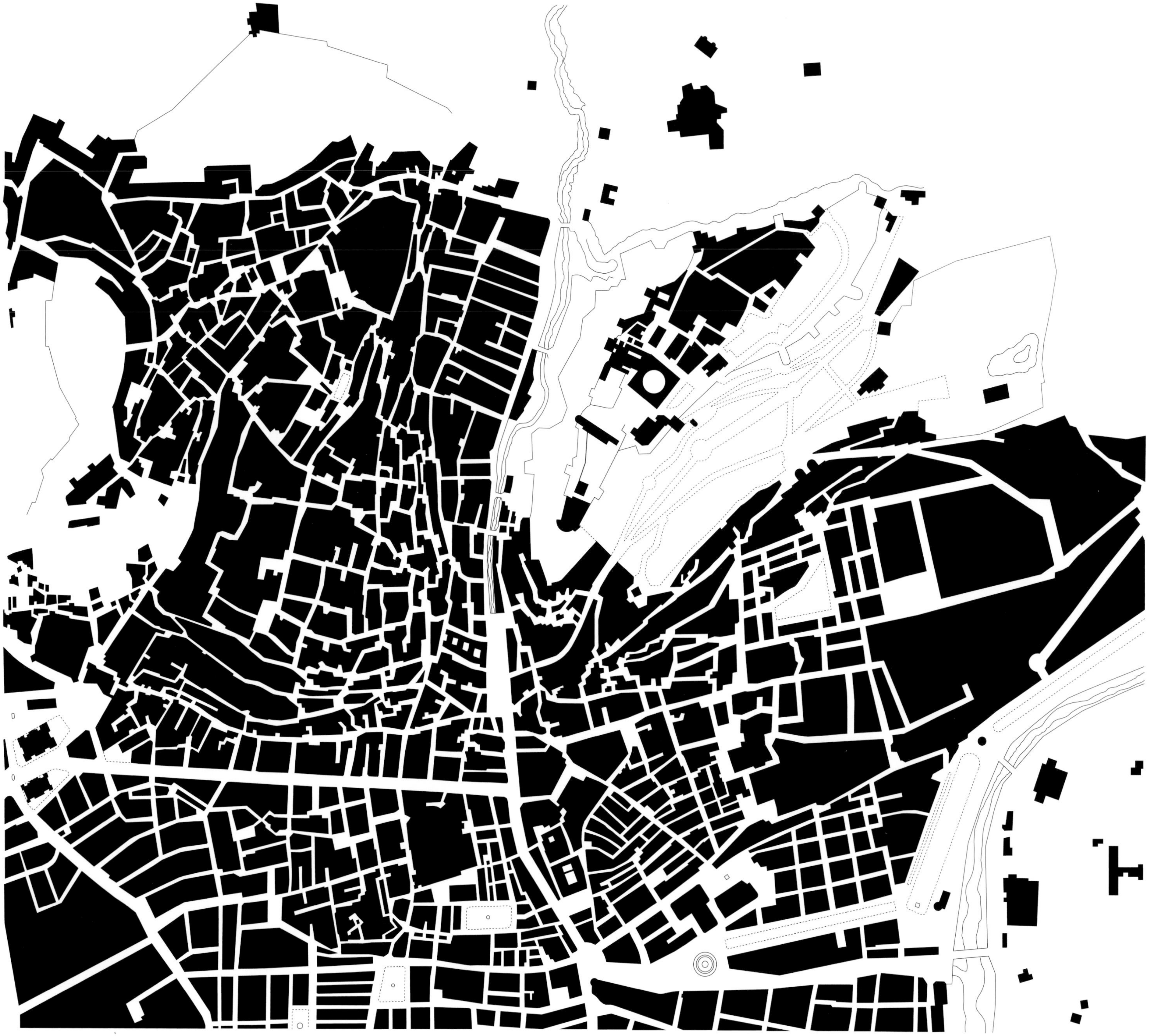

Granada, Spain 1906

city /country / date

scale comparison

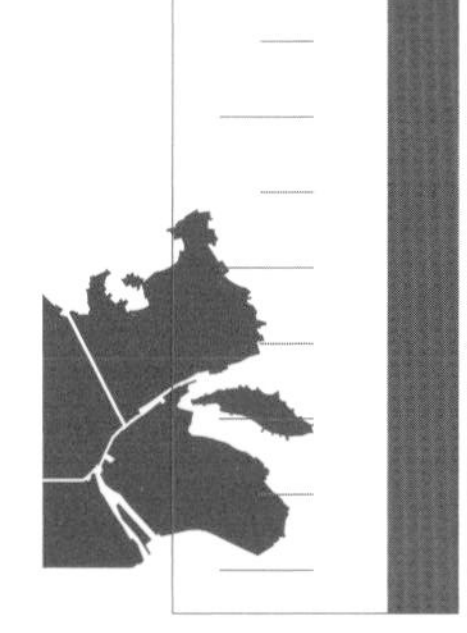

city / country / date

Hanau, Germany 1790

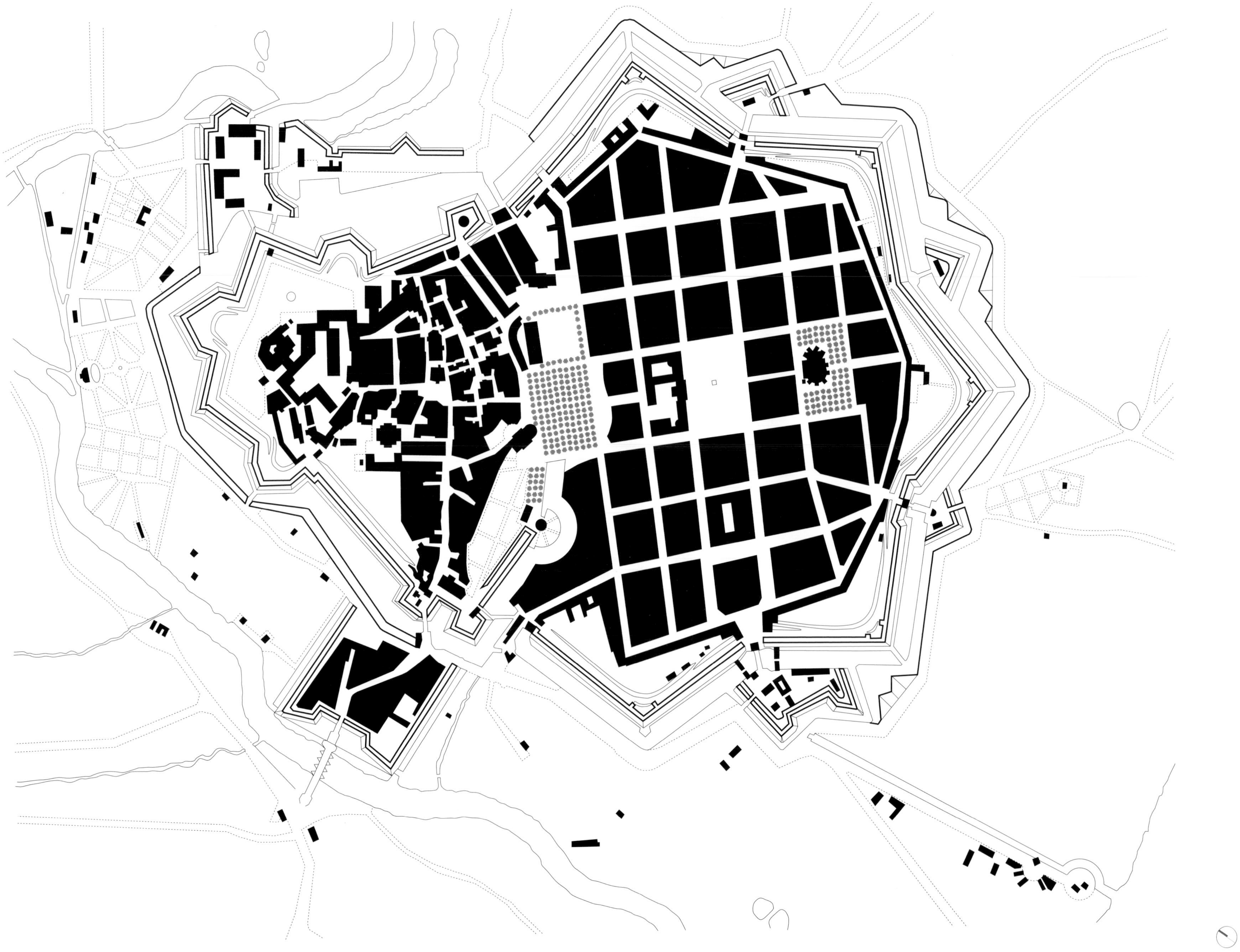

scale comparison

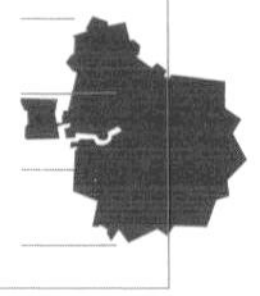

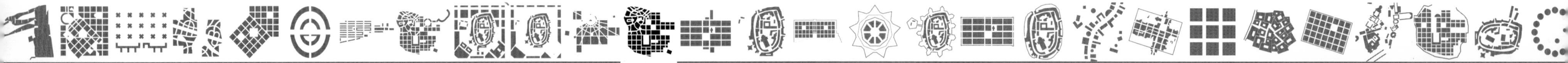

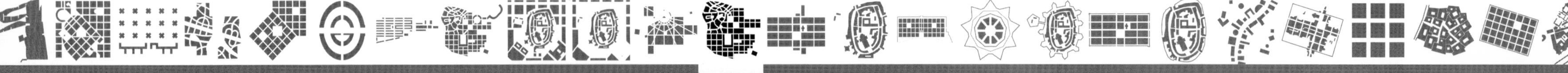

Herrnhut, Germany 1782

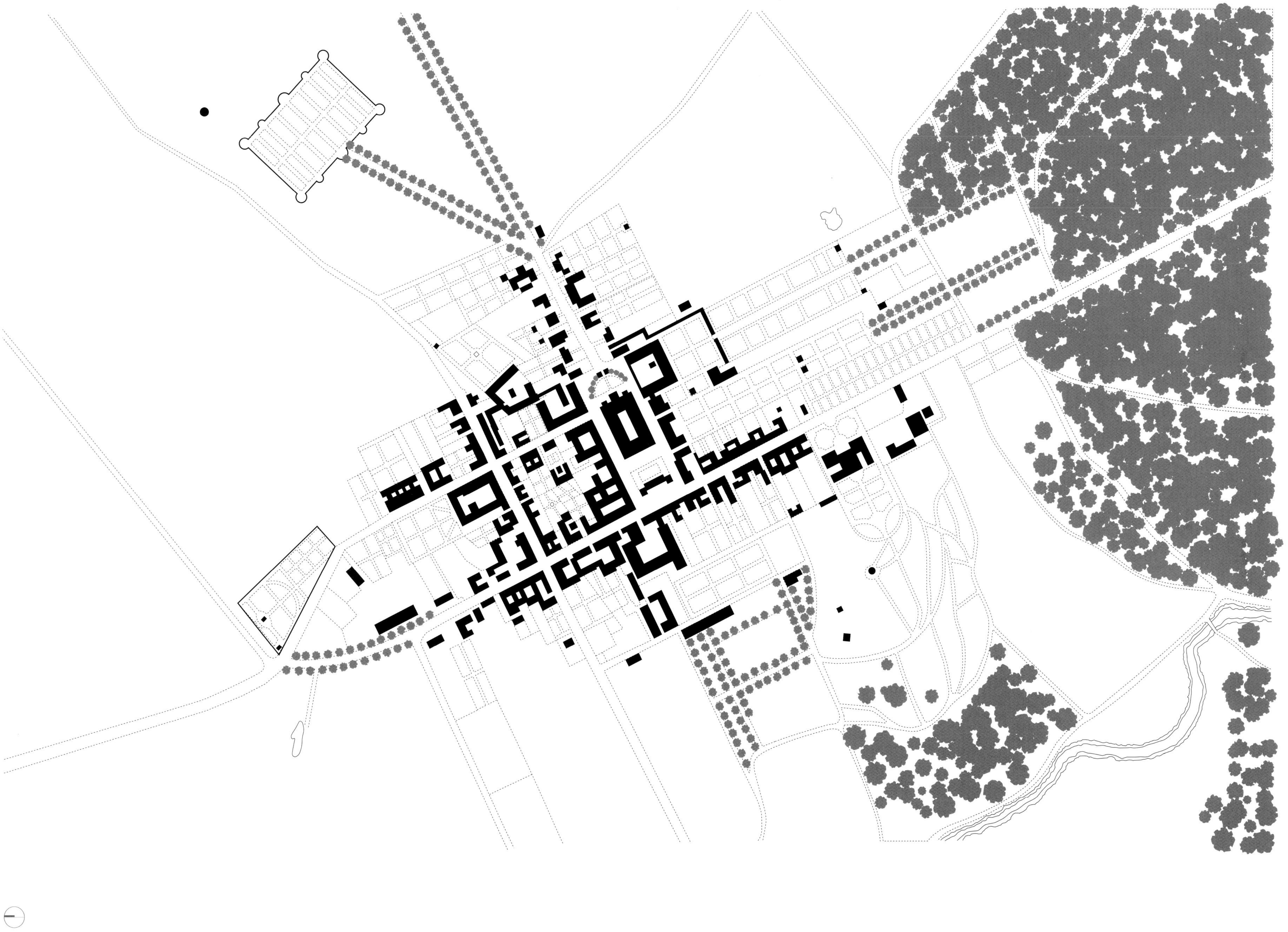

city /country / date

scale comparison

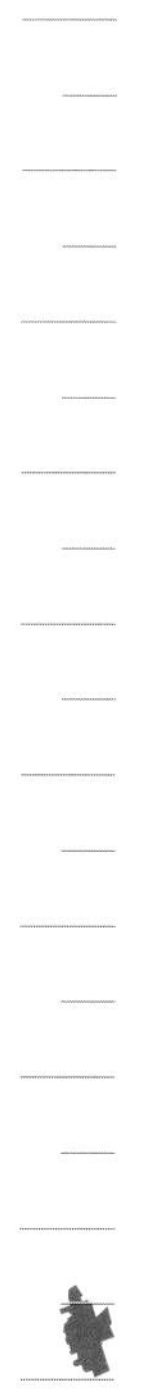

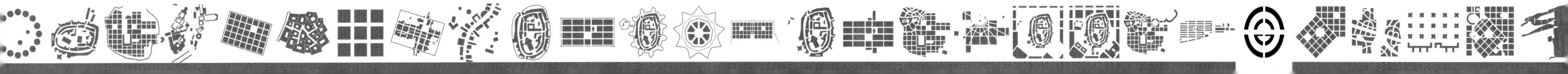

city / country / date

Hué in Annam, Vietnam 1800

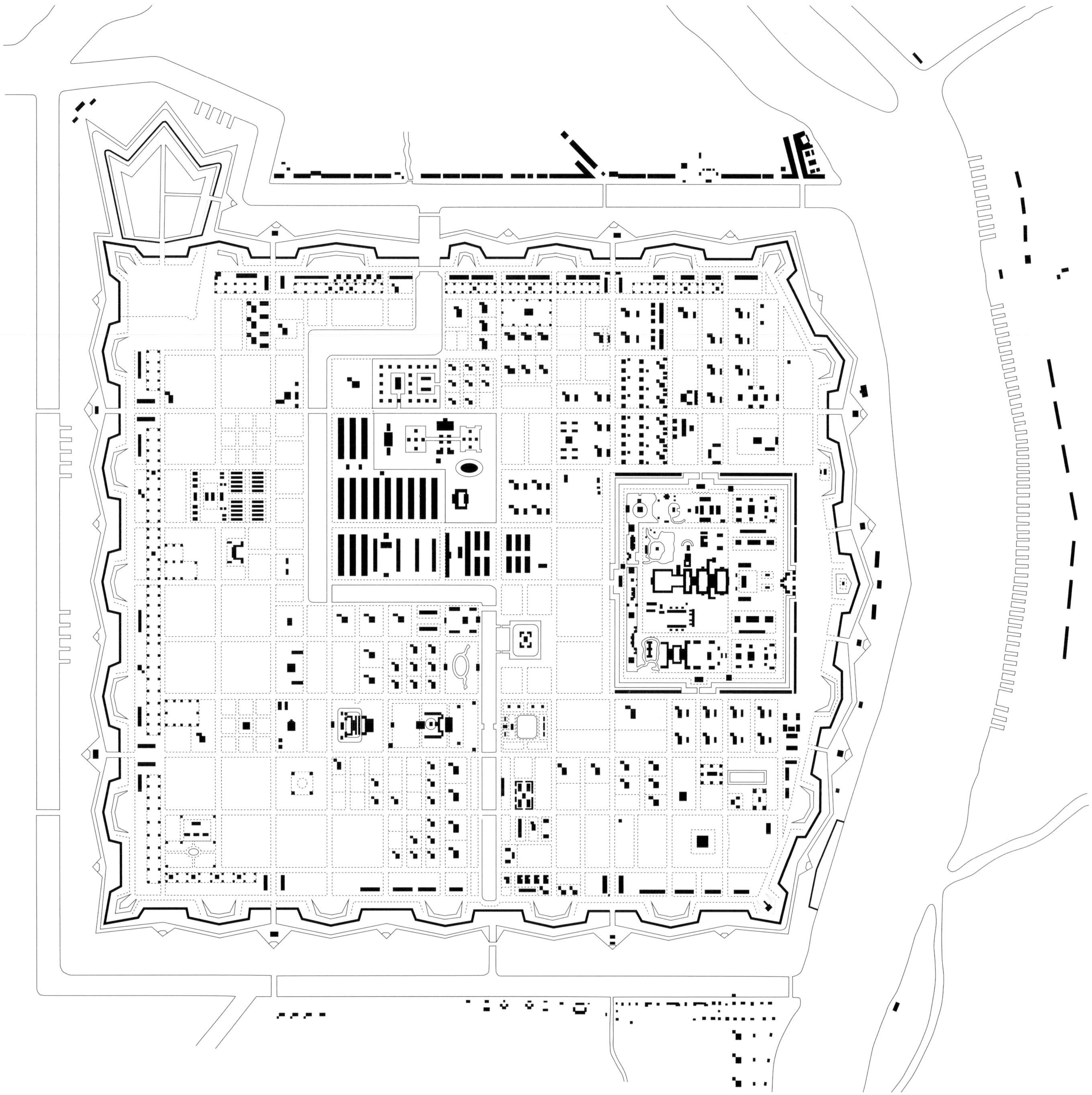

scale comparison

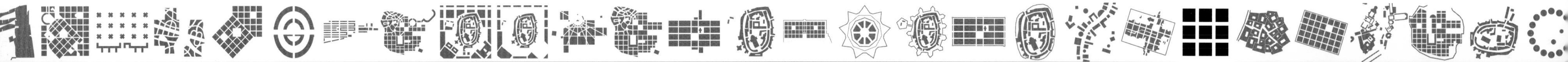

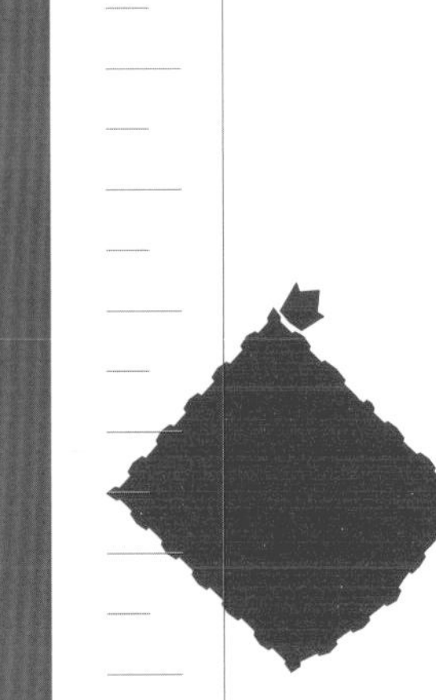

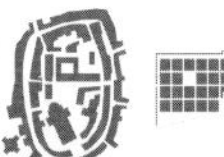

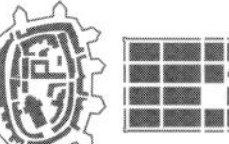

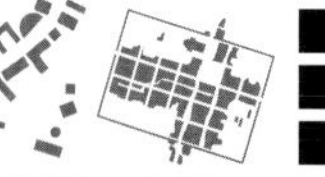
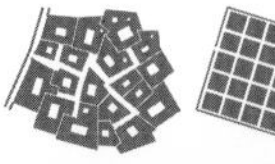

Hygeia, KY, USA (design by I.B. Papworth) 1827

city / country / date

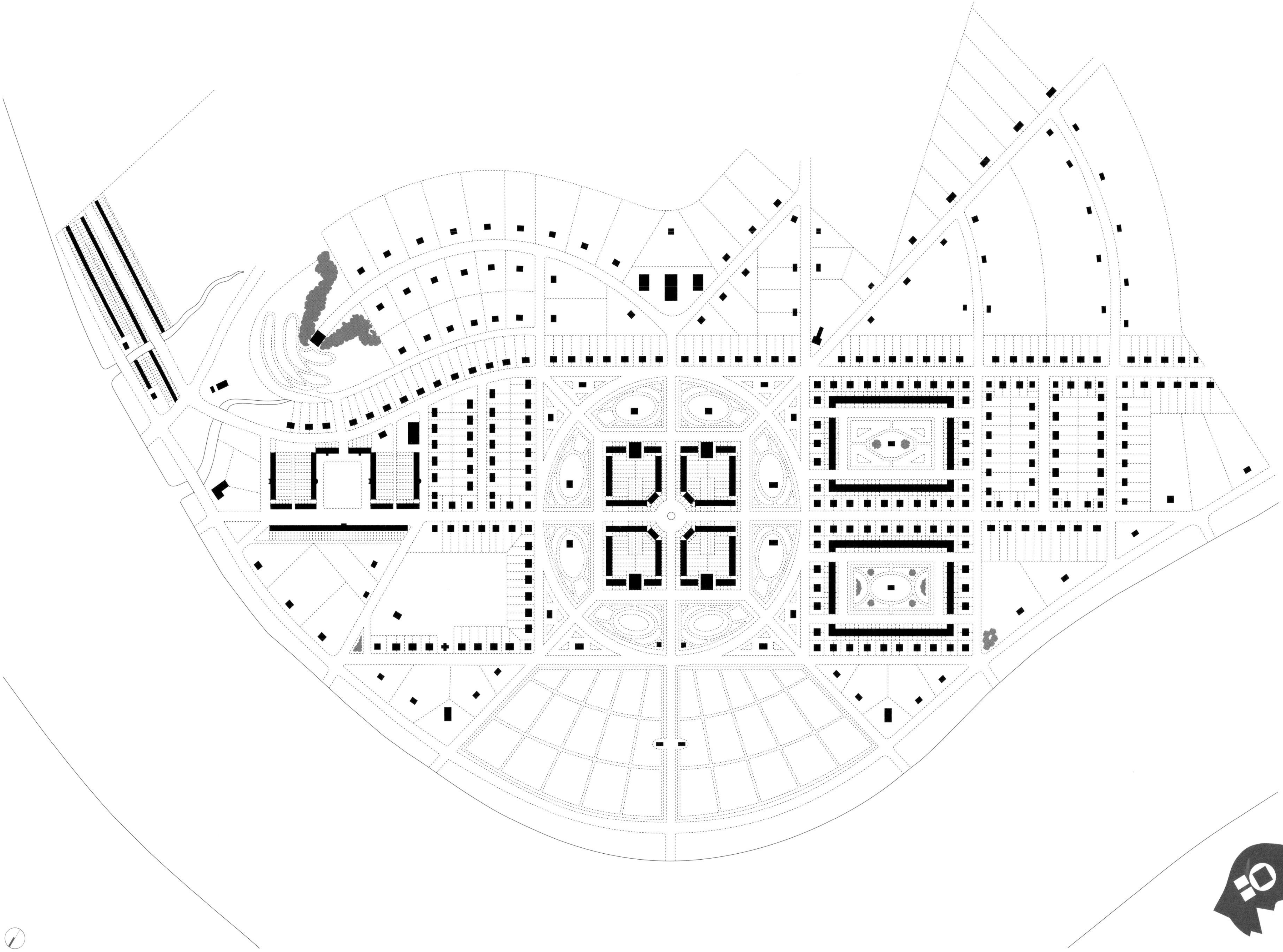

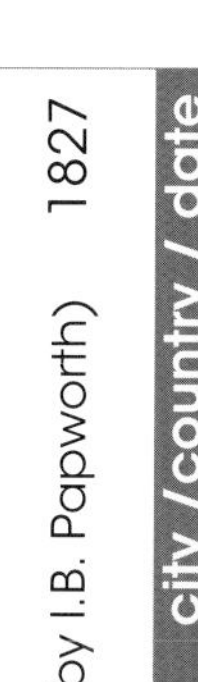

scale comparison

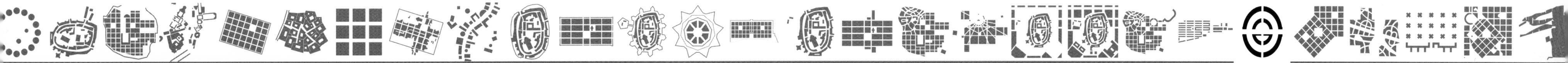

city / country / date

Ideal Town, Germany (Designed by Joseph Furttenbach the Younger) 1650

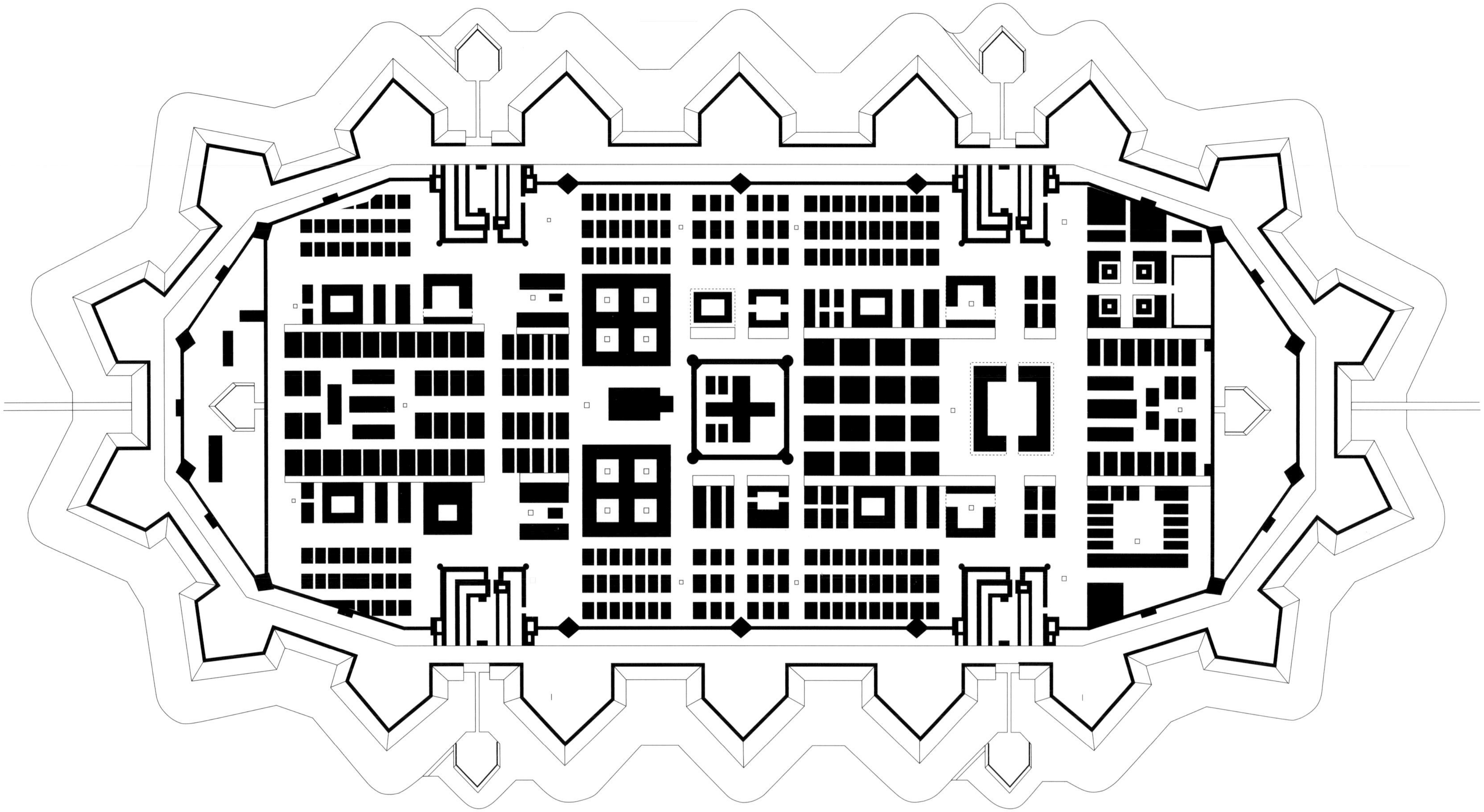

scale comparison

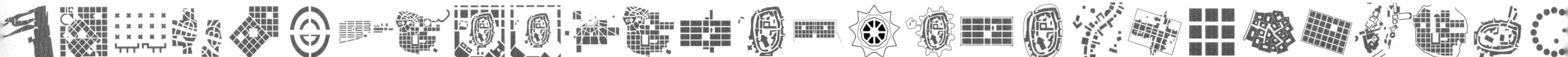

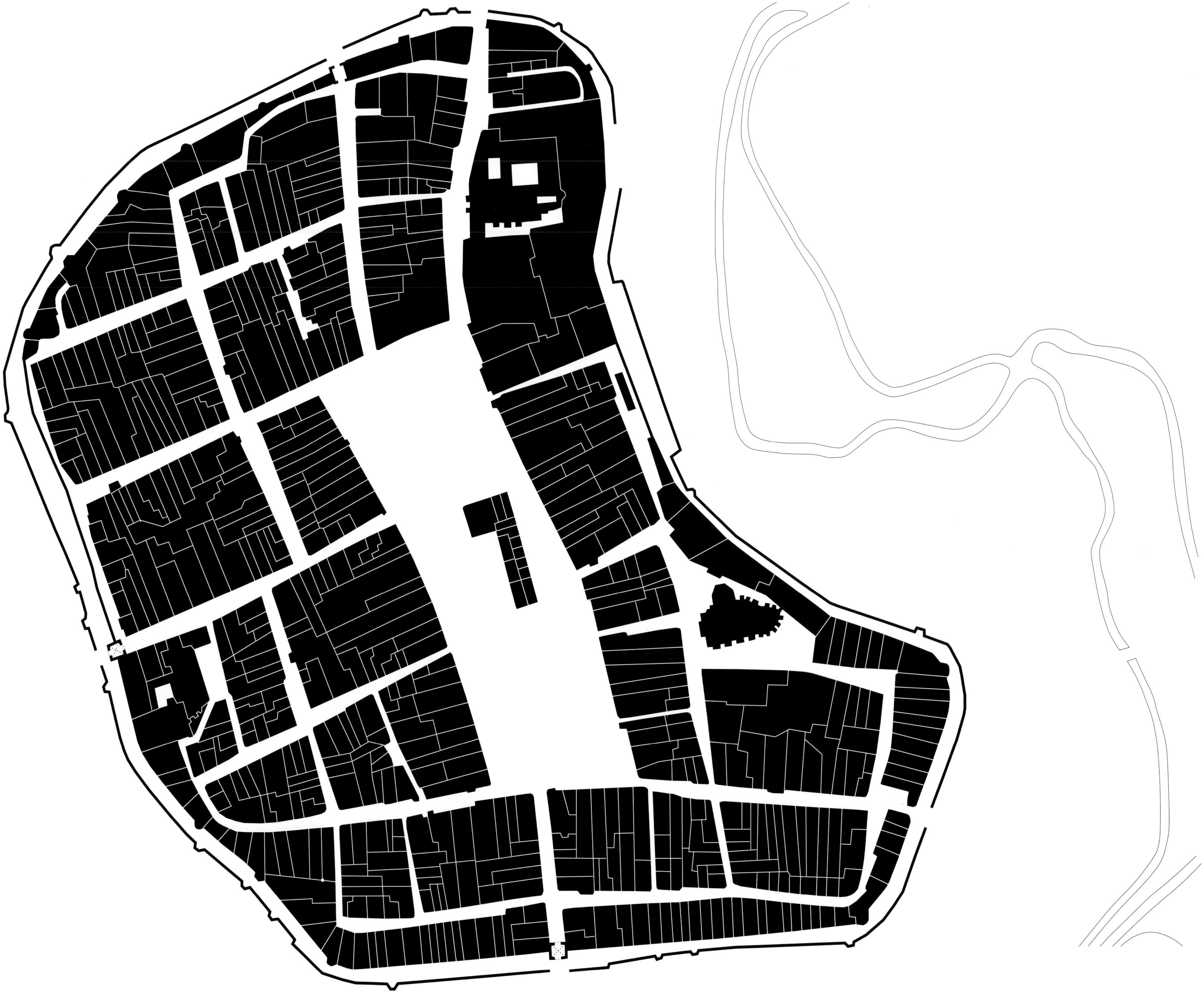

Iglau, Czech Republic [1974]

city /country / date

scale comparison

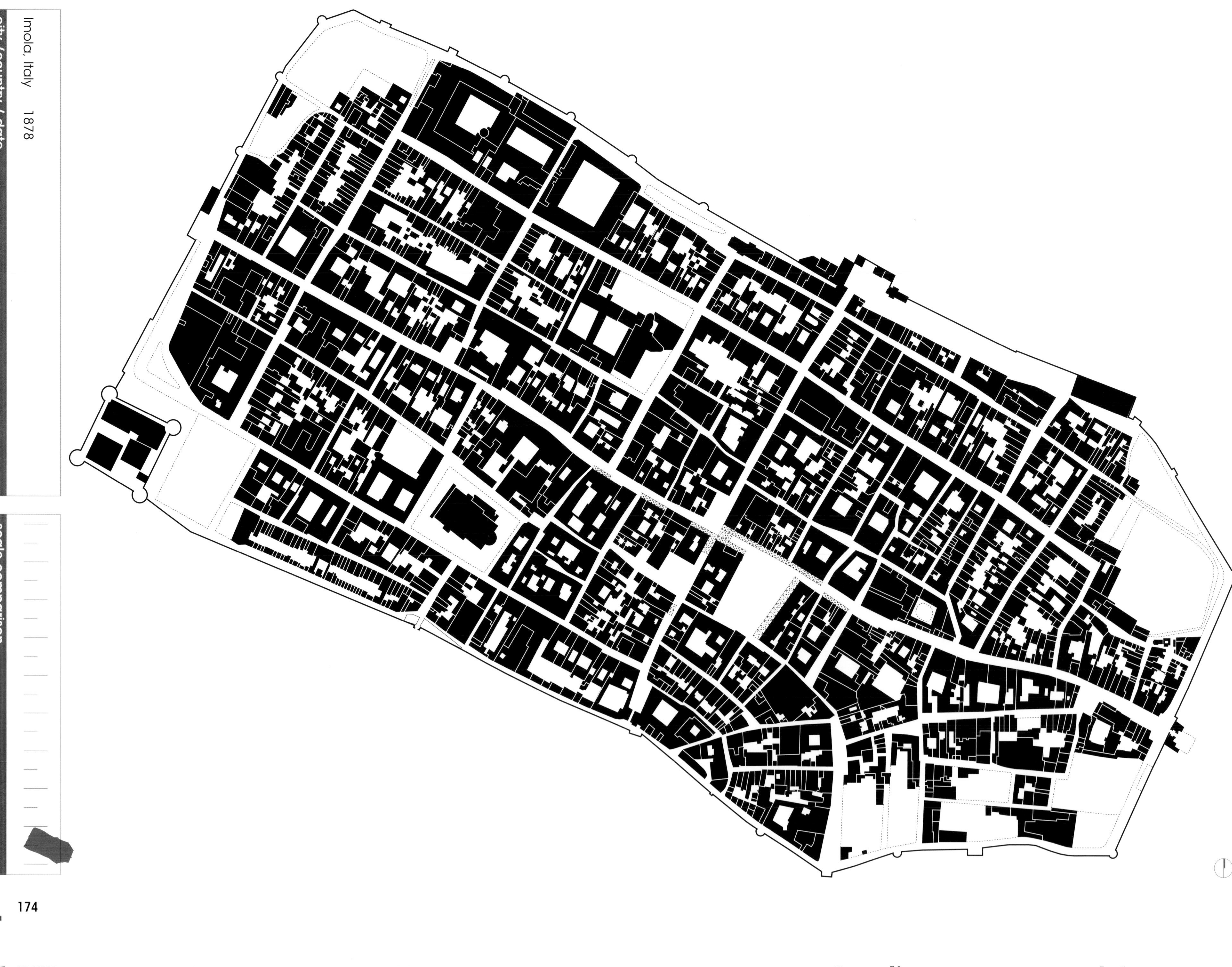

city / country / date

Imola, Italy 1878

scale comparison

Indianapolis, IN, USA 1821

city /country / date

scale comparison

100M

city / country / date

Ipswich, MA, USA 1872

scale comparison

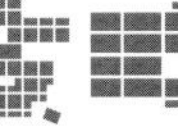

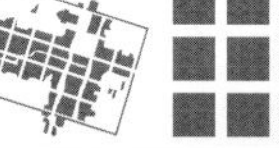
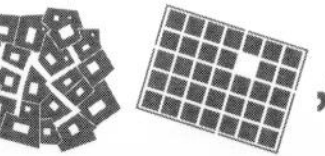

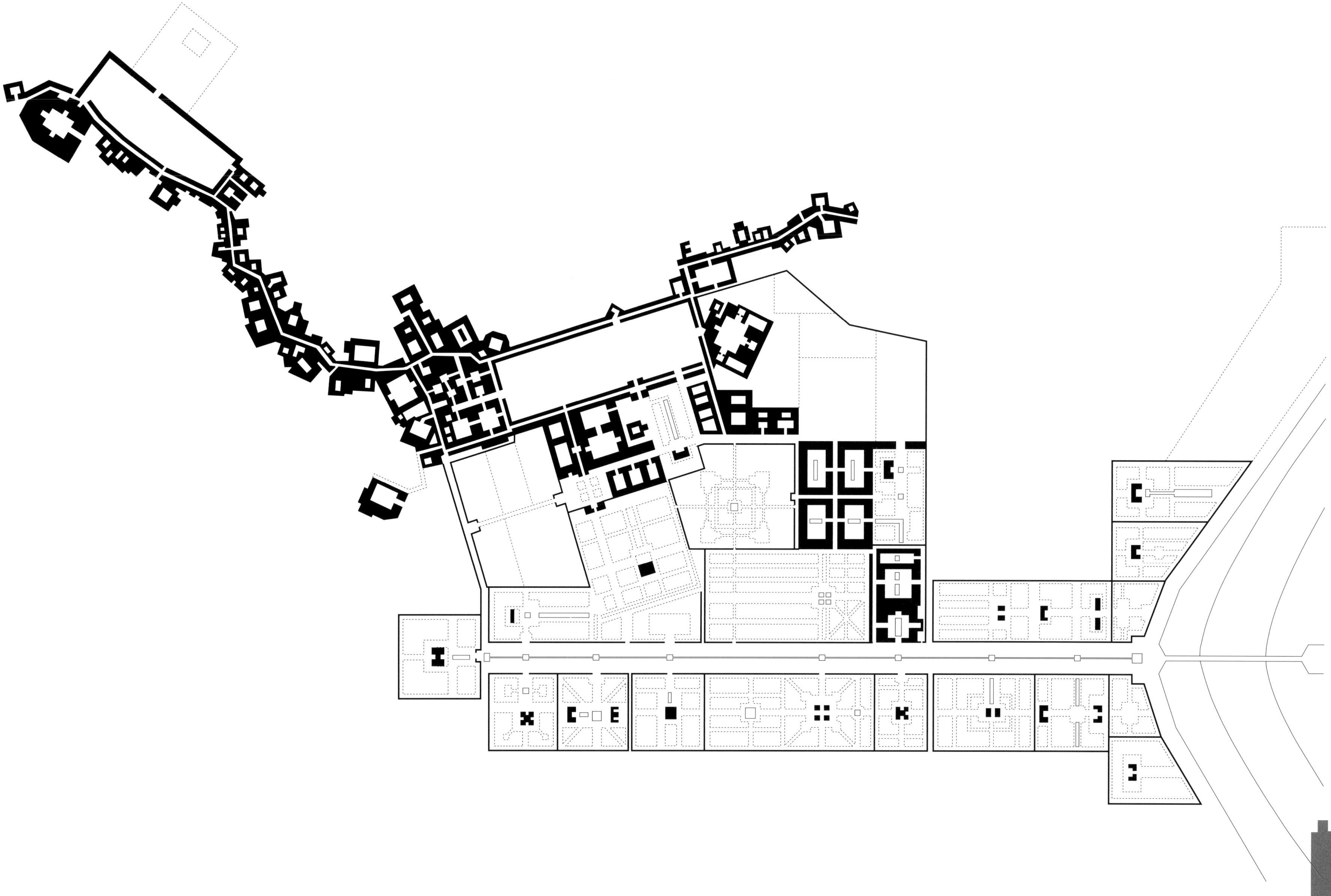

100M

Ishfahan, Iran (The Gridded gardens of Safavid Ishfahan) 1627

city / country / date

scale comparison

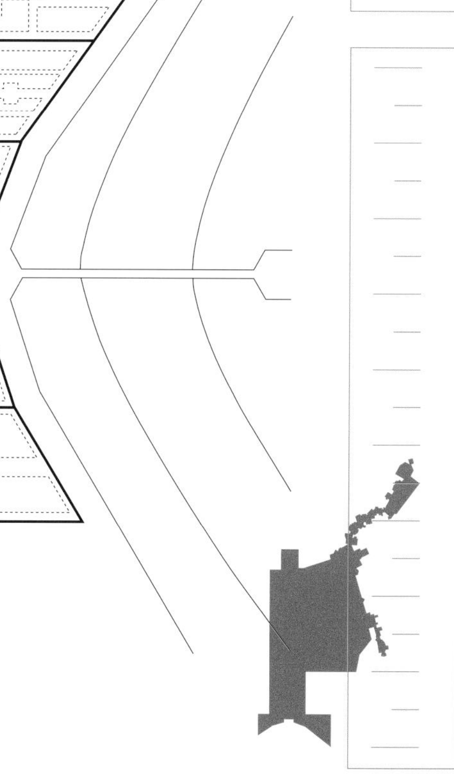

100M

city / country / date

Jaipur, India 1950

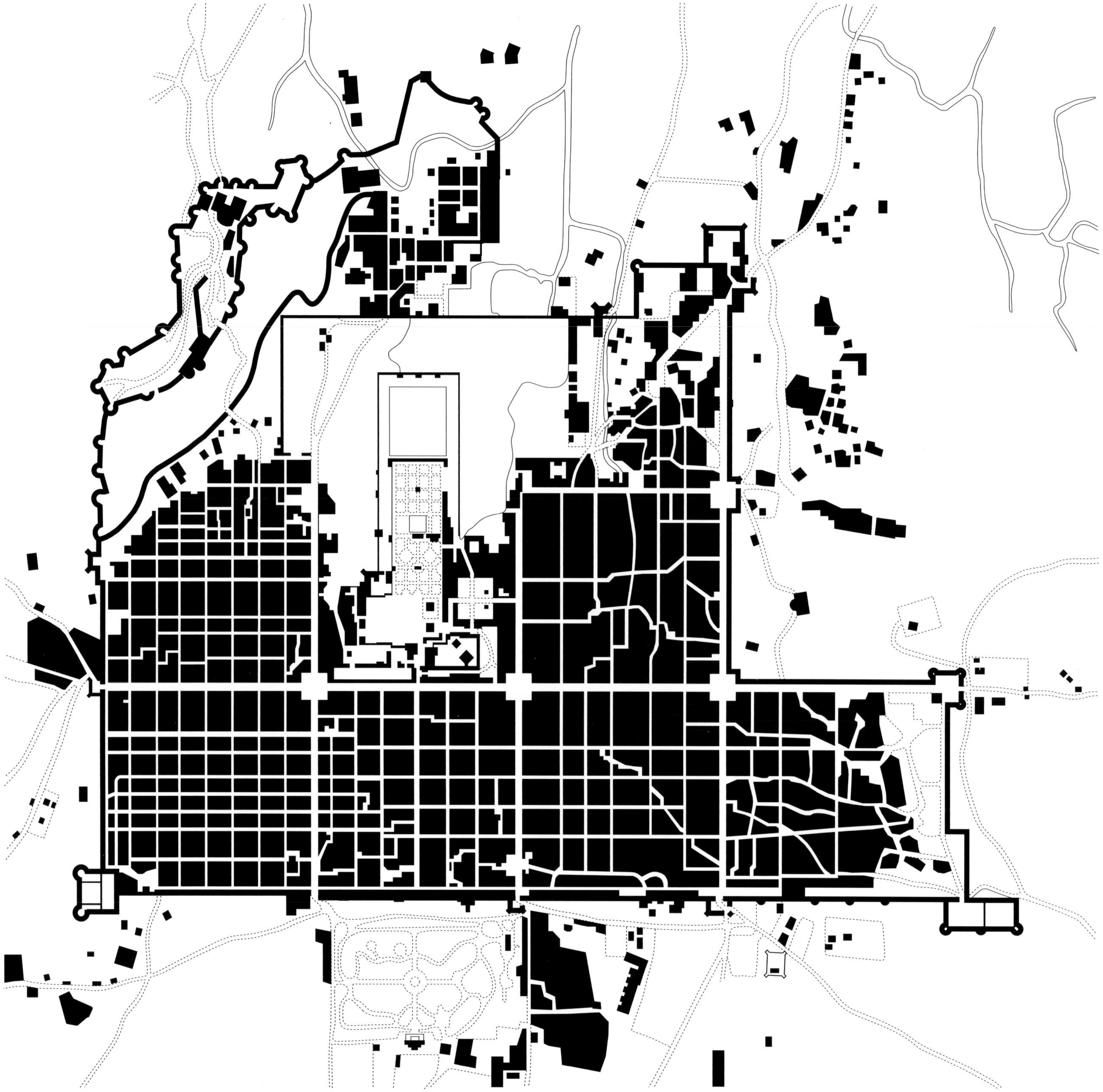

scale comparison

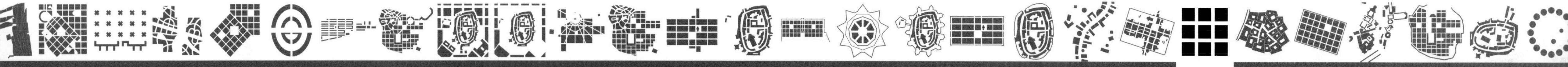

100M

city / country / date

Jerusalem, Israel 1912

scale comparison

100M
city / country / date
Karlsruhe, Germany
1896
scale comparison
K

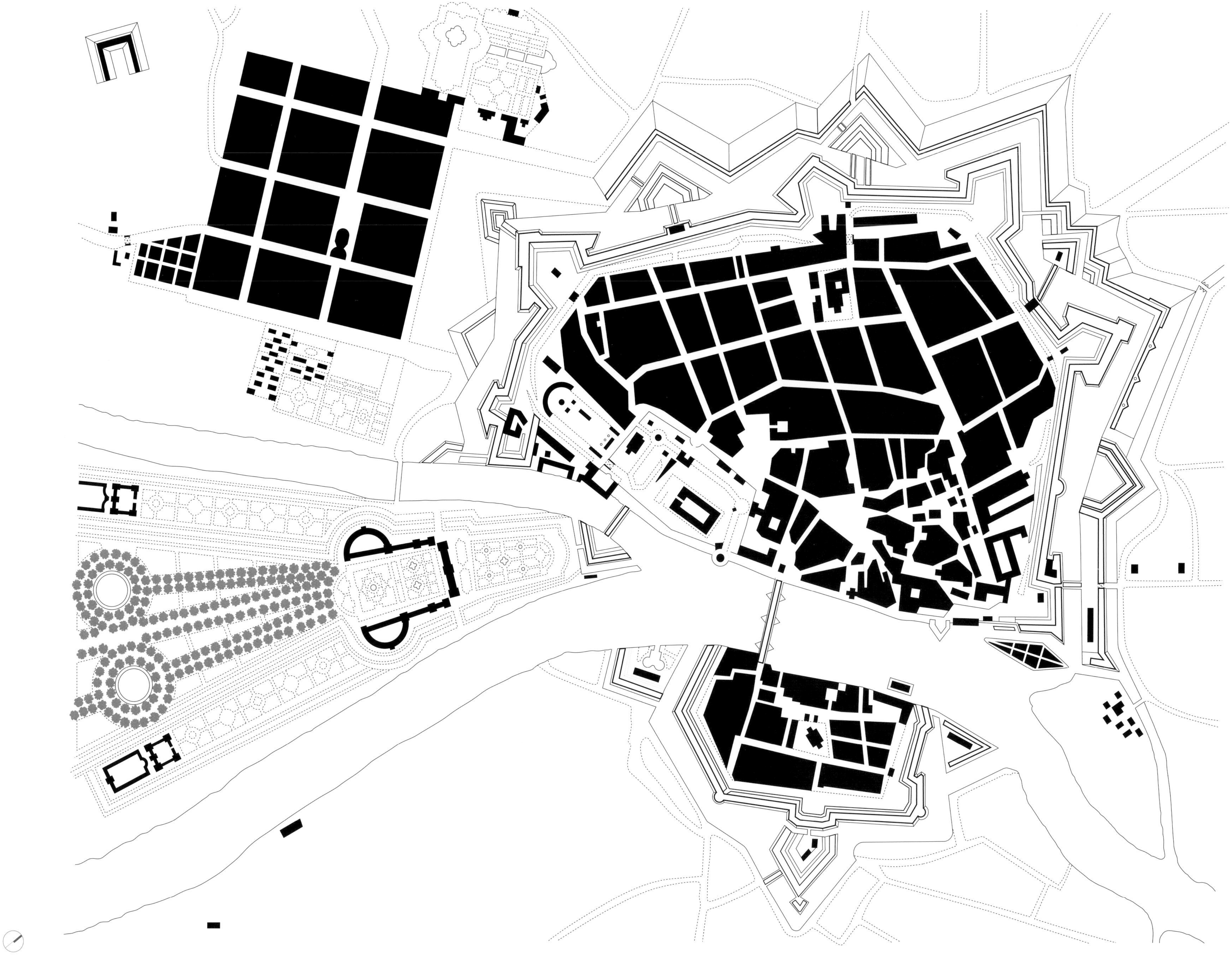

100M

Kassel (Cassel), Germany 1750

city / country / date

scale comparison

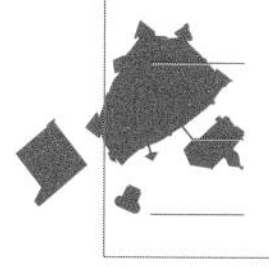

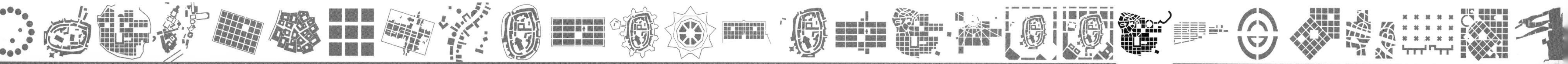

K

100M

city / country / date

Khiva (inner city), Uzbekistan 1970

scale comparison

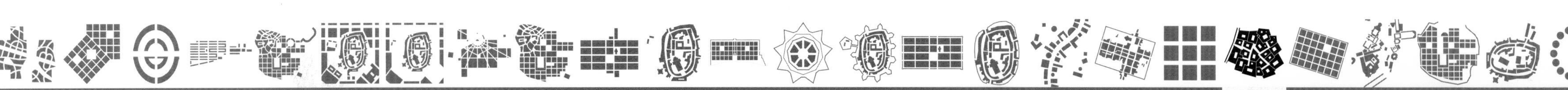

100M

Kimbolton, England 1946

city / country / date

scale comparison

100M

city / country / date

La Rochelle, France 1914

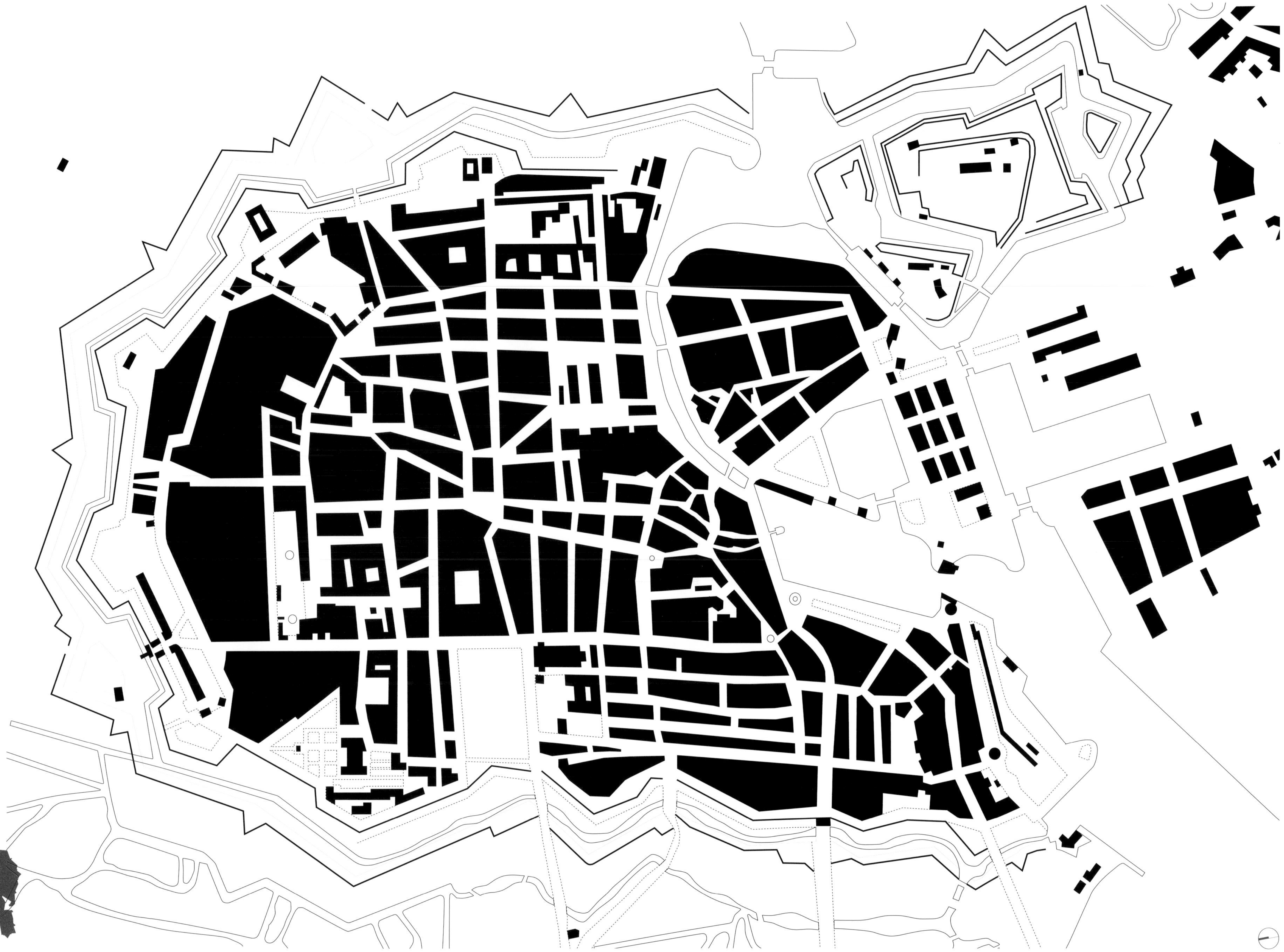

scale comparison

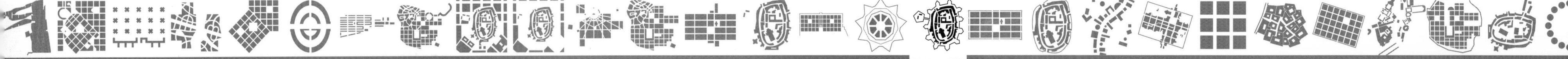

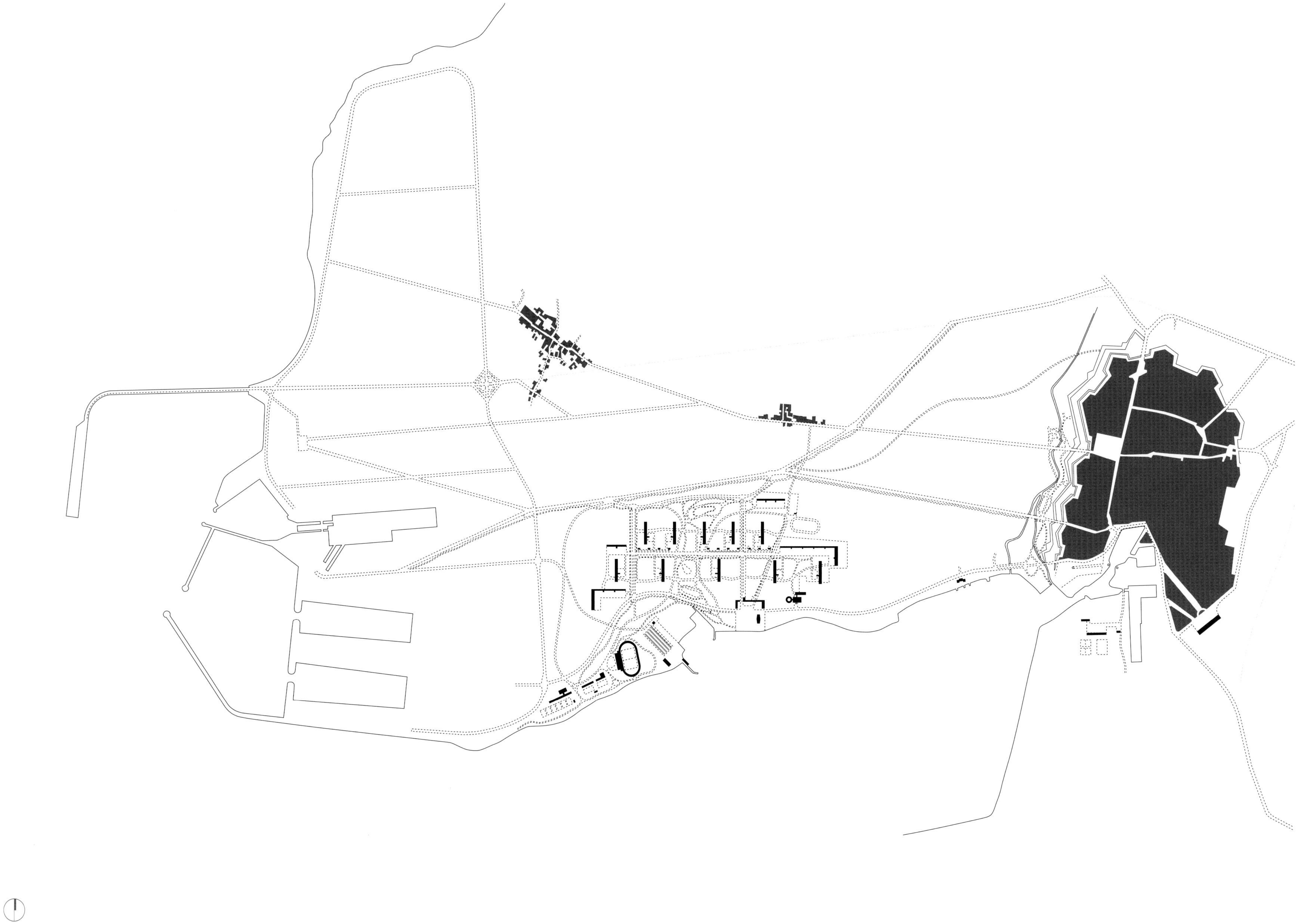

100M

La Rochelle-Pallice, France (proposal by Le Corbusier) 1946

city / country / date

scale comparison

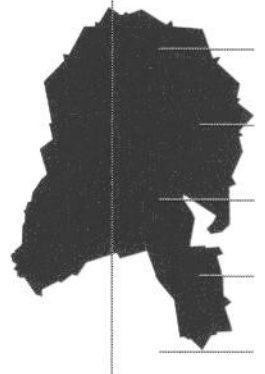

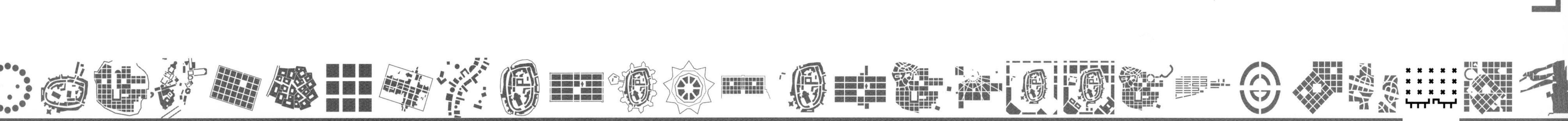

100M

city / country / date

Las Vegas Strip, NV, USA 1972

scale comparison

100M

Latina, Italy 1940

city / country / date

scale comparison

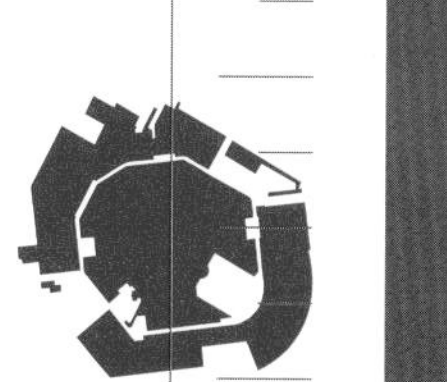

100M
city / country / date
Lille, France 1909
scale comparison

100M

Lisbon, Portugal 1833

scale comparison

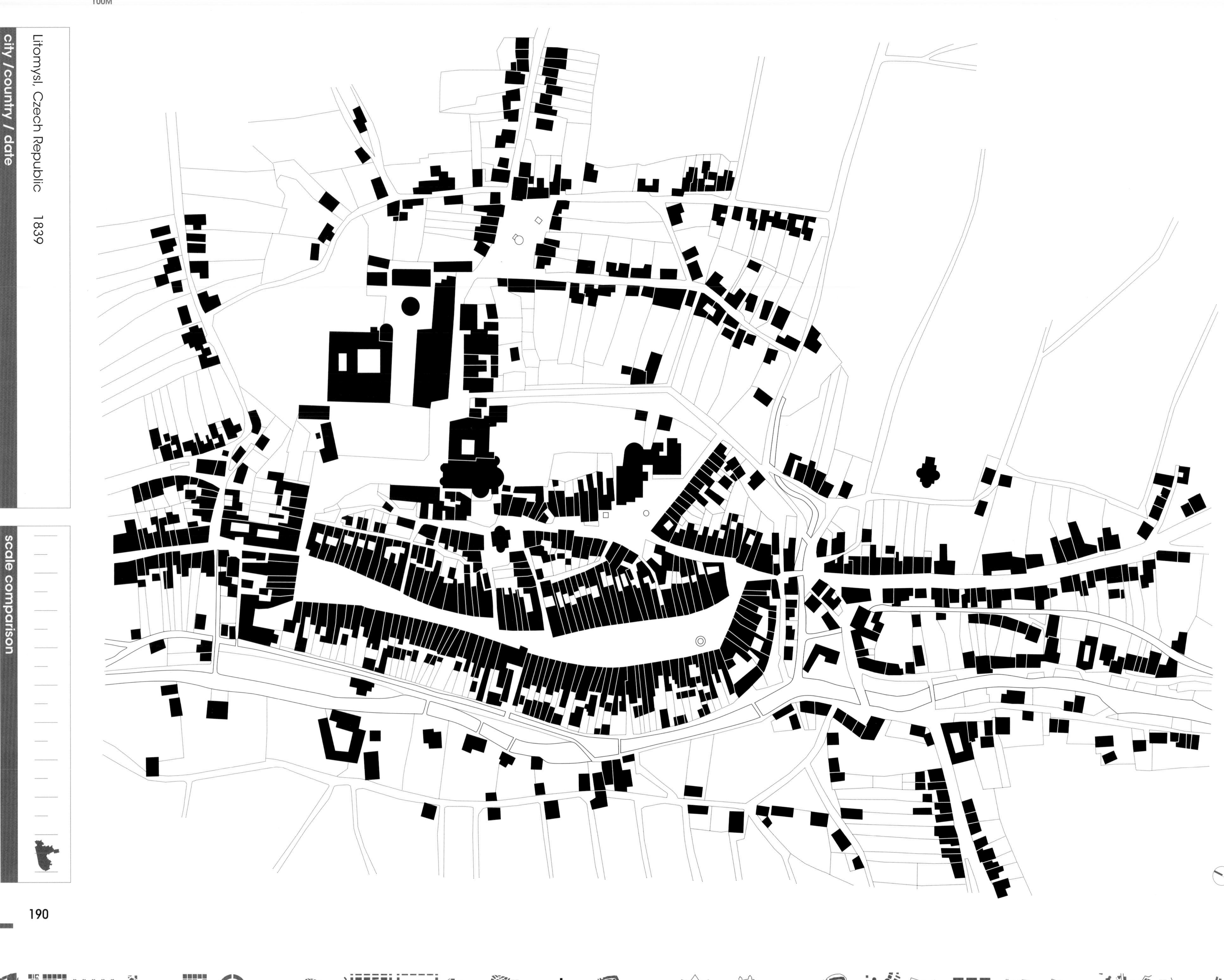
100M
Litomysl, Czech Republic
1839
city / country / date
scale comparison

100M

Liverpool, England 1863

city / country / date

scale comparison

100M
Livorno, Italy 1913
city / country / date
scale comparison

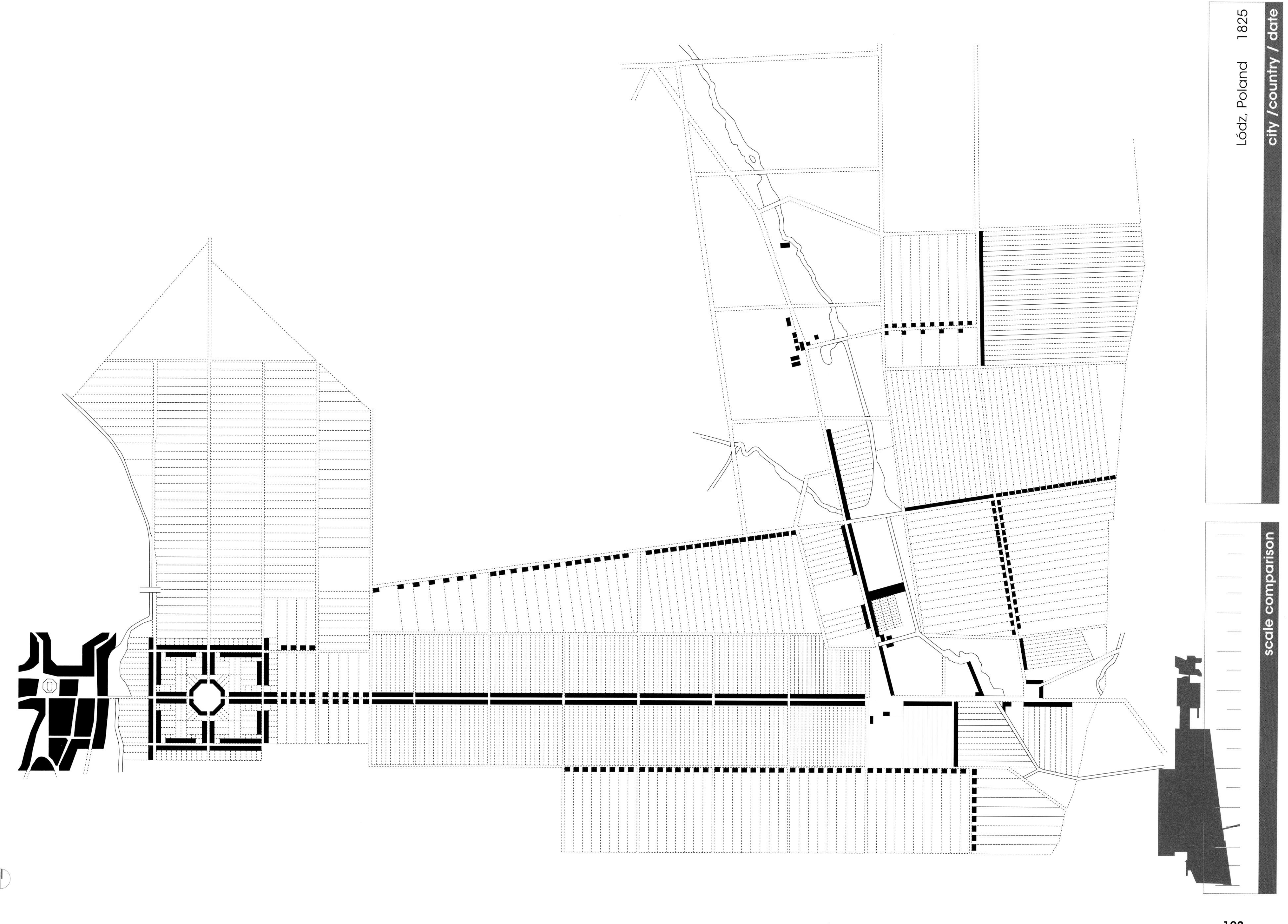
100M
Lódz, Poland 1825
city / country / date
scale comparison

100M

London, England (gray area represents the area destroyed in the fire of 1666) 1666

scale comparison

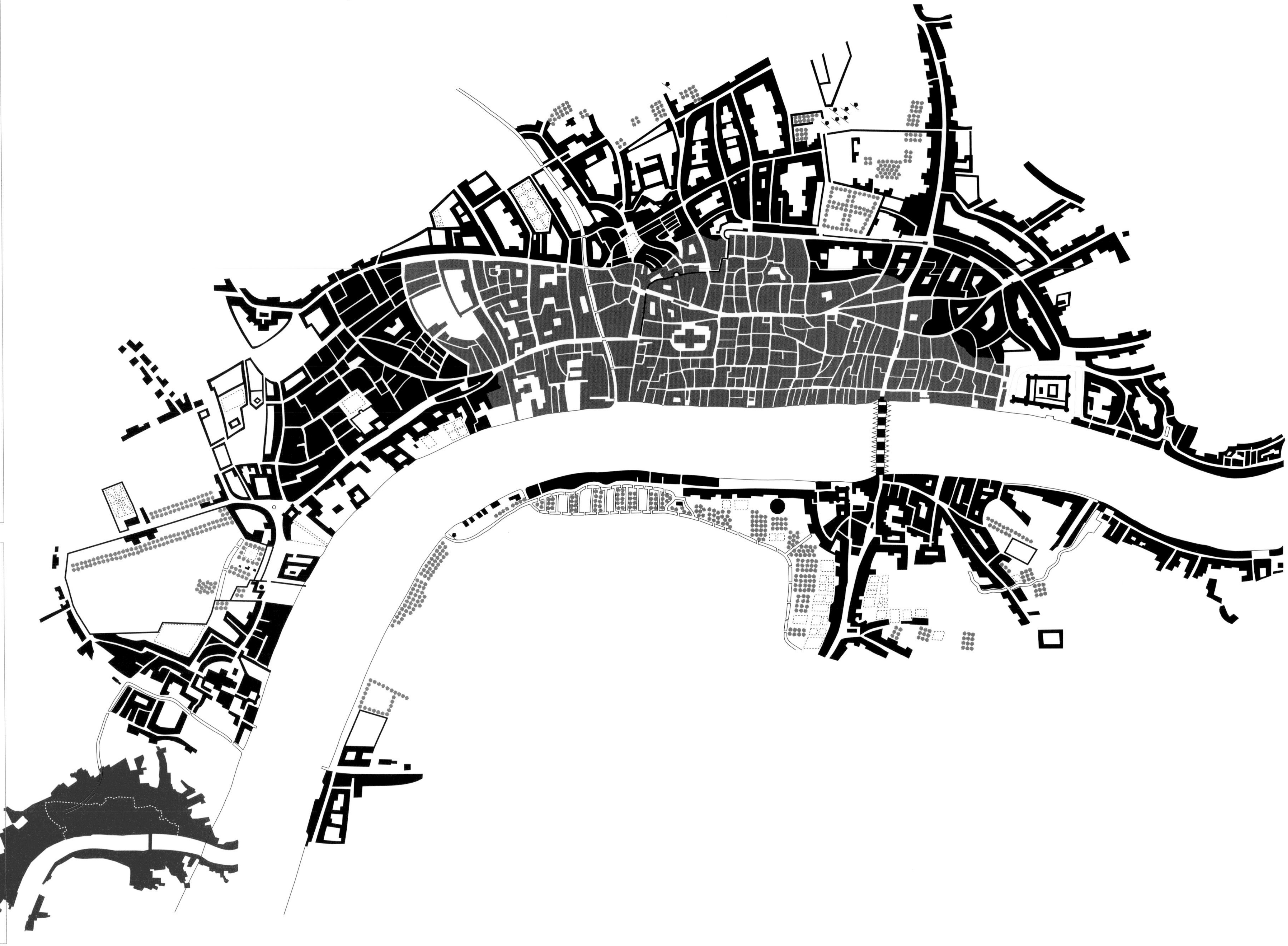

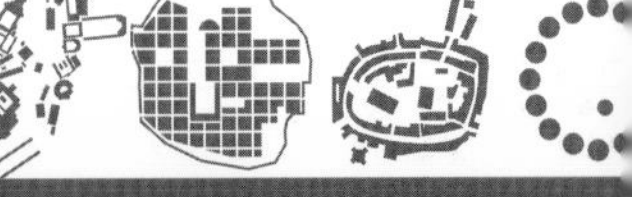

London, England (proposals for redesign of Central London) 1666

city / country / date

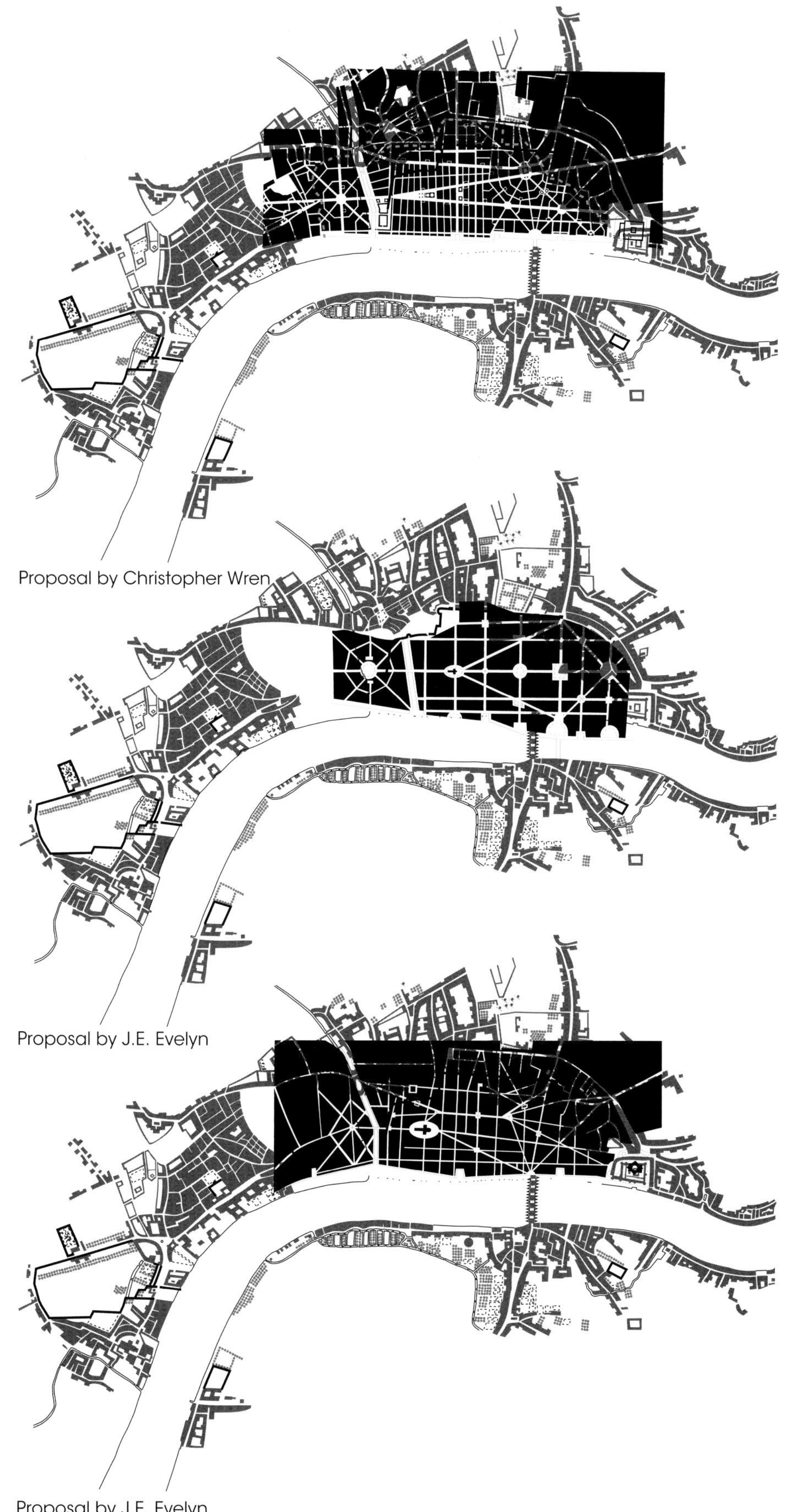

Proposal by Christopher Wren

Proposal by J.E. Evelyn

Proposal by J.E. Evelyn

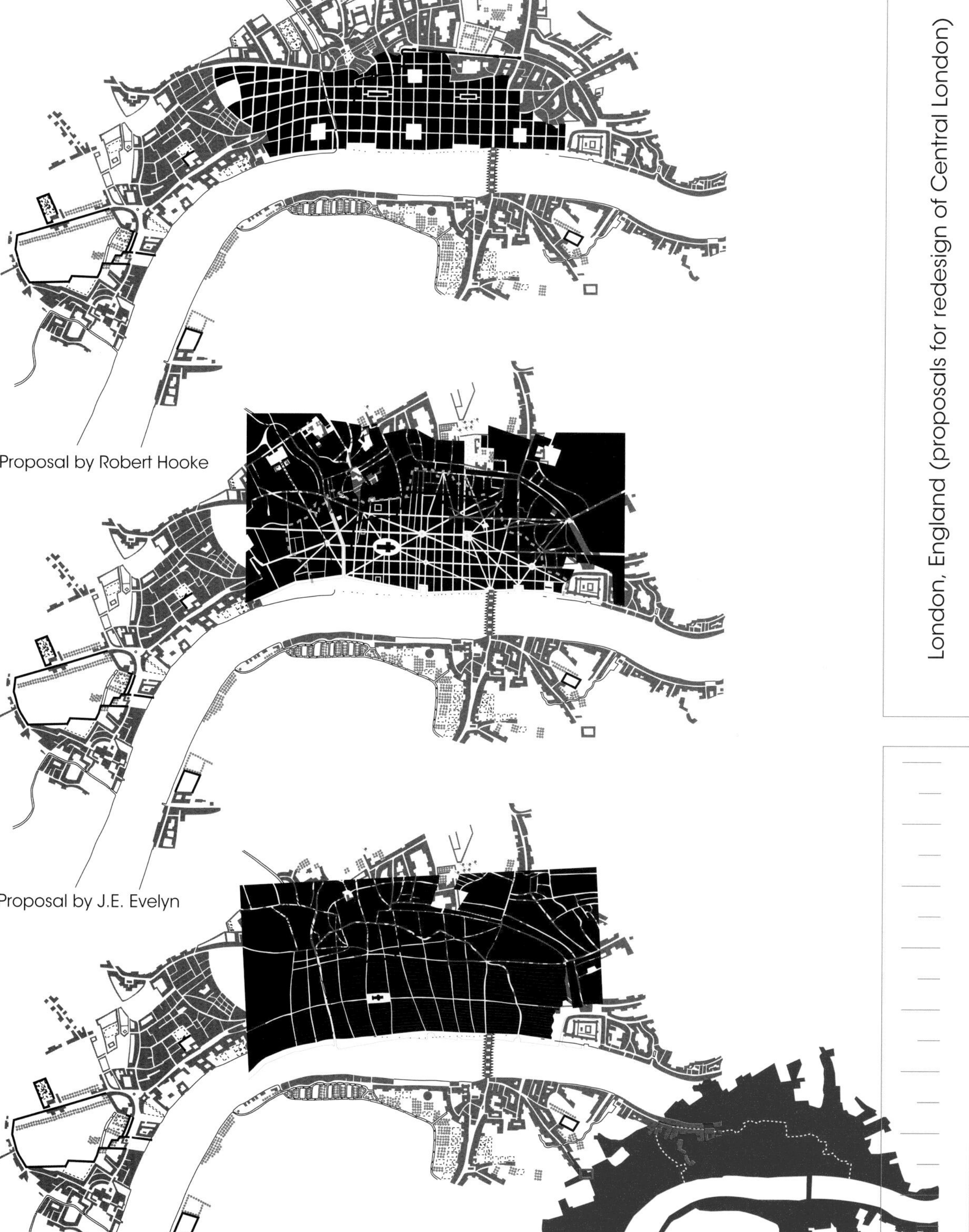

Proposal by Robert Hooke

Proposal by J.E. Evelyn

Proposal by Valentine Knight

scale comparison

city / country / date

London, England 1746

scale comparison

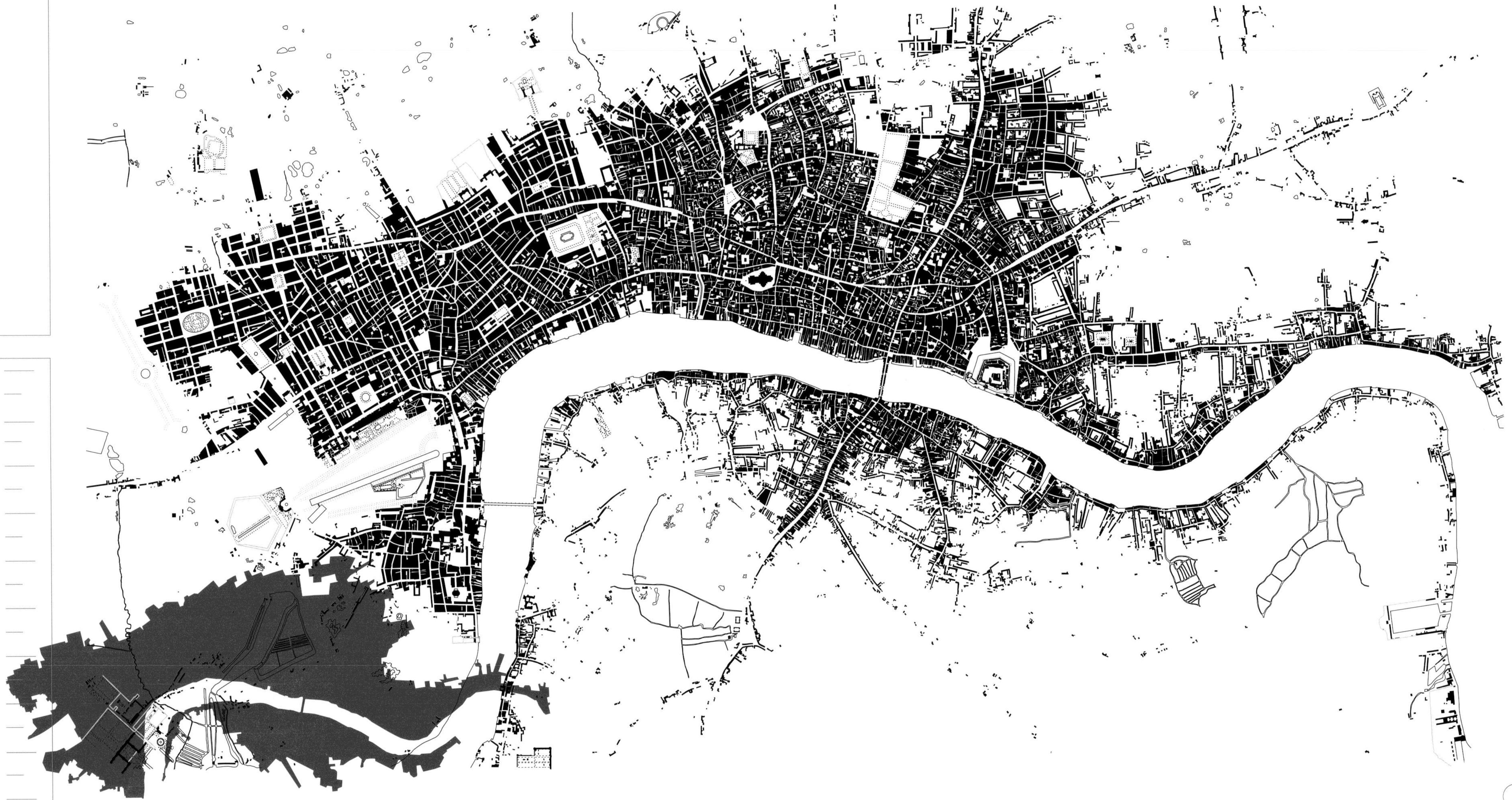

London, England 1843
city / country / date
scale comparison

100M

city / country / date

London, England (design by John Nash & as Regents Park was built) 1811 & 1843

scale comparison

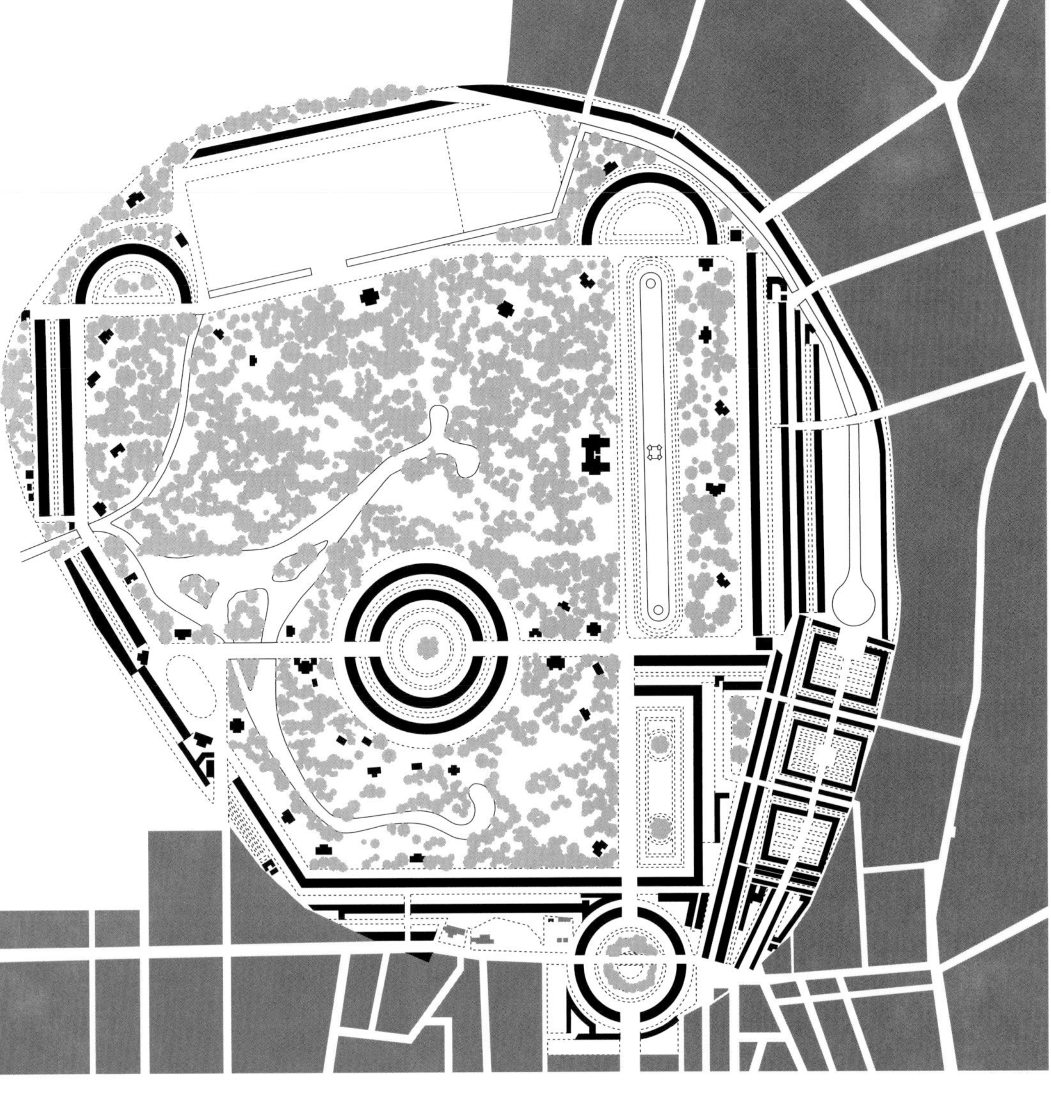

London, Marylebone District, England (proposal by Steven Fong) 1979

city / country / date

scale comparison

100M

city / country / date

London, Blackwall Peninsula (proposal by Koetter/Kim Associates) 1988

scale comparison

Blackwall Peninsula, *Collision Model*

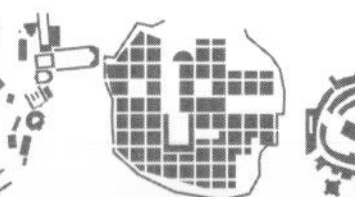
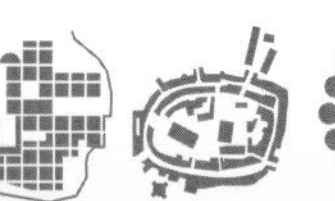

Blackwall Peninsula, *Little Cities Model*

Blackwall Peninsula, *Central Park Model*

Blackwall Peninsula, *The Parks & Canals, German Model*

Blackwall Peninsula, *Manhattan Model*

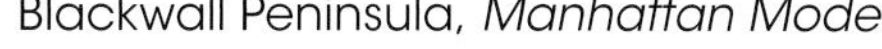

London, Blackwall Peninsula (proposal by Koetter/Kim Associates) 1988

city / country / date

scale comparison

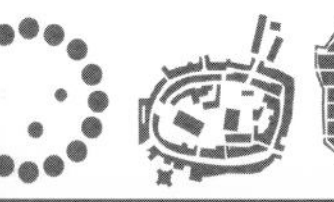

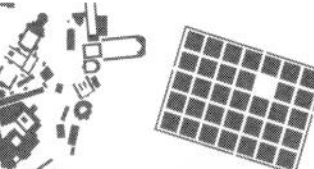
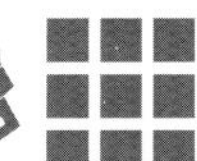

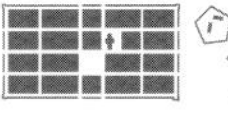

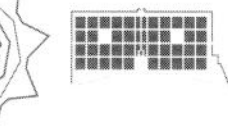

100M

city / country / date

London, Corydon Initiative, England (proposal by Dixon-Jones Architects) 1992

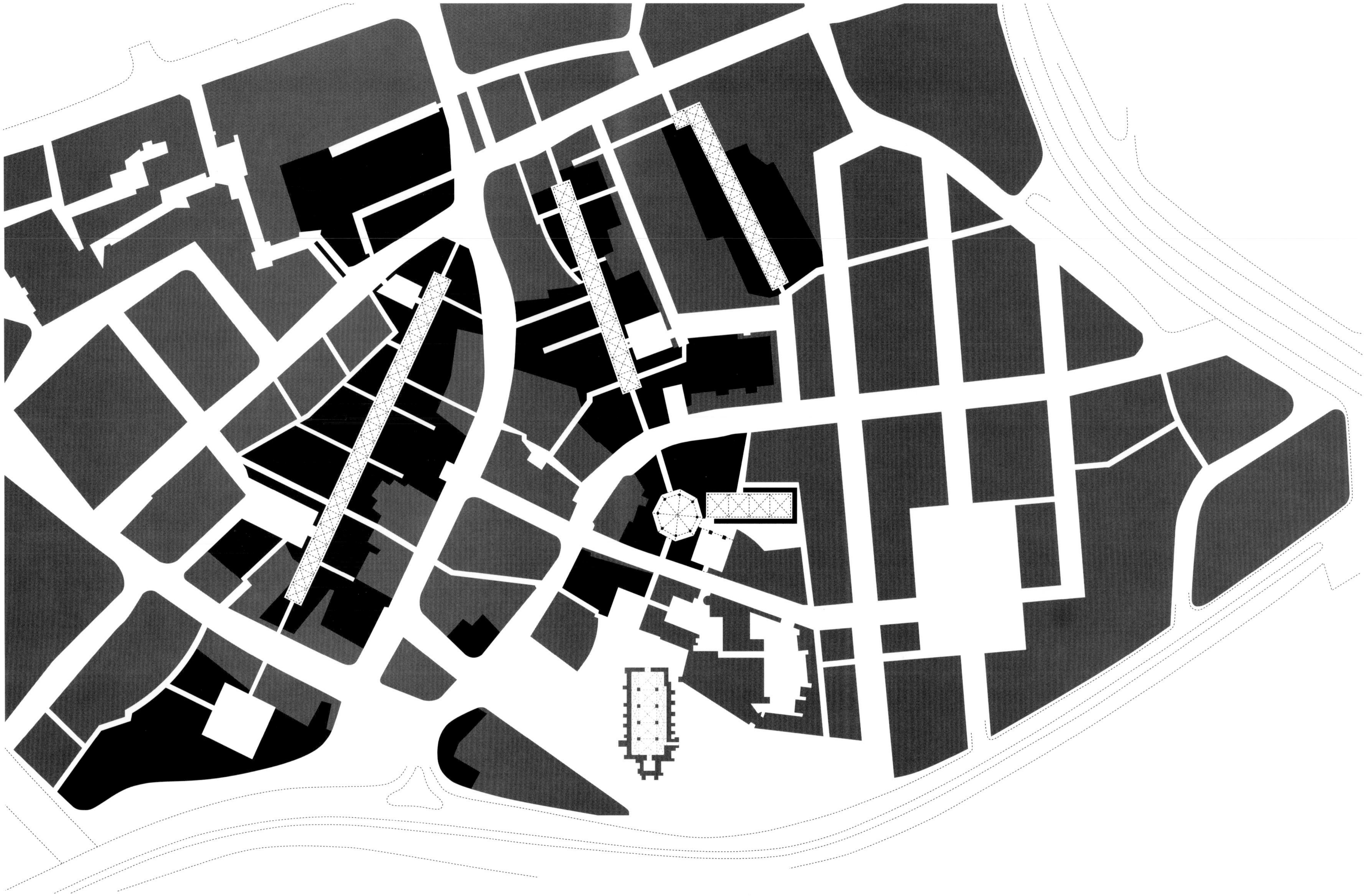

scale comparison

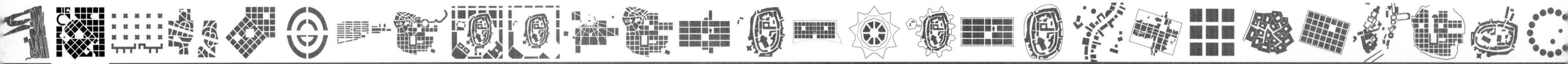

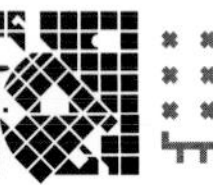

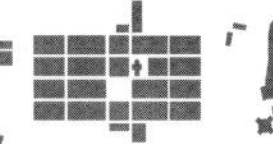
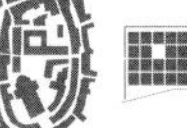

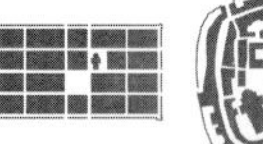

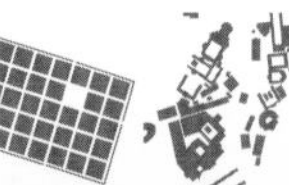

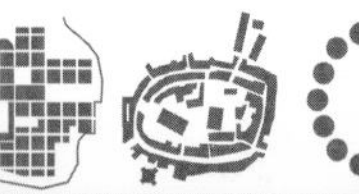

100M

Los Angeles, Getty Center, CA, USA (design by Richard Meier) 1997

city / country / date

scale comparison

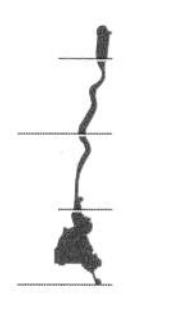

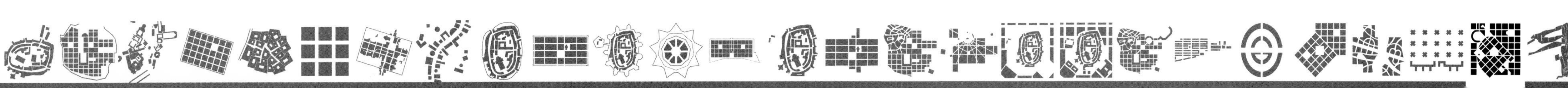

100M

city / country / date

Lowell, MA, USA 1832

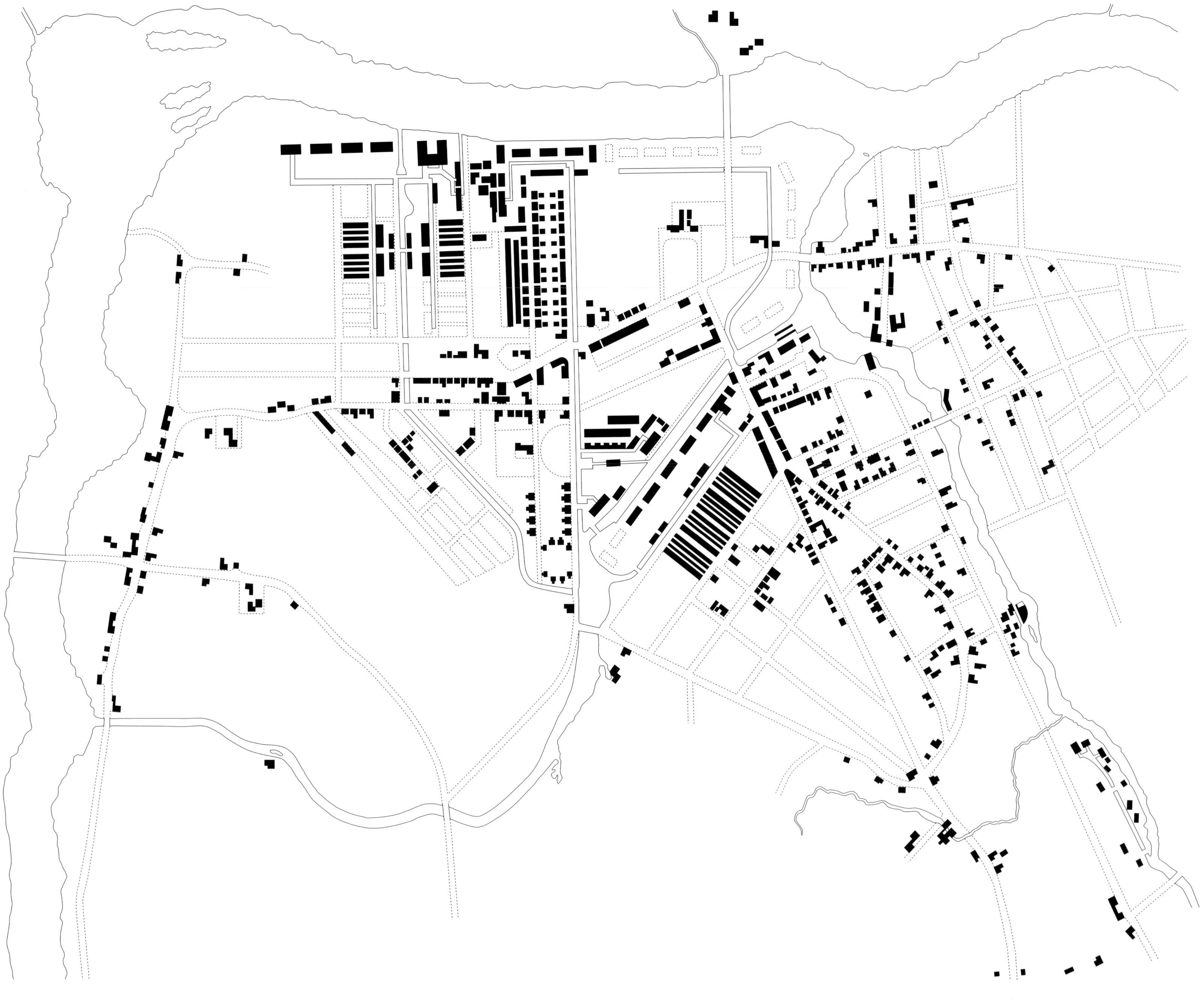

scale comparison

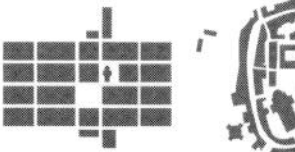
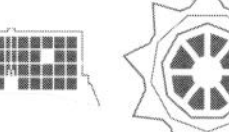

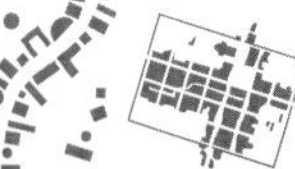

100M

Lucignano, Italy [1979]

city /country / date

scale comparison

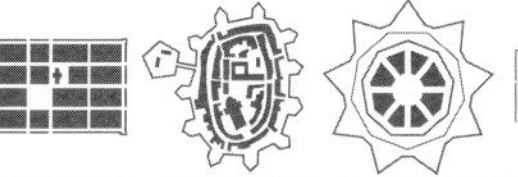

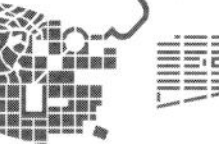

Luxembourg, Luxembourg 1906
city / country / date
scale comparison
100M

Luxembourg, Luxembourg (proposal by Léon Krier) 1978

city / country / date

scale comparison

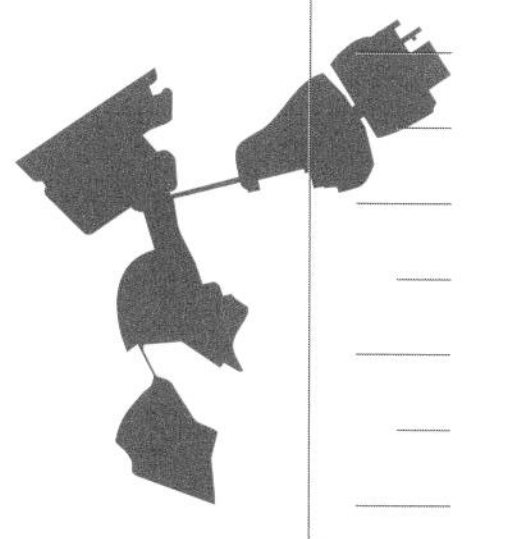

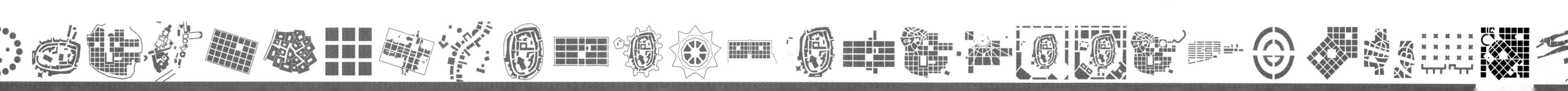

Lyon, France 1894
city /country / date
scale comparison
100M

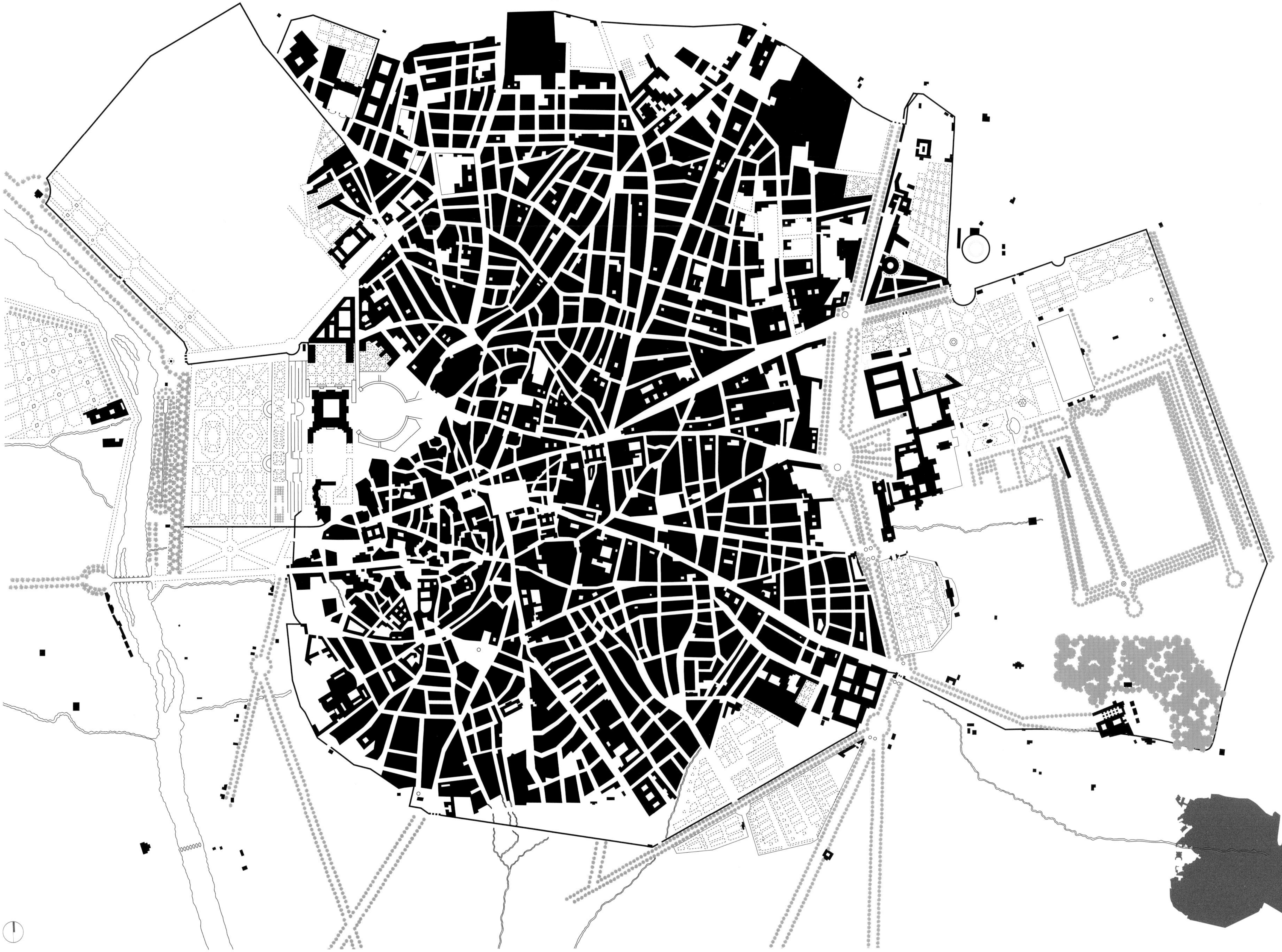

Madrid, Spain 1831

city /country / date

scale comparison

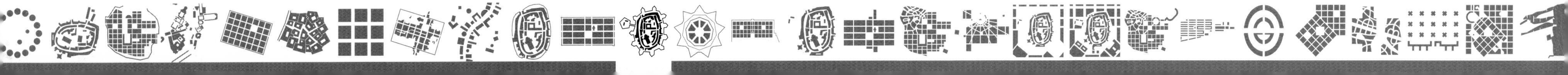

100M

city / country / date

Madrigal de las Altas Torres, Spain 1050

scale comparison

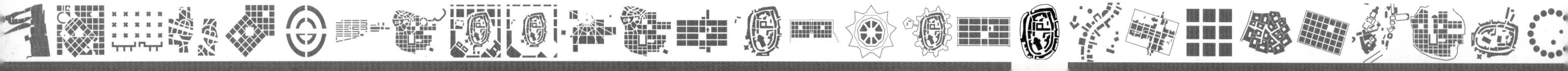

M

Maidan-e-Naghsh-e-Jahan, Ishfahan, Iran 1970

city / country / date

scale comparison

100M

M

100M

city / country / date

Mannheim, Germany

1645

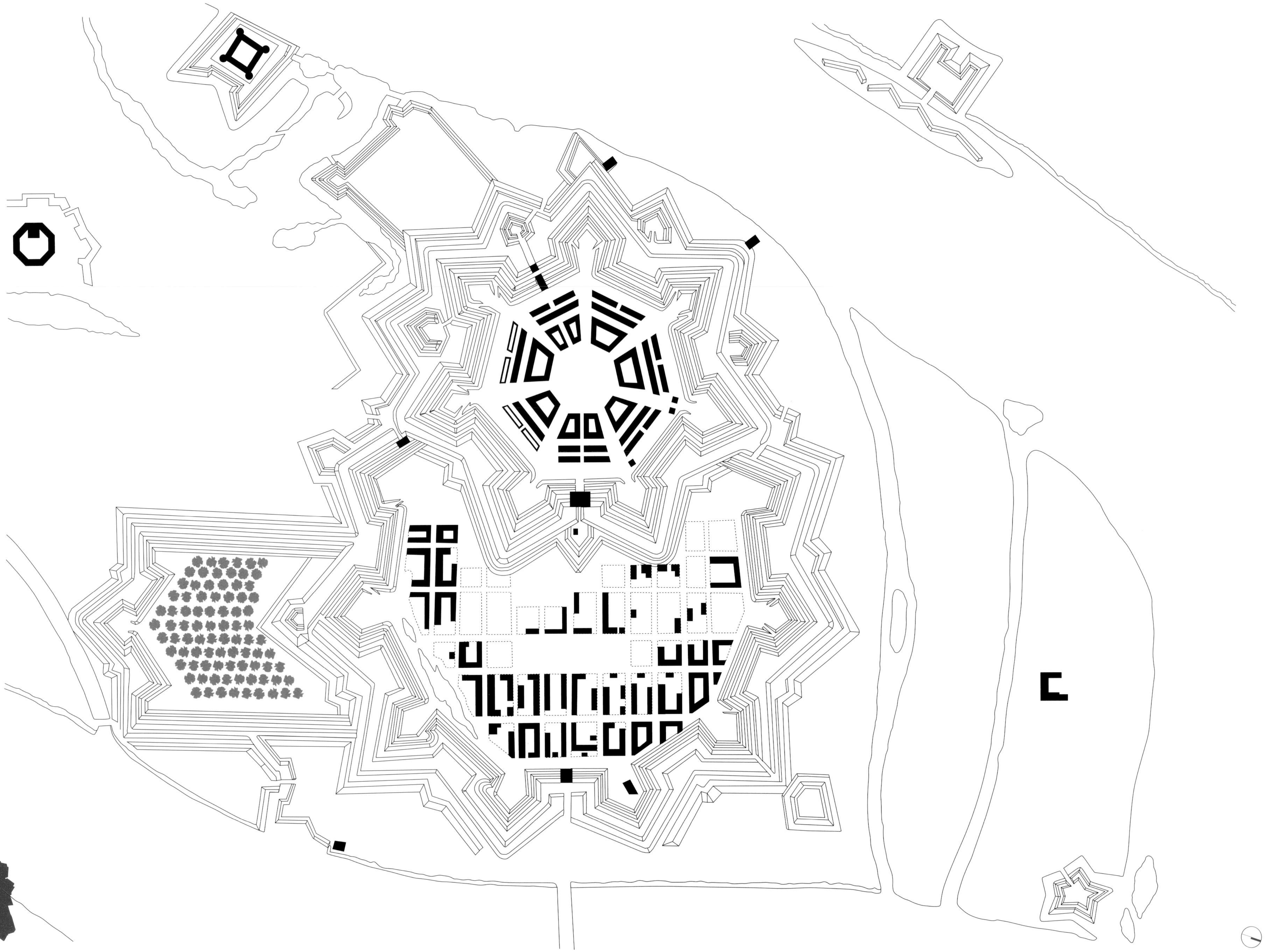

scale comparison

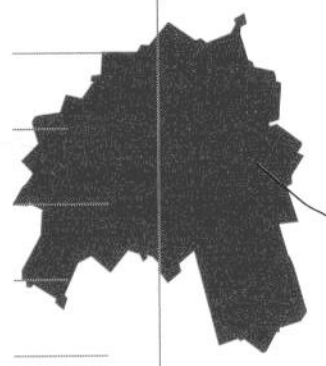

100M

city / country / date

Mantova, Italy [1963]

scale comparison

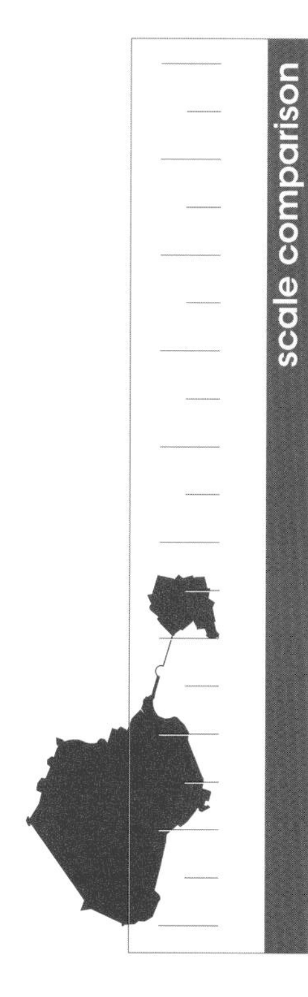

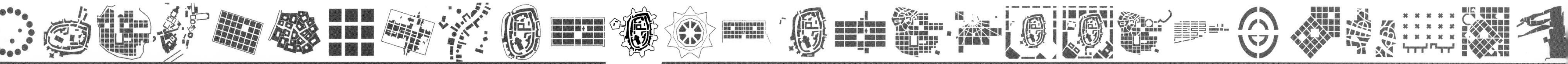

100M

city / country / date

Mardin, Turkey 1920

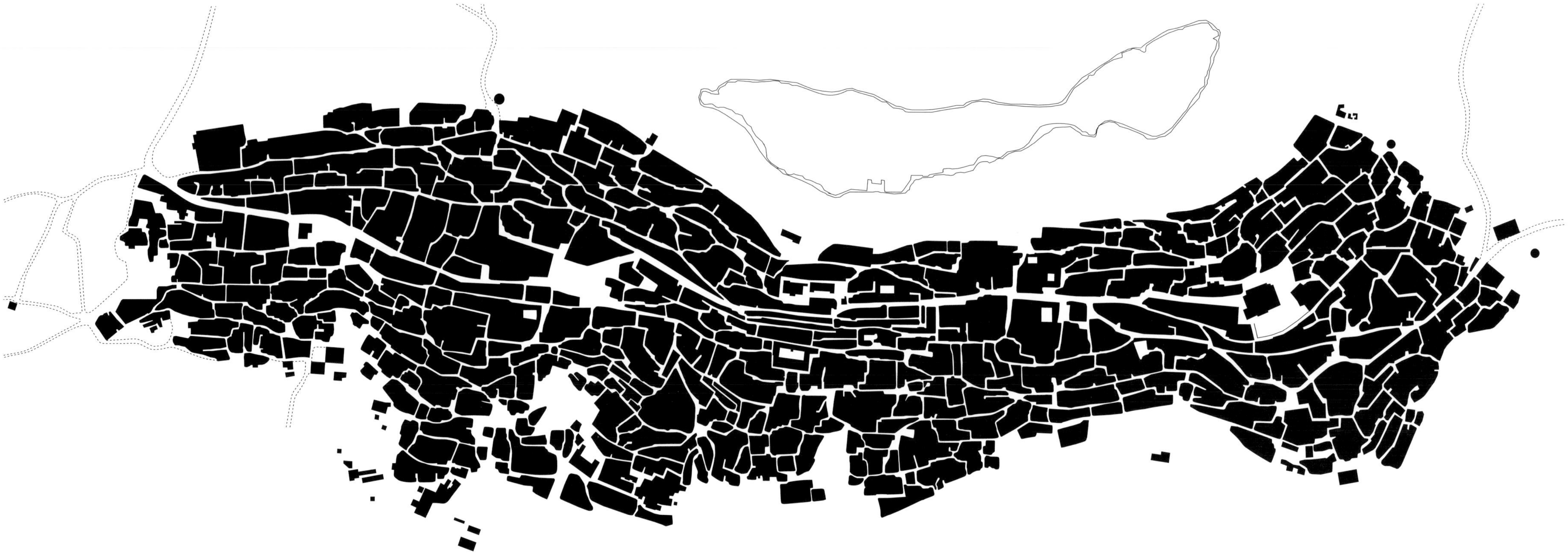

scale comparison

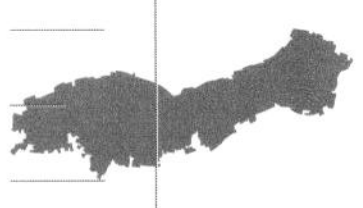

M

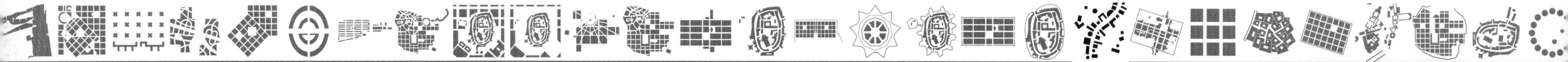

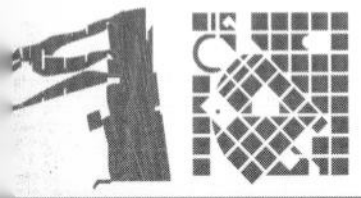

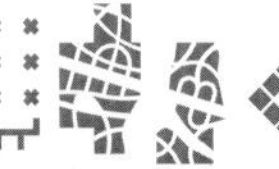

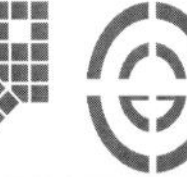

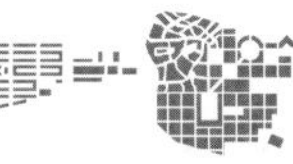

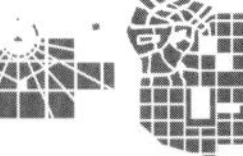

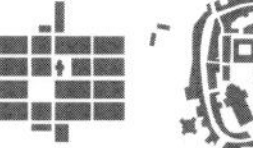

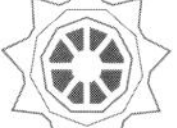

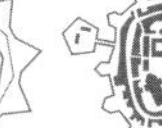

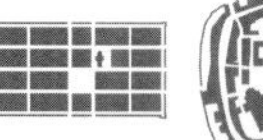

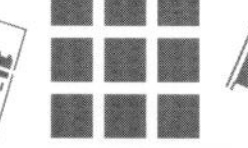

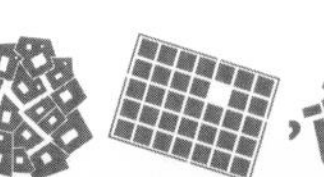

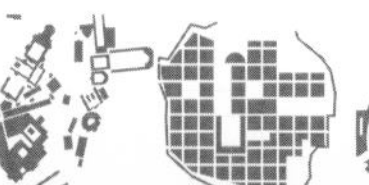

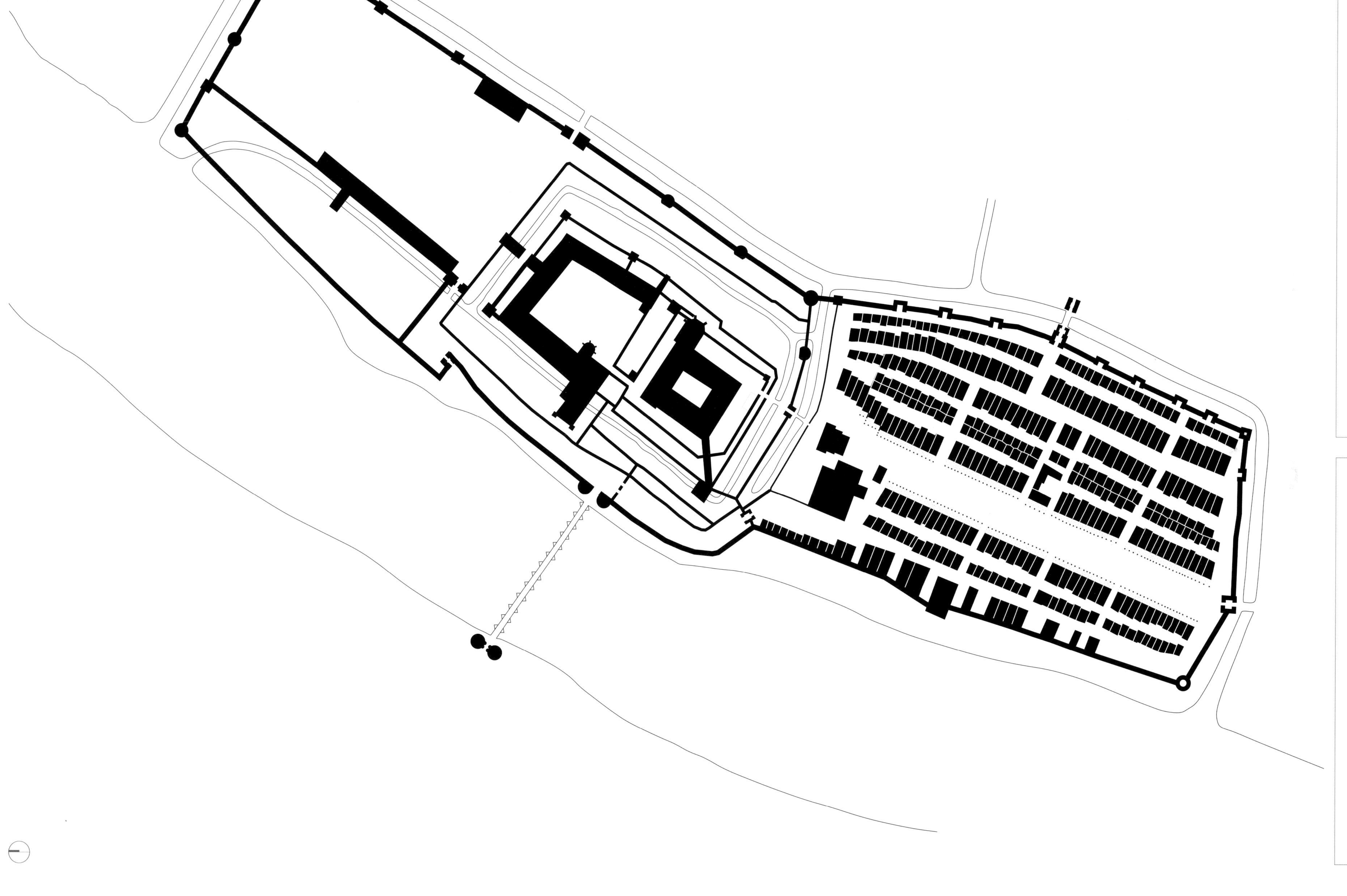

Marienburg, Germany 1276

city / country / date

scale comparison

100M

city / country / date

Marietta, OH, USA (Ancient Native American Works)

Date Unknown

scale comparison

100M

city / country / date

Marietta, OH, USA 1837

scale comparison

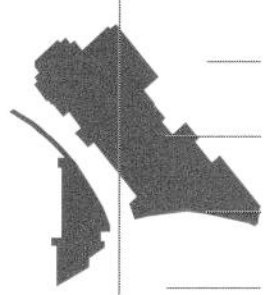

M

100M

city / country / date

Marseille, France 1840

scale comparison

100M

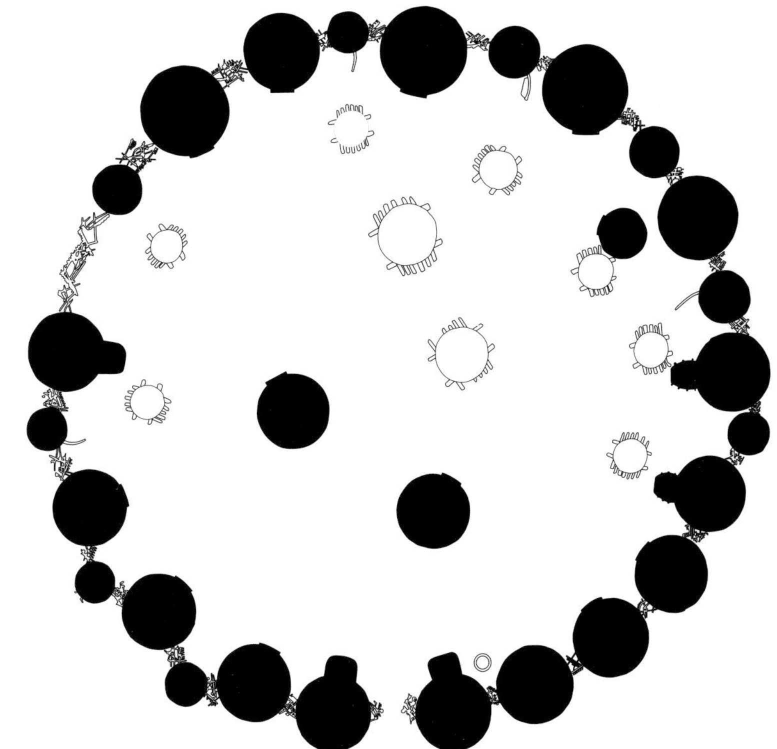

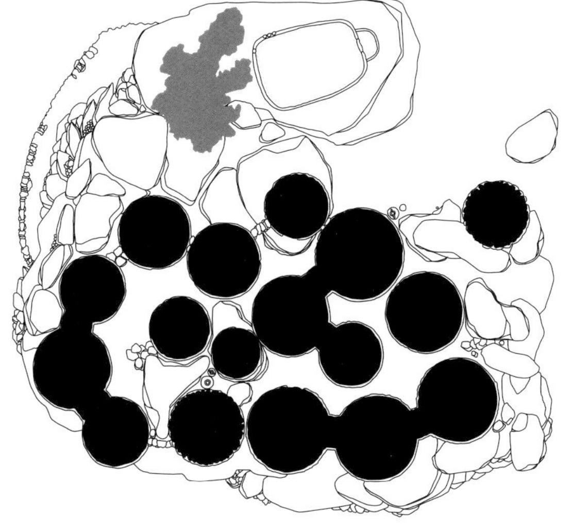

Massa & Matakam Homesteads, Cameroon, Africa [1979]

city / country / date

scale comparison

city / country / date

Meaux, France (proposal by Le Corbusier) 1956

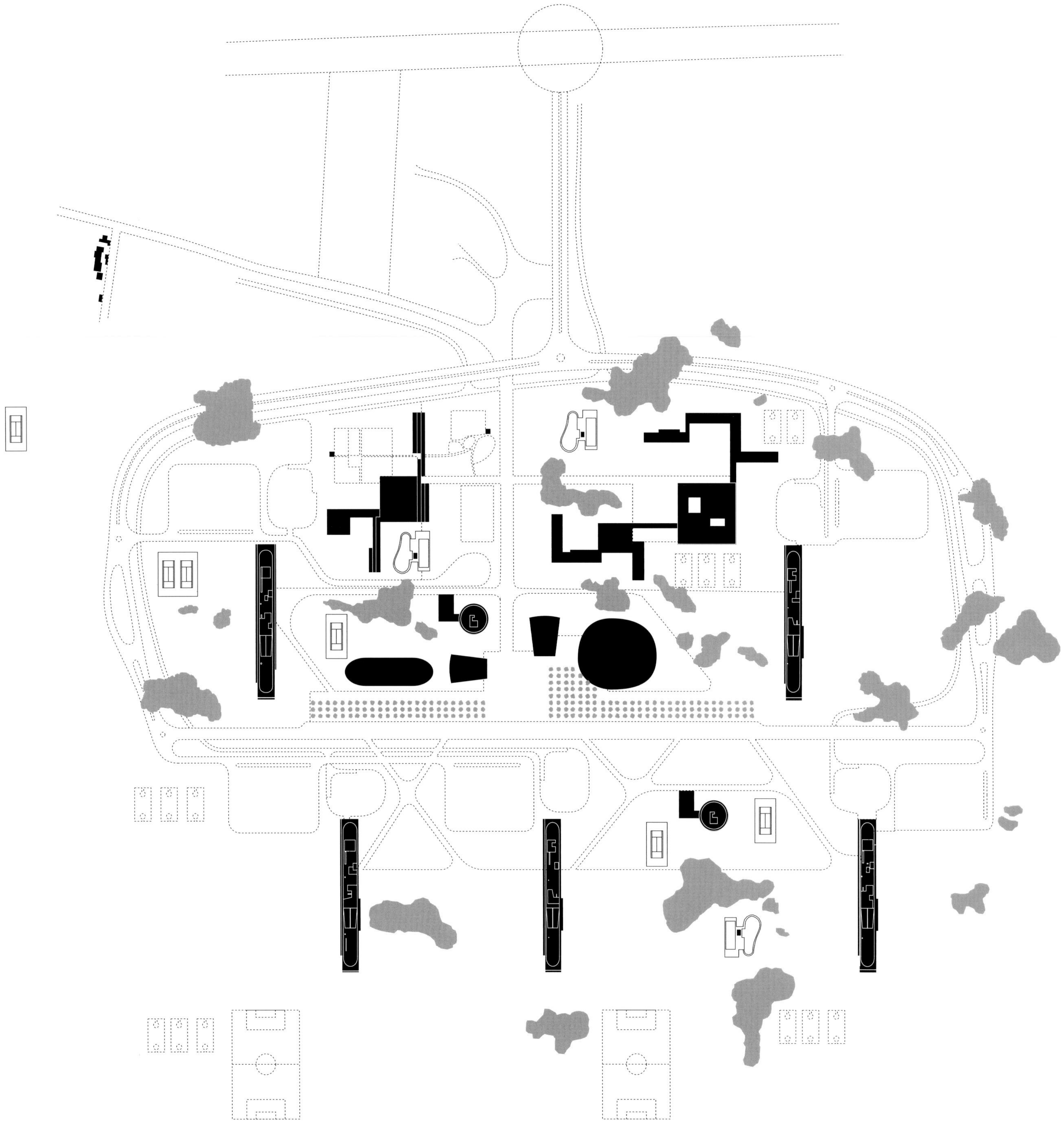

scale comparison

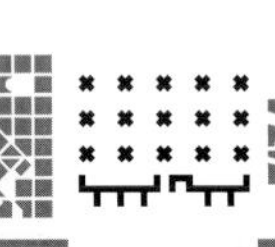

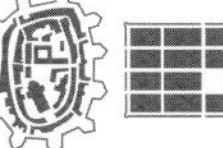

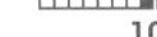

Melk, Austria [1974]

city /country / date

scale comparison

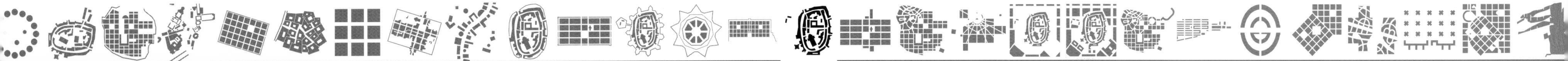

M

100M

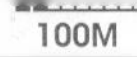

city / country / date

Milano, Italy 1832

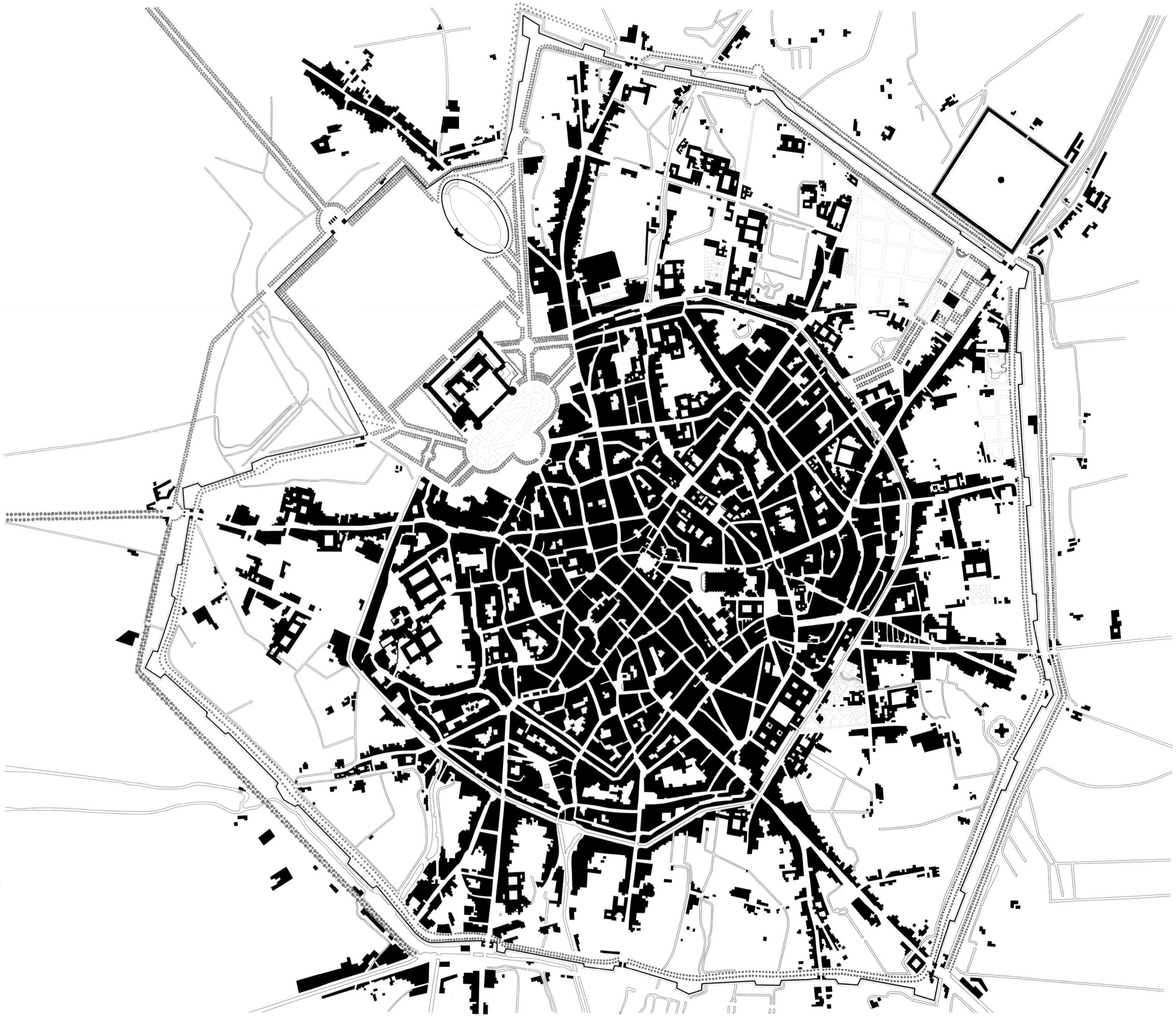

scale comparison

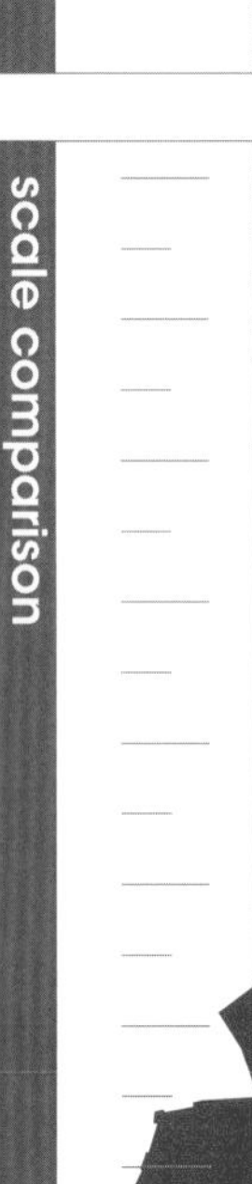

M

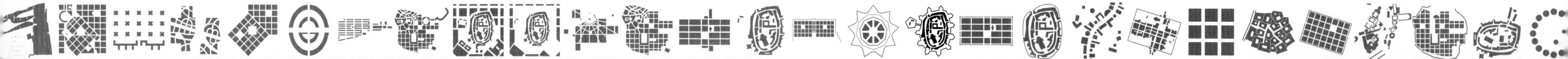

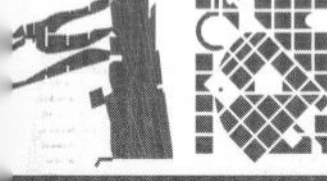

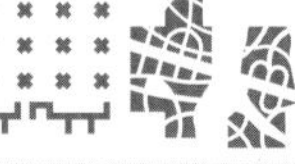

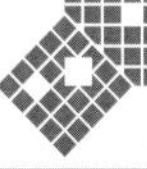

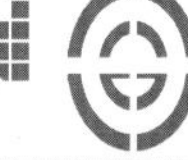

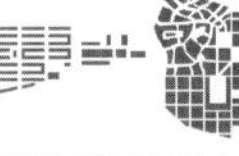

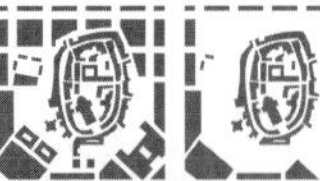

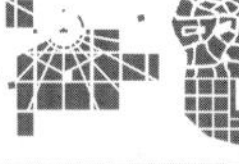

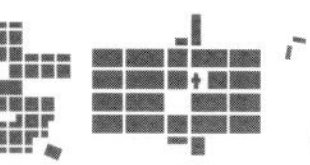

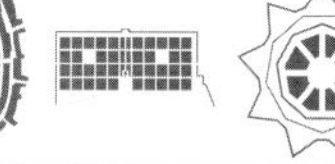

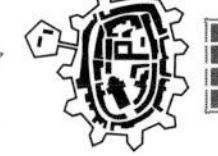

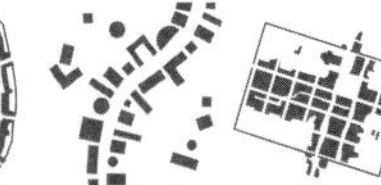

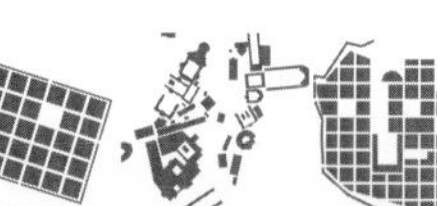

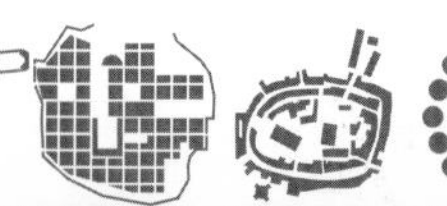

100M

city /country / date

Milano, Italy (proposal by Steven Holl) 1995

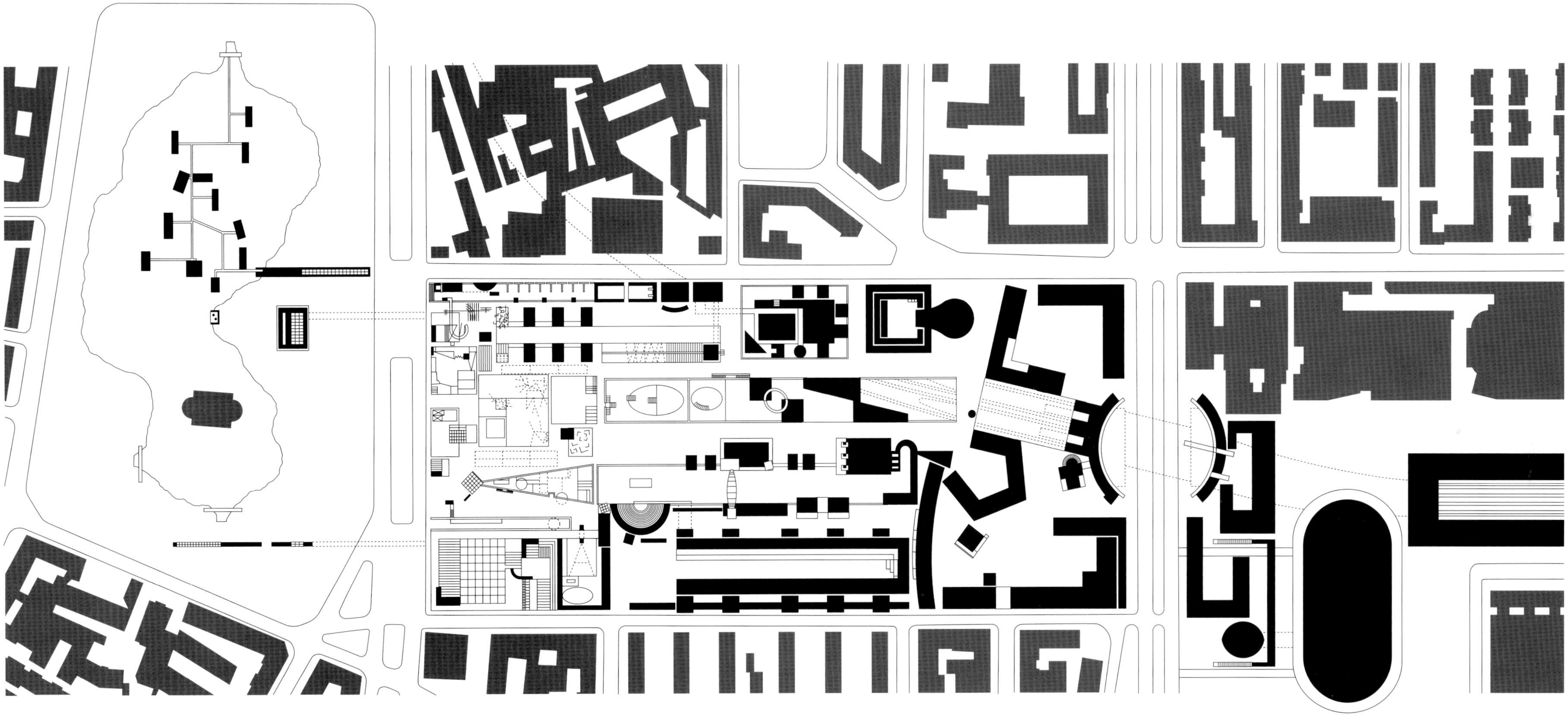

scale comparison

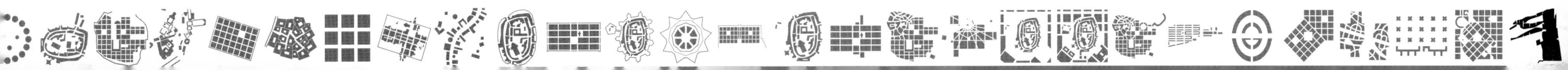

100M
city / country / date
Milburn, England
1946
scale comparison

100M

Miletus, Turkey 400 BC

city / country / date

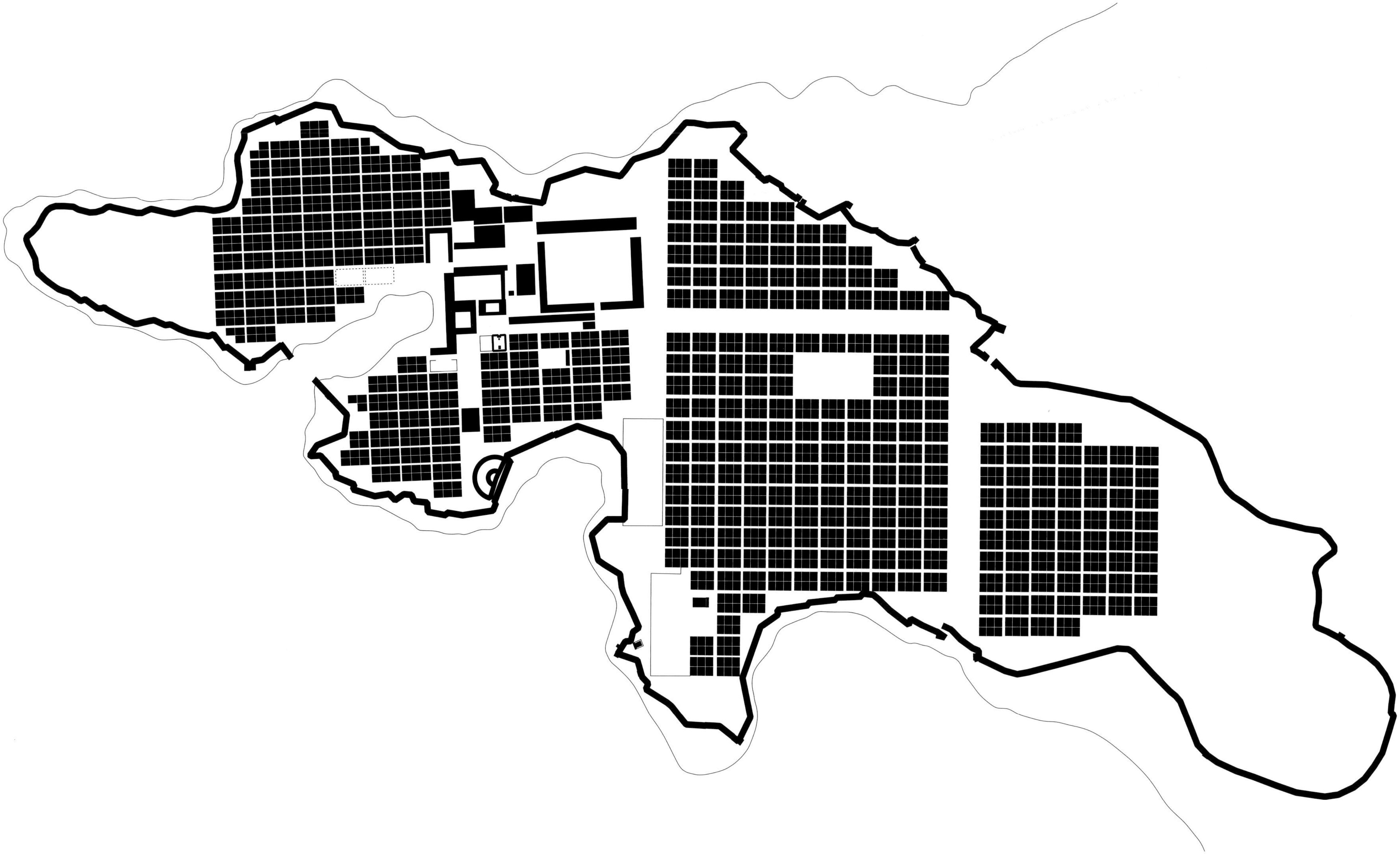

scale comparison

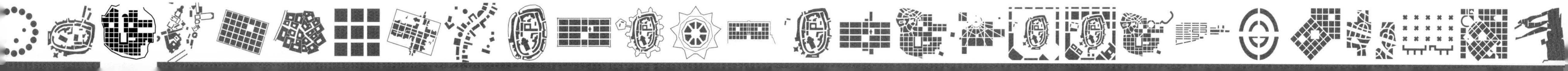

Milton Abbas, England 1946

city / country / date

scale comparison

100M

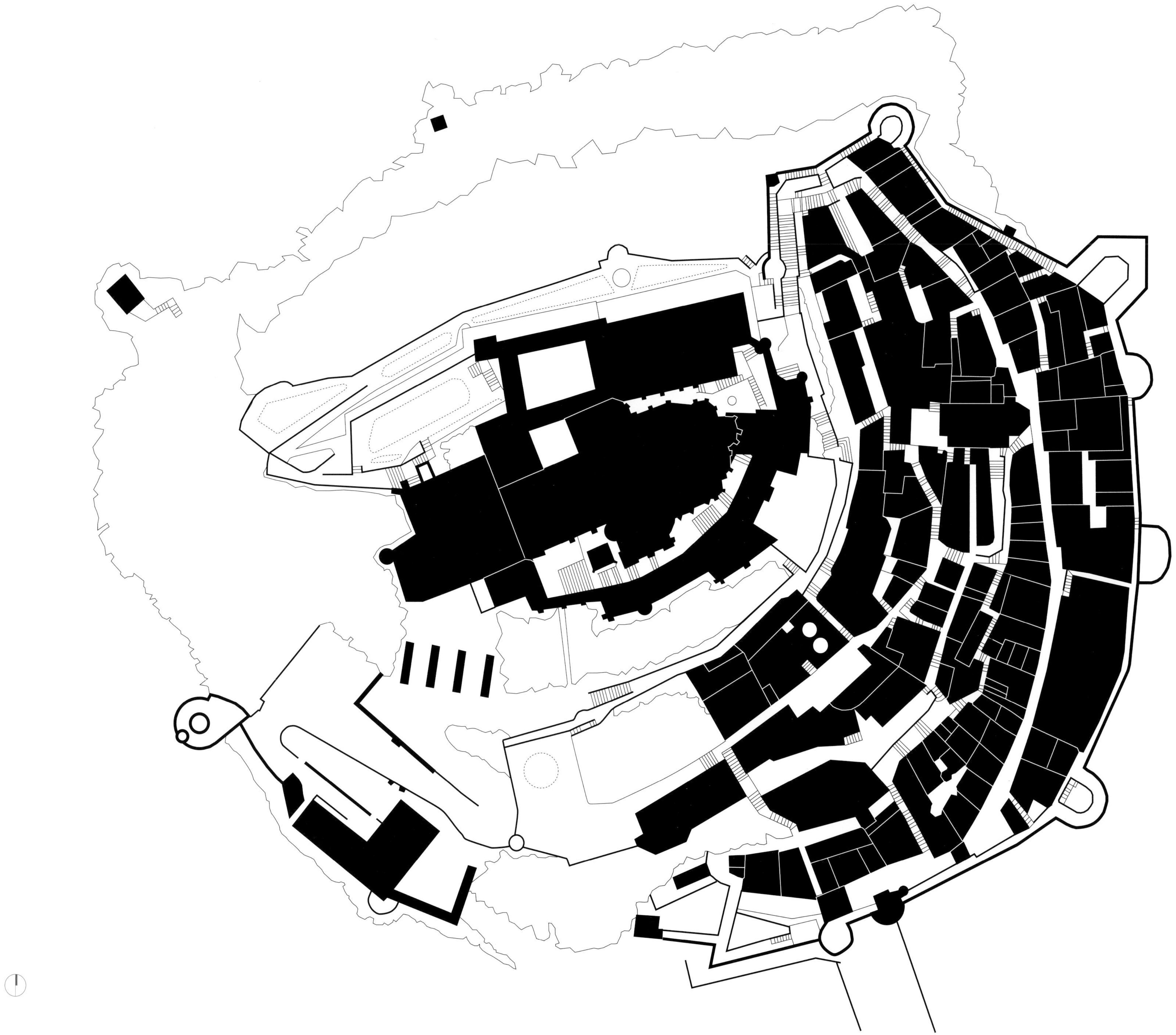

Mont St. Michel, France 1955

city /country / date

scale comparison

M

100M

city / country / date

Moscow, Russia 1836

scale comparison

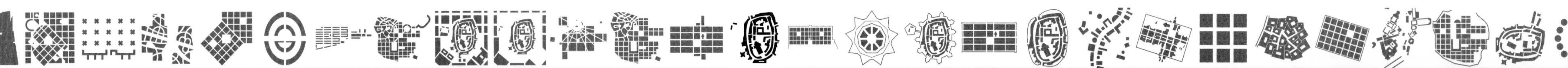

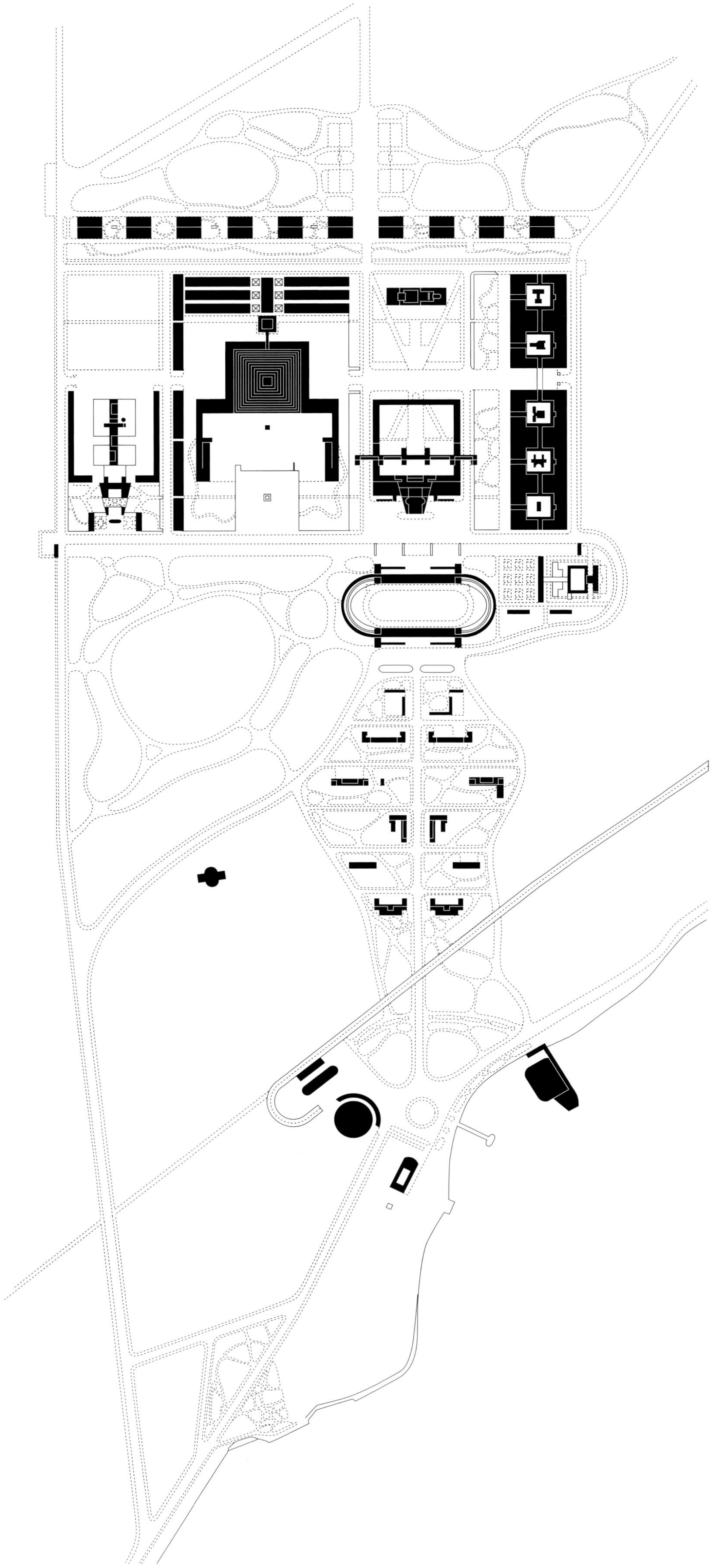

100M

city / country / date

Mundaneum, Belgium (proposal by Le Corbusier) 1929

scale comparison

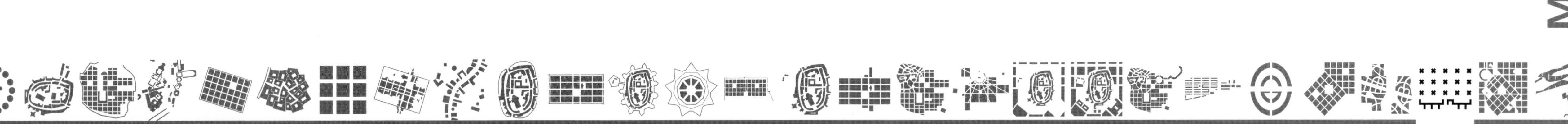

100M

city / country / date

Münich, Germany 1858

scale comparison

M

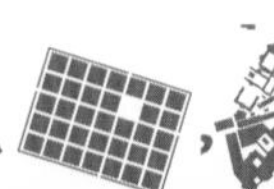

Nancy, France (outline in red shows early boundaries of Nancy) 1909

city / country / date

scale comparison

100M

city / country / date

Naples, Italy 1835

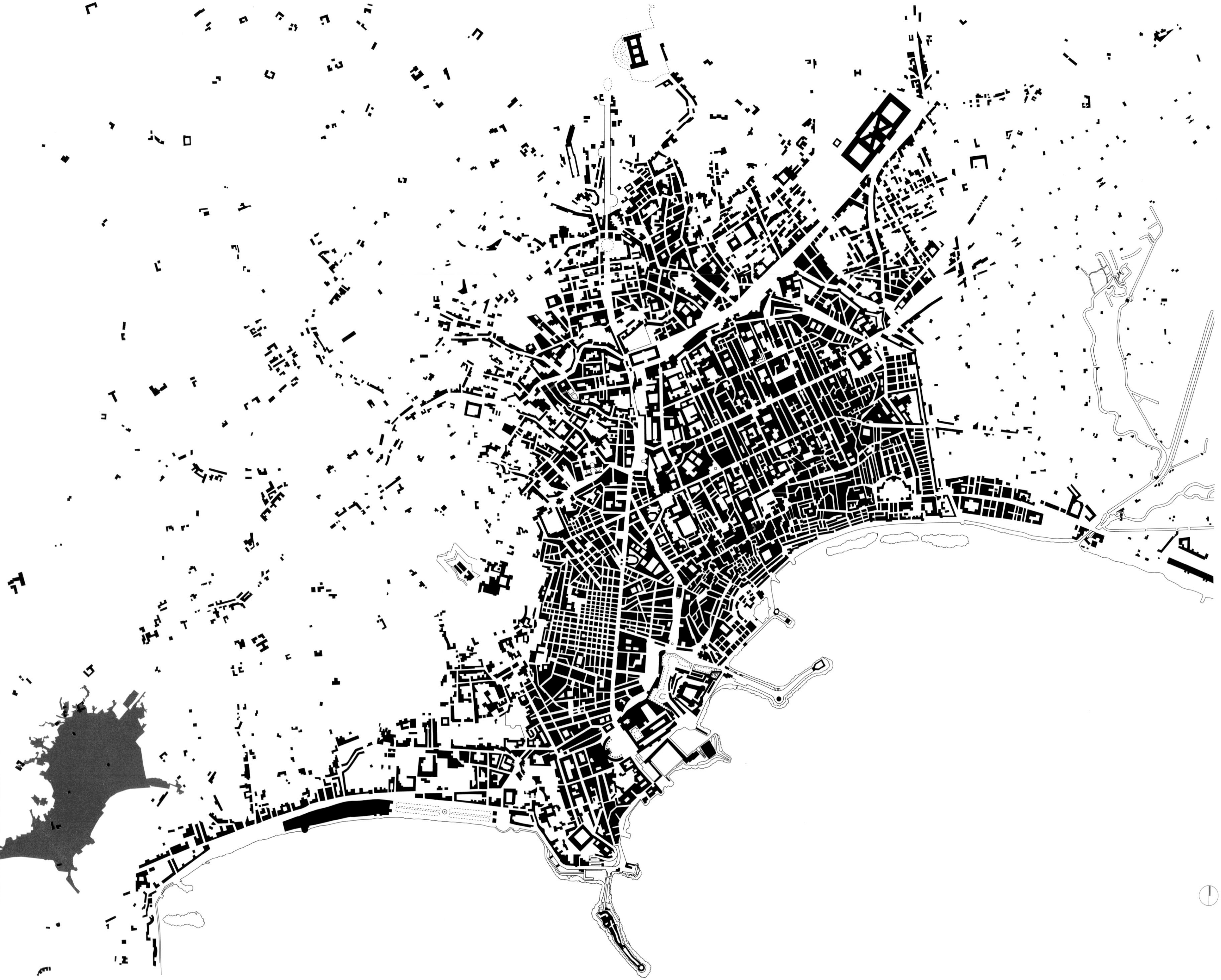

scale comparison

N

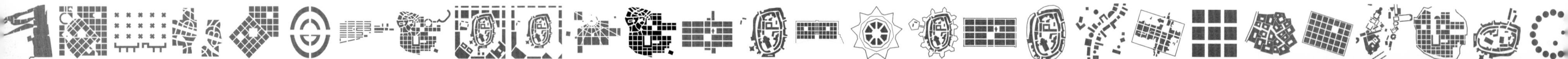

100M

Neuf-Brisach, France 1729

city / country / date

scale comparison

N

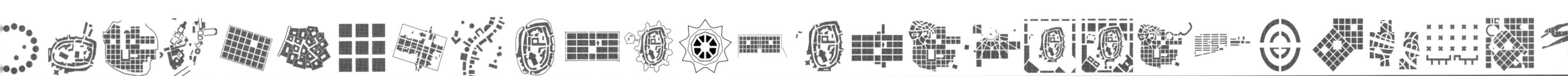

New Delhi, India (design by Edward Lutyens)
1911-1931
city /country / date
scale comparison
100M
N

100M

city / country / date

New Orleans, LA, USA 1770

scale comparison

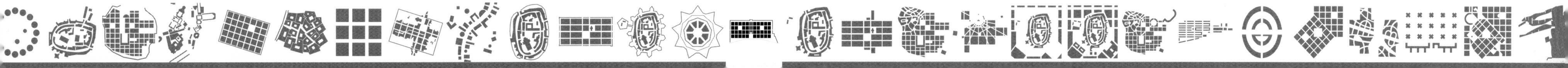

100M

city / country / date

New York, NY, USA 1731, 1763 & 1767

scale comparison

N

100M

New York, NY, USA 1797 & 1838

city /country / date

scale comparison

N

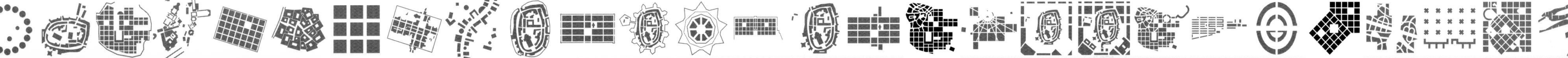

100M

city / country / date

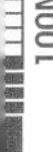

New York, NY, USA (proposal by Thom Mayne for the CCA) 1999

scale comparison

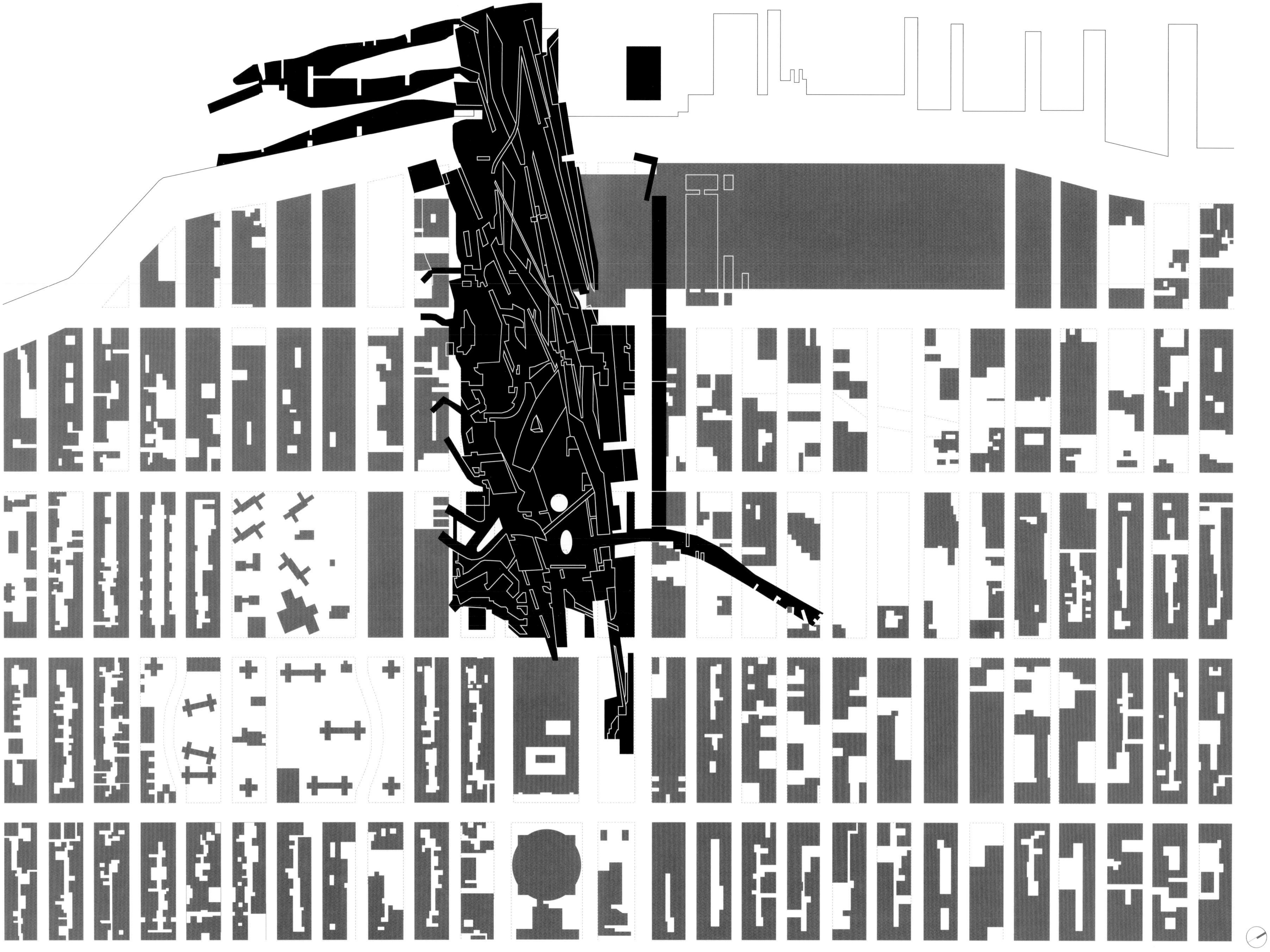

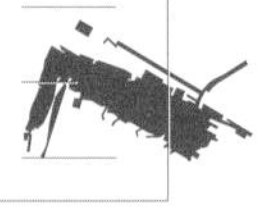

N

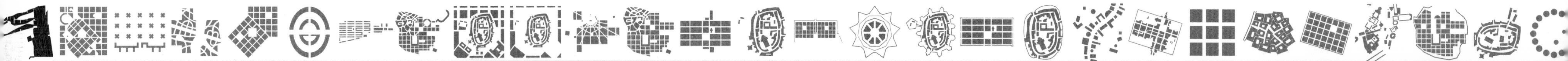

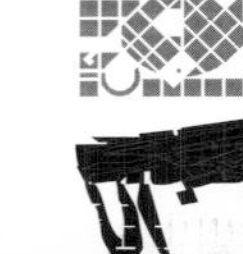

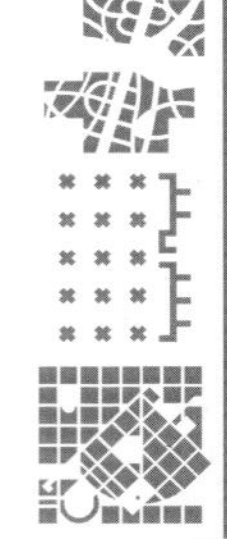

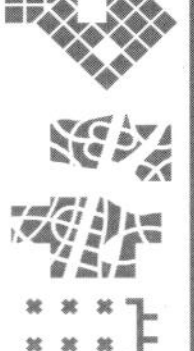

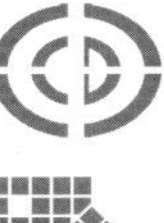

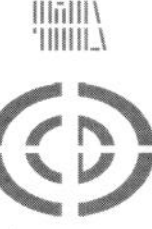

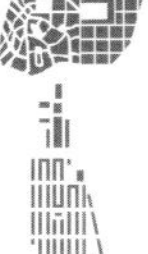

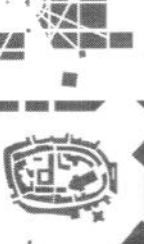

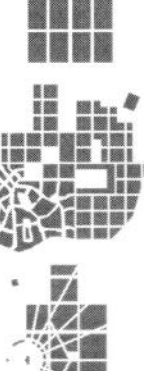

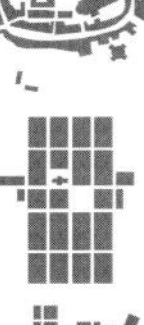

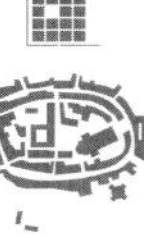

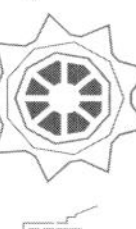

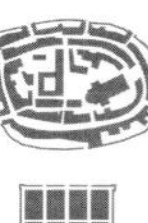

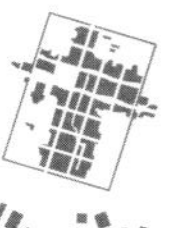

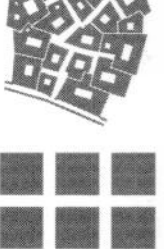

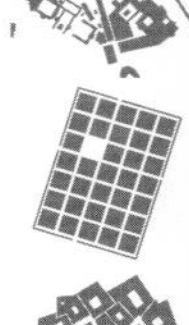

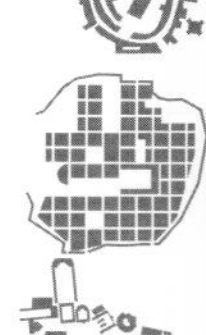

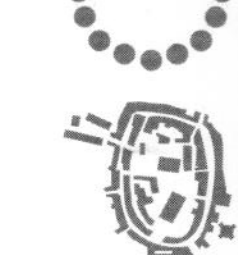

100M

Newport, RI, USA 1777

city / country / date

scale comparison

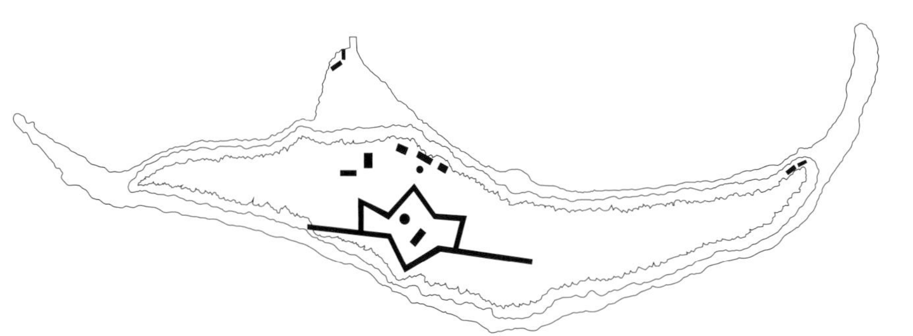

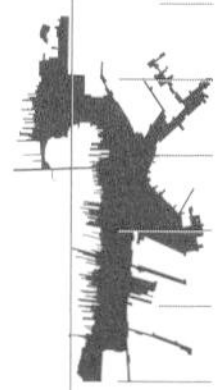

100M

city / country / date

Nisky, Germany 1782

scale comparison

N

scale comparison
Norwich, England 1800
city / country / date
100M
N

Nottingham, England 1800

city / country / date

scale comparison

100M

N

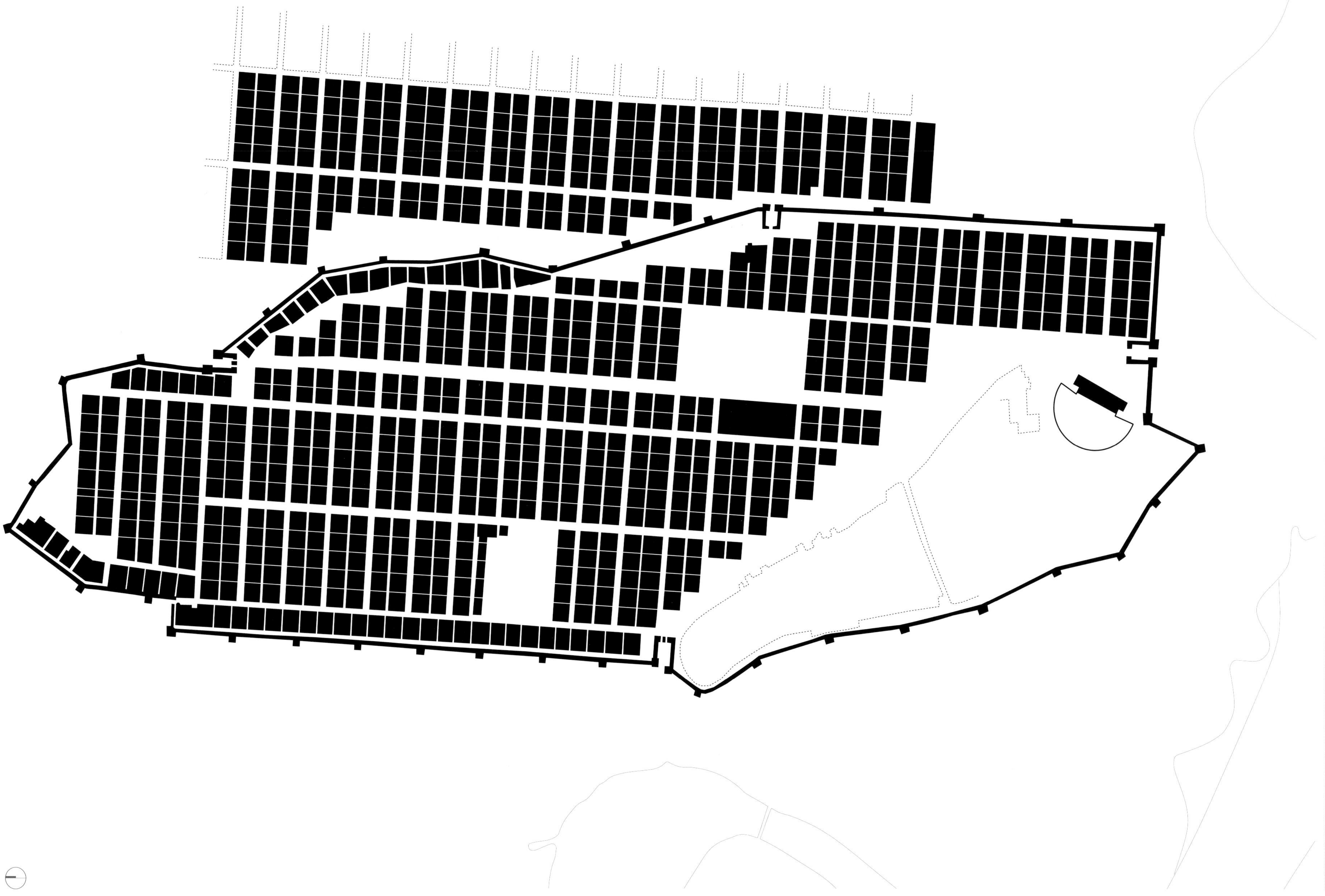

Olynthus, Greece 397BC

city /country / date

scale comparison

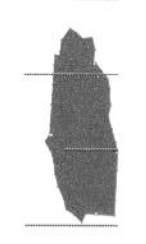

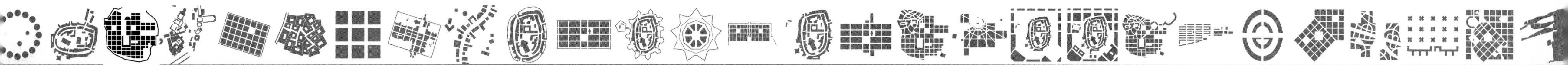

100M

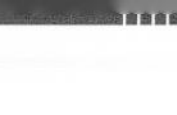

city / country / date

Oxford, England 1800

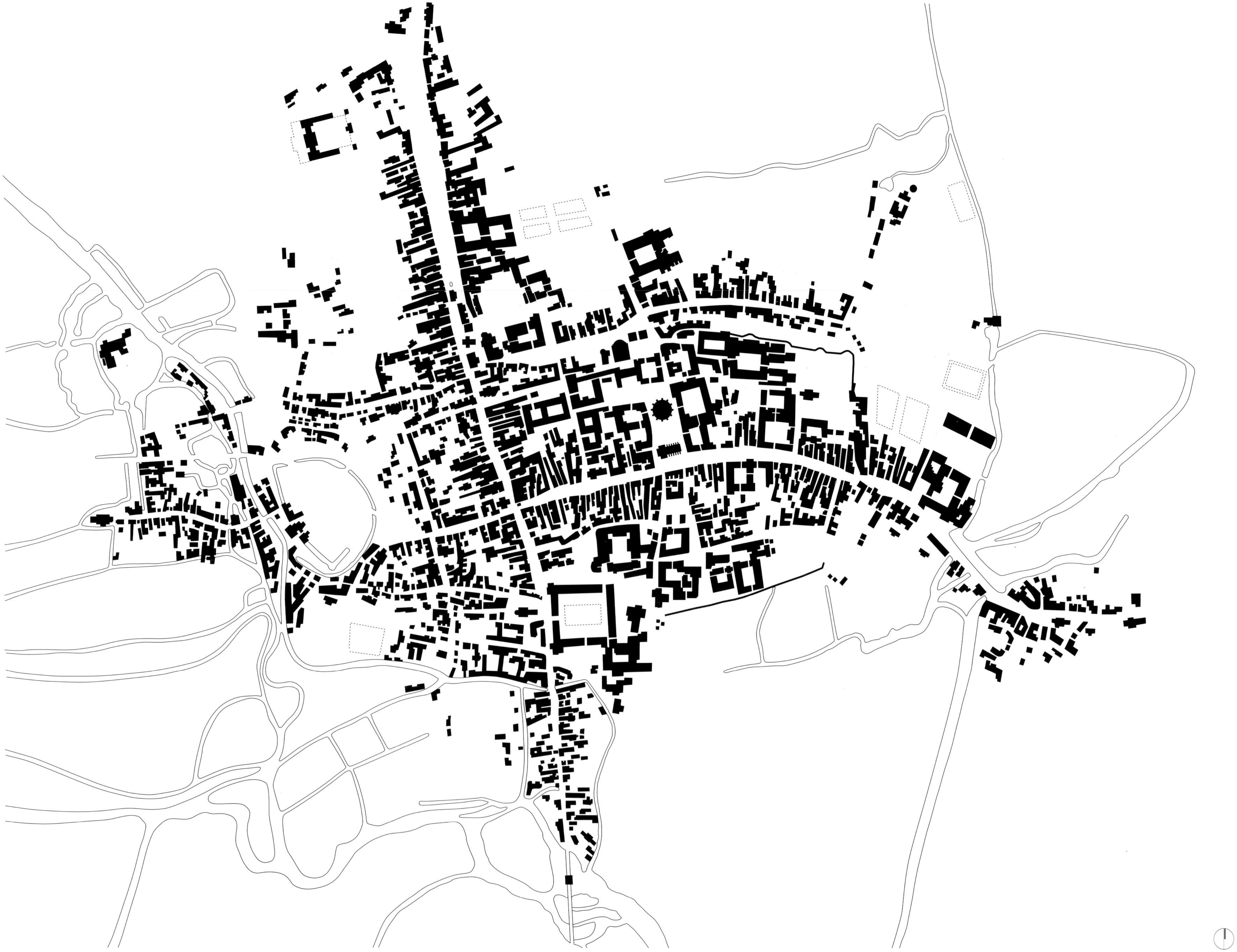

scale comparison

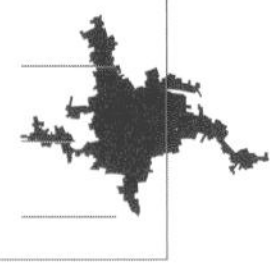

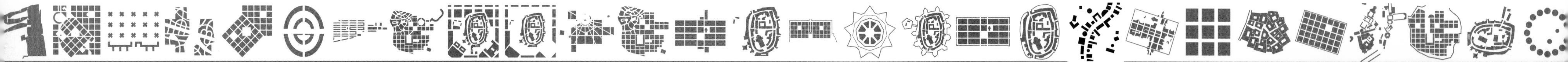

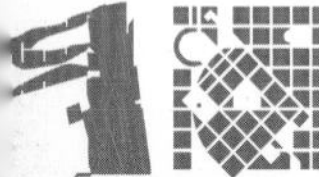

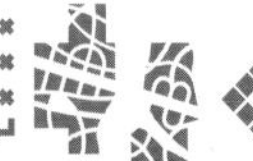

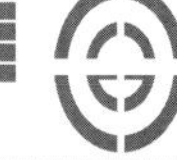

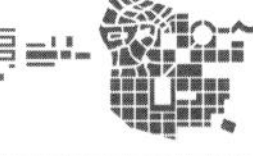

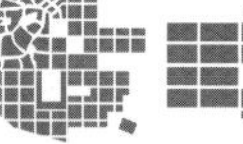

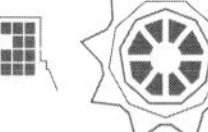

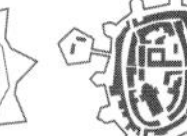

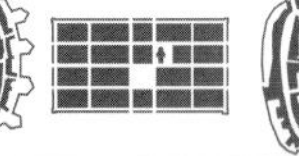

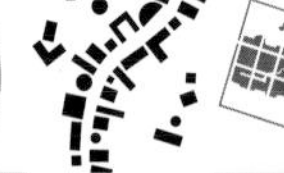

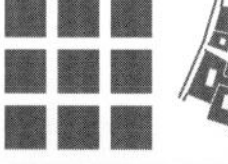

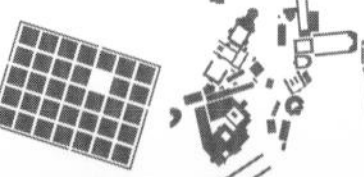

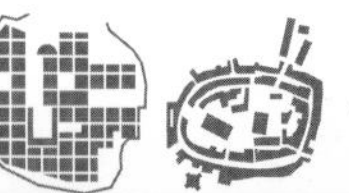

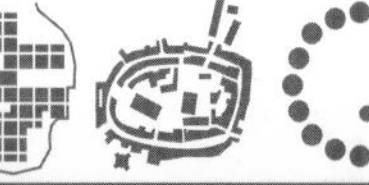

100M

city /country / date

Palermo, Italy 1906

scale comparison

city / country / date

Palmanova, Italy 1845

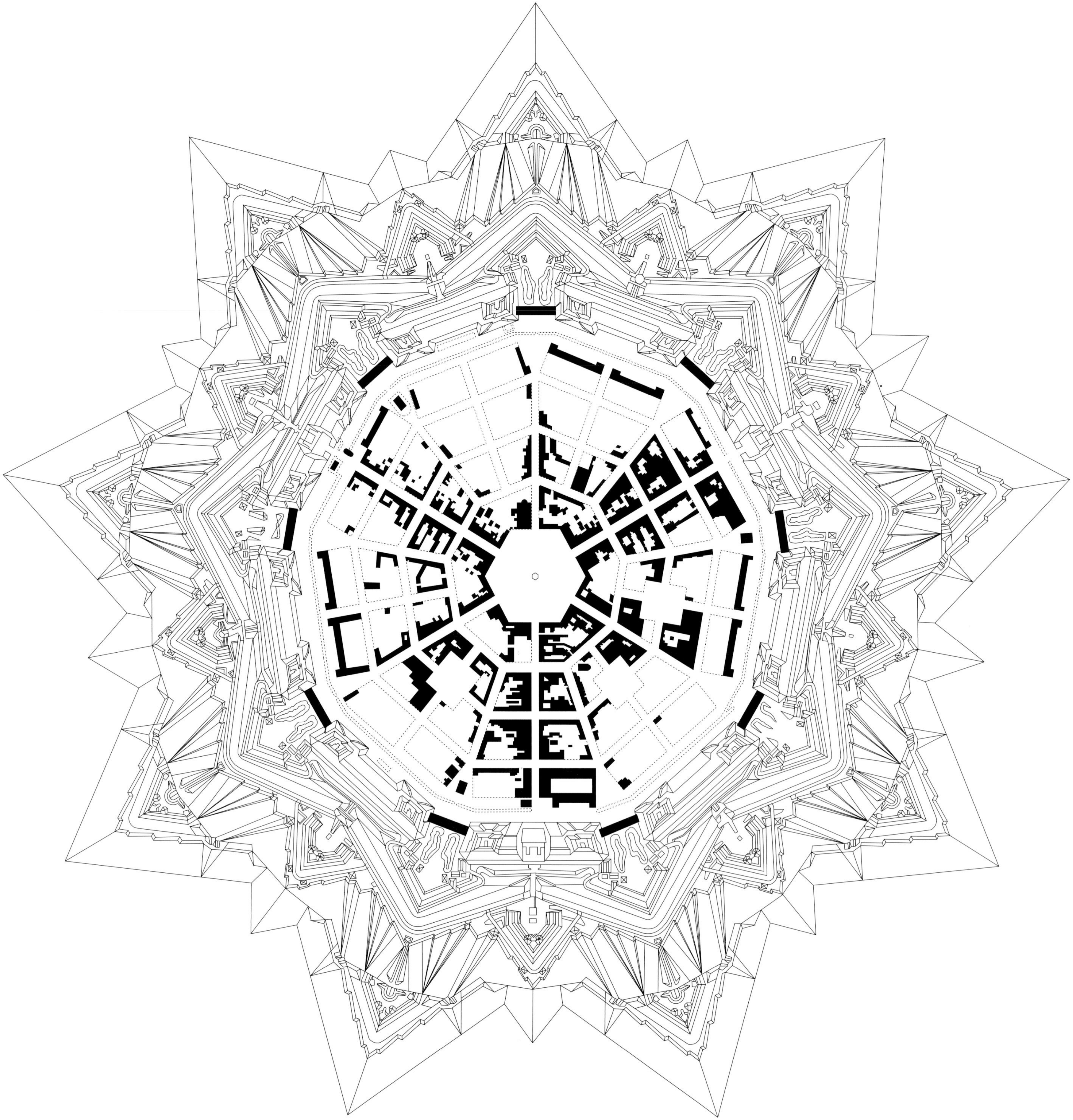

scale comparison

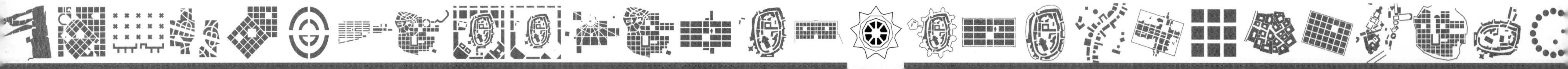

100M

Paris, France (L'île de la Cité) 1754

city /country / date

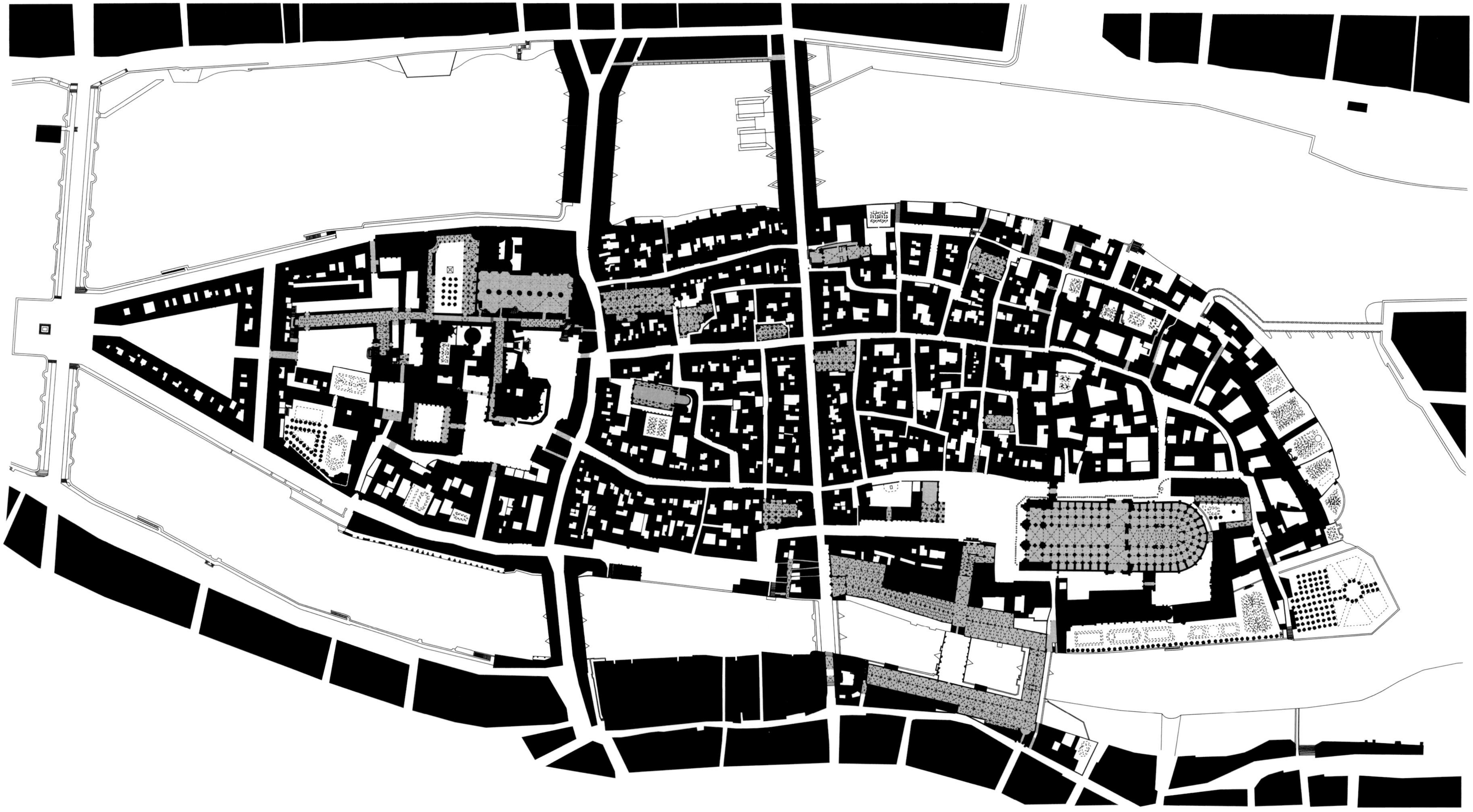

scale comparison

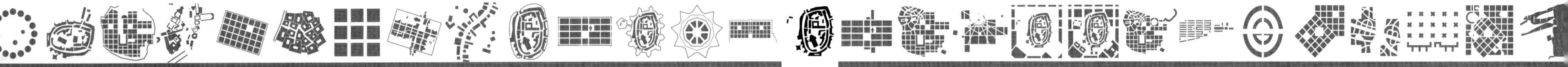

100M

city /country / date

Paris, France 1180 & 1779

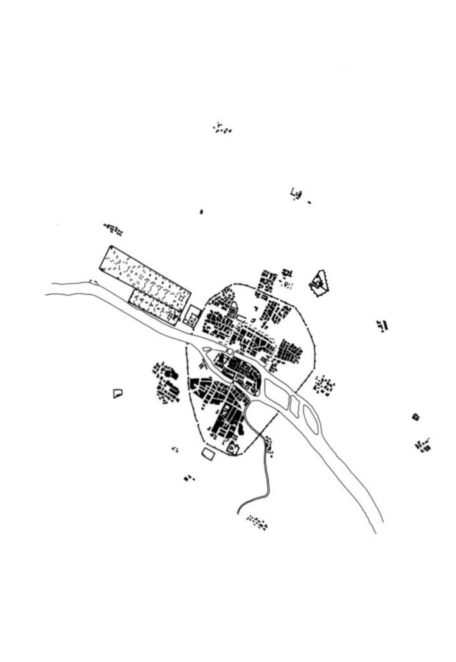

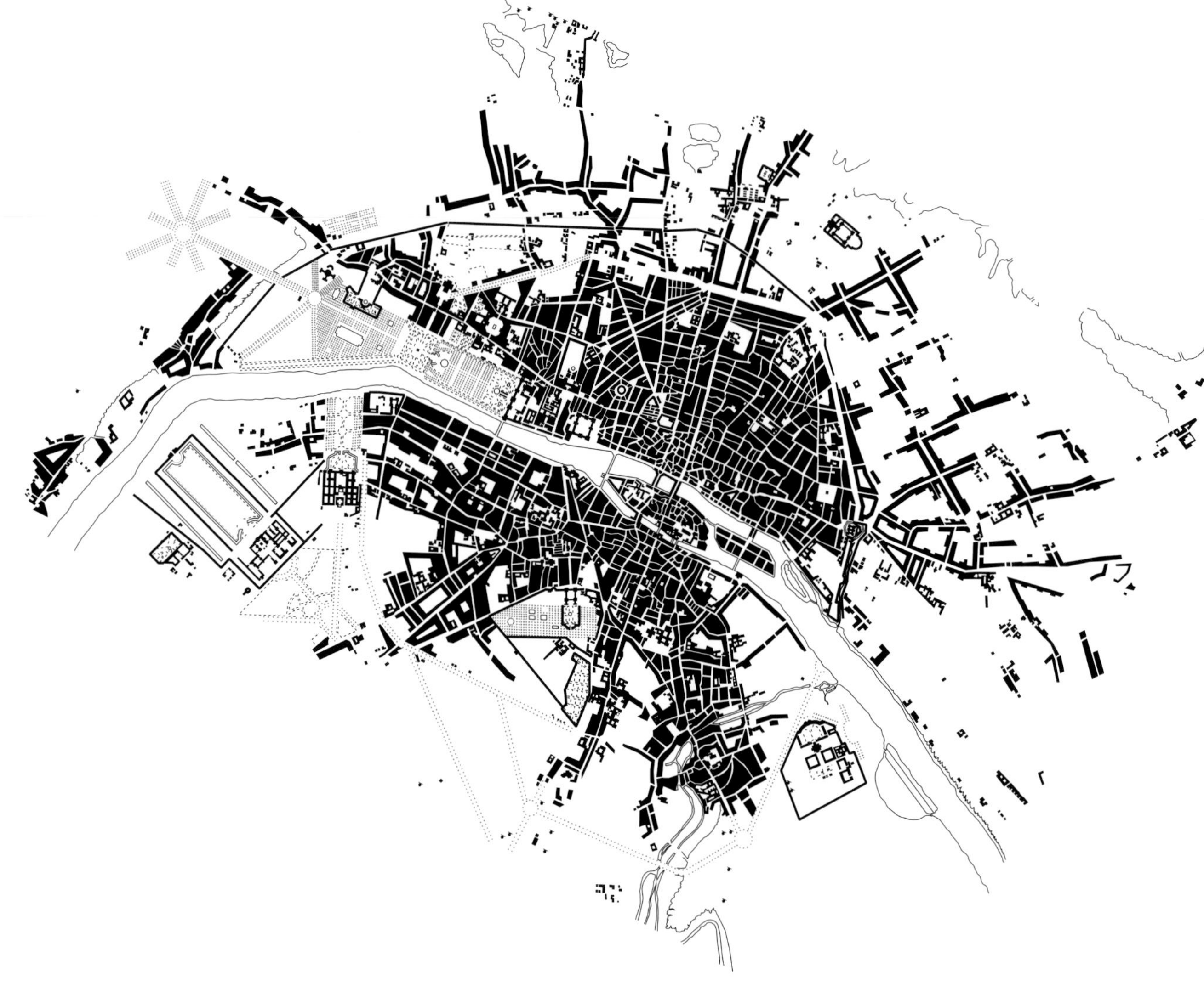

scale comparison

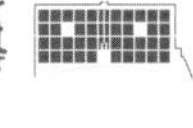

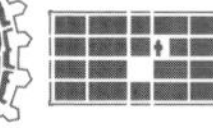

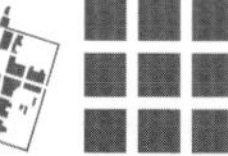

100M

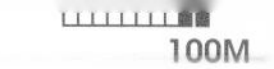

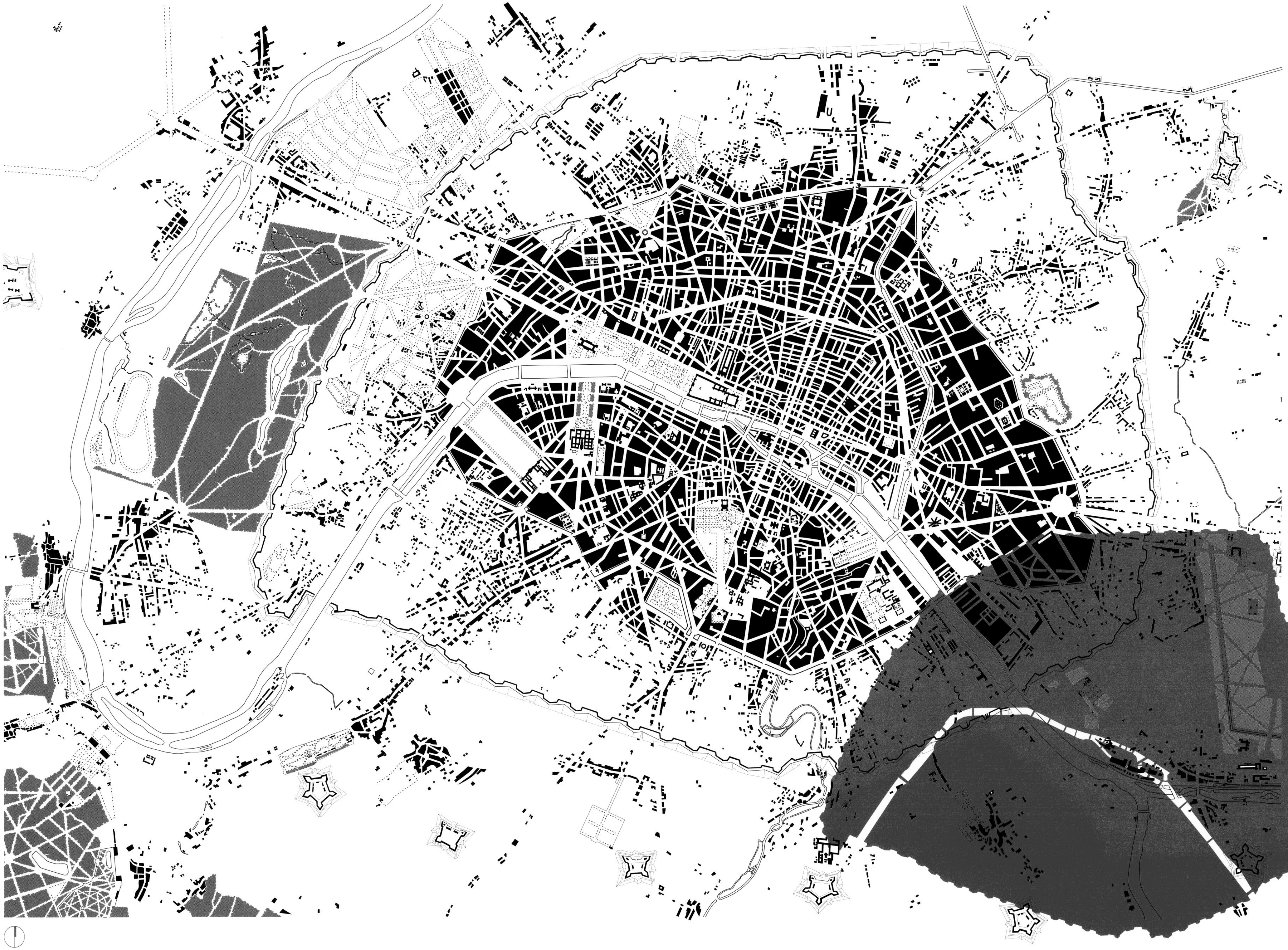

Paris, France 1863

city /country / date

scale comparison

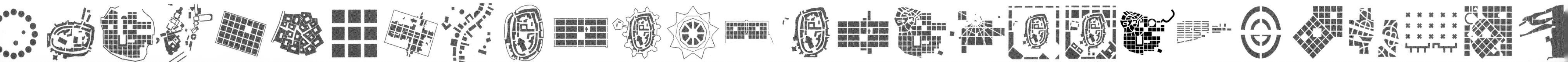

100M

city / country / date

Paris, Parc de la Villette, France (design by Leon Krier) 1982

scale comparison

100M

city / country / date

Paris, Parc de la Villette, France (design by Bernard Tschumi) 1982

scale comparison

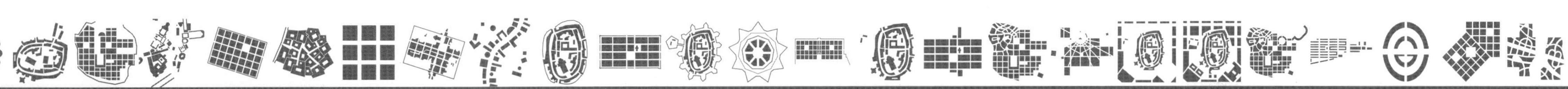

100M

city / country / date

Parma, Italy 1840

scale comparison

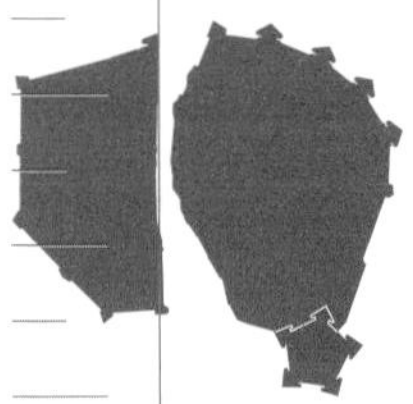

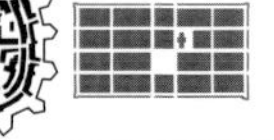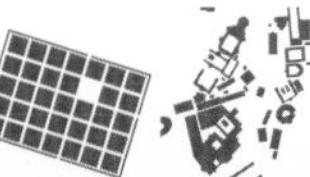

100M

Pesaro, Italy 1909

city / country / date

scale comparison

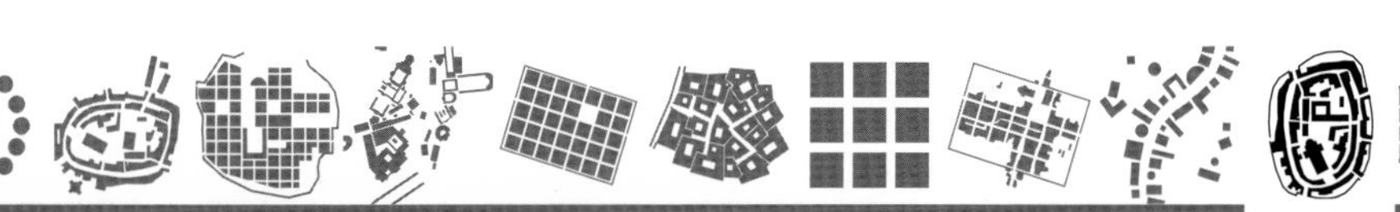

Philadelphia, PA, USA 1802

city / country / date

scale comparison

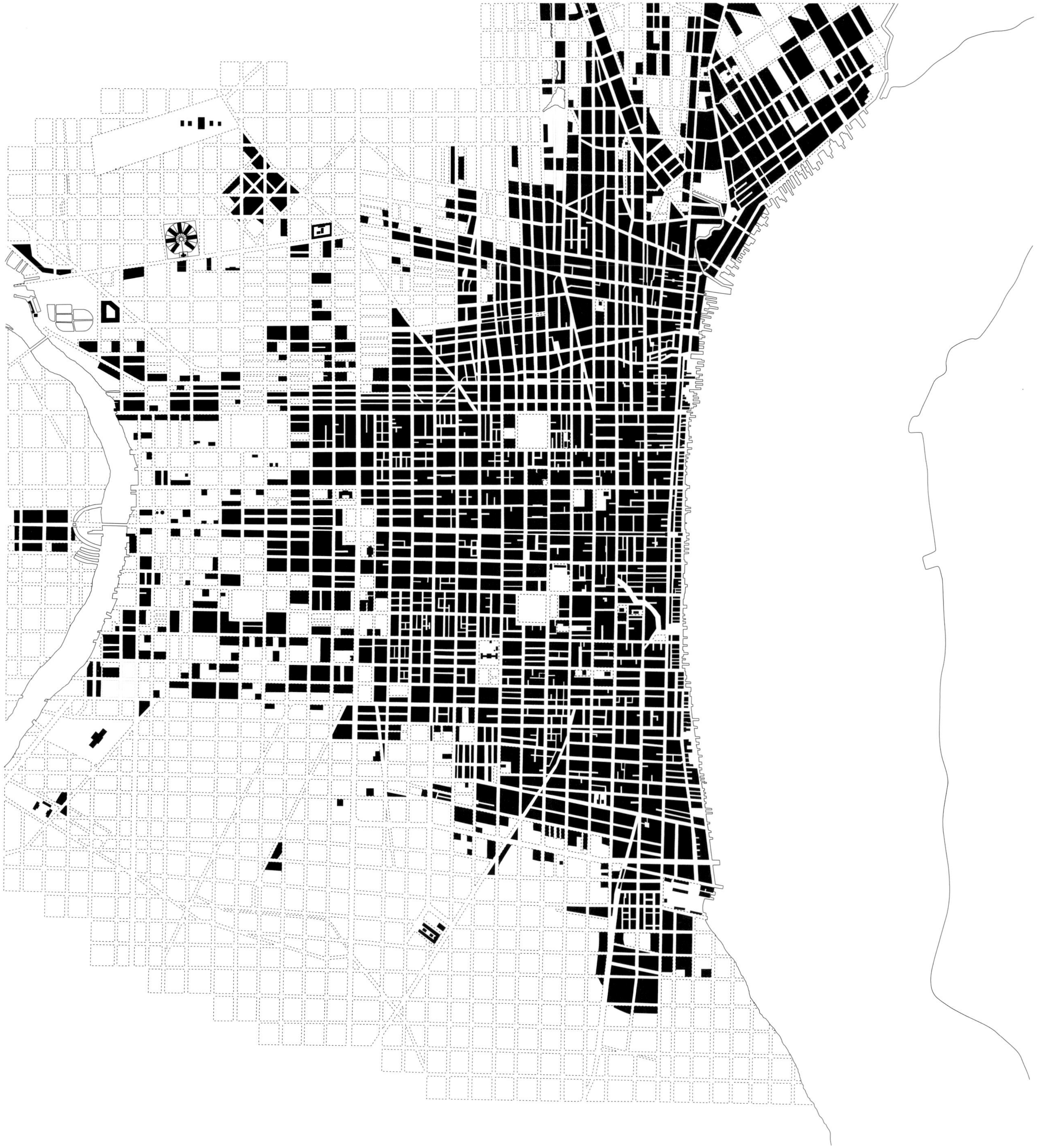

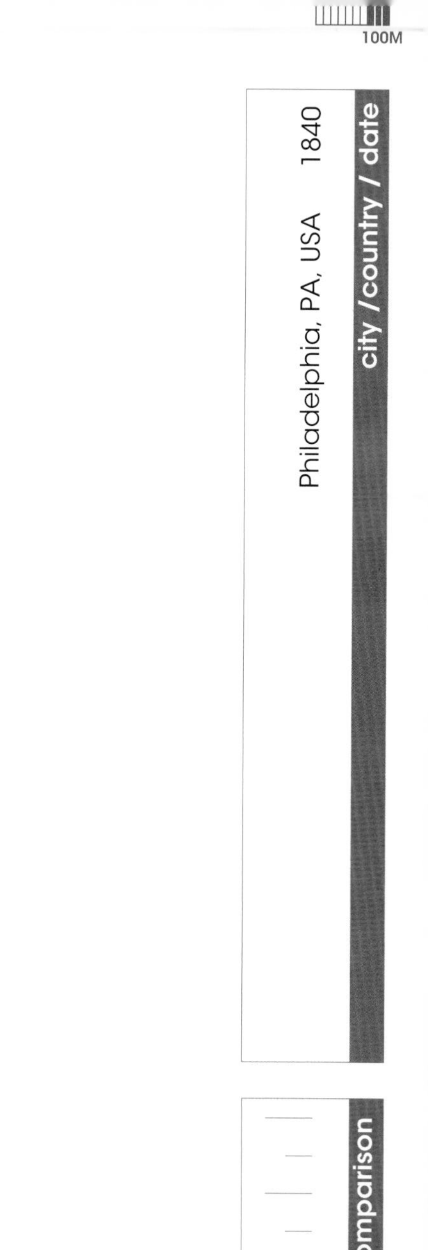
Philadelphia, PA, USA 1840
city / country / date

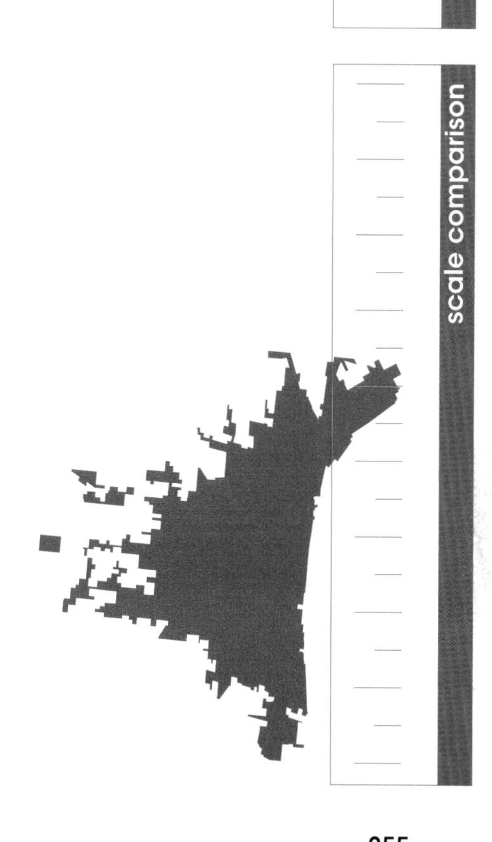
scale comparison

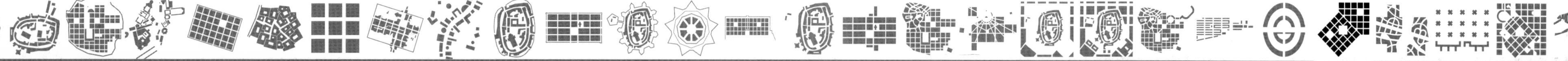

100M

Pietrasanta, Italy 1963

city / country / date

scale comparison

city /country / date

Pitigliano, Italy 1963

scale comparison

Pittsburgh, PA, USA 1795
city / country / date
scale comparison
100M
P

city / country / date

Pittsburgh, PA, USA (proposal for Carnegie Mellon by M. Dennis & J. Clark) 1987

scale comparison

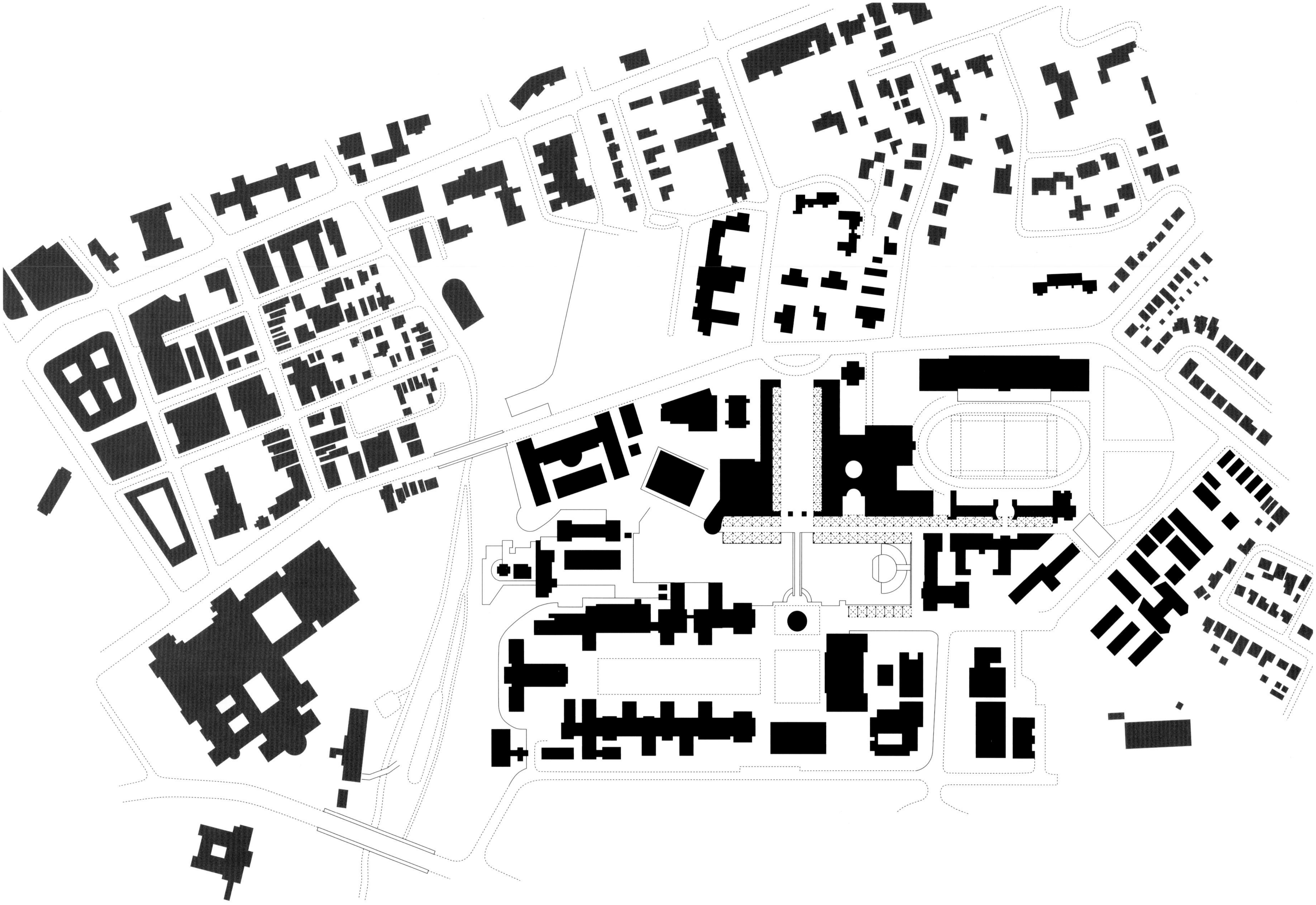

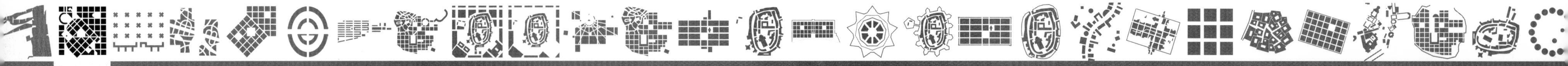

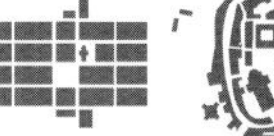
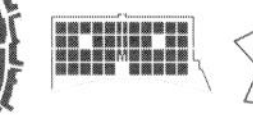

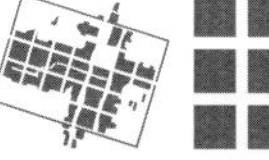

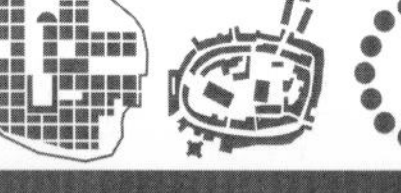

100M

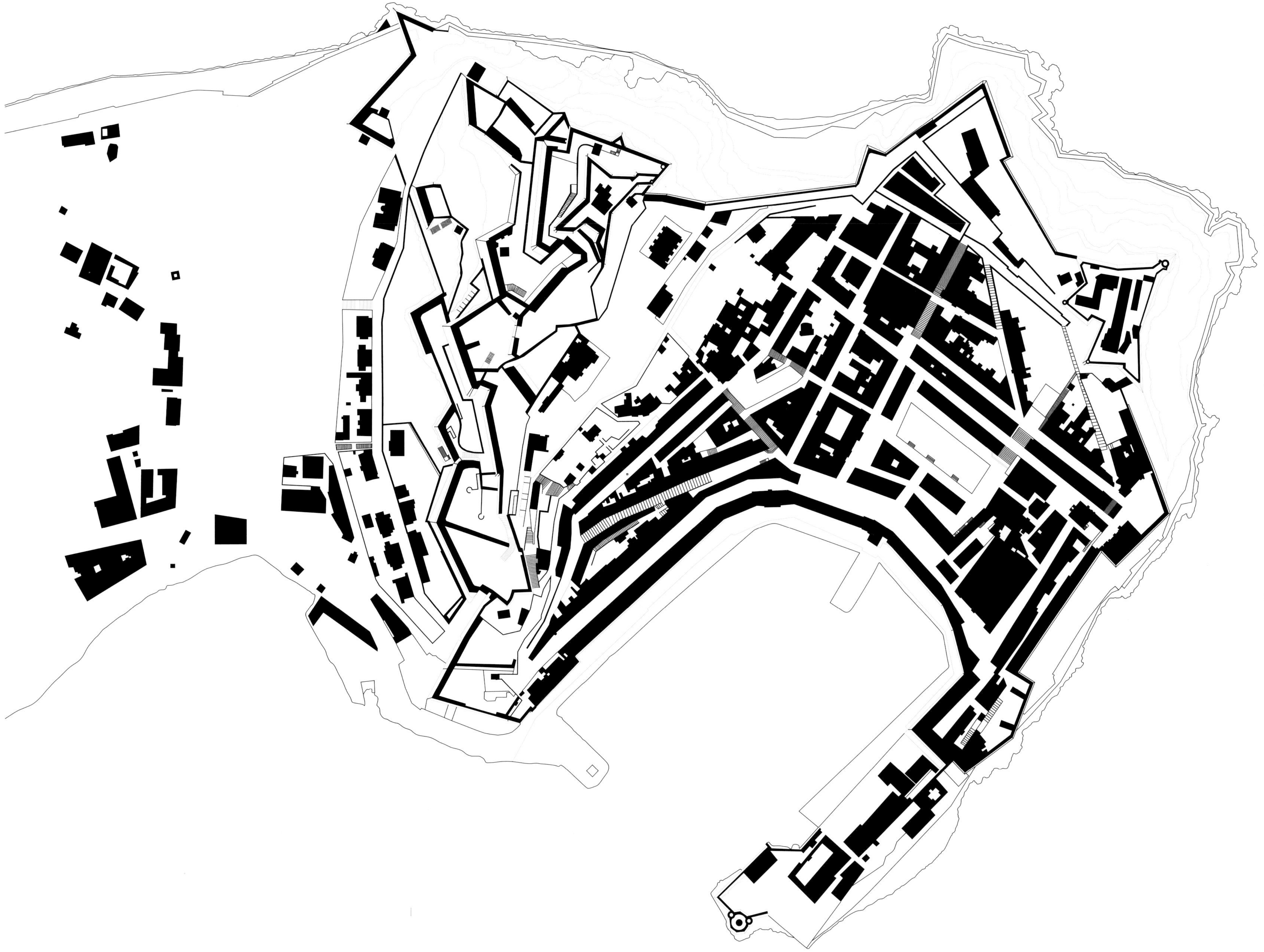

Portoferraio, Italy 1990

city /country / date

scale comparison

100M

city / country / date

Potsdam, Germany 1800

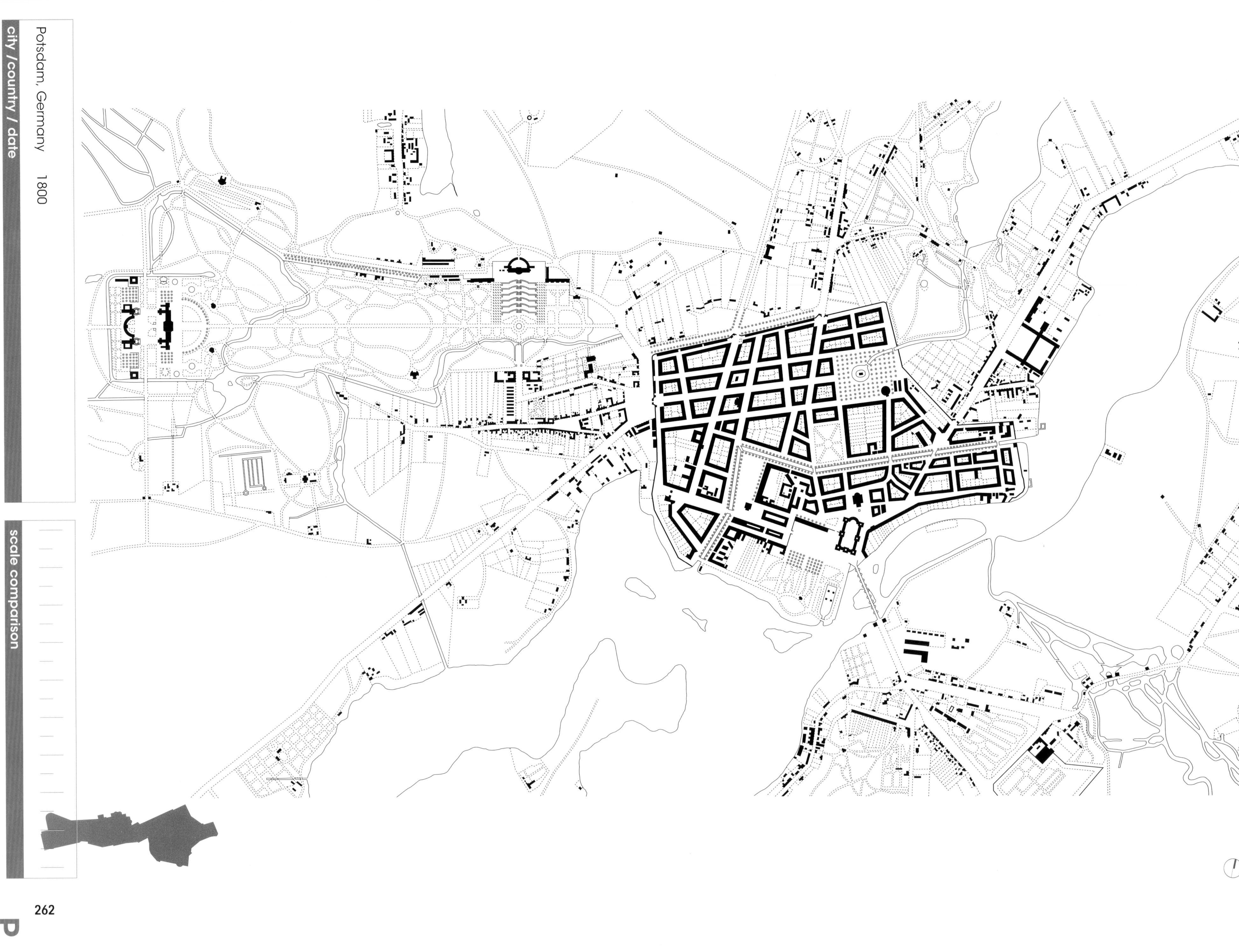

scale comparison

Priene, Turkey 350 BC

city /country / date

scale comparison

P

100M

city / country / date

Pullman, IL, USA 1885

scale comparison

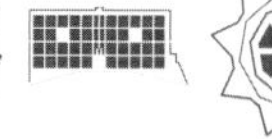

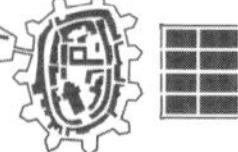
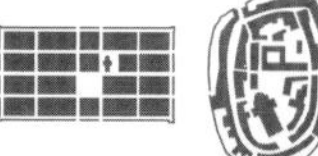

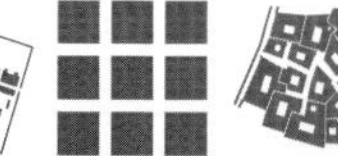

Quebec, Canada 1759

city /country / date

scale comparison

100M

city /country / date

Rhodes, Greece 408 BC

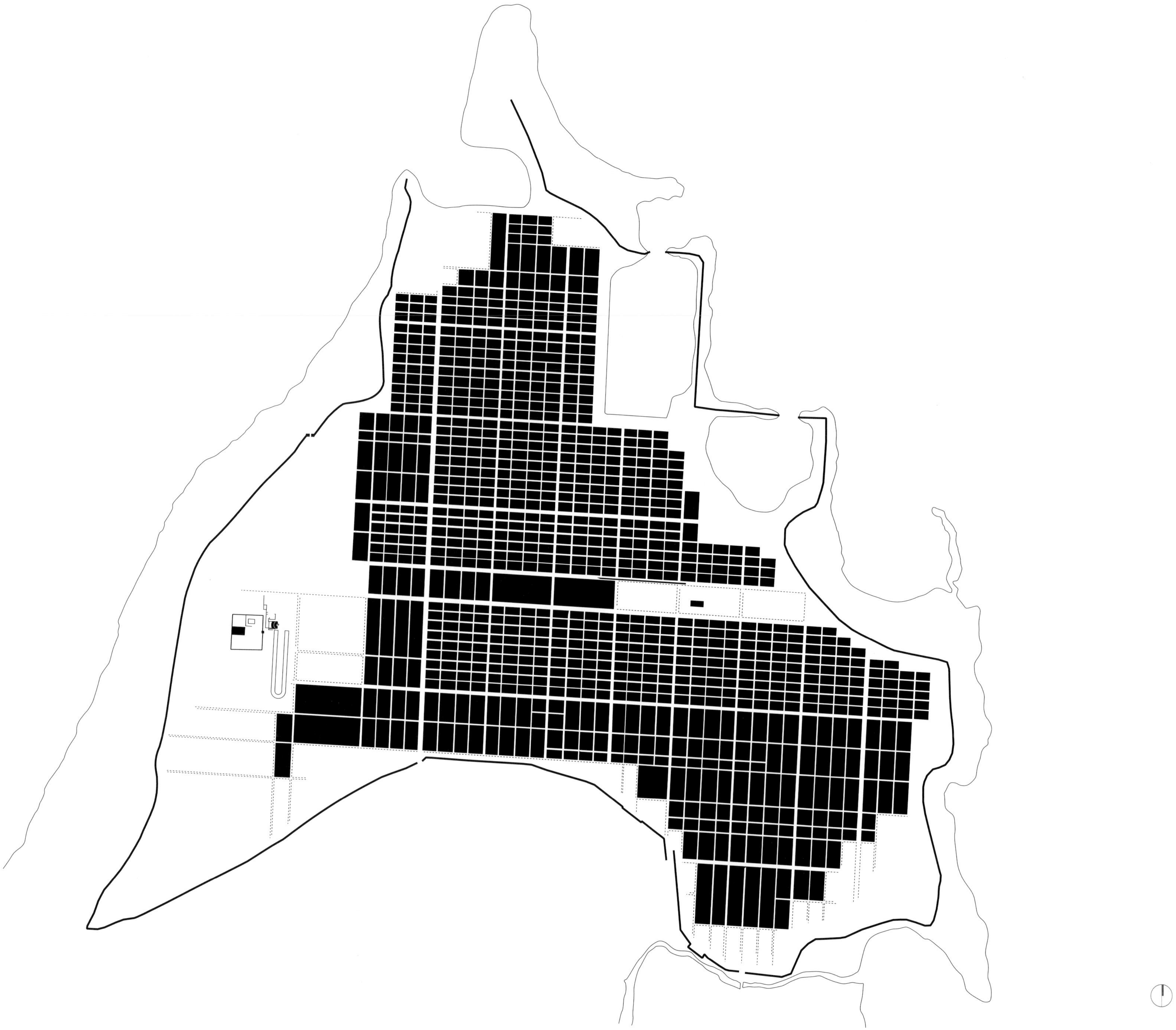

scale comparison

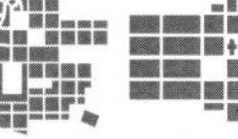

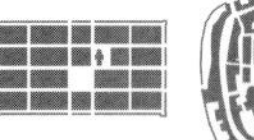

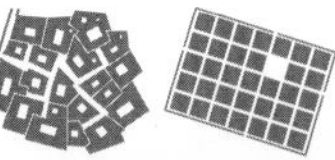
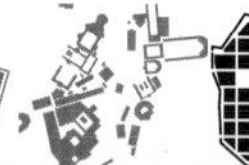
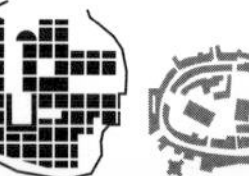
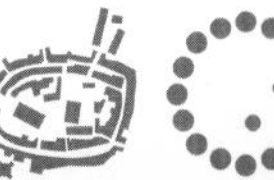

Rhodes, Greece 1906

city /country / date

scale comparison

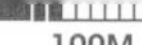

city /country / date

Ridley Park, PA, USA 1875

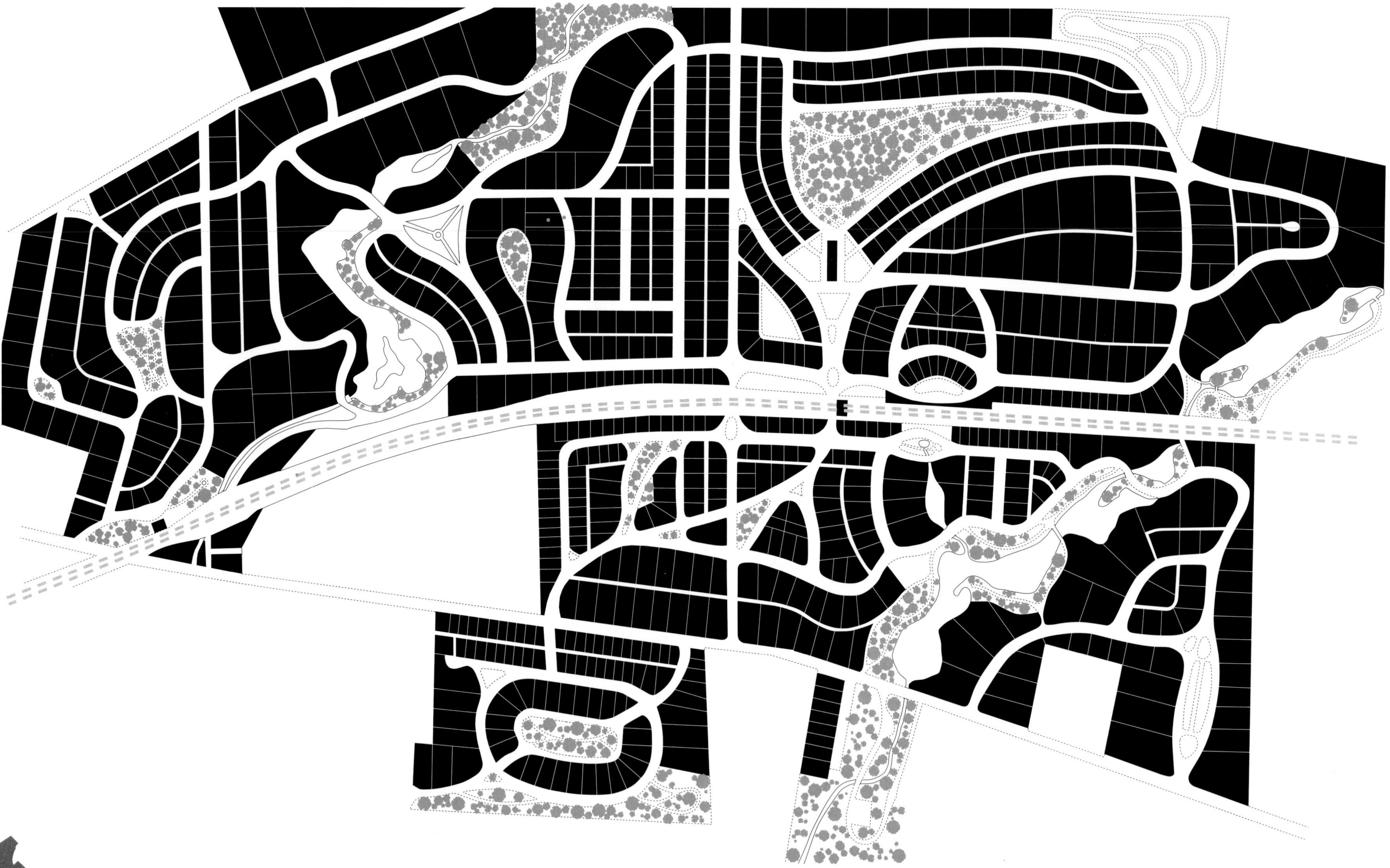

scale comparison

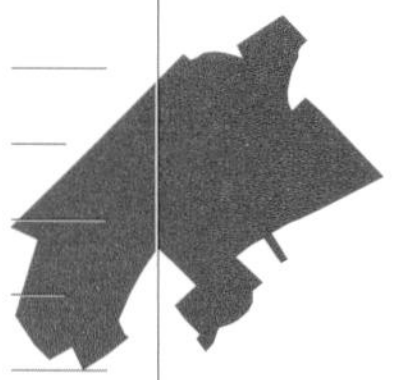

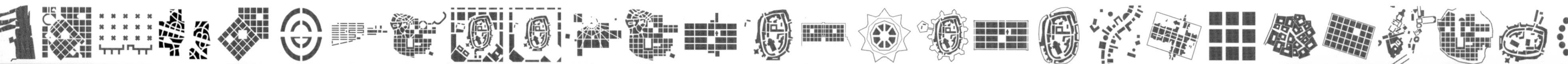

100M

Rieti, Italy 1990

city /country / date

scale comparison

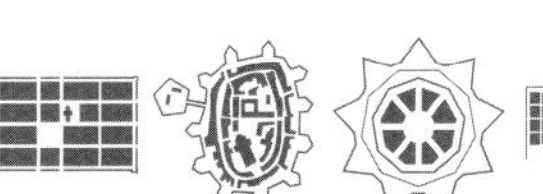

100M

city / country / date

Rio de Janeiro, Brazil 1831

scale comparison

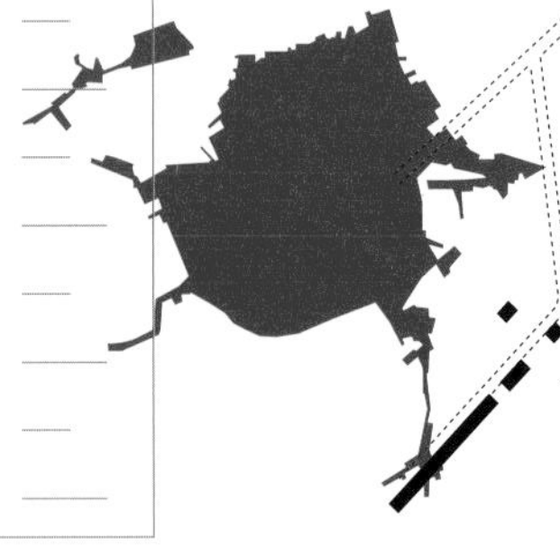

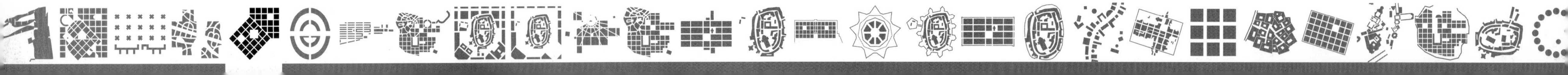

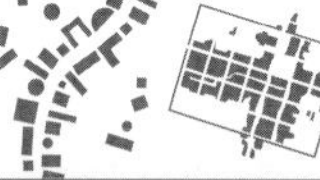
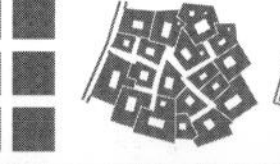

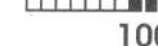

city / country / date

Rio de Janeiro, Brazil (proposal by Le Corbusier for a University) 1936

scale comparison

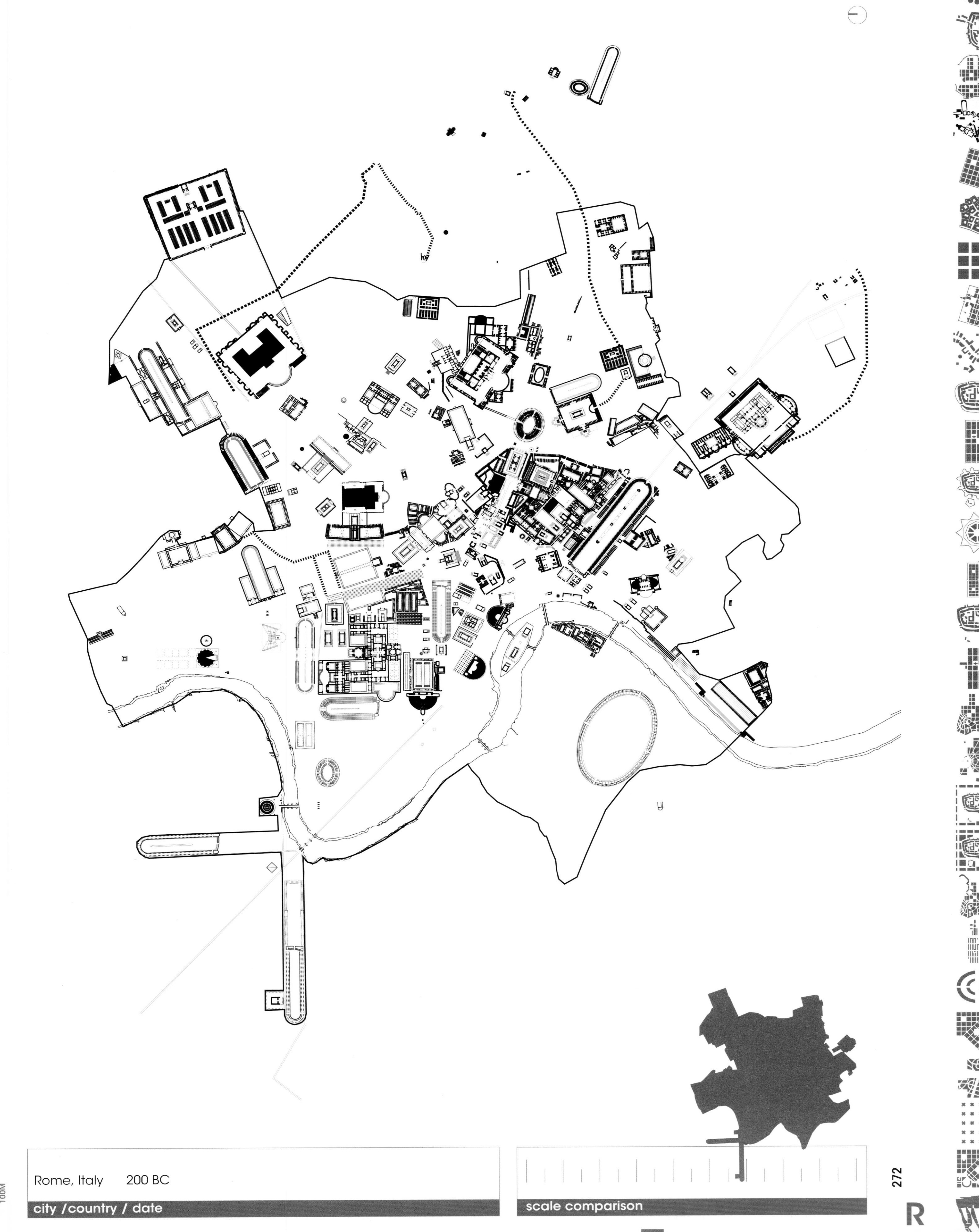
100M
Rome, Italy 200 BC
city / country / date
scale comparison
R

Rome, Italy 1551

city / country / date

scale comparison

100M

city / country / date

Rome, Italy (The Giambattista Nolli Plan) 1748

scale comparison

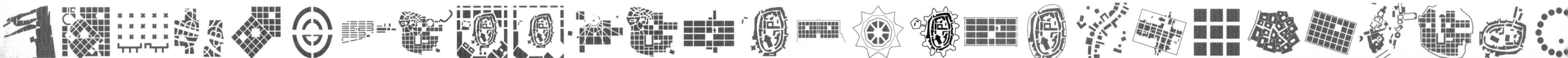

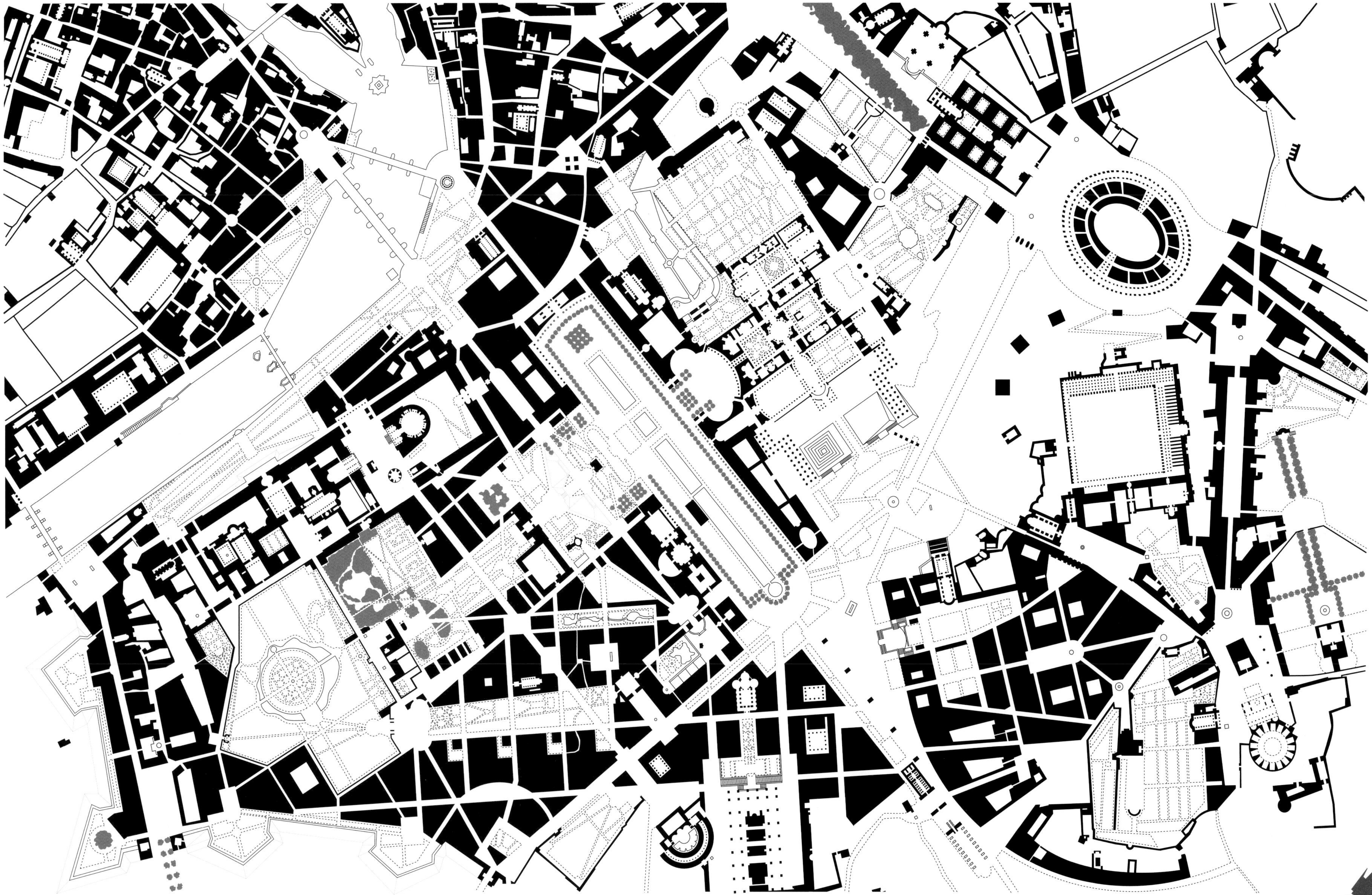

100M

Rome, Italy ("Roma Interrota" proposal by Colin Rowe & Group) 1979

city /country / date

scale comparison

100M

Rothenburg, Germany [1974]

city / country / date

scale comparison

R

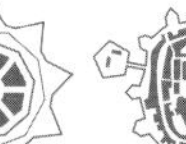
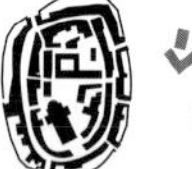
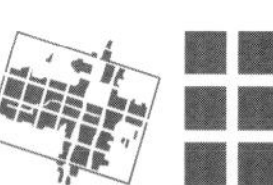
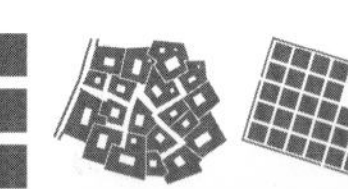

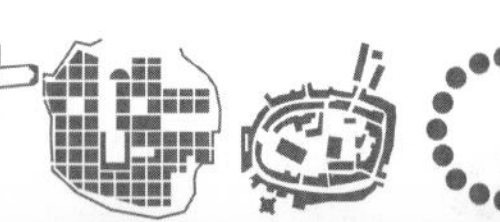

100M

city / country / date

Rotterdam, Kop va Zuid, Netherlands (master-plan by OMA) 1987

scale comparison

100M

city / country / date

Sabaudia, Italy 1940

scale comparison

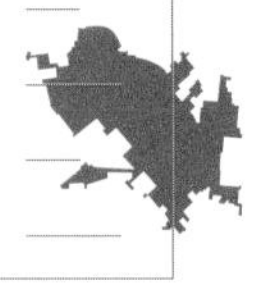

Sabbioneta, Italy 1560

city / country / date

scale comparison

100M

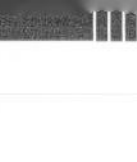

city / country / date

Saint Die, France 1935

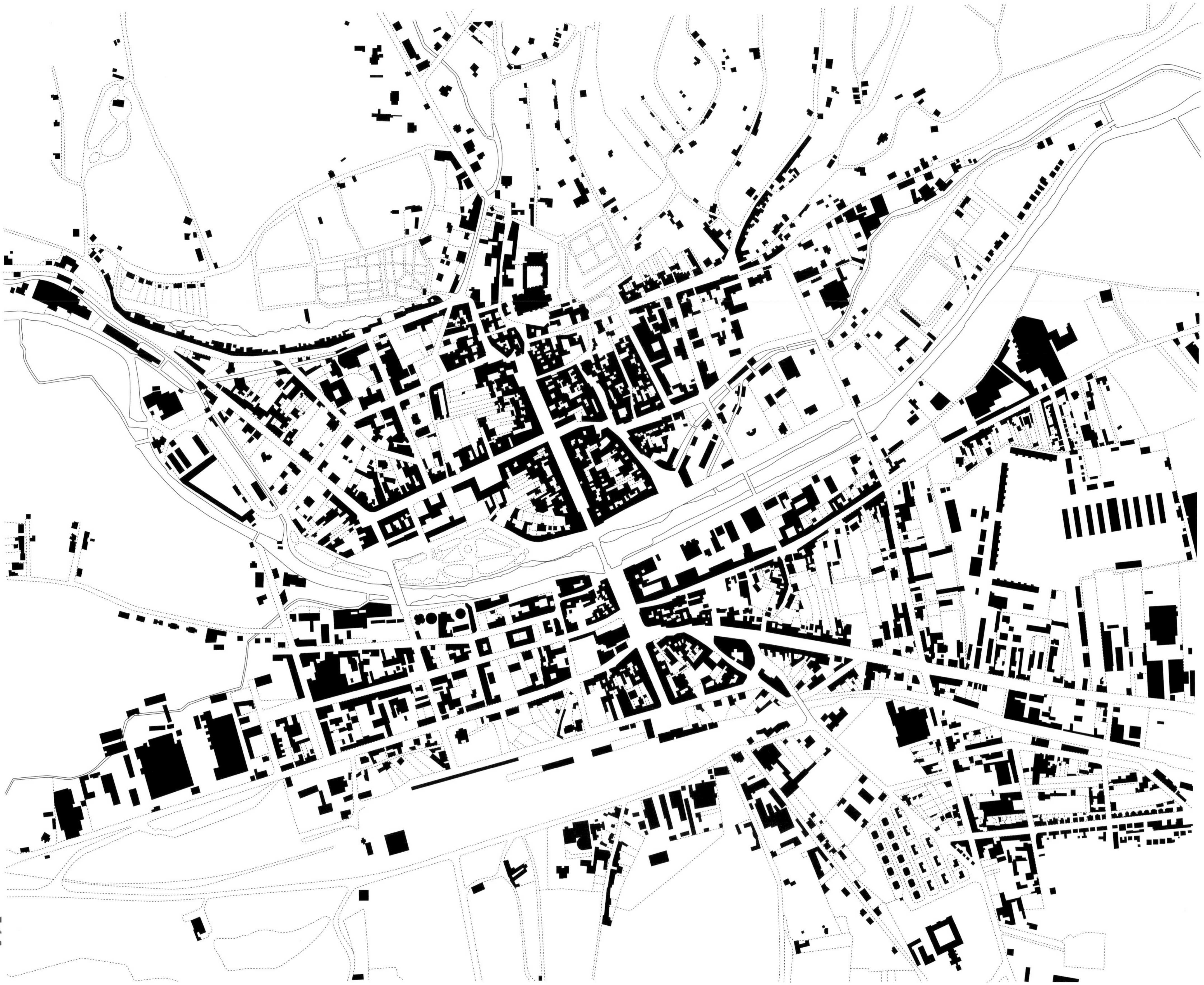

scale comparison

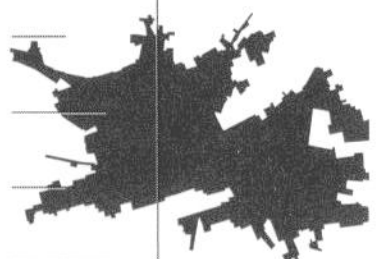

S

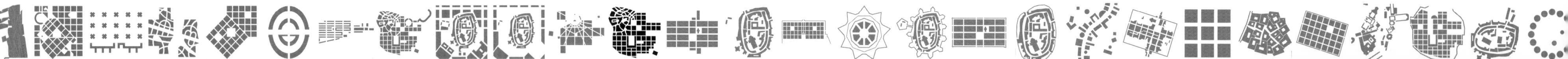

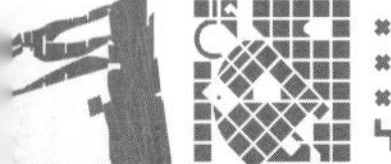

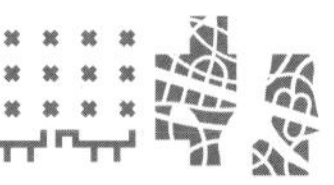

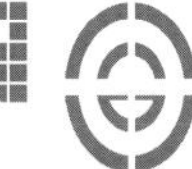

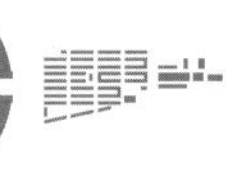

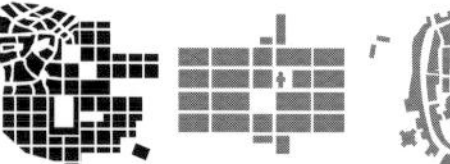

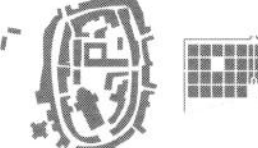

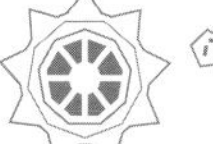

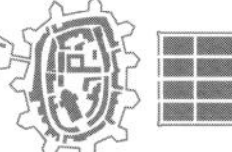

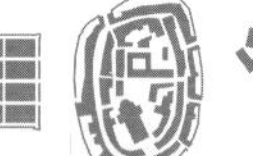

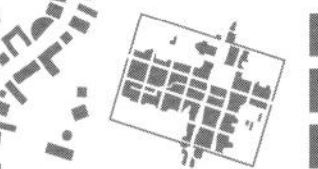

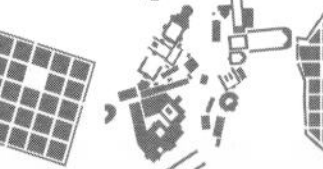

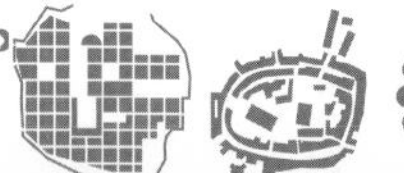

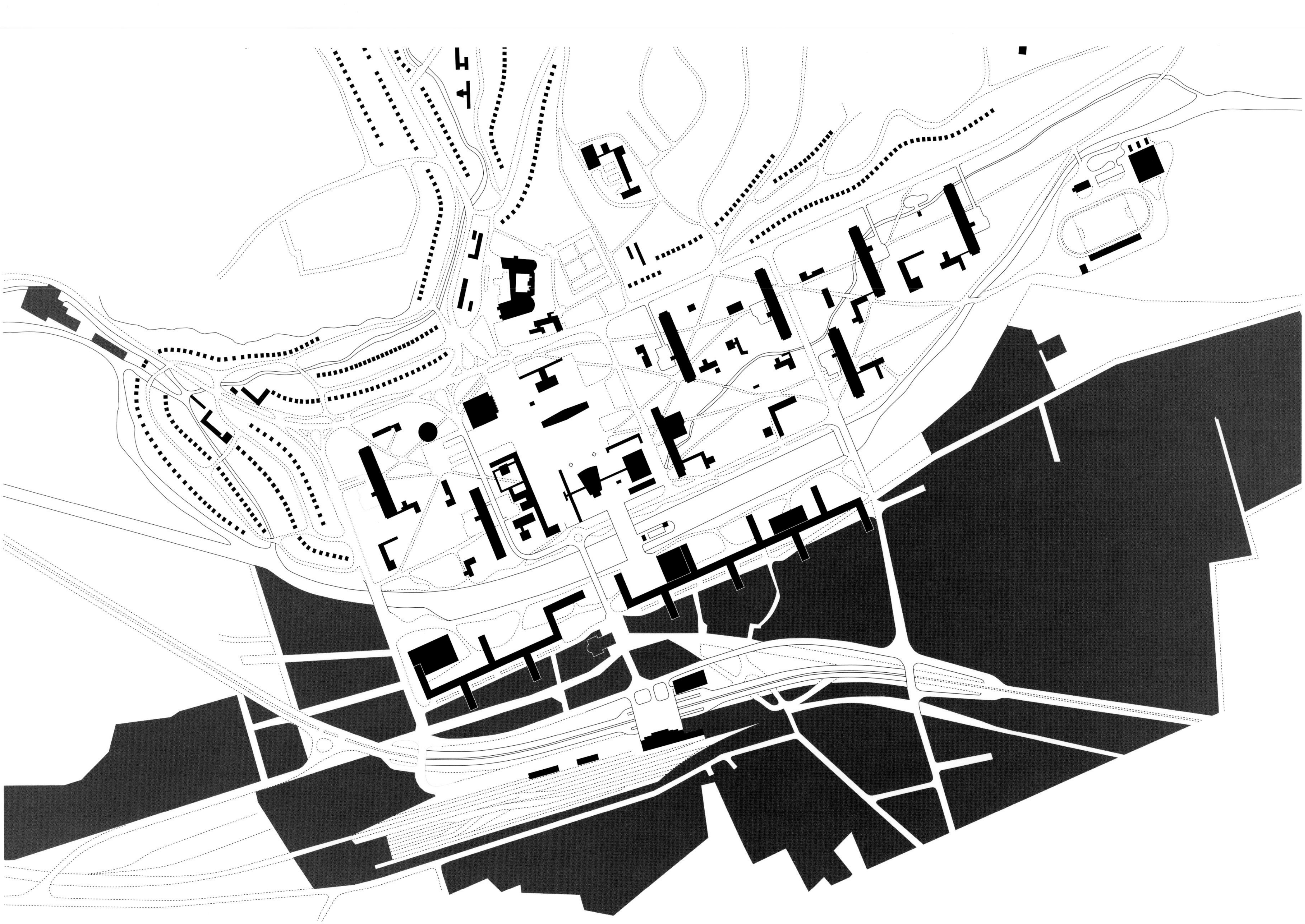

Saint Die, France (proposal by Le Corbusier) 1945

city / country / date

scale comparison

100M

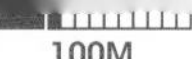

city /country / date

Saint Malo, France 1909

scale comparison

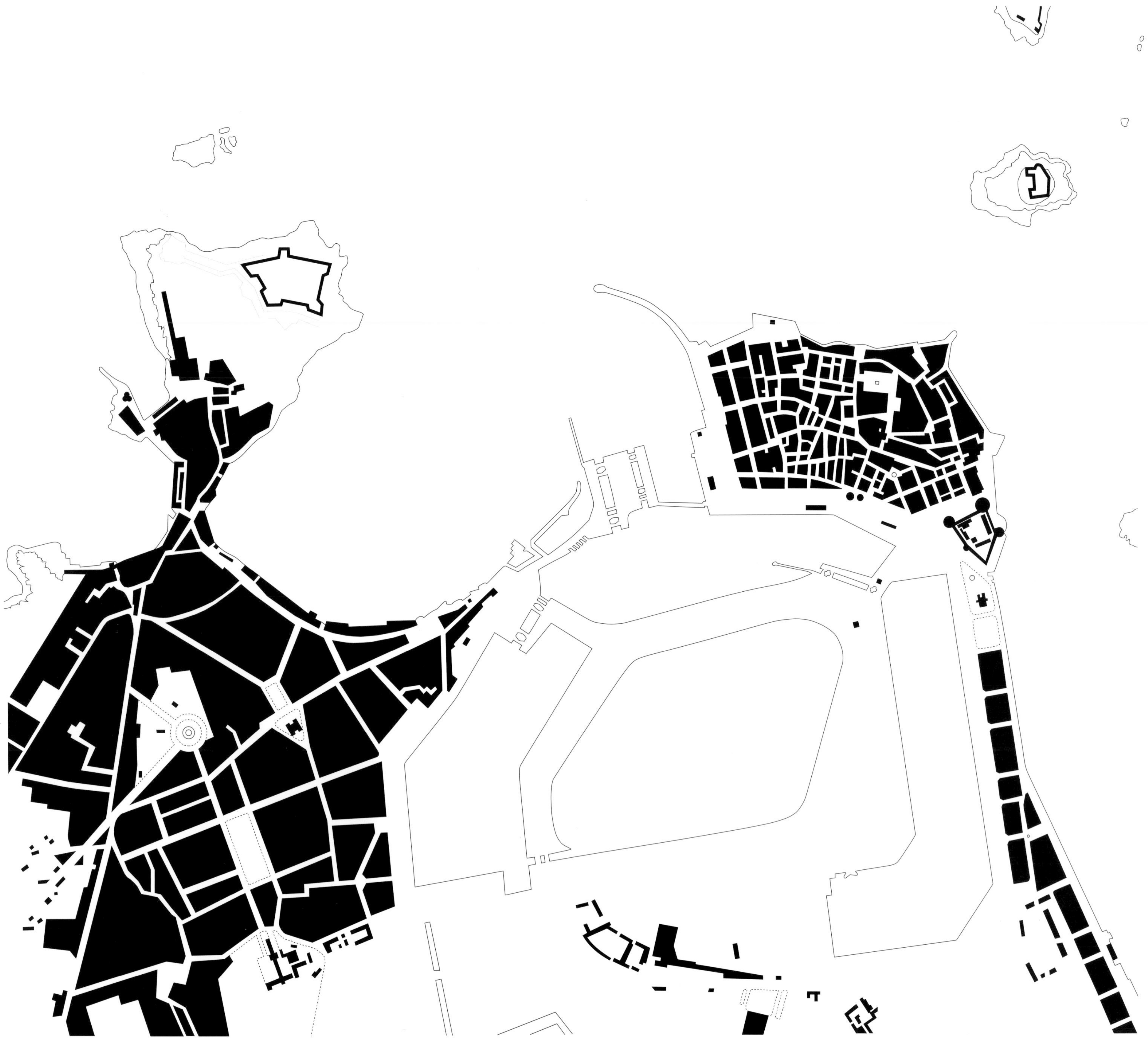

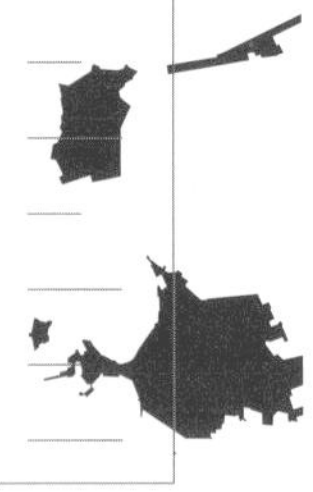

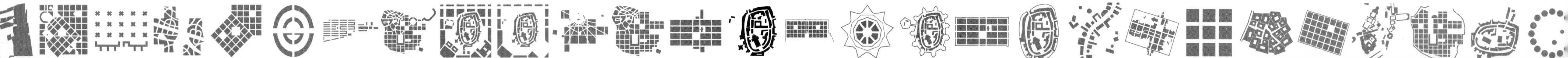

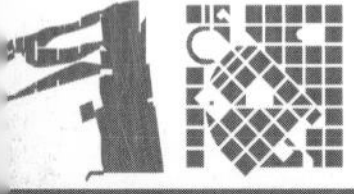

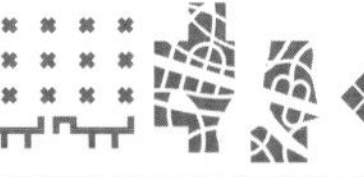

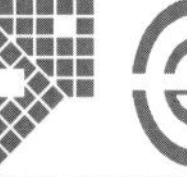

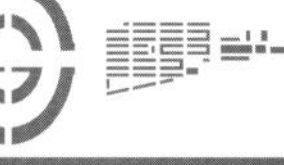

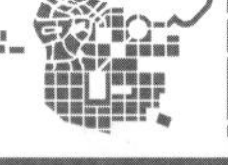

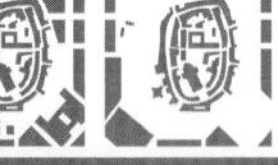

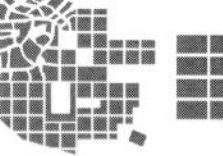

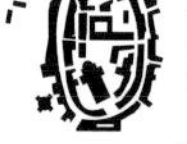

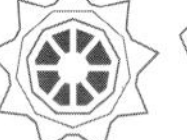

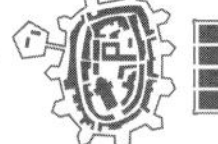

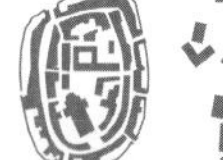

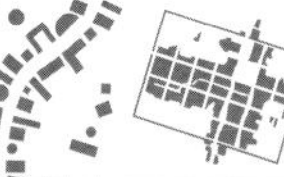

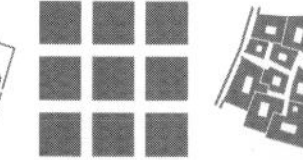

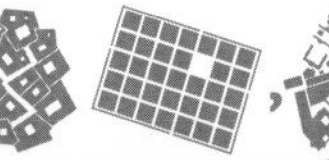

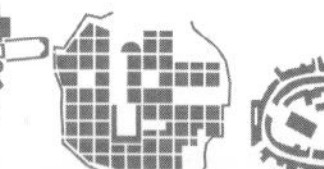

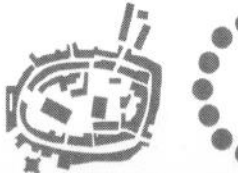

scale comparison

S

city / country / date

Saline de Chaux, France (proposal by Claude-Nicolas Dedoux) 1804

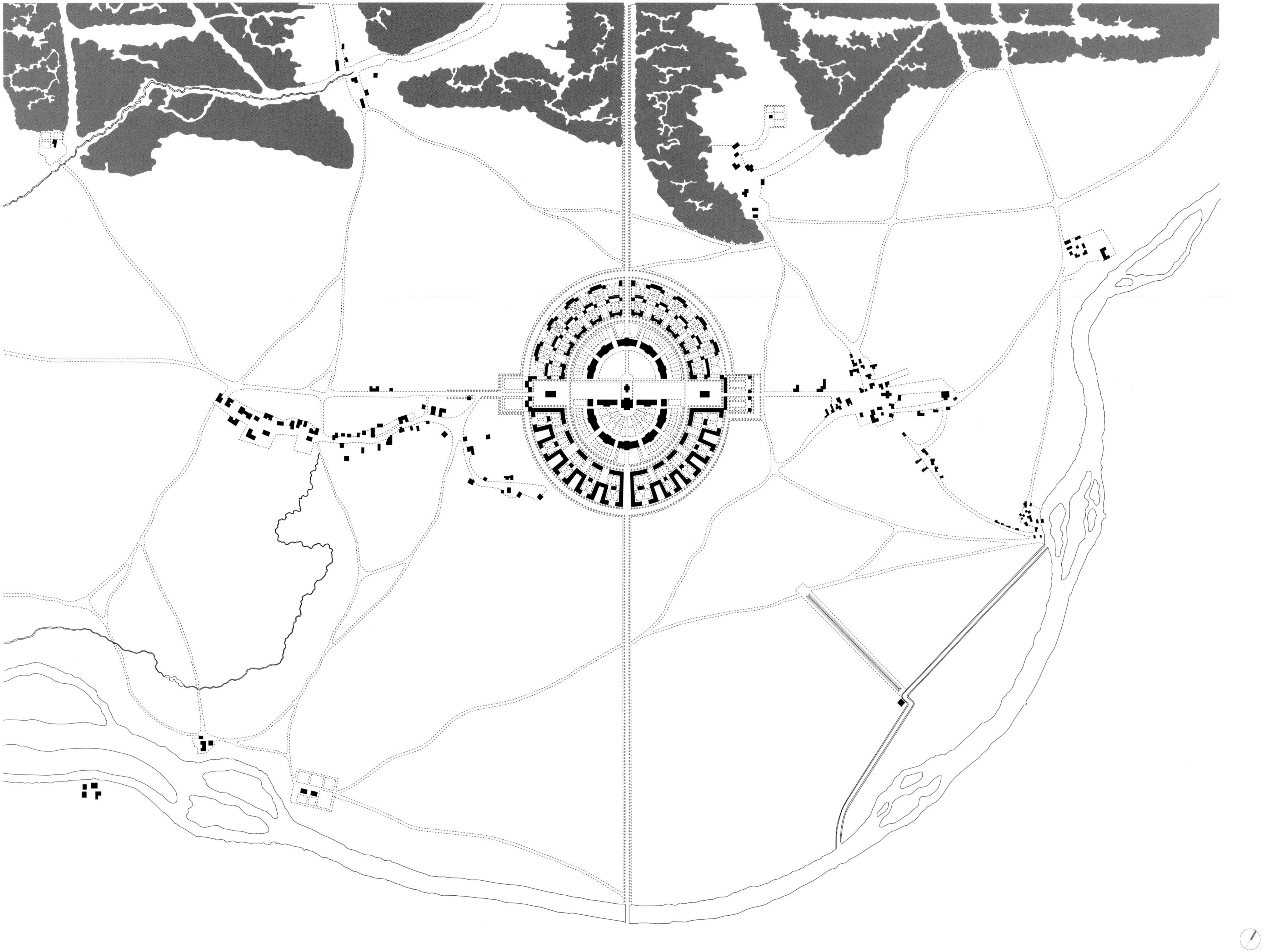

scale comparison

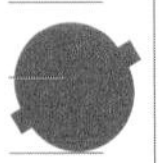

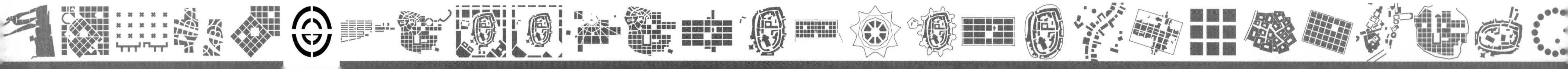

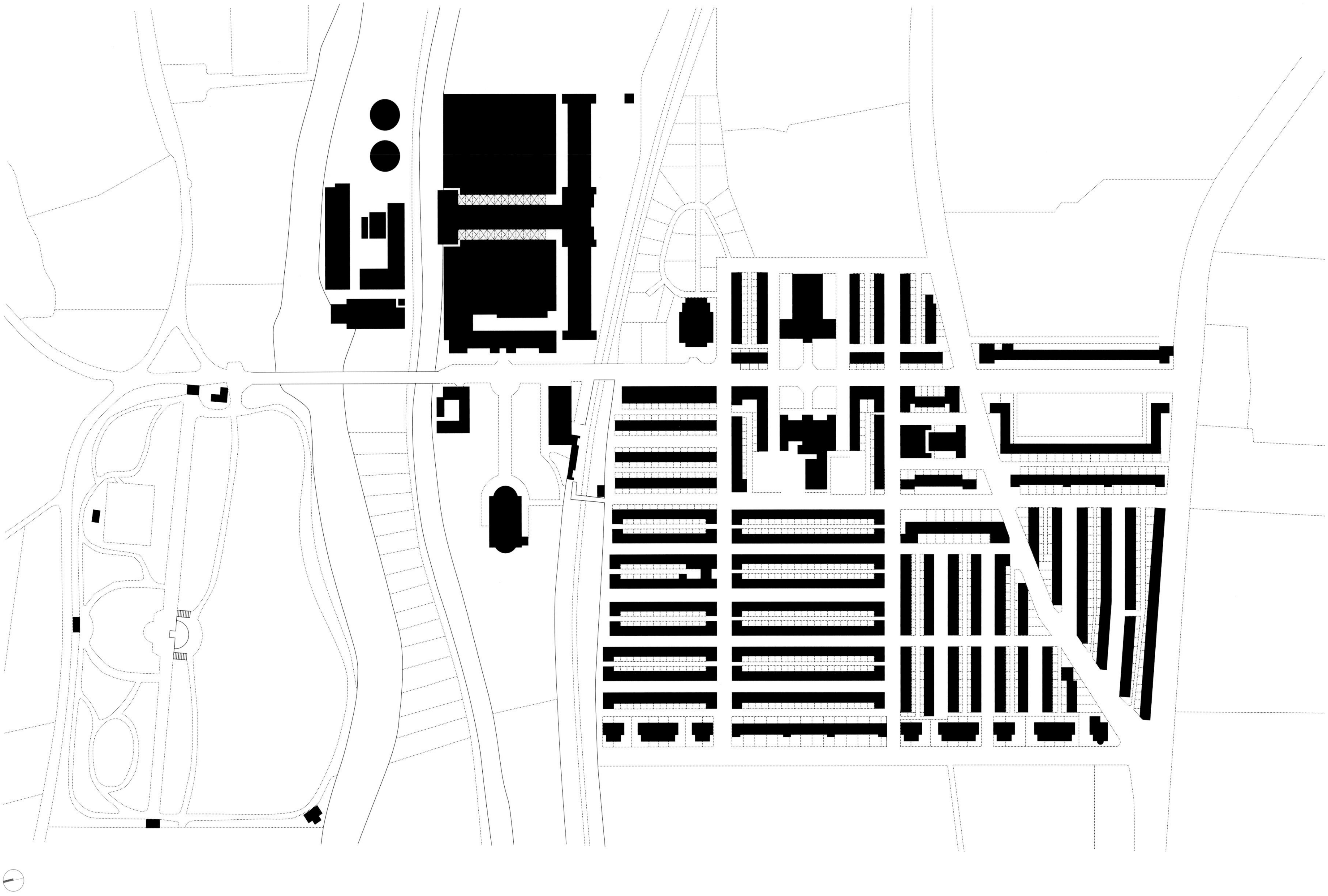

Saltaire, England 1851

city /country / date

scale comparison

100M

city / country / date

San Antonio, TX, USA (Plan of the Pueblo of San Fernando de Béxar) 1777

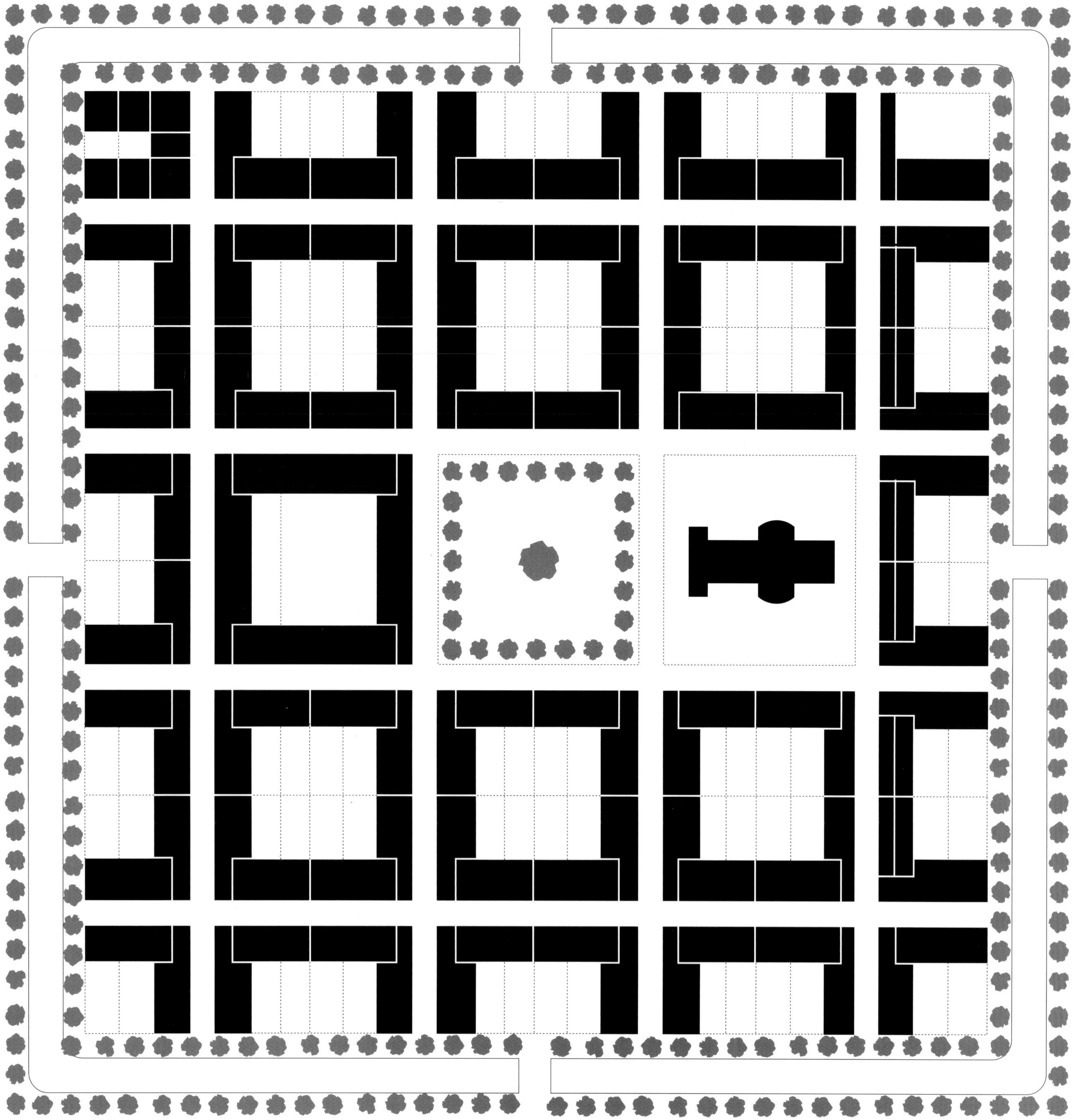

scale comparison

S

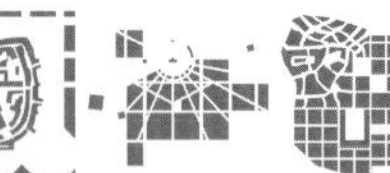
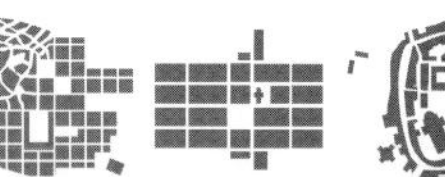
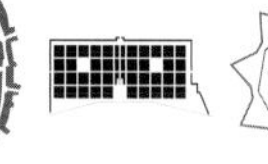

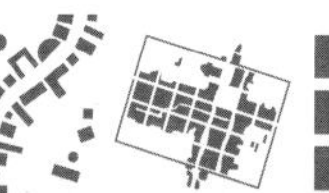
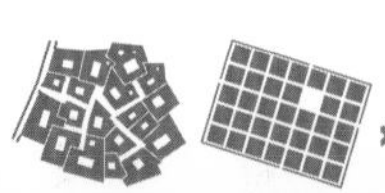

100M

San Gimignano, Italy 1990

city / country / date

scale comparison

100M

city / country / date

San Giovanni Valdarno, Italy 1800

scale comparison

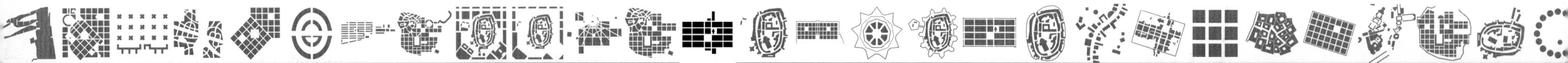

S

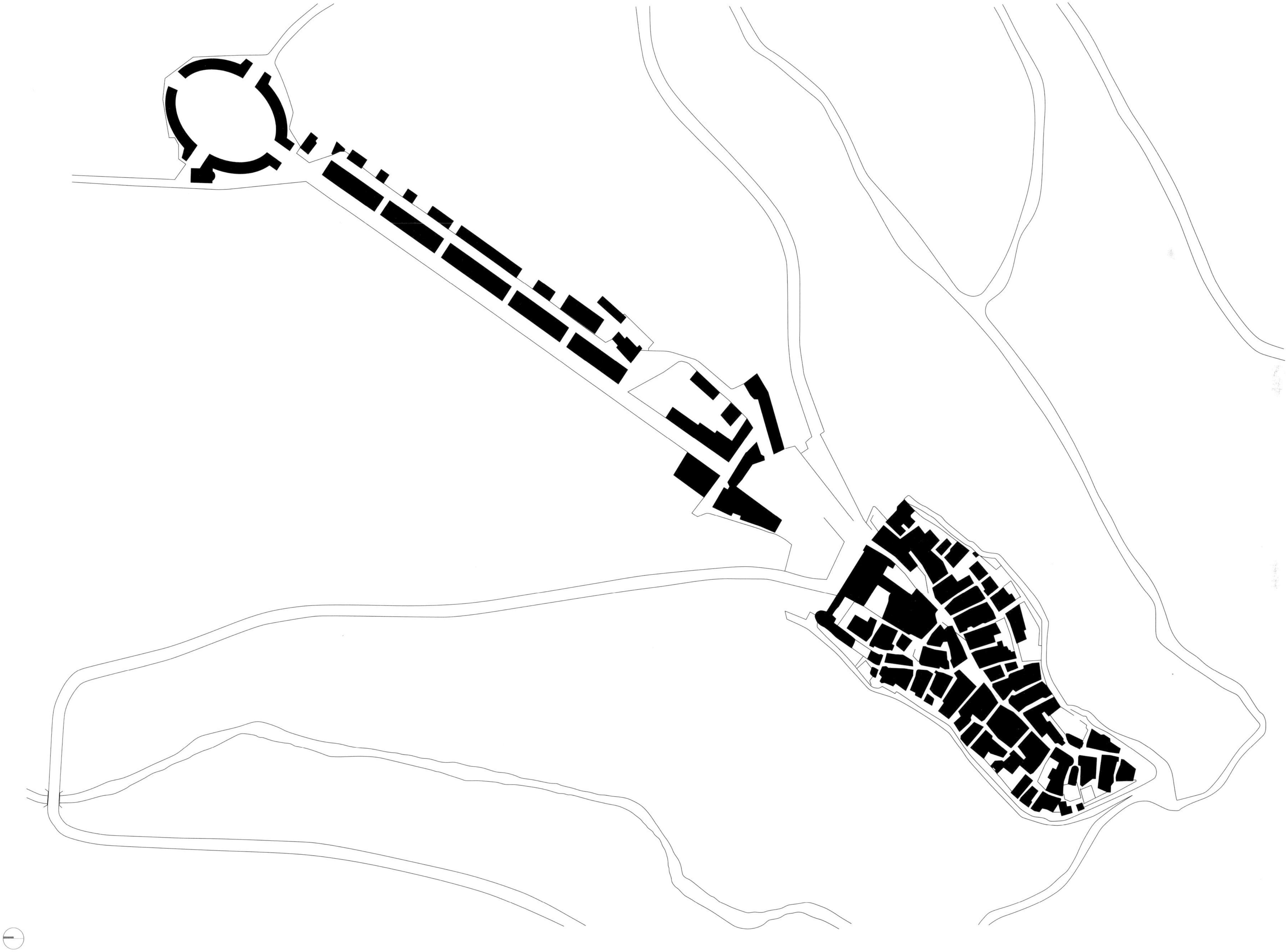

San Gregorio da Sassola, Italy 1970

city / country / date

scale comparison

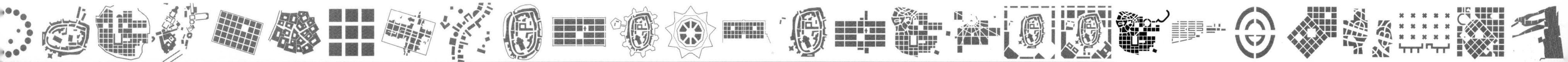

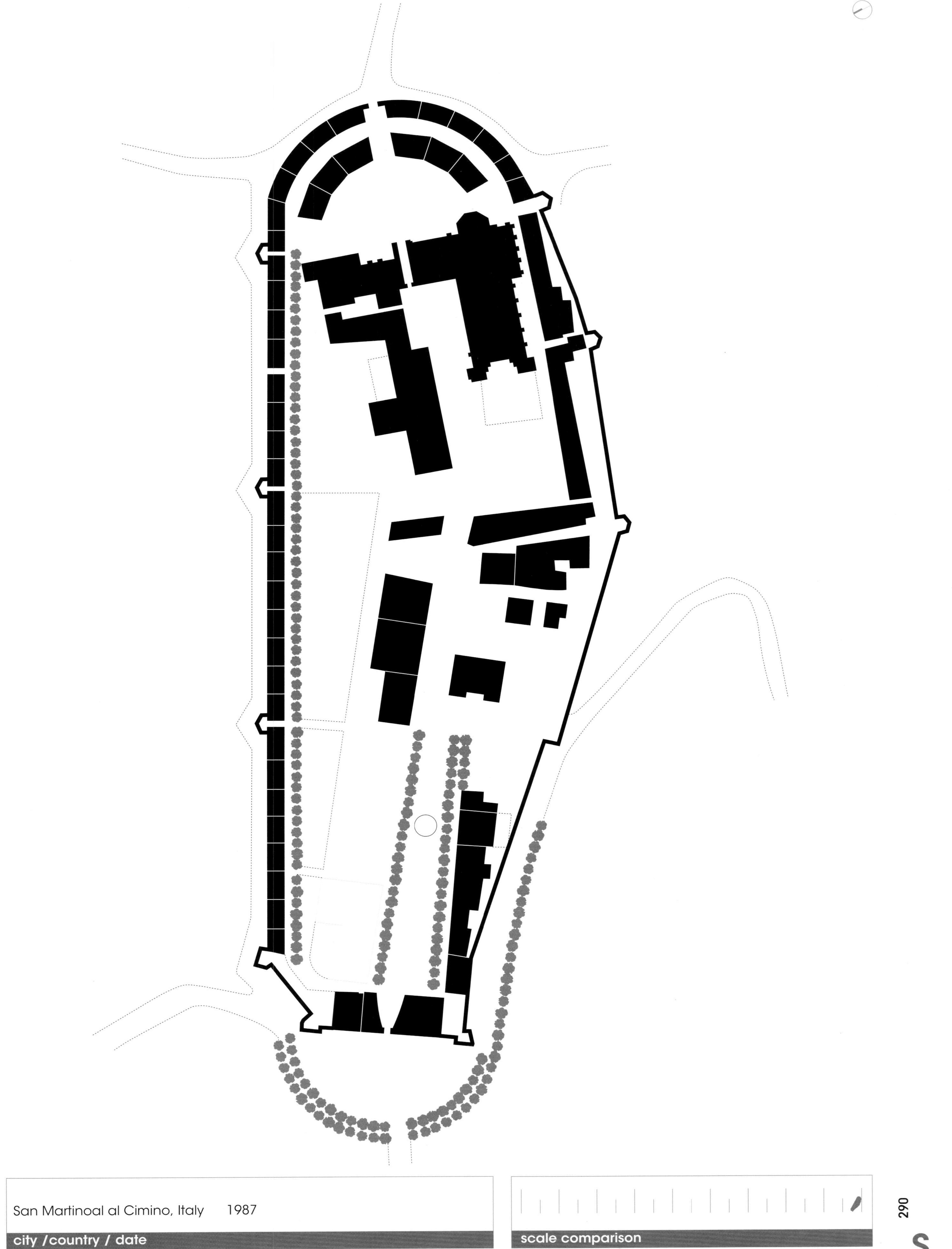
100M
San Martinoal al Cimino, Italy
1987
city /country / date
scale comparison
S

100M

city /country / date

San Miniato, Italy 1963

scale comparison

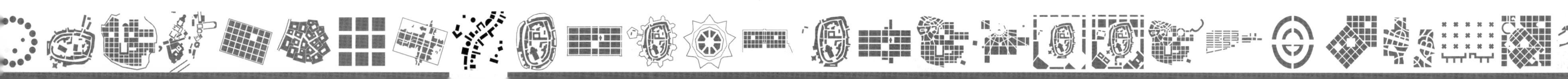

100M

city / country / date

Seaside, FL, USA 1984

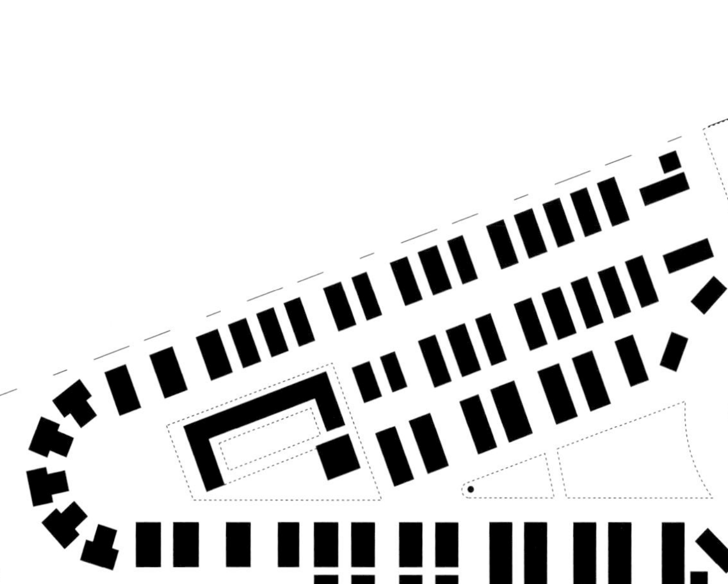

scale comparison

Selinus, Italy 628 BC

city / country / date

scale comparison

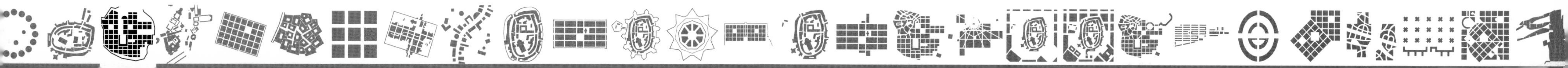

city / country / date
Seville, Spain 1906
scale comparison

Siena, Italy 1909

city /country / date

scale comparison

city / country / date

Sroda Slaska, Poland 1860

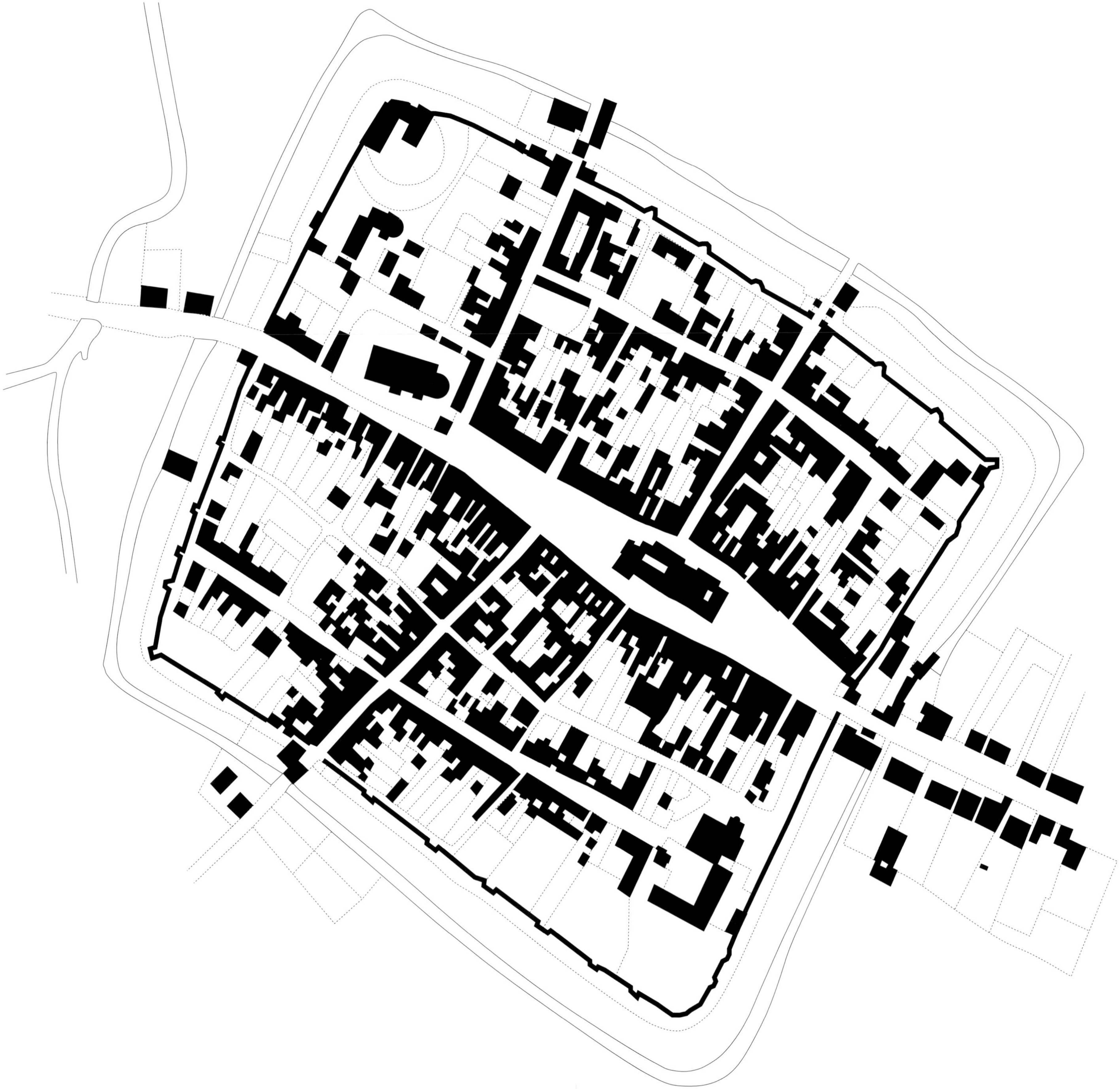

scale comparison

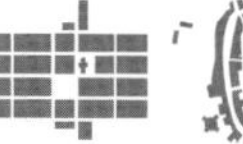

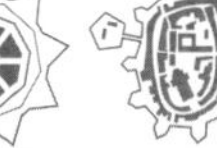

100M

Stanislawów, Ukraine 1792

city /country / date

scale comparison

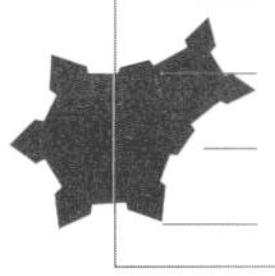

S

100M

city / country / date

Stockholm, Sweden 1838

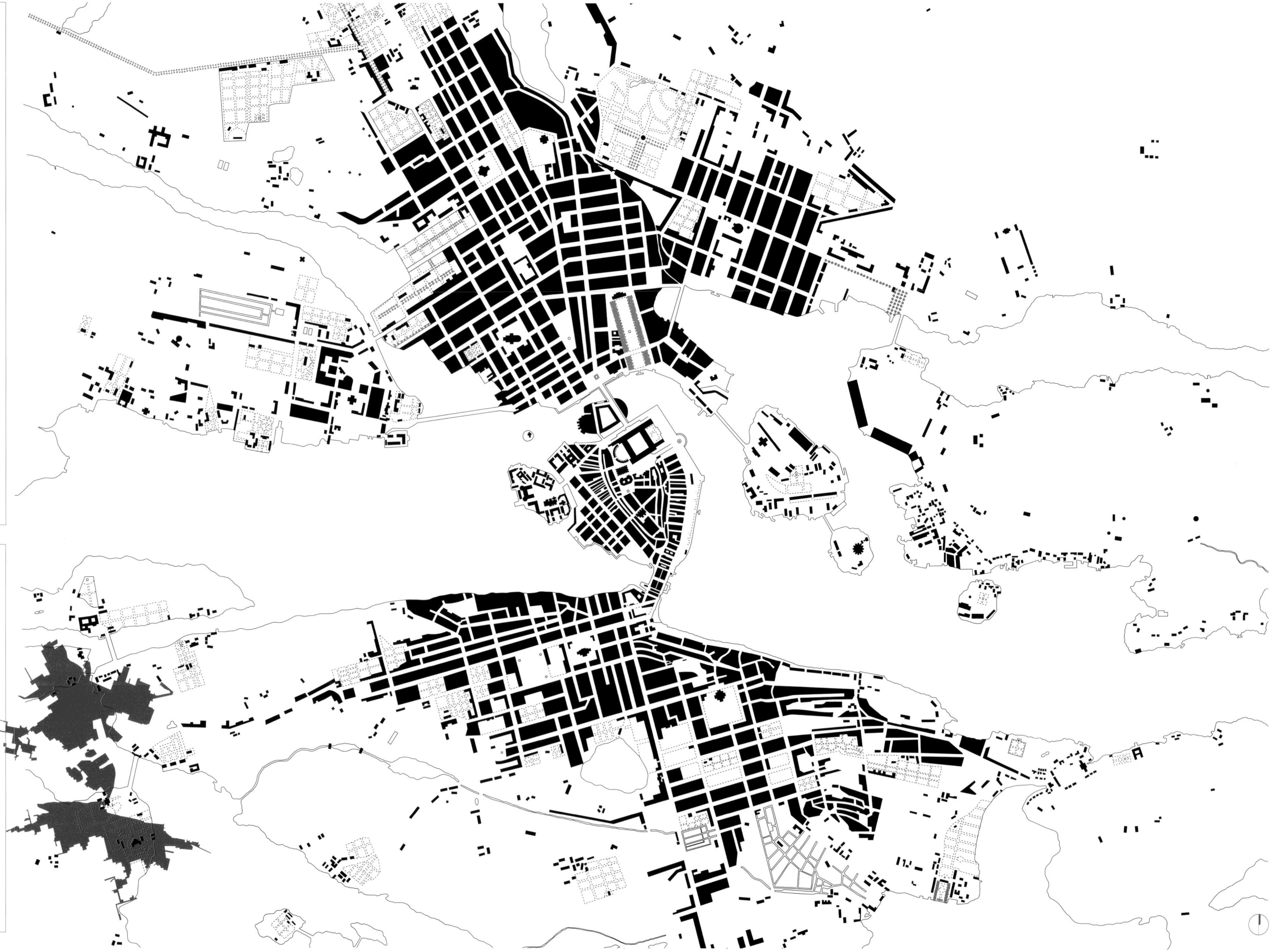

scale comparison

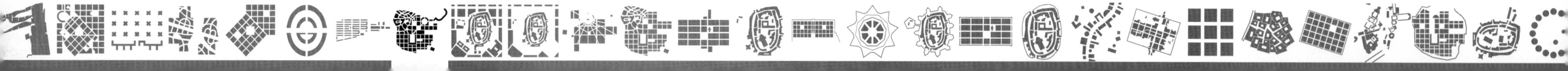

Stockholm, Sweden (proposal for the Royal Chancellery by Gunnar Asplund) 1922

city /country / date

scale comparison

100M

city / country / date

Stuttgart, Germany 1902

scale comparison

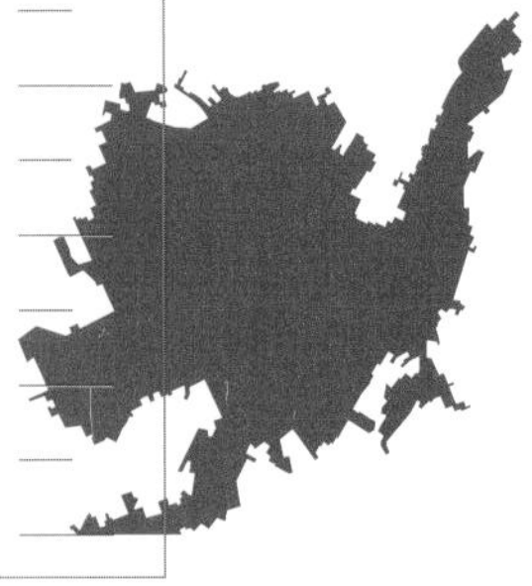

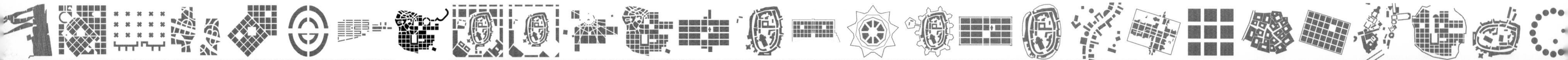

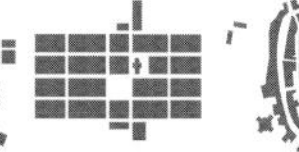
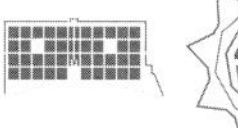

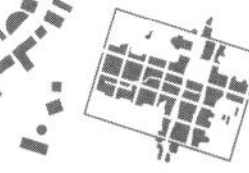
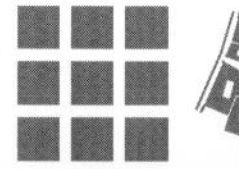
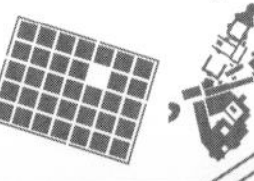

100M

city /country / date

Tanger, Morocco 1909

scale comparison

100M

city / country / date

Taranto, Italy 1940

scale comparison

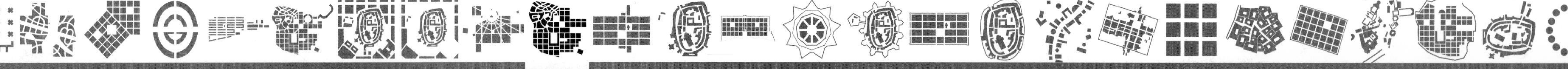

Timgad, Algeria 100

city /country / date

scale comparison

100M

city / country / date

Turin, Italy 28, 1590, 1620, & 1670

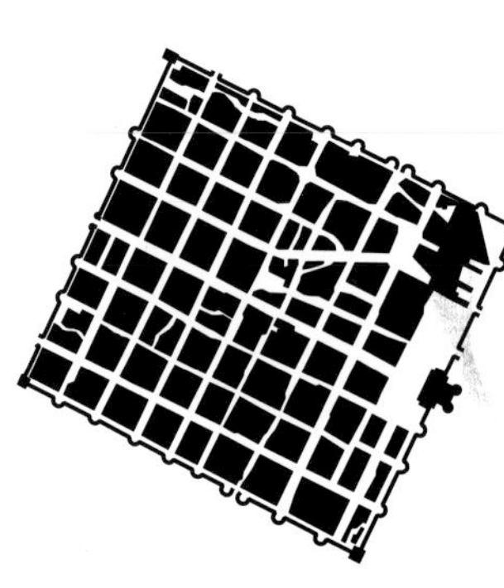

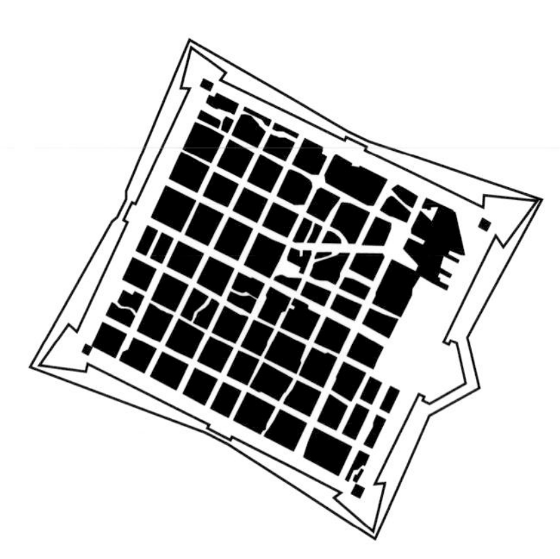

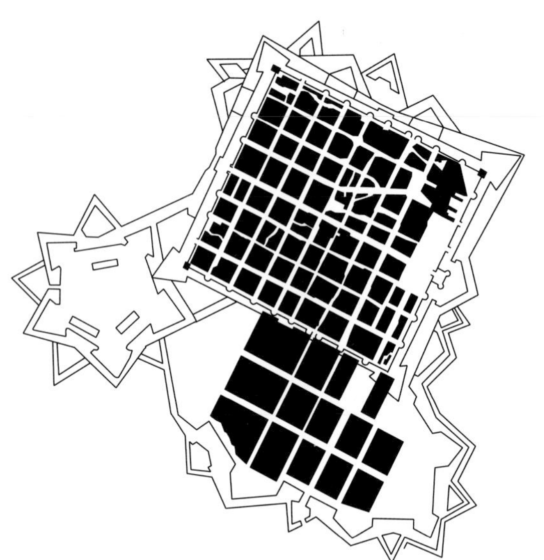

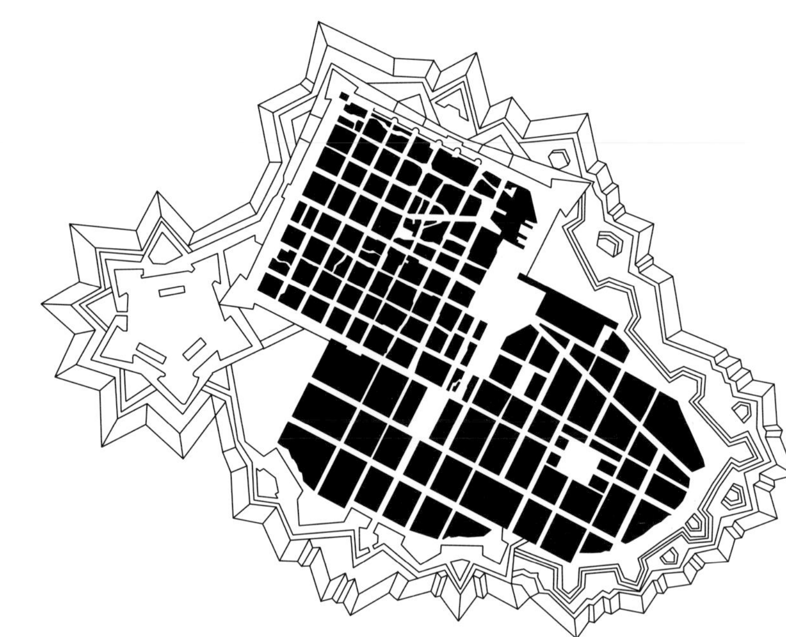

scale comparison

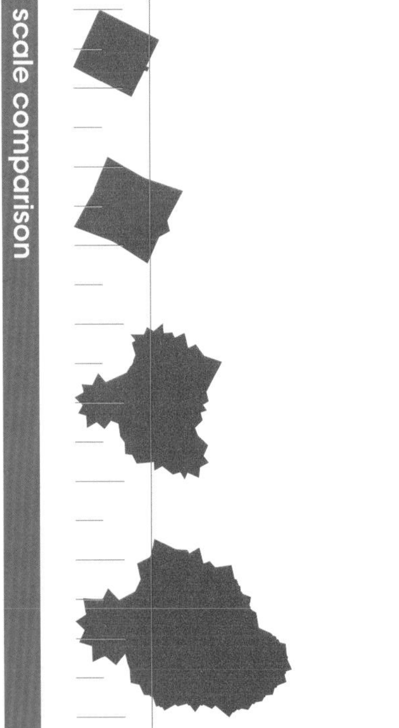

             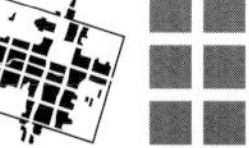 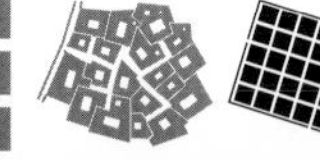   

100M

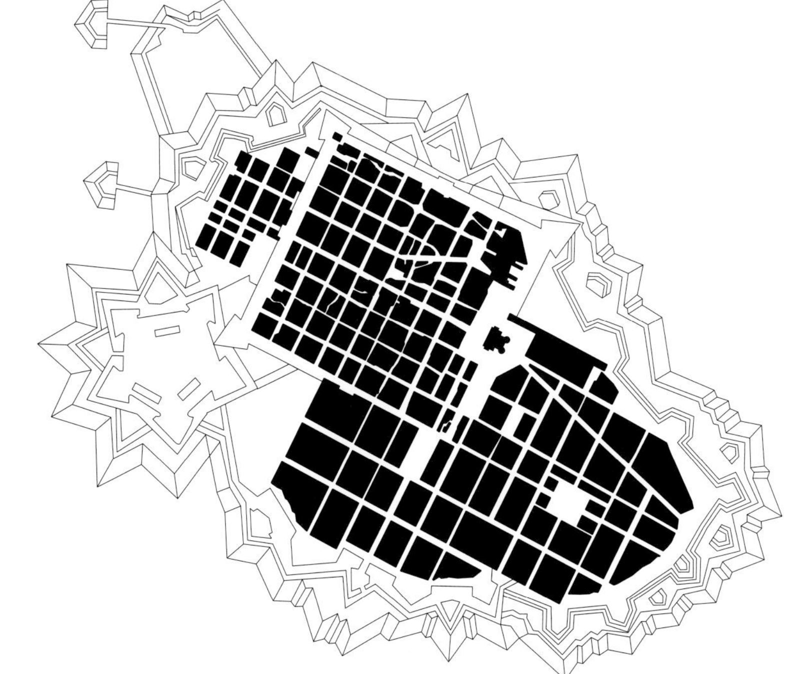

city / country / date

Turin, Italy 1720 & 1914

scale comparison

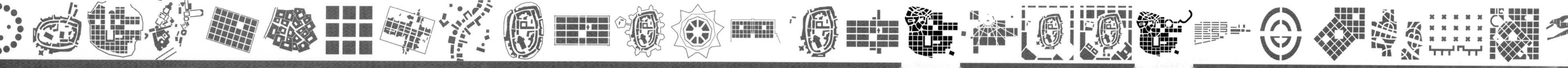

100M
city / country / date
Tripoli, Libya
1929
scale comparison

Urbino, Italy 1963

city / country / date

scale comparison

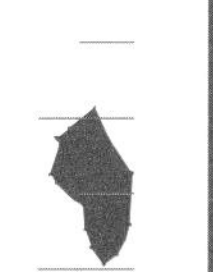

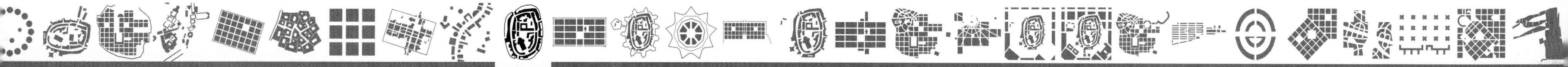

100M

city / country / date

Vallette, Malta 1963

scale comparison

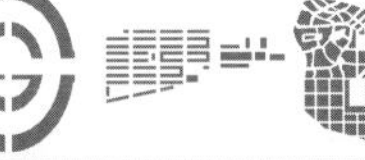

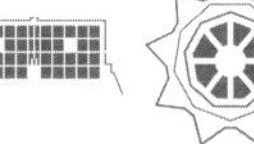

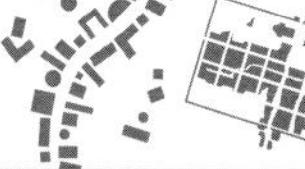

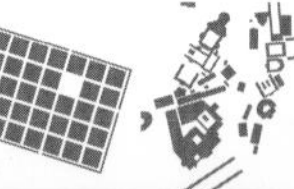
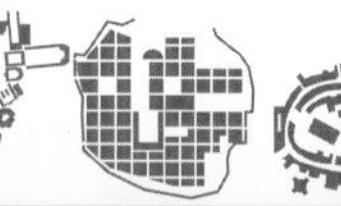

100M
Vaux-le-Vicomte, France 1990
city / country / date
scale comparison

Venice, Italy 1950
city / country / date
scale comparison
100M

100M

Venzone, Italy 1255

scale comparison

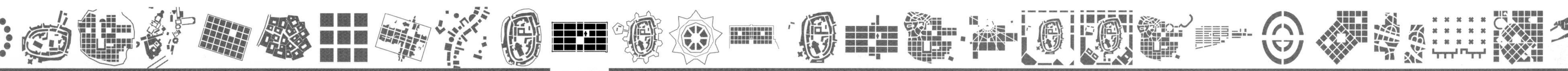

city / country / date

Verona, *municipium*, Italy 49 BC

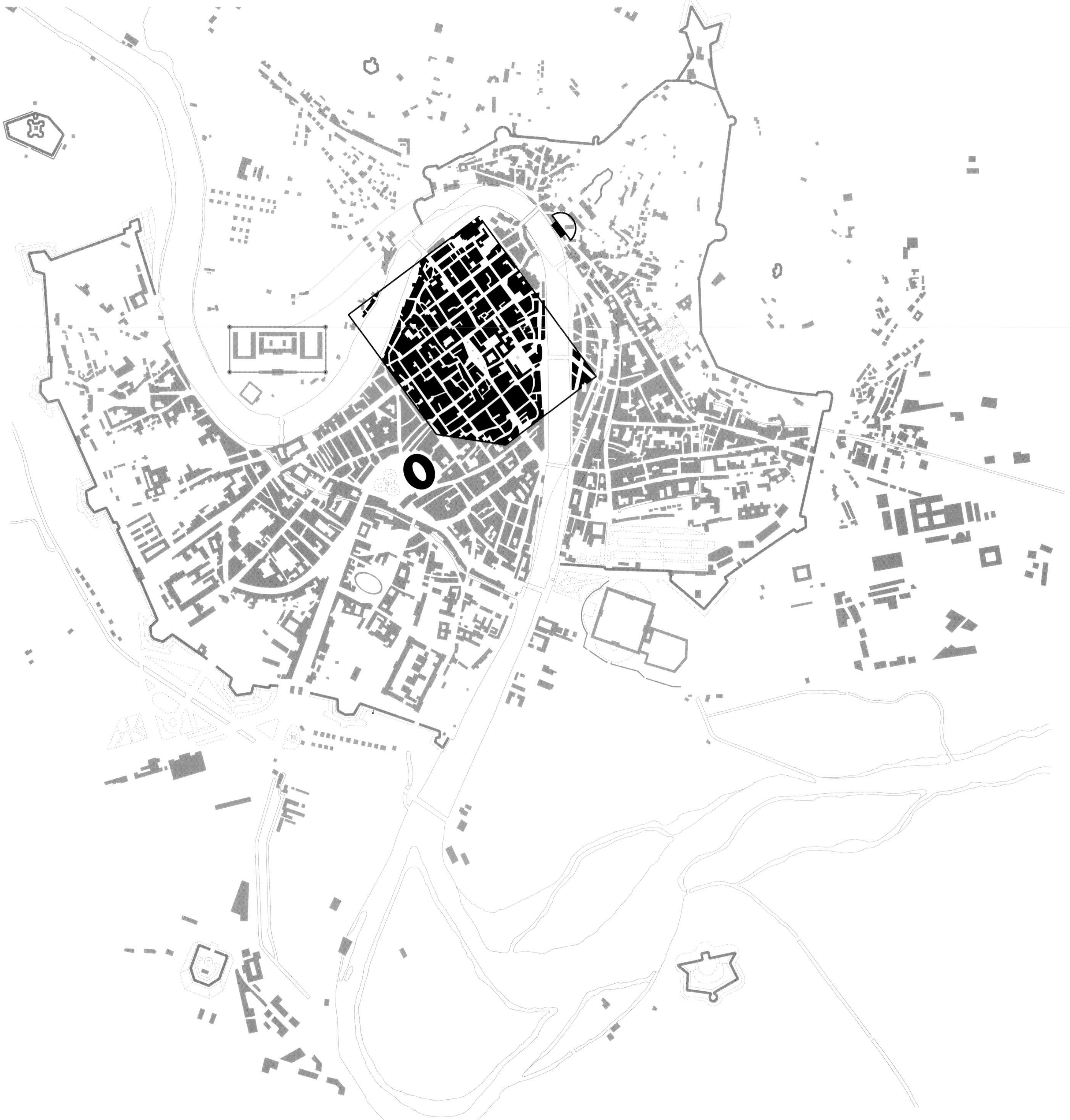

scale comparison

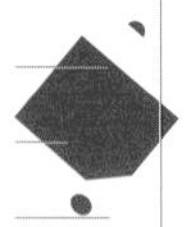

100M

Verona, Italy 1925

city / country / date

scale comparison

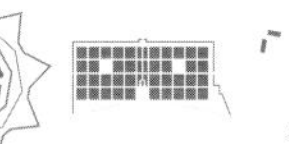

Versailles, France 1746 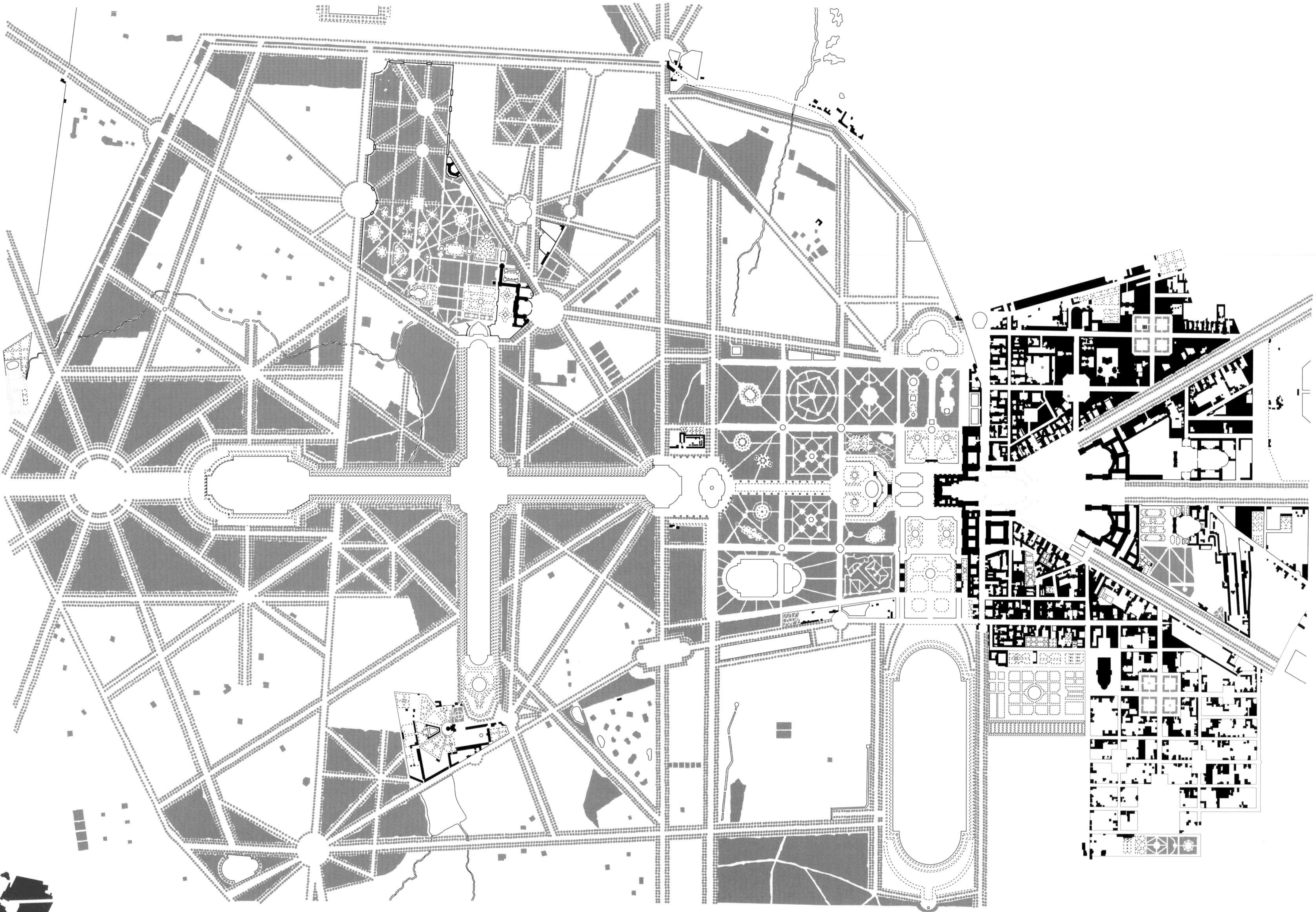
city / country / date
scale comparison

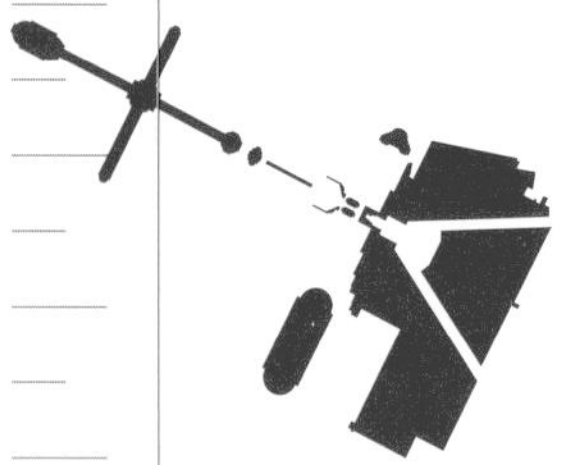

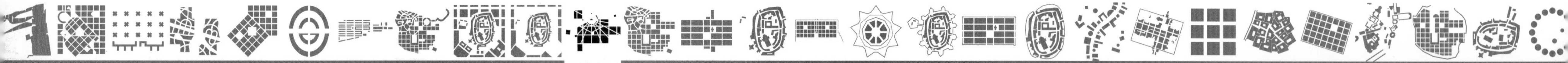

100M

Vienna, Austria 1547

city /country / date

scale comparison

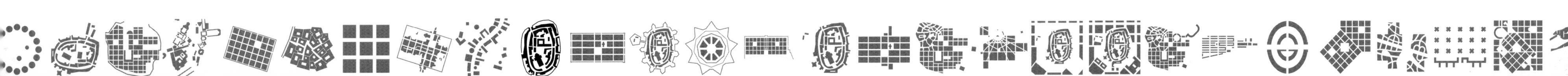

V

100M

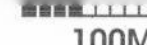

city / country / date

Vienna, Austria 1833

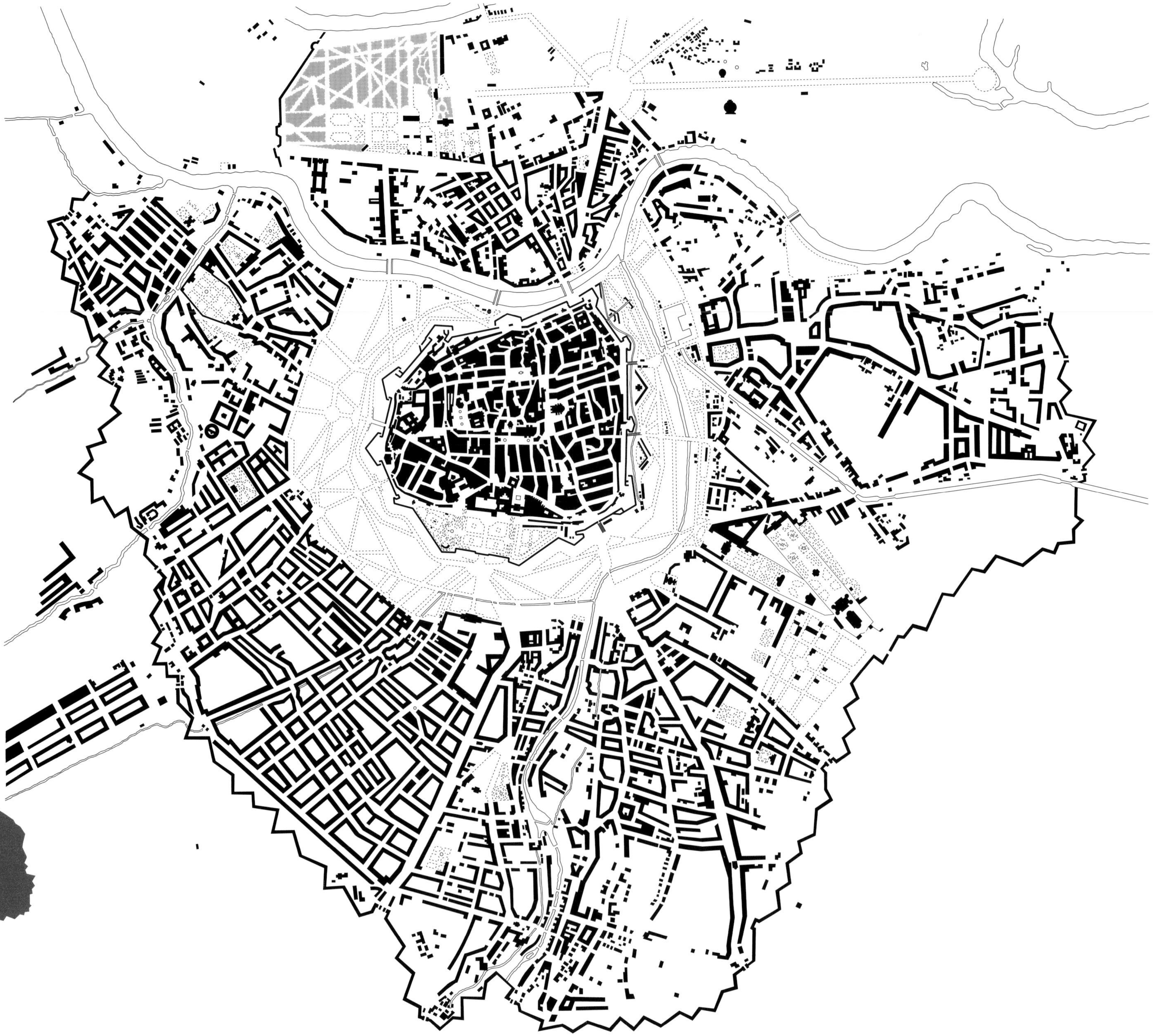

scale comparison

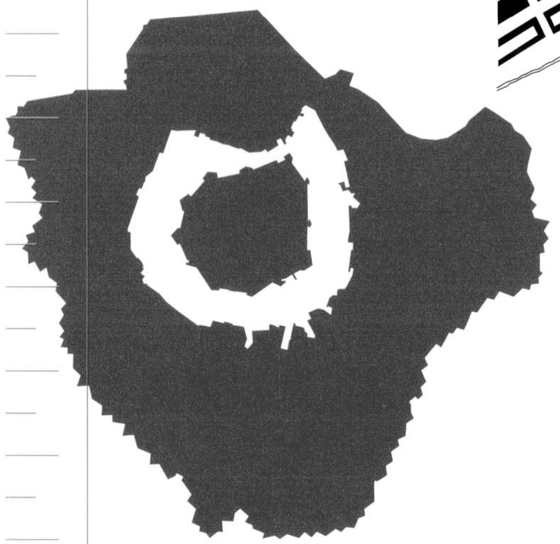

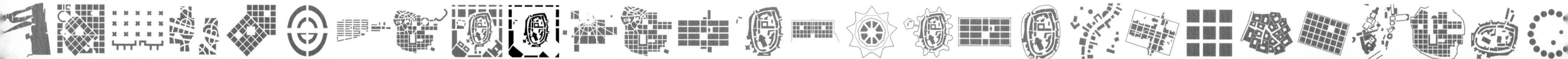

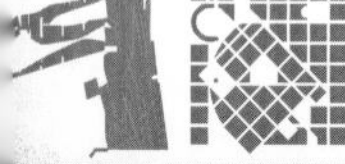

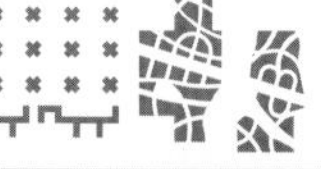

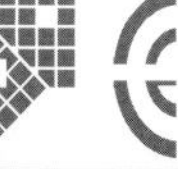

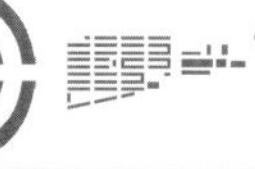

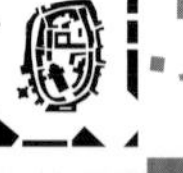

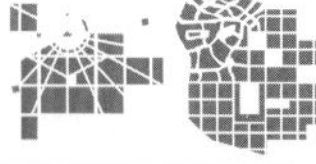

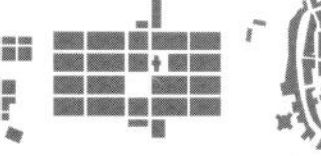

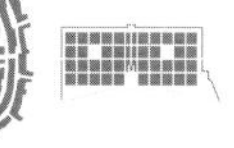

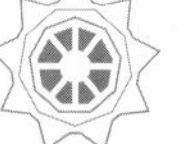

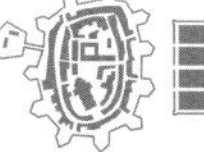

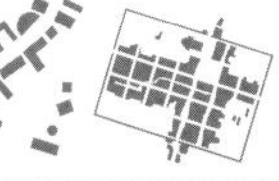

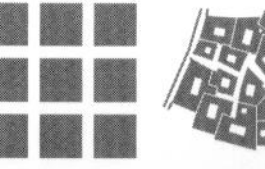

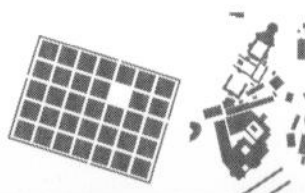

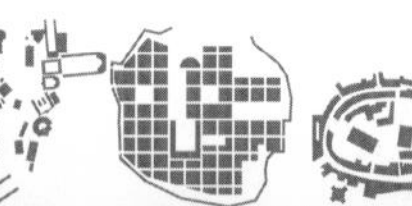

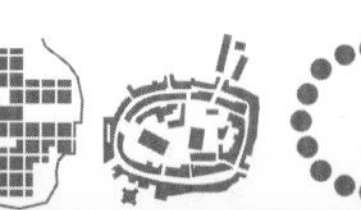

100M

Vienna, Hofburg, Austria 1914

city / country / date

scale comparison

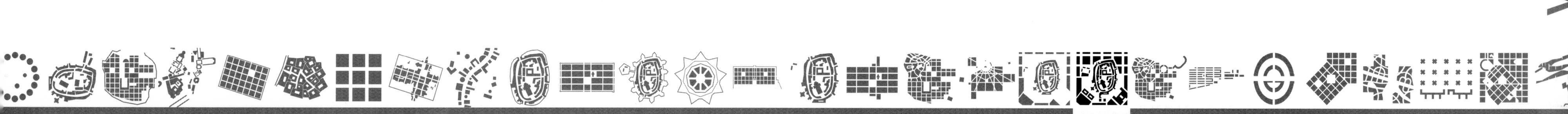

100M

city / country / date

Warsaw, Poland 1831

scale comparison

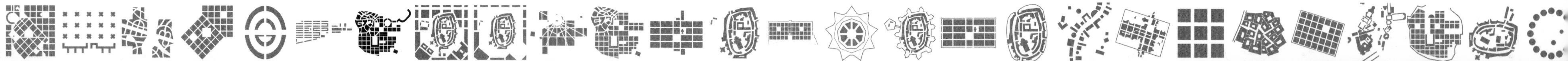

scale comparison
Washington D.C., USA (proposal by L'Enfant) 1791
city /country / date
100M
W

100M

city / country / date

Wiesbaden, Germany 1896

scale comparison

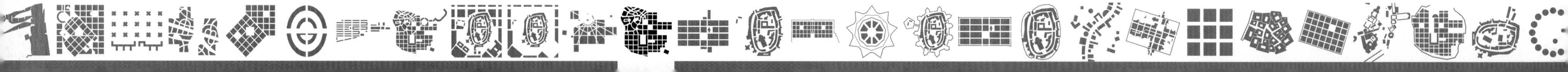

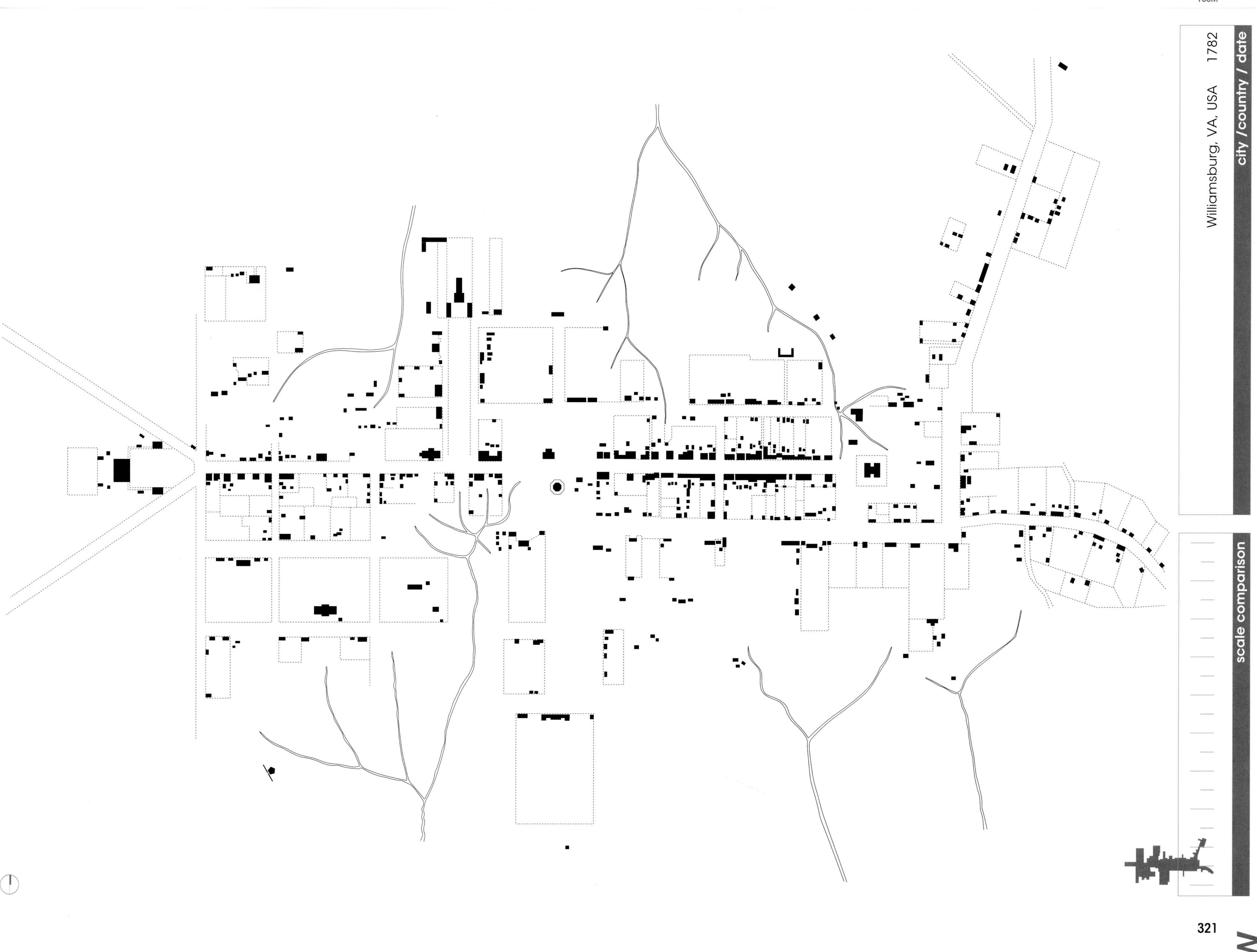
100M
Williamsburg, VA, USA 1782
city /country / date
scale comparison

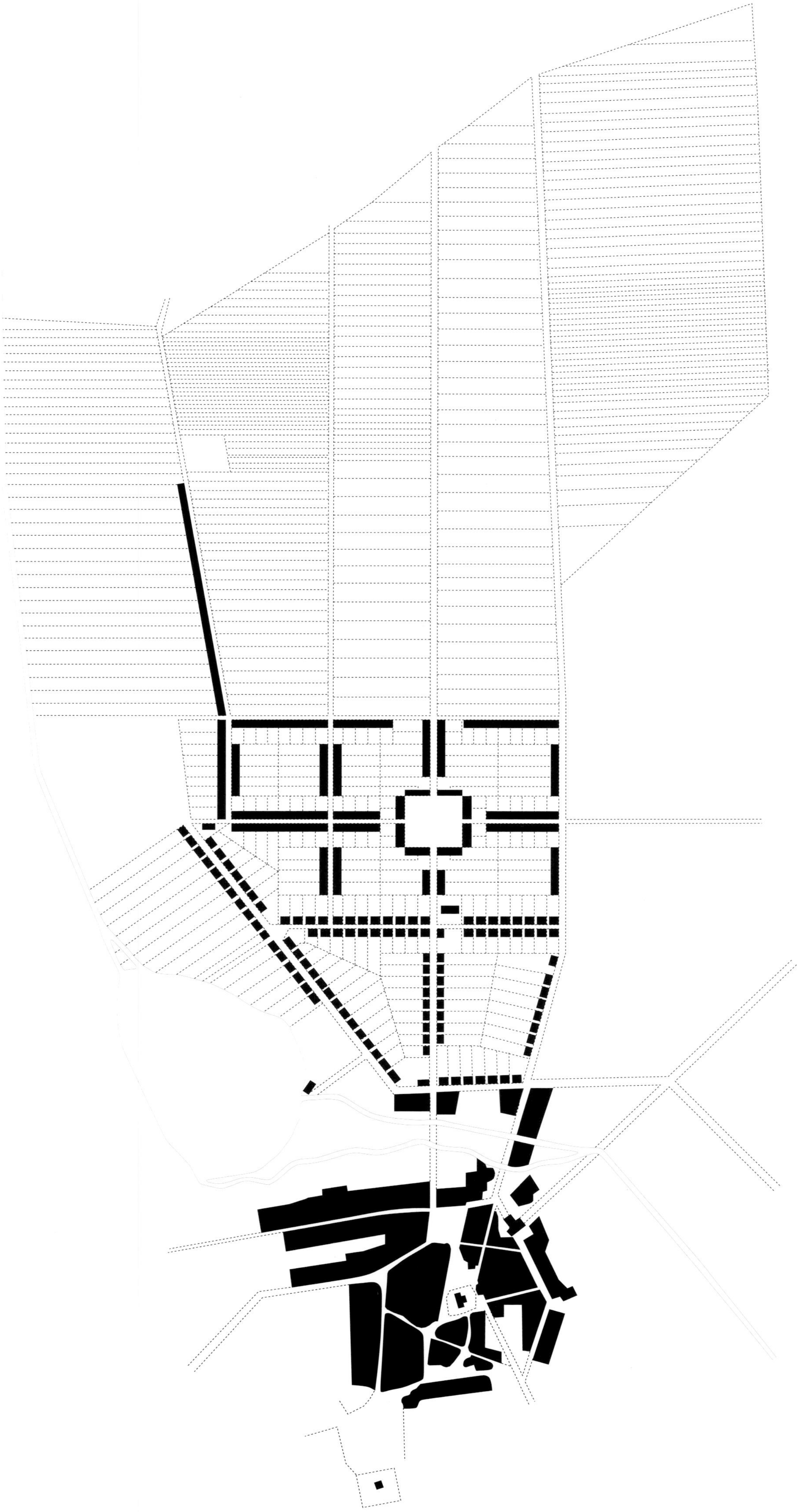

100M

city /country / date

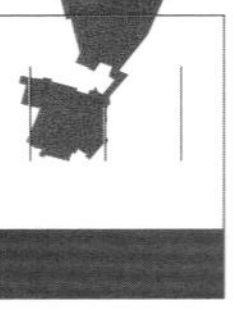

Zgierz, Russia 1821

scale comparison

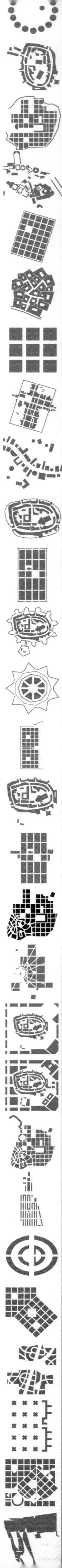

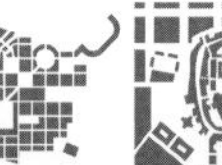

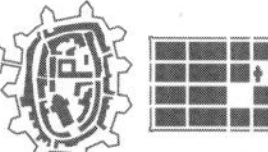

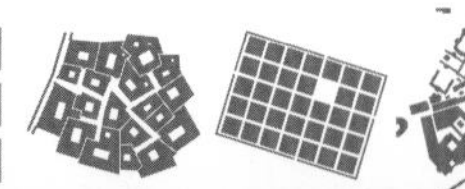

100M

Zürich, Switzerland 1907

city / country / date

scale comparison

N

Typological Icons Representing City Makeup

While researching and constructing the 1,000-plus city plans, I saw recurring series of patterns of various conditions. I observed that there were four major headings under which the city plans, or typologies, fell: urban forms, urban conditions, urban assemblages, and urban generators.

Using these four major groups, I created a matrix representing the city fabrics and, similar to the icons representing the historic periods, icons for the typologies representing city makeup. The following chart shows the breakdown of the fabrics and provides definitions and examples for each icon. The city plans in this section used to represent the examples are all drawn at the same scale for comparison.

It is important to note that these city makeup typologies do not represent everything that a city was or will be made up of. This is simply an exercise in clearly defining what makes up a city and by no means is this the final word.

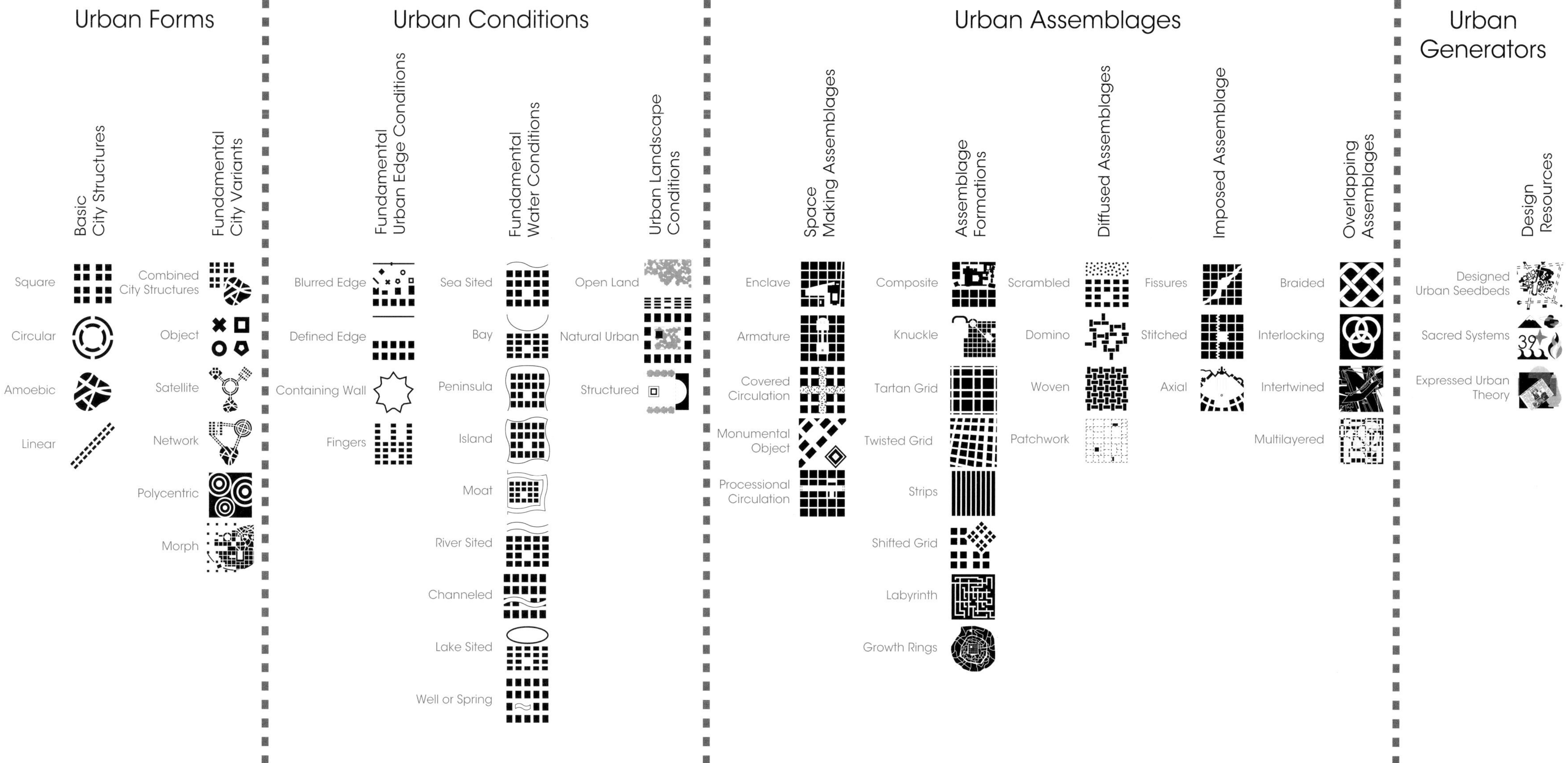

Urban Forms
Basic City Structures
Square
Circular
Amoebic
Linear
Fundamental City Variants
Combined City Structures
Object
Satellite
Network
Polycentric
Morph
Urban Conditions
Fundamental Urban Edge Conditions
Blurred Edge
Defined Edge
Containing Wall
Fingers
Fundamental Water Conditions
Sea Sited
Bay
Peninsula
Island
Moat
River Sited
Channeled
Lake Sited
Well or Spring
Urban Landscape Conditions
Open Land
Natural Urban
Structured
Urban Assemblages
Space Making Assemblages
Enclave
Armature
Covered Circulation
Monumental Object
Processional Circulation
Assemblage Formations
Composite
Knuckle
Tartan Grid
Twisted Grid
Strips
Shifted Grid
Labyrinth
Growth Rings
Diffused Assemblages
Scrambled
Domino
Woven
Patchwork
Imposed Assemblage
Fissures
Stitched
Axial
Overlapping Assemblages
Braided
Interlocking
Intertwined
Multilayered
Urban Generators
Design Resources
Designed Urban Seedbeds
Sacred Systems
Expressed Urban Theory

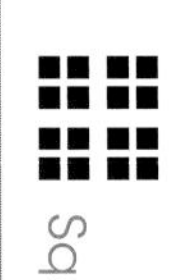

Square

An urban setting having the form of a rectilinear shape in plan, w/ a network of linear urban space forming horizontal and perpendicular lines.

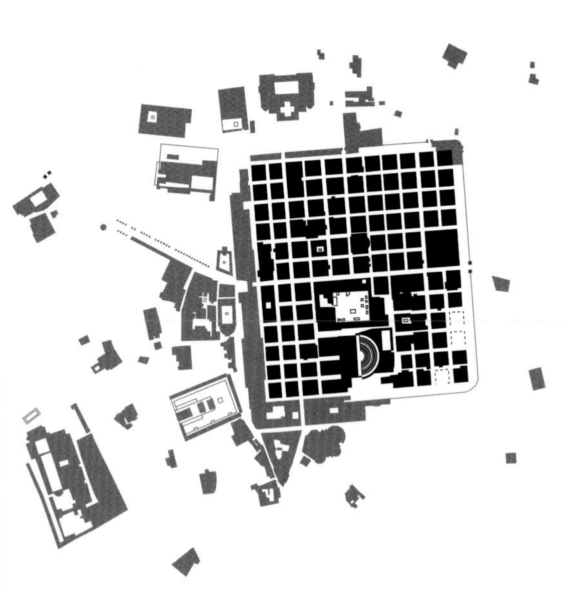

Timgad, Algeria 100

New Orleans, LA, USA 1770

Circular

An urban setting having the form of a round shape in plan.

Madrigal de las Altas Torres, Spain 1050

Saline de Chaux, France 1804 (designed by LeDoux)

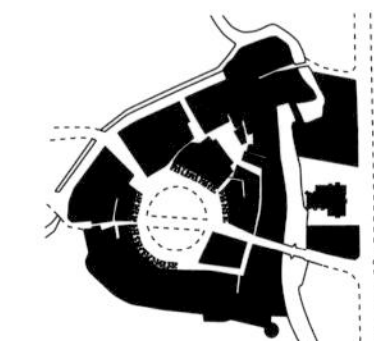

Fourcés, France [1974]

Amoebic

Urban form appearing to not have definite design, direction, rule, or method.

Hannover, Germany, circa 1200

Ferentino, Italy 1984

Linear

Urban form giving the appearance of being laid out from point to point in a line.

Magliano Percorareccio, Italy 1983

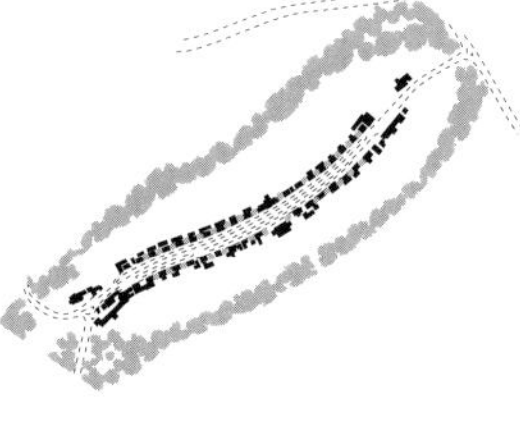

Milton Abbas, England 1946

Combined City Structures

Discernible urban fabric(s) adjacent to, or within, other recognizable urban fabrics.

Bari, Italy 1893

Object

The object city typically contains off-set urban fabric, and is commonly a focal point. Placed too far apart in a grouping they can cause a lack of urban space.

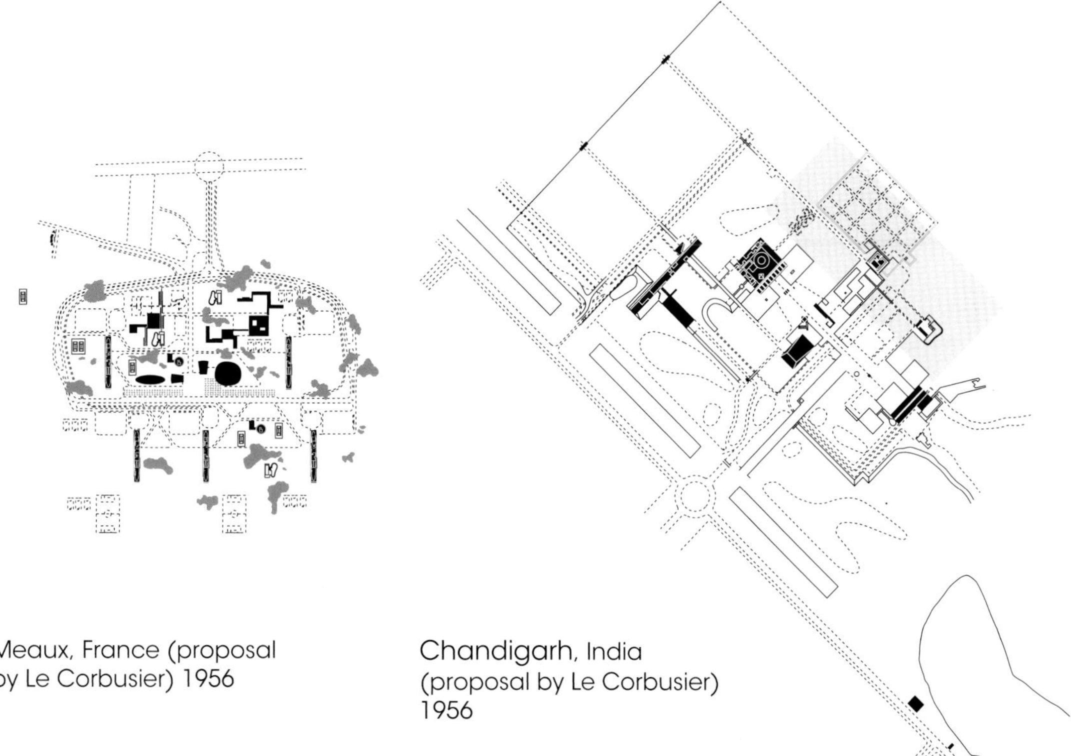

Meaux, France (proposal by Le Corbusier) 1956

Chandigarh, India (proposal by Le Corbusier) 1956

Satellite

Urban fabric situated near, but not immediately adjacent to, a large urban fabric.

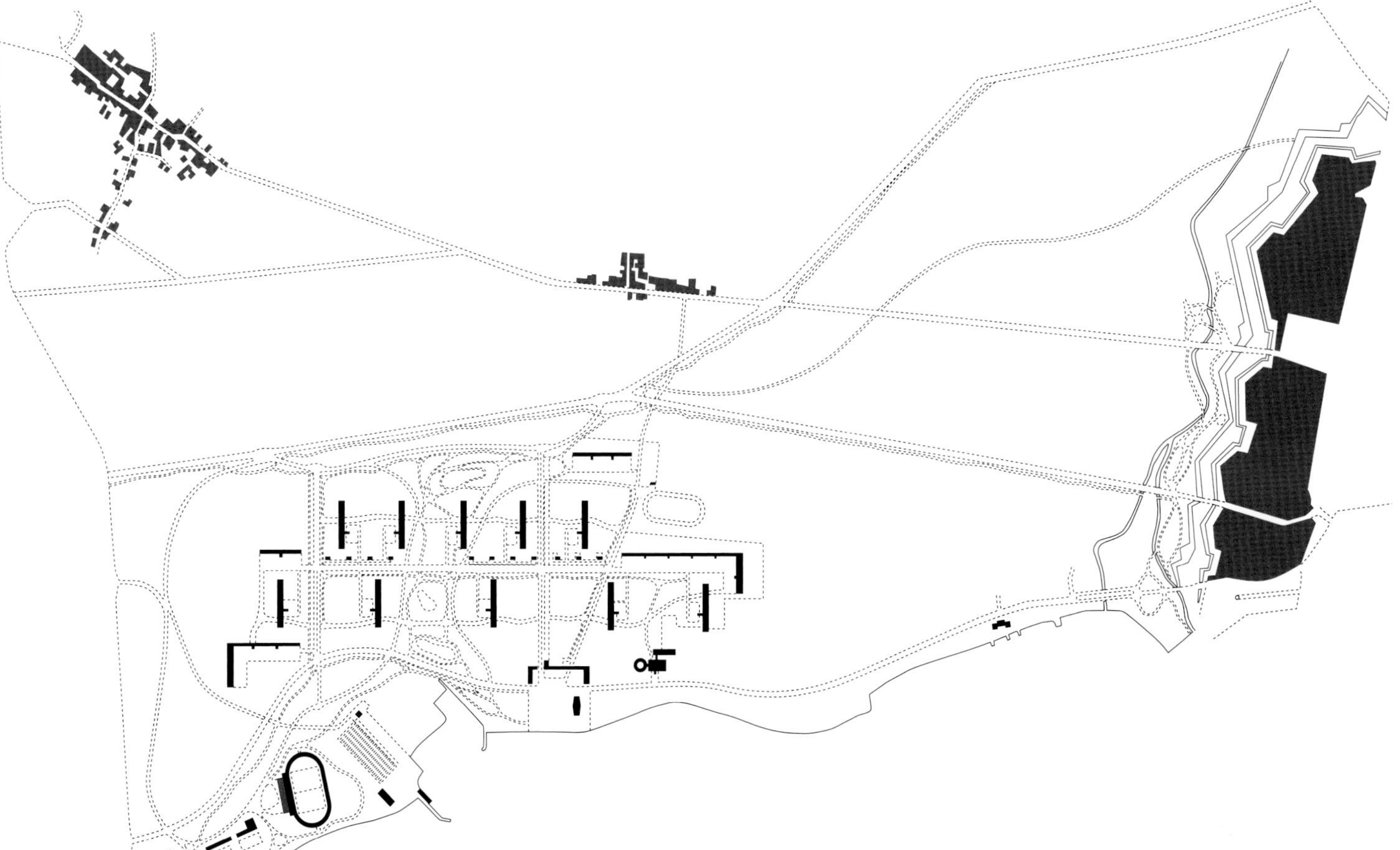

La Rochelle-Pallice, France (proposal by Le Corbusier) 1946

Typographical Make-Up

Network

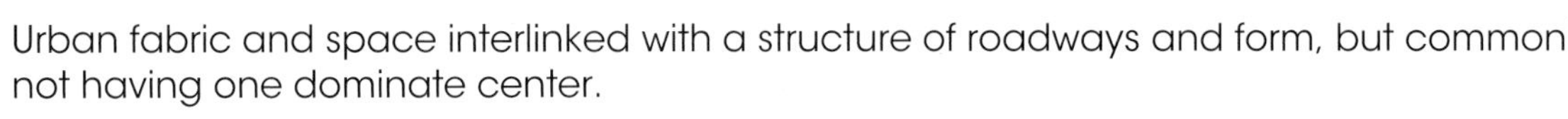

Urban fabric and space interlinked with a structure of roadways and form, but commonly not having one dominate center.

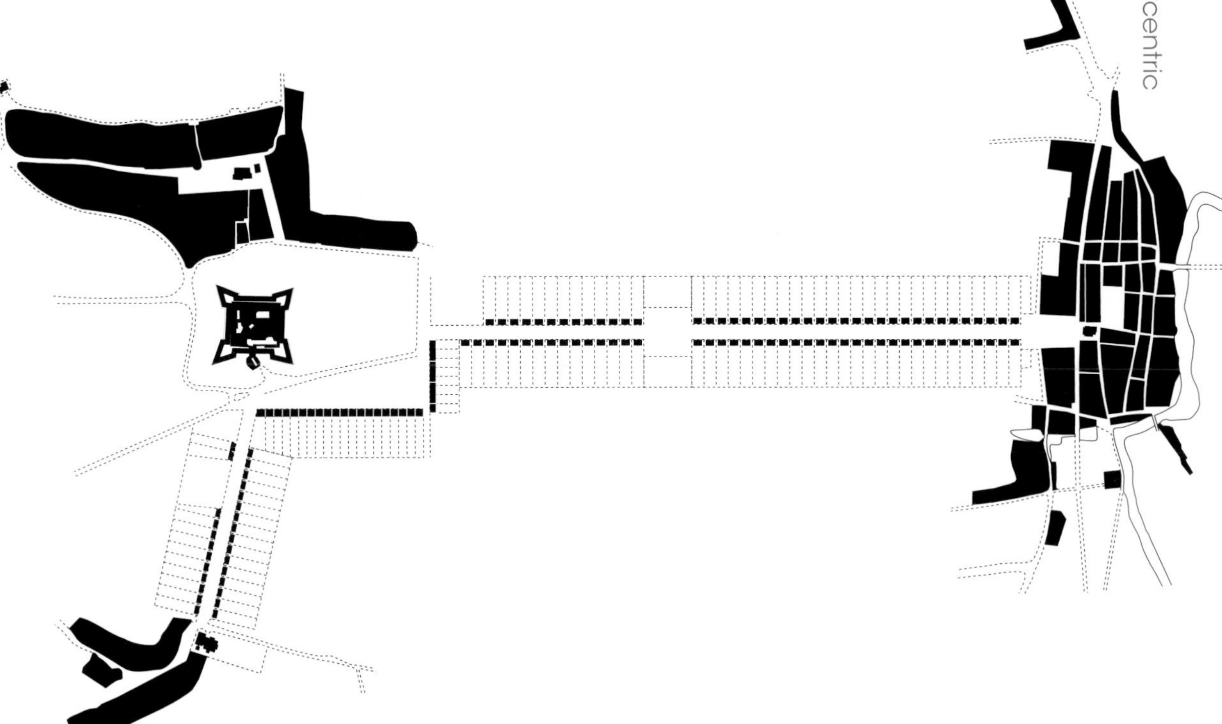

Czestochowa, Poland 1823

Polycentric

An urban setting having more than one visual center.

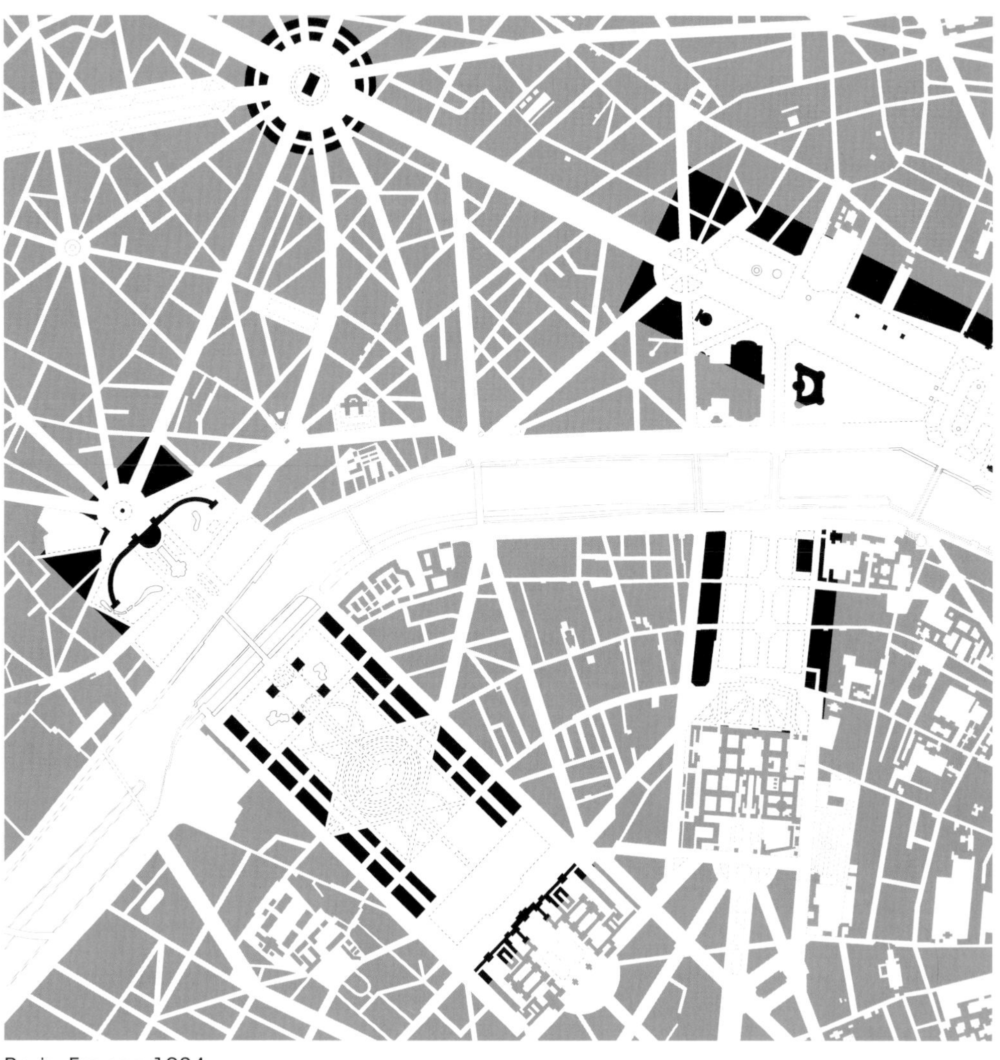

Paris, France 1924

Morph

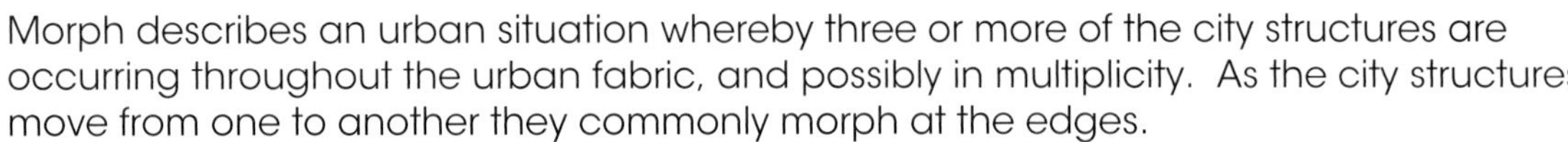

Morph describes an urban situation whereby three or more of the city structures are occurring throughout the urban fabric, and possibly in multiplicity. As the city structures move from one to another they commonly morph at the edges.

Cairo, Egypt 1914

Blurred Edge

An urban edge which appears indistinct, or vague due to the spacing of urban fabric

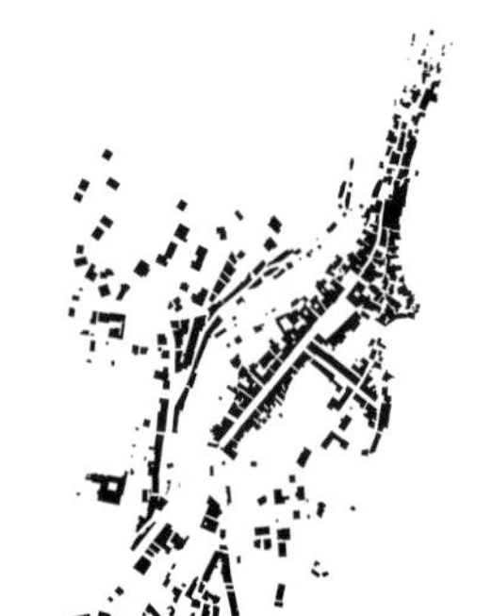

Campagnano, Italy 1983

Assen, Netherlands 1800

An urban edge, which appears distinct due to fixed or marked limits of an urban fabric.

Defined Edge

Lucca, Italy 1913

Zatec, Czech Republic 1843

Urban mass formed in a linear direction, typically attached to another urban mass, and spaced with an equal sized void.

Finger

Zwolle, Netherlands 1800

A thick structure enclosing an urban setting for protective purposes.

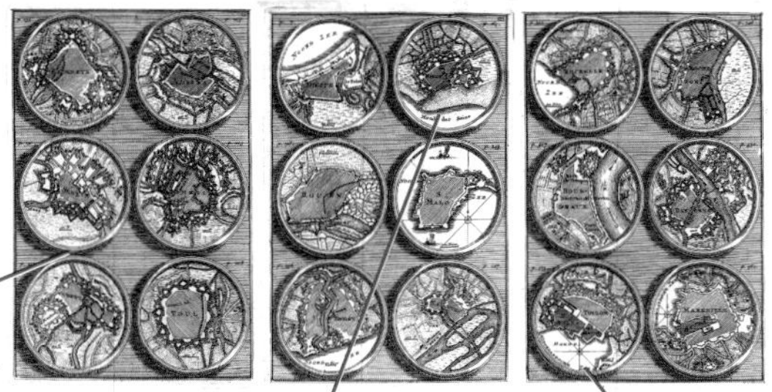

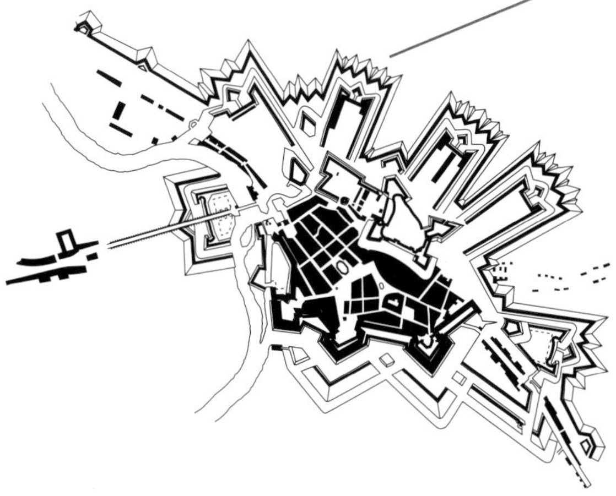

Containing Wall

Sedan, France 1702

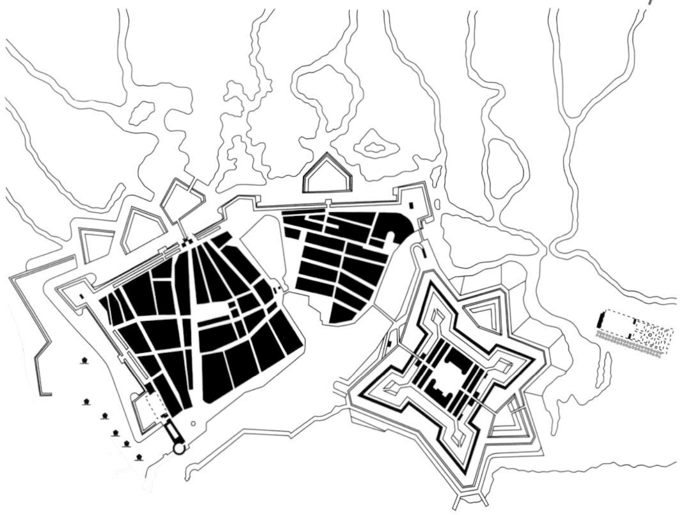

Le Havre, France 1645

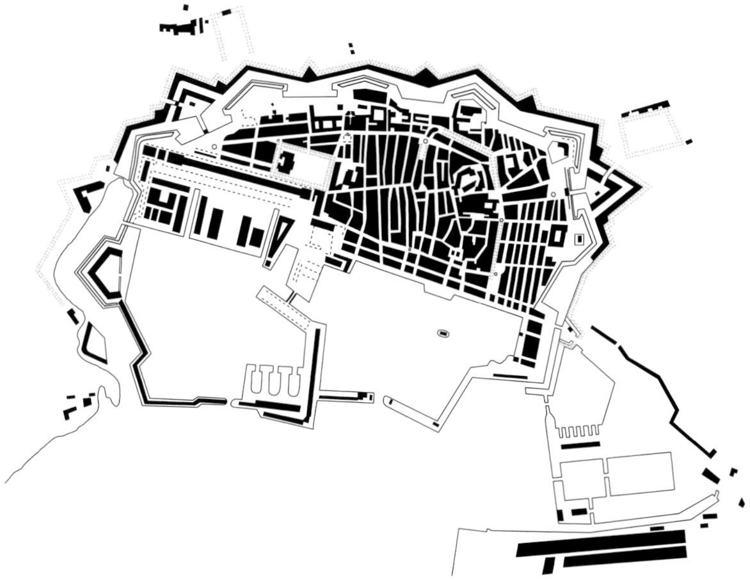

Toulon, France 1840

Sea Sited

An urban setting located on a vast body of water with the edge commonly running in a straight line.

Salerno, Italy 1940

Bay

An urban setting located on an inlet of a sea, or other body of water, typically smaller than a gulf.

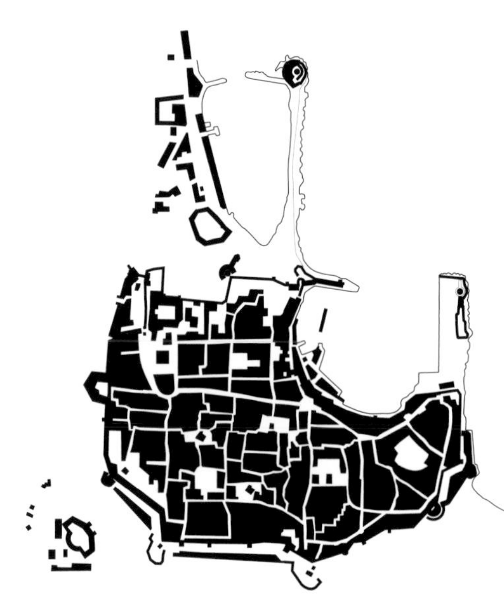

Rhodes, Greece 1906

Peninsula

An urban setting located on a portion of land nearly surrounded by water and connected with a larger body by an isthmus.

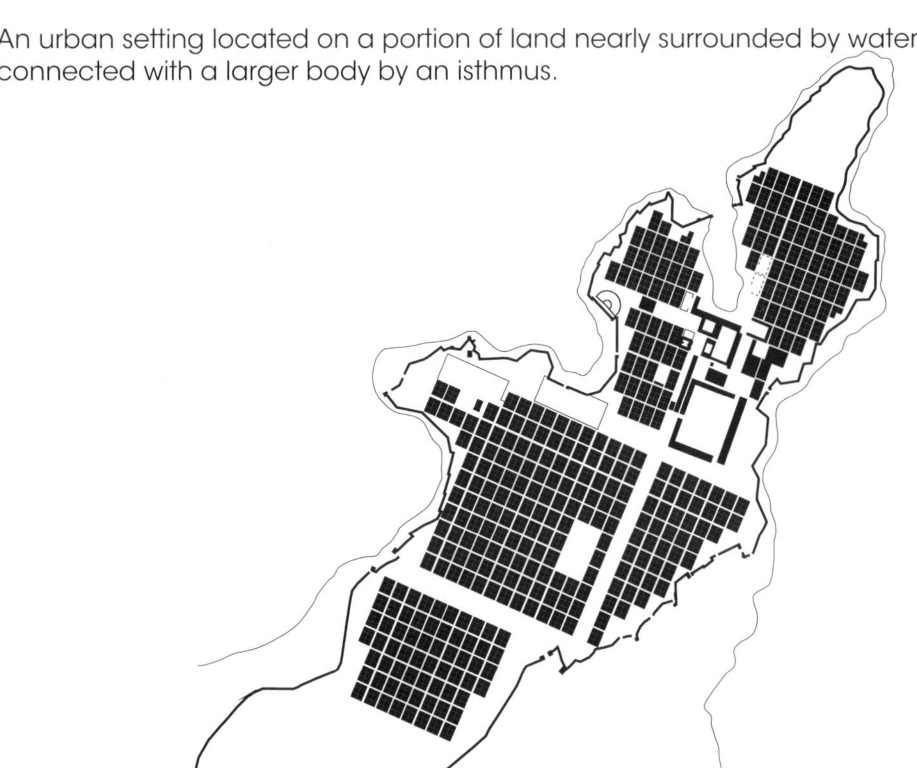

Miletus, Turkey 400 BC

Island

An urban setting located on a tract of land surrounded by water and adjacent to the majority of water to land edge.

Stockholm, Sweden 1838

Moat

A trench usually filled with water, surrounding the rampart of a fortified urban setting.

Middelburg, Netherlands 1927

Canal

An artificial waterway for navigation, and/or for draining, within the urban fabric.

Venice, Italy 1950

River Sited

An urban setting located near a body of water, which is typically traversed by a bridge.

Pisa, Italy 1913

Lake Sited

An urban setting occurring near, or next to, a body of water that is land locked.

Cleveland, Ohio 1990

Well

A hole for water obtained by natural or artificial means, commonly located within the urban fabric.

Venice, Italy 1950

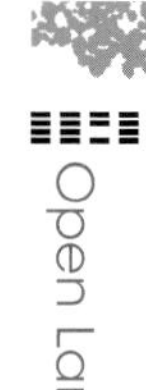

Open Land

A large body of land adjacent to or in-between urban fabric, but not enclosed on all sides.

Berlin, Germany 1863

Natural Urban

A body of wild or cultivated land enclosed by urban fabric.

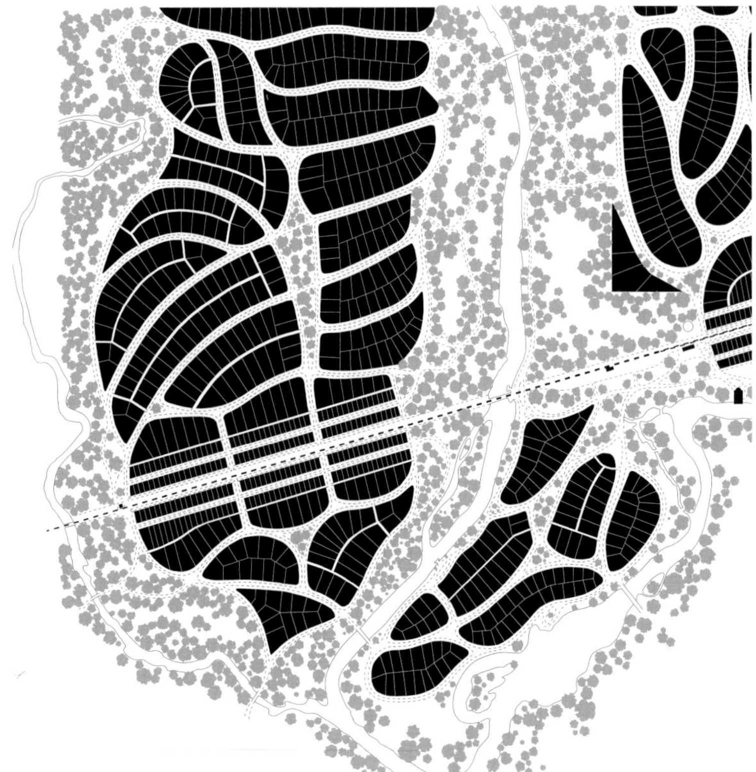

Riverside, IL, USA 1869

Structured

Space and/or mass, both natural and man-made, which is cultivated into a recognizable design.

Rome, Piazza del Popolo, Italy 1910

A distinct urban gathering space enclosed, or bounded, within the urban fabric.

Enclave

Rome, Italy 1748

The basic linear, urban armature links the sub-elements of the city, its urban magnets and/or attractors.

Armature

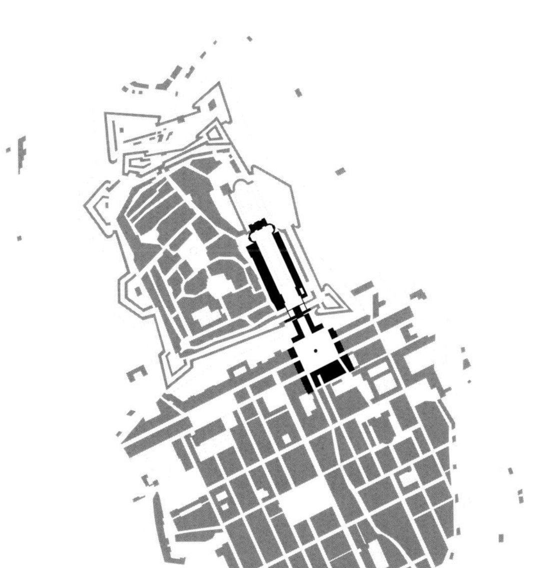

Nancy, France 1588

A covered gallery, passageway, avenue linking public spaces, and/or traffic movers, within an urban setting.

Covered Arcade

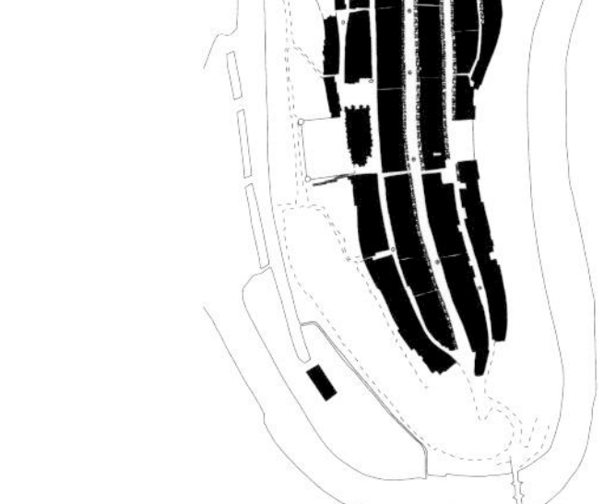

Bern, Switzerland 1191

Any large object, fountain, or monumental façade, that acts as a focal point within an urban setting.

Monumental Object

Rome, Piazza del Popolo, Italy 1910

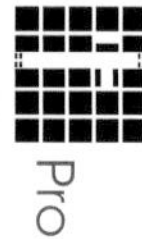

Processional Circulation

An urban setting used, or designed, for an organized body of people to advance in a formal, or ceremonial manner.

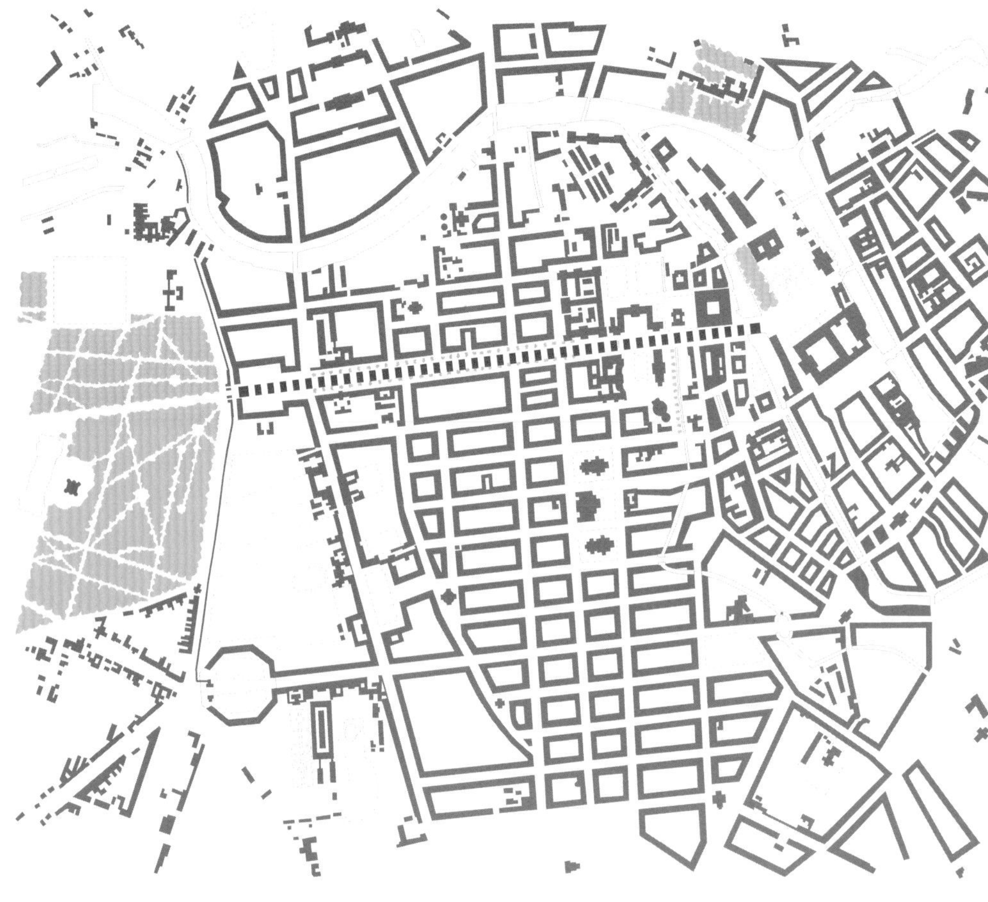

Berlin, Germany 1863

Composite

Composite buildings, or urban mega-structures, which work to define inside and outside space, and at times working as monumental context.

Florence, Italy 1843

Knuckle

An urban space or mass which gives the appearance of being a joint, hinge, or pivotal point between two or more other urban spaces or masses.

Bath, England 1775

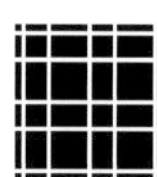

Tartan Grid

A pattern of weight varying parallel & perpendicular lines forming rectilinear shapes.

London, England 1748

Strips

Urban mass that is arranged in long narrow pieces and placed close together.

Brighton, England 1840

Twisted Grid

A pattern of parallel & perpendicular lines which appear twisted resulting in forming trapezoidal shapes.

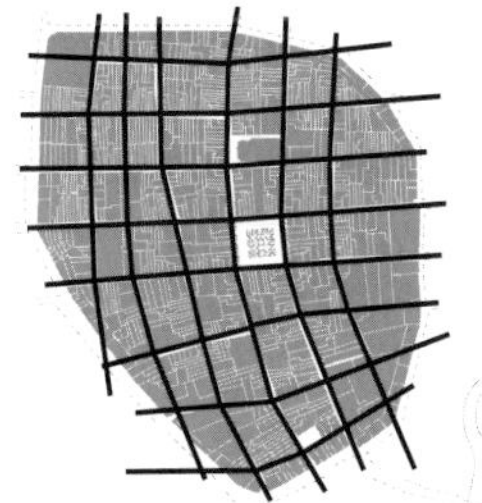

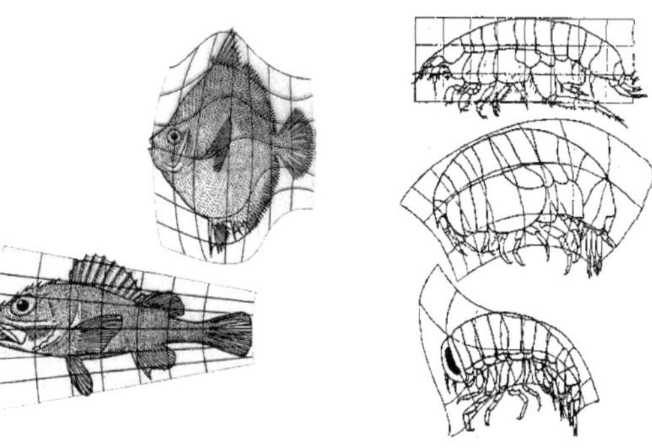

"On Growth and Form" published in 1917, the biologist D'Arcy Thompson (1860 - 1948)

Beaumont de Lomagne [1974]

Shifted Grid

A network of linear urban spaces forming horizontal and perpendicular lines, which changes it's place, position, or direction to the original grid.

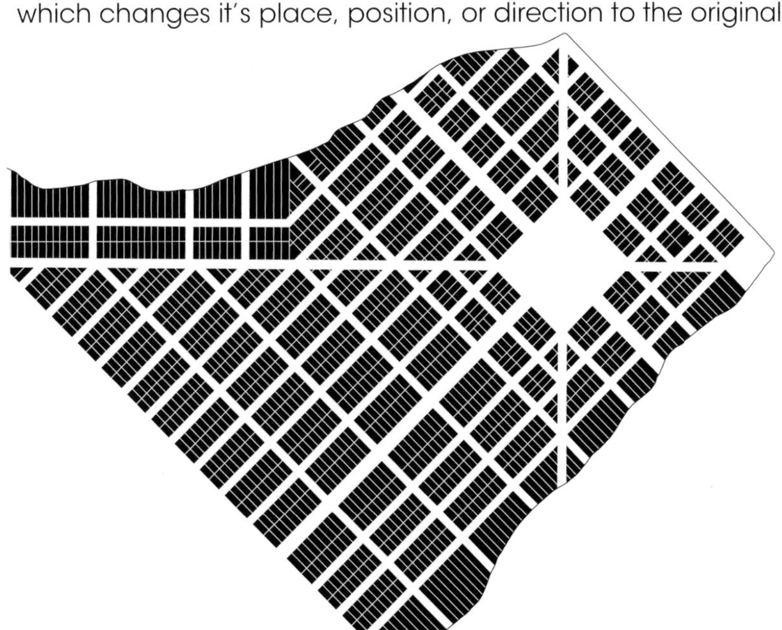

Madison, WI, USA 1836

Labyrinth

Urban mass and space which is constructed to form intricate passageways and blind alleys.

Algeri, Algeria 1837

Growth Rings

Discernible stages in the process of urban growth, most recognizable when the old wall is removed after external growth.

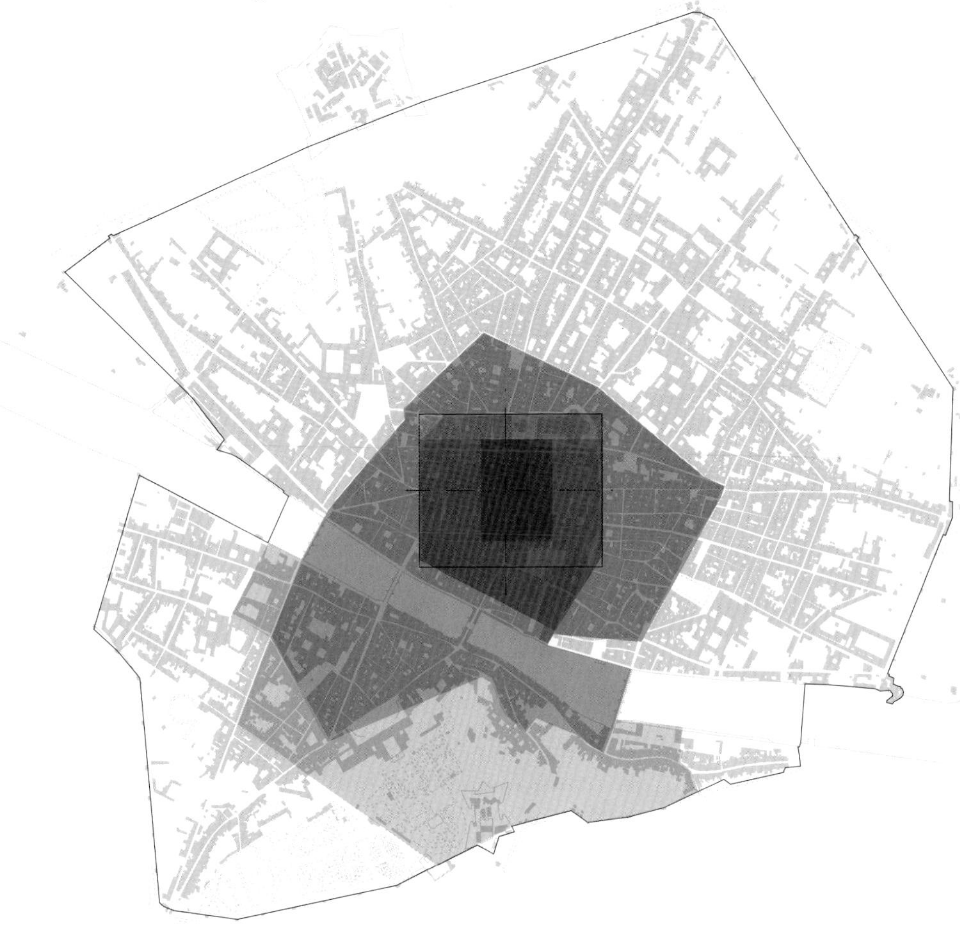

Florence, Italy 1843

Scrambled

Urban fabric that has spread or grown irregularly.

Wiesbaden, Germany 1896

Woven

Urban mass, or space, interlaced to form a texture, fabric, or design.

Frankfurt, Osthafen, Germany (proposal by David Chipperfield) 1994

Patchwork

Urban mass composed of miscellaneous or incongruous parts, spaced far apart, with property divisions visible in the plan.

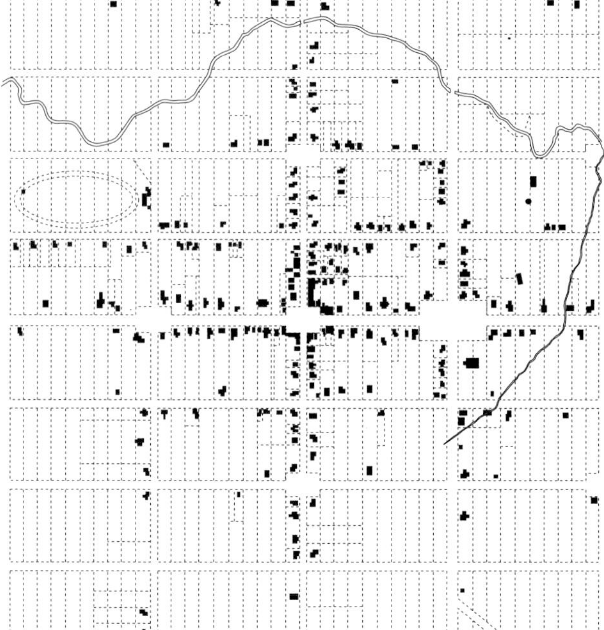

Jefferson, OH, USA 1874

Fissure

A fissure is an opening of considerable length and depth resulting in a breaking, or parting, of the urban fabric.

Parma, Italy 1840

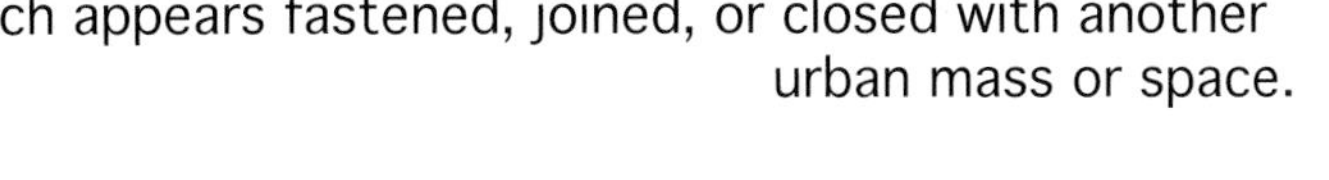

Stitched

Urban mass or space which appears fastened, joined, or closed with another urban mass or space.

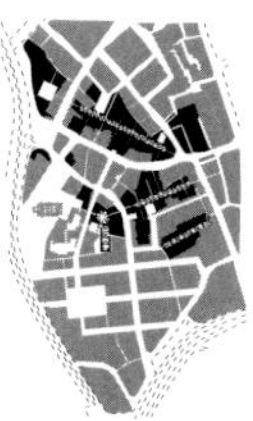

London, England (proposal by Dixon/Jones) 1992

Boston, MA, Prudential Center (designed by Koetter/Kim Associates) 1981

Axial

Typically urban space created by urban mass, which is situated around, in the direction of, on, or along an axis.

Karlsruhe, Germany 1910

Braided

The forming of an interlacing network of channels, roads and/or urban forms.

Cleveland, OH, USA 1990

Interlocking

To connect urban forms or spaces so that the apparent motion or operation of any part is constrained by another.

Milan, Italy (proposal by Steven Holl) 1995

Multilayered

An urban setting which has several distinct layers, strata, or levels.

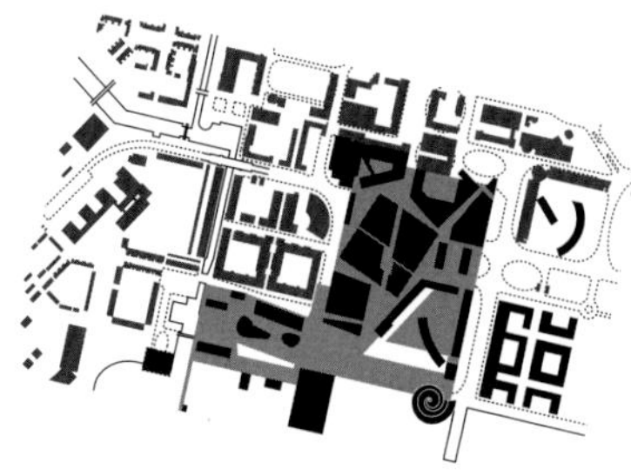

Almere, Netherlands, (proposed Urban Center by Rem Koolhaas) 1994

Intertwined

Urban mass and or space which is twined about itself to become by appearance one form/space combined

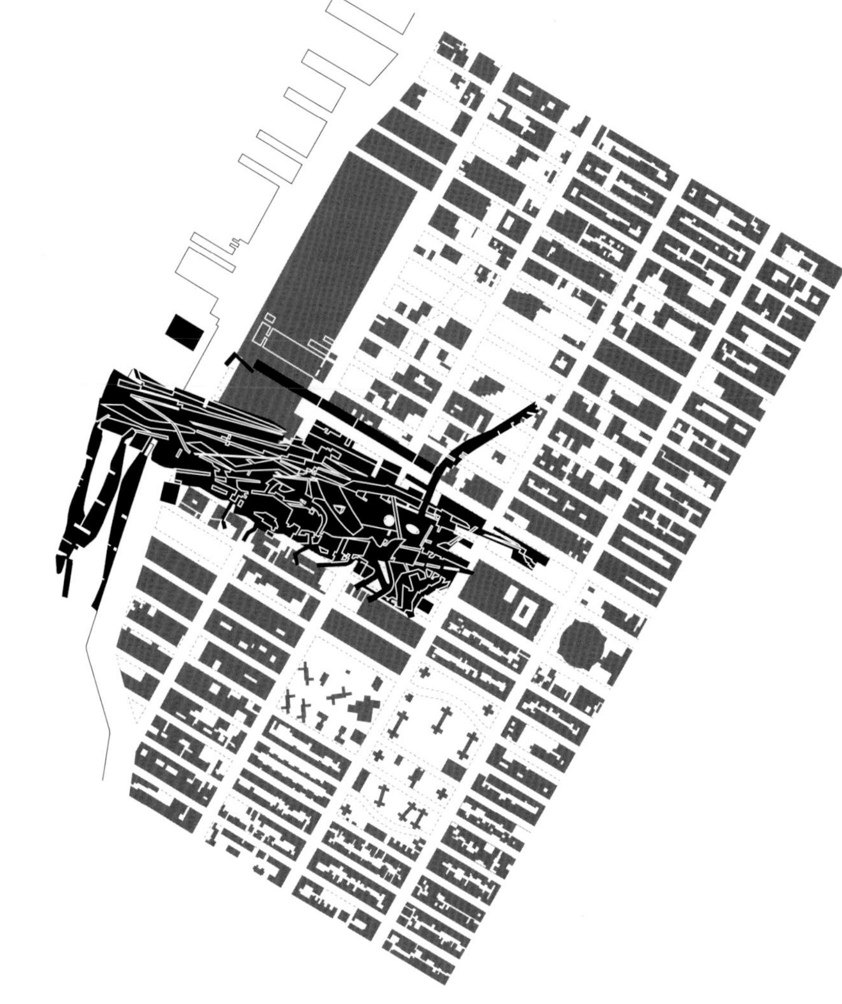

New York City, NY, USA (proposal by Thom Mayne) 1999

Preplanned urban moves which promote reactionary urban design.

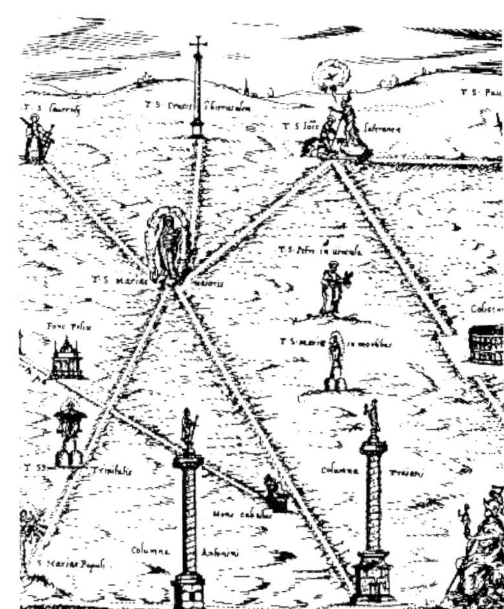

Sixtus V's plan for new streets in Rome, placed between monuments on the left bank of the Tiber. The drawing is from 1588

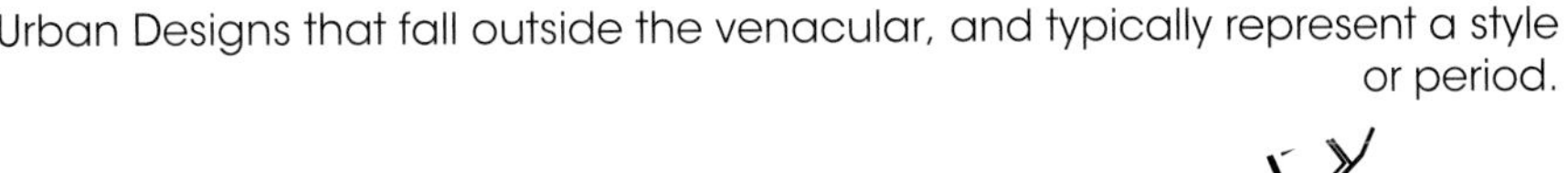

Urban Designs that fall outside the venacular, and typically represent a style or period.

Collage

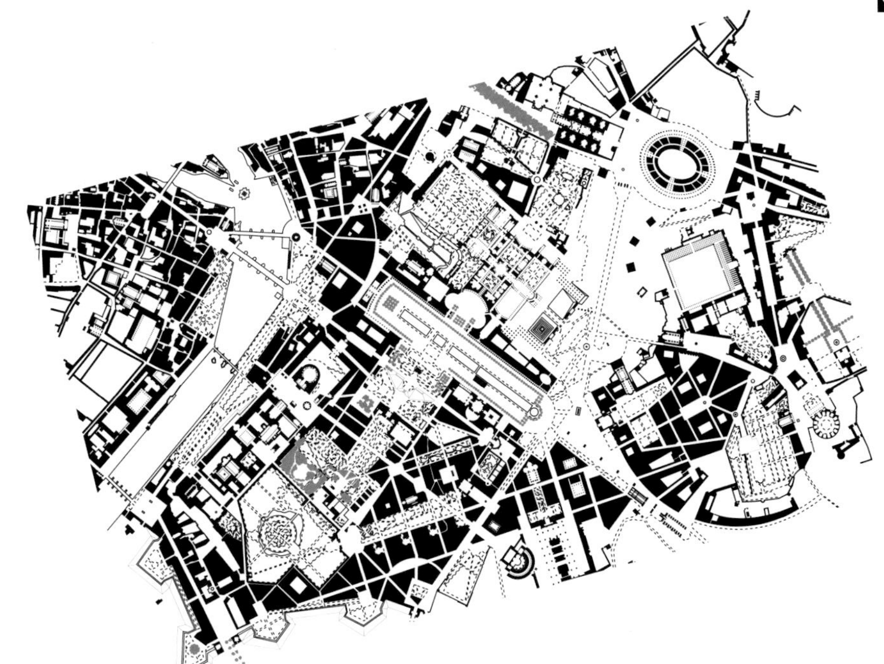

Rome, Italy (proposed by Colin Rowe) 1979

Urban setting designed via divination by means of figures, lines, astrology and/or geographic features.

Jaipur, India 1950

Appendix

City Plans and Historical Typologies

This appendix lists all the city plans included in the book and on the accompanying CD and the typology icons that correspond with the discussion of historical periods in the chapter "Historical Typologies for Urban Settings." Note that the historical typologies represent the style of the city fabric and not a period in time.

The city plans listed in red type appear in the book and on the CD; the black print indicates city plans that appear on the CD only.

City	Country	Date of Plan	1 Early Cities	2 Greek	3 Greek Colonial	4 Imperial Rome	5 Roman Colonial	6 Islamic	7 Indian, Asian	8 Medieval on Early Fabric	9 Medieval Linear, Spinal, or MultiArms	10 Medieval Circular or Free Growth	11 Medieval New Town	12 Renaissance on Earlier Fabric	13 Renaissance Ideal	14 Colonial Grid	15 Early New World Settlements or Late Renaissance	16 Grid Expansion	17 Grid Expansion Graphed onto Earlier Fabric	18 New Baroque	19 Growth Around Earlier Fabric w/Walls Removed	20 Growth Around Earlier Fabric w/Void Filled	21 Formal Expansion	22 Company Towns	23 Ideal, Religious, and Worker Towns	24 Colonial Expansion	25 Garden City	26 Early Modern and Fascist New Towns	27 Traditional Movement and the New Urbanism	28 New Modernism
Aachen (Aix-la-Chapelle)	Germany	1880										•																		
Aarau	Switzerland	[1974]										•																		
Abdera	Greece	545 BC			•																									
Acquasparta	Italy	[1963]										•																		
Agnano	Italy	1255									•																			
Aignes	France	[1974]																•												
Aigues Mortes	France	1246											•																	
Aix	France	1906																	•											
Aix-la-Chapelle (Aachen)	Germany	[1974]										•																		
Alan	France	[1974]											•																	
Alatri	Italy	1984										•																		
Albany	United States	1695														•														
Albenga	Italy	1983																•												
Albias	France	[1974]																•												
Alcamo	Italy	[1974]											•																	
Alés	France	[1974]										•																		
Alexandria	Egypt	100BC–100AD			•																									
Alexandria	Egypt	300AD–500AD			•																									
Alexandria, VA	United States	1749														•														
Alexandria	Egypt	1906																					•							
Algeri	Algeria	1837						•																						
Alghero	Italy	1984												•																
Alghero	Italy	1550																	•											
Alkmaar	Netherlands	1865												•																
Almenara	Spain	[1974]												•																
Almere (proposal by Rem Koolhaas)	Netherlands	1994																												•
Altamura	Italy	1984																	•											
Amarna	Egypt	1350 BC	•																											
Amatrice	Italy	1990																												
Amsterdam	Netherlands	1835												•																
Anagni	Italy	1984									•																			
Ancona	Italy	1909																	•											
Angers	France	1909																	•											
Anguillara Sabazia	Italy	1982										•																		
Annapolis	United States	1718																								•				
Antwerp	Belgium	1832												•																
Antwerp (proposal by Le Corbusier)	Belgium	1933																										•		
Anvers (See Antwerp)	Belgium	[1974]												•																
Aosta	Italy	1950								•																				
Arezzo	Italy	1909										•																		
Arles	France	1894								•																				
Arras	France	[1974]																	•											

City	Country	Date of Plan	1 Early Cities	2 Greek	3 Greek Colonial	4 Imperial Rome	5 Roman Colonial	6 Islamic	7 Indian, Asian	8 Medieval on Early Fabric	9 Medieval Linear, Spinal, or MultiArms	10 Medieval Circular or Free Growth	11 Medieval New Town	12 Renaissance on Earlier Fabric	13 Renaissance Ideal	14 Colonial Grid	15 Early New World Settlements or Late Renaissance	16 Grid Expansion	17 Grid Expansion Graphed onto Earlier Fabric	18 New Baroque	19 Growth Around Earlier Fabric w/Walls Removed	20 Growth Around Earlier Fabric w/Void Filled	21 Formal Expansion	22 Company Towns	23 Ideal, Religious, and Worker Towns	24 Colonial Expansion	25 Garden City	26 Early Modern and Fascist New Towns	27 Traditional Movement and the New Urbanism	28 New Modernism
Arthés	**France**	**[1974]**																•												
Asbury Park	United States	1990																											•	
Ascoli Piceno	**Italy**	**1924**								•																				
Asmara	Libya	1932																										•		
Asola	**Italy**	**[1963]**											•																	
Assen	Netherlands	1865									•																			
Assisi	Italy	1909									•																			
Athens	Greece	1909		•																										
Athens	Greece	477–431 BC																				•								
Augusta	Italy	1999																	•											
Auxonne	**France**	**[1974]**																•												
Aversa	Italy	[1963]																•												
Bagnaia (with Villa Lante)	Italy	1950																					•							
Bagnara di Romagna	Italy	[1963]											•																	
Baltimore	United States	1869																								•				
Baton Rouge	United States	1862																								•				
Barbarano Romano	Italy	1980																	•											
Barcelona	Spain	1492										•																		
Barcelona	Spain	1687												•																
Barcelona	Spain	1715												•																
Barcelona	Spain	1906																				•								
Barcelonne du Gers	France	[1979]											•																	
Bari	**Italy**	**1893**																	•											
Bassano del Grappa	Italy	1984															•													
Bassones	**France**	**[1974]**											•																	
Bath	England	1300										•																		
Bath	England	1720										•																		
Bath	England	1740																	•											
Bath	England	1775																					•							
Bath	England	1790																					•							
Batoufam Village, Bamileke	**Africa**	**Prehistory**	•																											
Bayonne	France	[1974]												•																
Beauchalot	**France**	**[1974]**											•																	
Beaumarchés	France	[1974]											•																	
Beaumont de Lomagne	France	[1974]											•																	
Beaumont de Lomagne	France	[1979]											•																	
Beaumont du Périgord	**France**	**[1974]**											•																	
Beaumont en Argonne	France	[1974]											•																	
Beaumont-en-Périgord	France	[1974]											•																	
Beaune	France	[1974]										•																		
Beauregard	**France**	**[1974]**											•																	
Beauvais	France	[1974]											•																	
Beijing	China	1950							•																					
Benicia	United States	1850																•												

City	Country	Date of Plan	1 Early Cities	2 Greek	3 Greek Colonial	4 Imperial Rome	5 Roman Colonial	6 Islamic	7 Indian, Asian	8 Medieval on Early Fabric	9 Medieval Linear, Spinal, or MultiArms	10 Medieval Circular or Free Growth	11 Medieval New Town	12 Renaissance on Earlier Fabric	13 Renaissance Ideal	14 Colonial Grid	15 Early New World Settlements or Late Renaissance	16 Grid Expansion	17 Grid Expansion Graphed onto Earlier Fabric	18 New Baroque	19 Growth Around Earlier Fabric w/Walls Removed	20 Growth Around Earlier Fabric w/Void Filled	21 Formal Expansion	22 Company Towns	23 Ideal, Religious, and Worker Towns	24 Colonial Expansion	25 Garden City	26 Early Modern and Fascist New Towns	27 Traditional Movement and the New Urbanism	28 New Modernism
Bergamo	Italy	1913											•																	
Bergues	France	1702												•																
Berlin	Germany	1688												•																
Berlin	Germany	1863																		•										
Berlin (proposal by Albert Speer)	Germany	1940																					•							
Berlin (proposal by Le Corbusier)	Germany	1961																										•		
Berlin, Potsdam (proposal by Augusto Romanano Burelli)	Germany	1991																											•	
Berlin-Tegel (proposals by Krier, Moore, Isozaki, Erskine, Behnisch, & Stavroproject)	Germany	1982																											•	
Bern	Switzerland	1191											•																	
Bern	Switzerland	1800												•																
Bern	Switzerland	1888																	•											
Besancon	France	1909												•																
Bettola	Italy	1909										•																		
Beziers	France	1909																	•											
Bieda	Italy	[1963]											•																	
Birmingham	England	1839																	•											
Bistagno	Italy	[1974]											•																	
Bitonto	Italy	1950																	•											
Blanchland	England	1946									•																			
Bologna	Italy	1913										•																		
Bonne	France	[1974]									•																			
Bonneville	France	[1974]											•																	
Bordeaux	France	1450																					•							
Bordeaux	France	1832																					•							
Borgomanero	Italy	1220											•																	
Bosa	Italy	1984																	•											
Boston	United States	1640															•													
Boston	United States	1852																								•				
Bouloc	France	[1974]											•																	
Boulogne	France	1909																	•											
Boulogne-sur-Gesse	France	[1974]											•																	
Bourges	France	1909										•																		
Bournville	England	1879																						•						
Brasilia	Brazil	1956																										•		
Braunschweig	Germany	1671										•																		
Breda	Netherlands	1865												•																
Bremen	Germany	1893																			•									
Brescia	Italy	1937										•																		
Breslau	Poland	1893																			•									
Breslavia	Germany	[1963]																•												

City	Country	Date of Plan	1 Early Cities	2 Greek	3 Greek Colonial	4 Imperial Rome	5 Roman Colonial	6 Islamic	7 Indian, Asian	8 Medieval on Early Fabric	9 Medieval Linear, Spinal, or MultiArms	10 Medieval Circular or Free Growth	11 Medieval New Town	12 Renaissance on Earlier Fabric	13 Renaissance Ideal	14 Colonial Grid	15 Early New World Settlements or Late Renaissance	16 Grid Expansion	17 Grid Expansion Graphed onto Earlier Fabric	18 New Baroque	19 Growth Around Earlier Fabric w/Walls Removed	20 Growth Around Earlier Fabric w/Void Filled	21 Formal Expansion	22 Company Towns	23 Ideal, Religious, and Worker Towns	24 Colonial Expansion	25 Garden City	26 Early Modern and Fascist New Towns	27 Traditional Movement and the New Urbanism	28 New Modernism
Brest	France	1909																	•											
Briatexte	France	[1974]											•																	
Brielle	Netherlands	1865												•																
Brighton	England	1840																•												
Brive	France	[1974]															•													
Briviesca	Spain	[1974]											•																	
Bruck an der Leitha	Austria	[1974]											•																	
Bruck an der Mur	Austria	[1974]											•																	
Bruges	Belgium	[1974]																•												
Brunswick	Germany	[1974]										•																		
Brussels	Belgium	1837															•													
Budweis	Czech Republic	[1963]											•																	
Buffalo	United States	1804																								•				
Buonalbergo	Italy	[1963]											•																	
Burlington	United States	1797																•												
Cadillac	France	[1974]																•												
Cairo	Egypt	1914						•																						
Calais	France	1909																			•									
Calcutta	India	1842															•													
Camaiore	Italy	1255											•																	
Cambrai	France	1938										•																		
Cambridge	England	1800									•																			
Cambridge, MA	United States	1637																												
Cambridge, MA (proposal by C. Graves)	United States	1977																											•	
Camerino	Italy	1984									•																			
Campagnano	Italy	1983									•																			
Campi	Italy	1380											•																	
Campobasso	Italy	1926										•																		
Canale	Italy	[1974]																•												
Canberra	Australia	1911																		•										
Candelo	Italy	[1974]											•																	
Canino	Italy	1982									•																			
Caparola (with Villa Farnese)	Italy	1983																					•							
Cape Town	South Africa	1764														•														
Capua	Italy	1928												•																
Carbonne	France	[1974]											•																	
Carcassonne	France	[1974]											•																	
Carmagnola	Italy	[1963]											•																	
Carrara	Italy	1916																	•											
Casale Monferrato	Italy	1700																	•											
Casale Monferrato	Italy	1984												•																
Castel Bolognese	Italy	[1974]											•																	
Castel S. Pietro	Italy	[1963]											•																	

City	Country	Date of Plan	1 Early Cities	2 Greek	3 Greek Colonial	4 Imperial Rome	5 Roman Colonial	6 Islamic	7 Indian, Asian	8 Medieval on Early Fabric	9 Medieval Linear, Spinal, or MultiArms	10 Medieval Circular or Free Growth	11 Medieval New Town	12 Renaissance on Earlier Fabric	13 Renaissance Ideal	14 Colonial Grid	15 Early New World Settlements or Late Renaissance	16 Grid Expansion	17 Grid Expansion Graphed onto Earlier Fabric	18 New Baroque	19 Growth Around Earlier Fabric w/Walls Removed	20 Growth Around Earlier Fabric w/Void Filled	21 Formal Expansion	22 Company Towns	23 Ideal, Religious, and Worker Towns	24 Colonial Expansion	25 Garden City	26 Early Modern and Fascist New Towns	27 Traditional Movement and the New Urbanism	28 New Modernism
Castelfranc	France	[1974]											•																	
Castelfranco di Sopra	Italy	1800											•																	
Castelfranco di Sotto	Italy	1280											•																	
Castelfranco Veneto	Italy	1984																•												
Castelnaud-de-Gratecambe	France	[1974]											•																	
Castelsarrasin	France	[1974]											•																	
Castillonnés	France	[1974]											•																	
Castle Acre	England	1946									•																			
Catania	Italy	1893																	•											
Caudecoste	France	[1974]											•																	
Caumont	France	[1974]											•																	
Caxéres-sur-Adour	France	[1974]											•																	
Cazéres-sur-Garonne	France	[1974]											•																	
Central Park, New York City	United States	1871																									•			
Certaldo	Italy	1984									•																			
Cesena	Italy	1984									•																			
Cesena	Italy	1909																	•											
Cesky Brod	Czech Republic	[1974]											•																	
Chandigarh-Le Corbusier (capitol)	India	1956																										•		
Chandigarh-Le Corbusier Master P.	India	1956																										•		
Charleston	United States	1739														•														
Charleston	United States	1704																•												
Charleville	France	1909																	•											
Charlieu	France	[1974]											•																	
Chateaux Meudon	France	1708																		•										
Chelmno (Kulm)	Poland	[1974]											•																	
Cherbourg	France	1909																	•											
Chester	England	1800								•																				
Chianciano	Italy	[1963]									•																			
Chiari	Italy	1963															•													
Chicago (proposal by Burnham)	United States	1909																								•				
Chicago World's Columbian Exposition	United States	1893																								•				
Chichester	England	1800								•																				
Chilham	England	1946									•																			
Chioggia	Italy	[1963]								•																				
Chioggia	Italy	1984									•																			
Chiusi	Italy	1984										•																		
Christiania	Norway	[1963]													•															
Christianopel	Sweden	[1963]													•															
Christianstad	Sweden	[1963]													•															
Cincinnati	United States	1815																								•				
Cingoli	Italy	1984									•																			

City	Country	Date of Plan	1 Early Cities	2 Greek	3 Greek Colonial	4 Imperial Rome	5 Roman Colonial	6 Islamic	7 Indian, Asian	8 Medieval on Early Fabric	9 Medieval Linear, Spinal, or MultiArms	10 Medieval Circular or Free Growth	11 Medieval New Town	12 Renaissance on Earlier Fabric	13 Renaissance Ideal	14 Colonial Grid	15 Early New World Settlements or Late Renaissance	16 Grid Expansion	17 Grid Expansion Graphed onto Earlier Fabric	18 New Baroque	19 Growth Around Earlier Fabric w/Walls Removed	20 Growth Around Earlier Fabric w/Void Filled	21 Formal Expansion	22 Company Towns	23 Ideal, Religious, and Worker Towns	24 Colonial Expansion	25 Garden City	26 Early Modern and Fascist New Towns	27 Traditional Movement and the New Urbanism	28 New Modernism
Circleville	United States	1820–56																								•				
Citta della Pieve	Italy	1984									•																			
Citta di Castello	Italy	1984									•																			
Cittadella	Italy	1984								•																				
Cittaducale	Italy	1309											•																	
City for 3 Million (proposal by Le Corbusier)		1924																										•		
Civitavecchia	Italy	1984																	•											
Clare	England	1946									•																			
Cleveland	United States	1835																								•				
Cleveland	United States	1990																								•				
Cluny	France	1650										•																		
Coaña	Spain	1100 BC	•																											
Coblenz	Germany	1907																					•							
Coevorden	Netherlands	1648													•															
Colchester	England	1800								•																				
Colle di Val d'Elsa	Italy	1984									•																			
Colmar	Germany	1820																	•											
Cologne	France	[1974]											•																	
Columbus	United States	1817																								•				
Como	Italy	1958								•																				
Compiegne	France	1974																					•							
Coneysthorpe	England	1946									•																			
Constantinople (Istanbul)	Turkey	1841						•																						
Copenhagen	Denmark	1535										•																		
Copenhagen	Denmark	1650												•																
Copenhagen	Denmark	1750																	•											
Copenhagen	Denmark	1837																	•											
Copenhagen	Denmark	1850																	•											
Cordes	France	[1974]									•																			
Cordova	Spain	1906						•																						
Corinaldo	Italy	1984										•																		
Cortemaggiore	Italy	[1963]											•																	
Cortona	Italy	1923										•																		
Cotignola	Italy	[1963]											•																	
Coventry	England	1800									•																			
Coxwold	England	1946									•																			
Cracovia	Germany	[1974]																•												
Crema	Italy	1984										•																		
Crema	Italy	[1963]																	•											
Créon	France	[1974]											•																	
Crevalcore	Italy	[1963]											•																	
Crotone	Italy	1999																	•											
Cuneo	Italy	1926																					•							
Curzola	Italy	[1963]											•																	

City	Country	Date of Plan	1 Early Cities	2 Greek	3 Greek Colonial	4 Imperial Rome	5 Roman Colonial	6 Islamic	7 Indian, Asian	8 Medieval on Early Fabric	9 Medieval Linear, Spinal, or MultiArms	10 Medieval Circular or Free Growth	11 Medieval New Town	12 Renaissance on Earlier Fabric	13 Renaissance Ideal	14 Colonial Grid	15 Early New World Settlements or Late Renaissance	16 Grid Expansion	17 Grid Expansion Graphed onto Earlier Fabric	18 New Baroque	19 Growth Around Earlier Fabric w/Walls Removed	20 Growth Around Earlier Fabric w/Void Filled	21 Formal Expansion	22 Company Towns	23 Ideal, Religious, and Worker Towns	24 Colonial Expansion	25 Garden City	26 Early Modern and Fascist New Towns	27 Traditional Movement and the New Urbanism	28 New Modernism
Czestochowa	Poland	1823																	•											
Damazan	France	[1974]											•																	
Denver	United States	1859																								•				
Derbent	Russia	1845									•																			
Detroit	United States	1830																								•				
Dieppe	France	1909																	•											
Digne	France	1938																	•											
Dijon	France	1909																				•								
Dole	France	1909										•																		
Domazlice	Czech Republic	1838											•																	
Domme	France	[1974]											•																	
Donzac	France	[1974]											•																	
Dordrecht	Netherlands	1867															•													
Doway	France	1743												•																
Dozza	Italy	[1963]									•																			
Dresde (Dresden)	Germany	[1974]											•	•																
Dresden	Germany	1800												•																
Dresden	Germany	1833																					•							
Dublin	Ireland	1836															•													
Dunes	France	[1974]											•																	
Dunkerque	France	1690												•																
Dura-Europos	Syria	300 BC			•																									
Düsseldorf	Germany	1896																				•								
Eden	United States	1736														•														
Edenton	United States	1769																•												
Edinburgh	Scotland	1860									•																			
Edinburgh	Scotland	1750																					•							
Eguisheim	Germany	[1963]										•																		
Elblag	Poland	[1974]																•												
Ellwanger	Germany	[1974]										•																		
Elyria	United States	1850																								•				
Emden	Germany	1904												•																
Erice	Italy	1984									•																			
Esperanza	United States	1794																								•				
EUR	Italy	1937																										•		
EUR	Italy	1995																										•		
Exeter	England	1802								•																				
Eymet	France	[1974]											•																	
Eyre Estate, St. Johns Wood	England	1794																									•			
Fabriano	Italy	1984																	•											
Faenza	Italy	1984								•																				
Faenza	Italy	1916																	•											
Fair Haven, CT	United States	1869									•																			
Fairfield, AL	United States	1910																									•			
Fairfield, CT	United States	1640																•												

City	Country	Date of Plan	1 Early Cities	2 Greek	3 Greek Colonial	4 Imperial Rome	5 Roman Colonial	6 Islamic	7 Indian, Asian	8 Medieval on Early Fabric	9 Medieval Linear, Spinal, or MultiArms	10 Medieval Circular or Free Growth	11 Medieval New Town	12 Renaissance on Earlier Fabric	13 Renaissance Ideal	14 Colonial Grid	15 Early New World Settlements or Late Renaissance	16 Grid Expansion	17 Grid Expansion Graphed onto Earlier Fabric	18 New Baroque	19 Growth Around Earlier Fabric w/Walls Removed	20 Growth Around Earlier Fabric w/Void Filled	21 Formal Expansion	22 Company Towns	23 Ideal, Religious, and Worker Towns	24 Colonial Expansion	25 Garden City	26 Early Modern and Fascist New Towns	27 Traditional Movement and the New Urbanism	28 New Modernism
Faleria	Italy	1983										•																		
Fano	Italy	[1974]																	•											
Feltre	Italy	1984									•																			
Ferentino	Italy	1984										•																		
Fermo	Italy	1984										•																		
Ferrara	Italy	[1963]												•																
Fiano Romano	Italy	[1963]										•																		
Figline	Italy	1360											•																	
Filacciano	Italy	[1963]									•																			
Finchingfield	England	1946									•																			
Firenzuola	Italy	1850											•																	
Firenzuola	Italy	1980											•																	
First Townships Survey, OH	United States	1796																								•				
Flagy	France	[1974]									•																			
Fleurance	France	[1974]																												
Florence	Italy	1843												•																
Foligno	Italy	1984																•												
Fondi	Italy	1990								•																				
Fontainebleau	France	1974																					•							
Fort Erie	Canada	1790														•														
Fort Michilmakinac	United States	1766														•														
Fort Niagaria	Canada	1755														•														
Fougéres	France	[1974]									•																			
Fourcés	France	[1974]										•																		
Francescas	France	[1974]										•																		
Francfort-sur-Oder	Germany	[1974]											•																	
Frankfurt	Germany	1837												•																
Frankfurt, Osthafen (proposal by David Chipperfield)	Germany	1994																												•
Fredericia	Denmark	[1963]													•															
Fredericksburg	United States	1721														•														
Freudenstadt	Germany	1800													•															
Fribourg	Switzerland	[1974]										•																		
Fribourg-en-Brisgau	Germany	[1974]											•																	
Friedberg	Germany	1200																•												
Friedeberg	Germany	[1963]											•																	
Friedland	Germany	1330											•																	
Frossasco	Italy	[1974]											•																	
Gaeta	Italy	1984									•																			
Gaeta	Italy	1928																	•											
Gainford	England	1946									•																			
Gallipoli	Italy	1984						•																						
Galvez	United States	1778														•														
Gan	France	[1974]											•																	

City	Country	Date of Plan	1 Early Cities	2 Greek	3 Greek Colonial	4 Imperial Rome	5 Roman Colonial	6 Islamic	7 Indian, Asian	8 Medieval on Early Fabric	9 Medieval Linear, Spinal, or MultiArms	10 Medieval Circular or Free Growth	11 Medieval New Town	12 Renaissance on Earlier Fabric	13 Renaissance Ideal	14 Colonial Grid	15 Early New World Settlements or Late Renaissance	16 Grid Expansion	17 Grid Expansion Graphed onto Earlier Fabric	18 New Baroque	19 Growth Around Earlier Fabric w/Walls Removed	20 Growth Around Earlier Fabric w/Void Filled	21 Formal Expansion	22 Company Towns	23 Ideal, Religious, and Worker Towns	24 Colonial Expansion	25 Garden City	26 Early Modern and Fascist New Towns	27 Traditional Movement and the New Urbanism	28 New Modernism
Gap	France	1938																	•											
Gdansk	Poland	[1974]											•																	
Geaune-en-Tursan	France	[1974]											•																	
Geneva	Switzerland	1841												•																
Genova	Italy	1836										•																		
Gensac	France	[1974]																												
Genzano	Italy	1979																		•										
Giglio Fiorentino	Italy	1350											•																	
Gimont	France	[1974]											•																	
Glasgow	Scotland	1860																					•							
Glogów Malopolski	Poland	1885																•												
Gloucester	England	1800								•																				
Glucholazy	Poland	[1974]											•																	
Göteborg	Sweden	1630													•															
Gourdon	France	[1974]															•													
Grammichele	Italy	1693													•															
Granada	Spain	1906															•													
Granges	France	[1974]																•												
Gransee	Germany	1838											•																	
Granville	France	1938									•																			
Gravina in Puglia	Italy	1984																	•											
Greenfield	United States	1774														•														
Grenade da Lavedan	France	[1974]											•																	
Grenade-sur-Adour	France	[1974]											•																	
Grenade-sur-Garonne	France	[1974]											•																	
Groningen	Netherlands	1865												•																
Groningen	Netherlands	1927																			•									
Grosseto	Italy	[1963]												•																
Guastalla	Italy	1984																			•									
Gubbio	Italy	1909								•																				
Haarlem	Netherlands	1865																	•											
Hadrian's Villa	Italy	1760				•																								
Halifax	Canada	1906																	•											
Halikarnassos	Turkey	364 BC			•																									
Hamburg	Germany	[1974]										•																		
Hamburg	Germany	1841																			•									
Hamm	Germany	1226											•																	
Hampton Court	England	1901																		•										
Hanau	Germany	1790																	•											
Hann-Münden	Germany	[1974]											•																	
Hannover	Germany	[1974]										•																		
Hardwick	United States	1754														•														
Harewood	England	1946									•																			
Hartford	United States	1640															•													
Hastingues	France	[1974]											•																	

City	Country	Date of Plan	1 Early Cities	2 Greek	3 Greek Colonial	4 Imperial Rome	5 Roman Colonial	6 Islamic	7 Indian, Asian	8 Medieval on Early Fabric	9 Medieval Linear, Spinal, or MultiArms	10 Medieval Circular or Free Growth	11 Medieval New Town	12 Renaissance on Earlier Fabric	13 Renaissance Ideal	14 Colonial Grid	15 Early New World Settlements or Late Renaissance	16 Grid Expansion	17 Grid Expansion Graphed onto Earlier Fabric	18 New Baroque	19 Growth Around Earlier Fabric w/Walls Removed	20 Growth Around Earlier Fabric w/Void Filled	21 Formal Expansion	22 Company Towns	23 Ideal, Religious, and Worker Towns	24 Colonial Expansion	25 Garden City	26 Early Modern and Fascist New Towns	27 Traditional Movement and the New Urbanism	28 New Modernism
Hatfield	United States	1887																								•				
Havre (Le Havre)	France	1702												•																
Heighington	England	1946									•																			
Herakleia Pontike	Turkey	400 BC			•																									
Hereford	England	1800									•																			
Herrenberg	Germany	1622										•																		
Herrnhut	Germany	1782																							•					
Hertogenbosch	Netherlands	1865												•																
Hesdin	France	1713												•																
Himera	Italy	480 BC			•																									
Hué in Annam	Vietnam	1800							•																					
Hugoton	United States	1887																								•				
Hygeia	United States	1827																							•					
Ideal Town (by Joseph Furttenbach the Younger)	Germany	1650													•															
Iglau (Jihlava)	Czech Republic	[1974]											•																	
Iglesias	Italy	1984																	•											
Imola	Italy	1878								•																				
Indianapolis	United States	1821																								•				
Inveraray	England	1946																					•							
Ipswich	United States	1872									•																			
Ishfahan	Iran	1627						•																						
Isola gei Pescatori	Italy	[1963]									•																			
Jaipur	India	1950							•																					
Jawor	Poland	[1963]											•																	
Jefferson	United States	1874																								•				
Jefferson Plan, Wash. DC	United States	1791																								•				
Jeffersonville	United States	1802																								•				
Jerusalem	Israel	1912						•																						
Jesi	Italy	[1990]																	•											
Jihlava (Iglau)	Czech Republic	[1974]											•																	
Jussy L'Evêque	Switzerland	[1974]										•																		
Kalisz	Poland	[1974]											•																	
Karlsruhe	Germany	1910																		•										
Karlsruhe	Germany	1896																		•										
Kaskaskia	United States	1770														•														
Kassel	Germany	1750																					•							
Kassope	Greece	380 BC			•																									
Kenzingen	Germany	1249											•																	
Khiva	Uzbekistan	1970						•																						
Kimbolton	England	1946									•																			
Kingston	United States	1695														•														
Klatovy (Klattau)	Czech Republic	[1974]											•																	
Klattau	Czech Republic	[1979]											•																	
Klein Welke	Germany	1782																							•					

City	Country	Date of Plan	1 Early Cities	2 Greek	3 Greek Colonial	4 Imperial Rome	5 Roman Colonial	6 Islamic	7 Indian, Asian	8 Medieval on Early Fabric	9 Medieval Linear, Spinal, or MultiArms	10 Medieval Circular or Free Growth	11 Medieval New Town	12 Renaissance on Earlier Fabric	13 Renaissance Ideal	14 Colonial Grid	15 Early New World Settlements or Late Renaissance	16 Grid Expansion	17 Grid Expansion Graphed onto Earlier Fabric	18 New Baroque	19 Growth Around Earlier Fabric w/Walls Removed	20 Growth Around Earlier Fabric w/Void Filled	21 Formal Expansion	22 Company Towns	23 Ideal, Religious, and Worker Towns	24 Colonial Expansion	25 Garden City	26 Early Modern and Fascist New Towns	27 Traditional Movement and the New Urbanism	28 New Modernism
Knidos	Turkey	380 BC			•																									
Kolin	Czech Republic	[1979]											•																	
Kosice	Czech Republic	[1974]											•																	
La Bastide-Clairence	France	[1974]											•																	
La Bastide-Clemont	France	[1974]											•																	
La Bastide-d'Armagnac	France	[1974]											•																	
La Bastide-de-Besplas	France	[1974]											•																	
La Bastide-de-Lévis	France	[1974]											•																	
La Bastide-de-Lordat	France	[1974]											•																	
La Bastide-Dénat	France	[1974]											•																	
La Bastide-du-Haut-Mont	France	[1974]											•																	
La Bastide-du-Temple	France	[1974]											•																	
La Bastide-du-Vert	France	[1974]											•																	
La Bastide-Marnhac	France	[1974]											•																	
La Bastide-Murat	France	[1974]											•																	
La Couvertoirade	France	[1974]										•																		
La Neuveville	Switzerland	[1974]											•																	
La Rochelle	France	1914												•																
La Rochelle-Pallice (proposal by Le Corbusier)	France	1946																										•		
La Salvetat d'Aveyron	France	[1974]										•																		
La Salvetat-de-Sainte-Foy	France	[1974]									•																			
La Sauvetat-du-Dropt	France	[1974]									•																			
La Selve	France	[1974]									•																			
Lalinda	France	[1974]											•																	
Lamontjoie	France	[1974]											•																	
Lanciano	Italy	1984																	•											
Langon	France	[1974]																												
Lanuvio	Italy	1990																												
Laparade	France	[1974]																												
Las Vegas Strip	United States	1972																										•		
Latina	Italy	1940																										•		
Lauzerte	France	[1974]											•																	
Lavardac	France	[1974]											•																	
Law of Indies Study 1		1573														•														
Law of Indies Study 2		1573														•														
Le Havre	France	1645												•																
Le Plan	France	[1974]											•																	
Lecce	Italy	1935																	•											
Lédergues	France	[1974]											•																	
Leeuwarden	Netherlands	1910																			•									
Leiden (Leyden)	Netherlands	1910																			•									
Leon	Spain	1906																					•							
Lestelle	France	[1974]											•																	
Lestelle-de-Saint-Martory	France	[1974]										•																		

City	Country	Date of Plan	1 Early Cities	2 Greek	3 Greek Colonial	4 Imperial Rome	5 Roman Colonial	6 Islamic	7 Indian, Asian	8 Medieval on Early Fabric	9 Medieval Linear, Spinal, or MultiArms	10 Medieval Circular or Free Growth	11 Medieval New Town	12 Renaissance on Earlier Fabric	13 Renaissance Ideal	14 Colonial Grid	15 Early New World Settlements or Late Renaissance	16 Grid Expansion	17 Grid Expansion Graphed onto Earlier Fabric	18 New Baroque	19 Growth Around Earlier Fabric w/Walls Removed	20 Growth Around Earlier Fabric w/Void Filled	21 Formal Expansion	22 Company Towns	23 Ideal, Religious, and Worker Towns	24 Colonial Expansion	25 Garden City	26 Early Modern and Fascist New Towns	27 Traditional Movement and the New Urbanism	28 New Modernism
Levoca	**Czech Republic**	**[1974]**											•																	
Libourne	**France**	**[1974]**											•																	
Liége	**France**	**1906**																	•											
Lignières	**France**	**[1974]**																	•											
Lille	France	1909												•																
Lisbon	Portugal	1833																	•											
Lisle d'Albi	**France**	**[1974]**											•																	
Litomysl	Czech Republic	1839																•												
Liverpool	England	1863																	•											
Livorno	Italy	1913															•													
Lódz	Poland	1825																	•											
London	England	1746																	•											
London	England	1843																					•							
London-Corydon Initiative, Community University (proposal by Dixon/Jones)	England	1992																											•	
London-Marylebone District (proposal by Fong)	England	1979																											•	
London-Regents Park (proposal by Nash)	England	1811																					•							
London-Regents Park as Built	England	1843																					•							
London Fire (plan & proposals by Wren, Hooke, Evelyn, & Knight)	England	1666															•		•				•							
London Medieval	**England**	**[1979]**										•																		
London (proposal by Koetter/Kim, 5 schemes)	England	1988																											•	
Longiano	**Italy**	**[1963]**															•													
Loreto	**Italy**	**1984**																	•											
Lorris	**France**	**[1974]**										•																		
Los Angeles	**United States**	**1857**																								•				
Los Angeles-Getty Center (proposal by Richard Meier)	United States	1984–97																											•	
Louisbourg	**Canada**	**1764**													•															
Louisville	**United States**	**1824**														•														
Louisville	**United States**	**1779**														•														
Louisville	**United States**	**1836**																								•				
Lowell	United States	1832																						•						
Lowther	**England**	**1946**																					•							
Lübeck	**Germany**	**1904**																			•									
Lucca	**Italy**	**1913**								•																				
Lucignano	Italy	[1979]										•																		
Luckau	**Germany**	**[1974]**										•																		
Luxembourg	Luxembourg	1906																			•									

City	Country	Date of Plan	1 Early Cities	2 Greek	3 Greek Colonial	4 Imperial Rome	5 Roman Colonial	6 Islamic	7 Indian, Asian	8 Medieval on Early Fabric	9 Medieval Linear, Spinal, or MultiArms	10 Medieval Circular or Free Growth	11 Medieval New Town	12 Renaissance on Earlier Fabric	13 Renaissance Ideal	14 Colonial Grid	15 Early New World Settlements or Late Renaissance	16 Grid Expansion	17 Grid Expansion Graphed onto Earlier Fabric	18 New Baroque	19 Growth Around Earlier Fabric w/Walls Removed	20 Growth Around Earlier Fabric w/Void Filled	21 Formal Expansion	22 Company Towns	23 Ideal, Religious, and Worker Towns	24 Colonial Expansion	25 Garden City	26 Early Modern and Fascist New Towns	27 Traditional Movement and the New Urbanism	28 New Modernism
Luxembourg (proposal by Léon Krier)	Luxembourg	1978																											•	
Lwówek	Poland	[1974]											•																	
Lyon	France	1894																	•											
Maastricht	Netherlands	1865												•																
Macerata	Italy	1924										•																		
Madison	United States	1836																								•				
Madrid	Spain	1831												•																
Madrigal de las Altas Torres	Spain	1050										•																		
Magliano Percorareccio	Italy	1983									•																			
Maidan-e-Naghsh-e-Jahan	Iran	1970						•																						
Malchin	Germany	[1974]											•																	
Manchester	England	1800																	•											
Manfredonia	Italy	[1963]											•																	
Mannheim	Germany	1645													•															
Mantova	Italy	[1963]												•																
Marciac	France	[1974]											•																	
Mardin	Turkey	1920									•																			
Marienburg	Germany	1276											•																	
Marietta	United States	1837																								•				
Marietta (Native American)	United States	unknown	•																											
Marlborough	United States	1691														•														
Marsala	Italy	1984																	•											
Marseille	France	1840																					•							
Martina Franca	Italy	1984																	•											
Massa Homestead, Cameroon	Africa	[1979]	•																											
Massa Lombarda	Italy	[1988]											•																	
Massa Marittima	Italy	1984																	•											
Masseube	France	[1974]											•																	
Matakam Homestead, Cameroon	Africa	[1979]	•																											
Mazara del Vallo	Italy	1984																	•											
Meaux (proposal by Le Corbusier)	France	1956																										•		
Melk	Austria	[1974]															•													
Merida	Spain	1906										•																		
Metz	France	1927											•																	
Meyenburg	Germany	[1963]										•																		
Middelburg	Netherlands	1927																			•									
Milano	Italy	1832												•																
Milano (proposal by Chambry/Zanuso/Pascoe Architects)	Italy	1988–98																											•	
Milano (proposal by Steven Holl)	Italy	1995																												•
Milburn	England	1946									•																			

City	Country	Date of Plan	1 Early Cities	2 Greek	3 Greek Colonial	4 Imperial Rome	5 Roman Colonial	6 Islamic	7 Indian, Asian	8 Medieval on Early Fabric	9 Medieval Linear, Spinal, or MultiArms	10 Medieval Circular or Free Growth	11 Medieval New Town	12 Renaissance on Earlier Fabric	13 Renaissance Ideal	14 Colonial Grid	15 Early New World Settlements or Late Renaissance	16 Grid Expansion	17 Grid Expansion Graphed onto Earlier Fabric	18 New Baroque	19 Growth Around Earlier Fabric w/Walls Removed	20 Growth Around Earlier Fabric w/Void Filled	21 Formal Expansion	22 Company Towns	23 Ideal, Religious, and Worker Towns	24 Colonial Expansion	25 Garden City	26 Early Modern and Fascist New Towns	27 Traditional Movement and the New Urbanism	28 New Modernism
Miletus	Turkey	400 BC			•																									
Milton Abbas	England	1946									•																			
Miramont-de-Guyenne	France	[1974]											•																	
Mirande	France	[1979]											•																	
Mirandola	Italy	1460													•															
Mirepoix	France	[1974]											•																	
Mobile	United States	1711														•														
Mobile	United States	1770														•														
Modena	Italy	1913																	•											
Monclar-d'Argenais	France	[1974]											•																	
Monflanquin	France	[1974]											•																	
Monpazier	France	[1979]											•																	
Monreale	Italy	1984									•																			
Mons	Belgium	1906																	•											
Monségur	France	[1974]											•																	
Mont St. Michel	France	1955															•													
Montagnana	Italy	1984																•												
Montalba	France	[1974]										•																		
Montalto di Castro	Italy	1980										•																		
Montastruc-la-Conseillére	France	[1974]											•																	
Montauban	France	[1974]											•																	
Montaut	France	[1974]											•																	
Montefalco	Italy	[1984]										•																		
Montepulciano	Italy	[1984]									•																			
Monteriggioni	Italy	1963											•																	
Montesquieui Lauragais	France	[1974]										•																		
Montesquieu-Volvestre	France	[1974]											•																	
Montevarchi	Italy	1254											•																	
Montezuma	United States	1887																								•				
Montferrand	France	[1974]								•																				
Montluçon	France	[1974]										•																		
Montpazier	France	[1974]											•																	
Montréal	Canada	1907																								•				
Montréal du Gers	France	[1974]											•																	
Montrejeau	France	[1974]											•																	
Monza	Italy	1984																	•											
Morat au milieu	Switzerland	[1974]											•																	
Moravska Trebova	Czech Republic	[1979]											•																	
Morgan Park	United States	1917																									•			
Moscow	Russia	1836															•													
Mousgourm Homestead, Gaia	Africa	Prehistory	•																											
Mülheim	Germany	1612													•															
Mundaneum (proposal by Le Corbusier)	Belgium	1929																										•		

City	Country	Date of Plan	1 Early Cities	2 Greek	3 Greek Colonial	4 Imperial Rome	5 Roman Colonial	6 Islamic	7 Indian, Asian	8 Medieval on Early Fabric	9 Medieval Linear, Spinal, or MultiArms	10 Medieval Circular or Free Growth	11 Medieval New Town	12 Renaissance on Earlier Fabric	13 Renaissance Ideal	14 Colonial Grid	15 Early New World Settlements or Late Renaissance	16 Grid Expansion	17 Grid Expansion Graphed onto Earlier Fabric	18 New Baroque	19 Growth Around Earlier Fabric w/Walls Removed	20 Growth Around Earlier Fabric w/Void Filled	21 Formal Expansion	22 Company Towns	23 Ideal, Religious, and Worker Towns	24 Colonial Expansion	25 Garden City	26 Early Modern and Fascist New Towns	27 Traditional Movement and the New Urbanism	28 New Modernism
Münich	Germany	2005																					•							
Münich	Germany	1858																					•							
Münich	Germany	1640												•																
Münich	Germany	1200										•																		
Münster	Germany	1893																			•									
Myslibórz	Poland	[1974]											•																	
Najac	France	[1974]									•																			
Nam-myeon, Yeongi-gun, and Chungcheongnam-do	South Korea	2007																												•
Namur	Belgium	1702												•																
Nancy	France	1909																					•							
Naples	Italy	1835																	•											
Narbonne	France	1909																	•											
Narni	Italy	[1984]									•																			
Navarrenx	France	[1974]											•																	
Nay	France	[1974]											•																	
Nègrepelisse	France	[1974]											•																	
Neuf-Brisach (design by Vauban)	France	1729													•															
Neubrandenburg	Germany	[1963]											•																	
Neuchâtel	France	1729										•																		
Neuf-Brisach	France	1776													•															
Neumarkt	Austria	[1974]									•																			
Neunkirch	Switzerland	1925											•																	
Neustadt	Germany	1265											•																	
Neuville-aux-Bois	France	[1974]								•																				
New Bern	United States	1769														•														
New Delhi	India	1911–31																		•										
New Haven	United States	1641														•														
New Orleans	United States	1770														•														
New Orleans	United States	1815																								•				
New York 1731	United States	1731															•													
New York 1763	United States	1763																	•											
New York 1767	United States	1767																	•											
New York 1797	United States	1797																	•											
New York 1838	United States	1838																								•				
New York (proposal by Thom Mayne)	United States	1999																												•
New York-Ground Zero Area	United States	2005																	•											
New York-GZ (proposal by Steven Peterson & Barbara Littenberg)	United States	2005																											•	
New York-GZ (proposal by Eisenman, Meier, Holl, & Gwathmey Siegel)	United States	2005																												•
Newcastle	England	1800									•																			
Newcastle upon Tyne	England	1946																	•											

City	Country	Date of Plan	1	2	3	4	5	6	7	8	9	10	11	12	13	14	15	16	17	18	19	20	21	22	23	24	25	26	27	28
			Early Cities	Greek	Greek Colonial	Imperial Rome	Roman Colonial	Islamic	Indian, Asian	Medieval on Early Fabric	Medieval Linear, Spinal, or MultiArms	Medieval Circular or Free Growth	Medieval New Town	Renaissance on Earlier Fabric	Renaissance Ideal	Colonial Grid	Early New World Settlements or Late Renaissance	Grid Expansion	Grid Expansion Graphed onto Earlier Fabric	New Baroque	Growth Around Earlier Fabric w/Walls Removed	Growth Around Earlier Fabric w/Void Filled	Formal Expansion	Company Towns	Ideal, Religious, and Worker Towns	Colonial Expansion	Garden City	Early Modern and Fascist New Towns	Traditional Movement and the New Urbanism	New Modernism
Newport	United States	1777																	•											
Niagara Falls	United States	1907																								•				
Nice	France	1906																		•										
Nieuwpoort	Belgium	1702												•																
Nijmegen	Netherlands	1865										•																		
Nimes	France	1894																					•							
Nisky	Germany	1782																							•					
Nizza Monferrato	Italy	[1974]											•																	
Norcia	Italy	1984										•																		
Norwich	England	1800										•																		
Nottingham	England	1800																	•											
Novy Bydzon	Czech Republic	[1974]											•																	
Novy Jicin	Czech Republic	[1974]											•																	
Nuremburg	Germany	1858												•																
Oak Bluffs	United States	1875																									•			
Olynthus	Greece	379 BC			•																									
O'Porto	Portugal	1833																	•											
Oppeln	Germany	[1963]											•																	
Orange	France	1926									•																			
Orbetello	Italy	1557												•																
Orléans	France	[1974]											•																	
Orvieto	Italy	1909									•																			
Orzinuovi	Italy	[1963]											•																	
Osimo	Italy	1984										•																		
Ostia	Italy	1970				•																								
Ostuni	Italy	1984																	•											
Oxford	England	1800									•																			
Paczkow	Poland	[1974]											•																	
Padua (Padova)	Italy	1913															•													
Palermo	Italy	1906																	•											
Pallazzo Castera	Italy	[1910]																				•								
Palmanova	Italy	1845													•															
Palmyra	United States	1885																								•				
Palombara Sabina	Italy	[1963]										•																		
Pampelonne	France	[1974]																												
Paris, Parc de la Villette-Krier	France	1982																											•	
Paris, Parc de la Villette-Tschumi	France	1982																												•
Paris (by Haussmann)	France	1871																					•							
Paris, L'île de la Cité	France	1754															•													
Paris 1180	France	1180										•																		
Paris 1779	France	1779																					•							
Paris 1863	France	1863																					•							
Paris (proposal by Le Corbusier)	France	1924																										•		

City	Country	Date of Plan	1 Early Cities	2 Greek	3 Greek Colonial	4 Imperial Rome	5 Roman Colonial	6 Islamic	7 Indian, Asian	8 Medieval on Early Fabric	9 Medieval Linear, Spinal, or MultiArms	10 Medieval Circular or Free Growth	11 Medieval New Town	12 Renaissance on Earlier Fabric	13 Renaissance Ideal	14 Colonial Grid	15 Early New World Settlements or Late Renaissance	16 Grid Expansion	17 Grid Expansion Graphed onto Earlier Fabric	18 New Baroque	19 Growth Around Earlier Fabric w/Walls Removed	20 Growth Around Earlier Fabric w/Void Filled	21 Formal Expansion	22 Company Towns	23 Ideal, Religious, and Worker Towns	24 Colonial Expansion	25 Garden City	26 Early Modern and Fascist New Towns	27 Traditional Movement and the New Urbanism	28 New Modernism
Parma	Italy	1840												•																
Parthanon	Greece	1793								•																				
Pavia	Italy	1913								•																				
Pavie	France	[1974]											•																	
Payerne	Switzerland	[1974]										•																		
Penne	Italy	1984									•																			
Pensacola	United States	1778																												
Perth	Scotland	1800								•																				
Perugia	Italy	1909									•																			
Pesaro	Italy	1909										•																		
Philadelphia	United States	1662														•														
Philadelphia	United States	1794														•														
Philadelphia	United States	1802																•												
Philadelphia	United States	1840																								•				
Philippeville	Belgium	1710													•															
Piacenza	Italy	1916								•																				
Piazza della Signoria	Italy	1960															•													
Piazza Popolo	Italy	[1910]																					•							
Pienza	Italy	[1979]												•																
Pietrasanta	Italy	1963																•												
Pignerol	Italy	1702												•																
Pisa	Italy	1913								•																				
Písek	Czech Republic	[1974]											•																	
Pistoia	Italy	1913								•																				
Pitigliano	Italy	1963										•																		
Pitschen	Germany	[1963]											•																	
Pittsburgh	United States	1795																•												
Pittsburgh	United States	1815																								•				
Pittsburgh	United States	1893																								•				
Pittsburgh, Carnegie-Mellon University (proposal by M. Dennis & J. Clark)	United States	1987																											•	
Pizzighettone	Italy	[1963]												•																
Plaisance-du-Gers	France	[1974]											•																	
Plaisance-du-Touch	France	[1974]											•																	
Plymouth	England	1800																	•											
Plzen (Pilsen)	Czech Republic	[1979]											•																	
Poli	Italy	[1963]									•																			
Polperro	England	1946									•																			
Pompei	Italy	1882				•																								
Pontassieve	Italy	1382									•																			
Ponte dell'Olio	Italy	[1963]									•																			
Pontecurone	Italy	[1963]											•																	
Portoferraio	Italy	1990												•																
Portogruaro	Italy	1984																	•											

City	Country	Date of Plan	1 Early Cities	2 Greek	3 Greek Colonial	4 Imperial Rome	5 Roman Colonial	6 Islamic	7 Indian, Asian	8 Medieval on Early Fabric	9 Medieval Linear, Spinal, or MultiArms	10 Medieval Circular or Free Growth	11 Medieval New Town	12 Renaissance on Earlier Fabric	13 Renaissance Ideal	14 Colonial Grid	15 Early New World Settlements or Late Renaissance	16 Grid Expansion	17 Grid Expansion Graphed onto Earlier Fabric	18 New Baroque	19 Growth Around Earlier Fabric w/Walls Removed	20 Growth Around Earlier Fabric w/Void Filled	21 Formal Expansion	22 Company Towns	23 Ideal, Religious, and Worker Towns	24 Colonial Expansion	25 Garden City	26 Early Modern and Fascist New Towns	27 Traditional Movement and the New Urbanism	28 New Modernism
Potsdam	Germany	1800																					•							
Potsdam Burelli	Germany	1991																											•	
PotsDamer Platz	Germany	1994																											•	
Prague	Czech Republic	[1974]															•													
Prato	Italy	1916								•																				
Presidio of San Francisco	United States	1820														•														
Priene	Turkey	350 BC			•																									
Providence	United States	1638															•													
Pullman	United States	1885																						•						
Puybrun	France	[1974]											•																	
PuyMirol	France	[1974]											•																	
Pyramids of Cheops	Egypt	2566 BC	•																											
Pyrzyce	Poland	[1974]											•																	
Quebec	Canada	1759												•																
Quito	Ecuador	1700														•														
Rabastens	France	[1974]											•																	
Racanati	Italy	1984									•																			
Radstadt	Austria	1280											•																	
Ravenna	Italy	1913																•												
Réalmont	France	[1974]											•																	
Réalville	France	[1974]											•																	
Recanati	Italy	[1963]									•																			
Regensburg	Germany	1800												•																
Reims	France	1909																			•									
Retz	Austria	[1974]											•																	
Revel	France	[1974]											•																	
Rhodes	Greece	408 BC			•																									
Rhodes	Greece	1906								•																				
Richmond	United States	1893																								•				
Ridley Park	United States	1875																									•			
Rieti	Italy	1990															•													
Rieumes	France	[1974]										•																		
Riga	Latvia	1927																			•									
Rimini	Italy	1901																					•							
Rio de Janeiro	Brazil	1831																								•				
Rio de Janeiro (Uni. proposal by Le Corbusier)	Brazil	1936																										•		
Riverside	United States	1869																									•			
Rivolta d'Adda	Italy	[1963]																•												
Rochefort	France	1600													•															
Rome-Buffalini	Italy	1551								•																				
Rome-Nolli plan	Italy	1748												•																
Rome Imperial	Italy	200 BC				•																								
Rome-Interrota (proposal by Colin Rowe & team)	Italy	1979																											•	

City	Country	Date of Plan	1 Early Cities	2 Greek	3 Greek Colonial	4 Imperial Rome	5 Roman Colonial	6 Islamic	7 Indian, Asian	8 Medieval on Early Fabric	9 Medieval Linear, Spinal, or MultiArms	10 Medieval Circular or Free Growth	11 Medieval New Town	12 Renaissance on Earlier Fabric	13 Renaissance Ideal	14 Colonial Grid	15 Early New World Settlements or Late Renaissance	16 Grid Expansion	17 Grid Expansion Graphed onto Earlier Fabric	18 New Baroque	19 Growth Around Earlier Fabric w/Walls Removed	20 Growth Around Earlier Fabric w/Void Filled	21 Formal Expansion	22 Company Towns	23 Ideal, Religious, and Worker Towns	24 Colonial Expansion	25 Garden City	26 Early Modern and Fascist New Towns	27 Traditional Movement and the New Urbanism	28 New Modernism
Ronda	Spain	1906																	•											
Rostock	Germany	1904																			•									
Rothenburg	Germany	[1974]										•																		
Rotterdam	Netherlands	1865																				•								
Rotterdam (project by OMA)	Netherlands	1987																												•
Rottweil	Germany	1564											•																	
Rottweil	Germany	1823															•													
Rouen	France	[1974]											•																	
Rudelle	France	[1974]											•																	
Rydzyna	Poland	1703																					•							
Sabaudia	Italy	1940																										•		
Sabbioneta	Italy	1560													•															
Sacramento	United States	1849																								•				
Sacrofano	Italy	[1963]									•																			
Sagunto	Spain	1906								•																				
Saint Albans	England	1800									•																			
Saint Aubin-du-Cormier	France	[1974]											•																	
Saint Aubin-du-Saissac	France	[1974]											•																	
Saint Augustine	United States	1770														•														
Saint Clar	France	[1974]											•																	
Saint Croix Island	United States	1604														•														
Saint Die	France	1935																	•											
Saint Die (proposal by Le Corbusier)	France	1945																										•		
Saint Félix-Lauragais	France	[1974]											•																	
Saint Flour	France	[1974]											•																	
Saint Foy de Peyroliéres	France	[1974]																•												
Saint Foy-la-Grande	France	1255											•																	
Saint Gallen	Switzerland	1888																	•											
Saint Livrade-sur-Lot	France	[1974]										•																		
Saint Louis	United States	1780														•														
Saint Lys	France	[1974]											•																	
Saint Malo	France	1909															•													
Saint Pastour	France	[1974]											•																	
Saint Petersburg	Russia	1834																					•							
Saint Quentin	France	1909																	•											
Saint Sardos	France	[1974]										•																		
Saint Surlpice-sur-Léze	France	[1974]											•																	
Saint Suzanne	France	[1974]										•																		
Salerno	Italy	1940																	•											
Saline de Chaux	France	1804																							•					
Saltaire	England	1851																						•						
San Agata dé Goti	Italy	[1963]									•																			
San Antonio	United States	1777														•														
San Casciano	Italy	1356									•																			

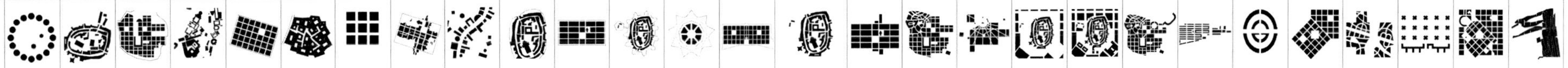

City	Country	Date of Plan	1 Early Cities	2 Greek	3 Greek Colonial	4 Imperial Rome	5 Roman Colonial	6 Islamic	7 Indian, Asian	8 Medieval on Early Fabric	9 Medieval Linear, Spinal, or MultiArms	10 Medieval Circular or Free Growth	11 Medieval New Town	12 Renaissance on Earlier Fabric	13 Renaissance Ideal	14 Colonial Grid	15 Early New World Settlements or Late Renaissance	16 Grid Expansion	17 Grid Expansion Graphed onto Earlier Fabric	18 New Baroque	19 Growth Around Earlier Fabric w/Walls Removed	20 Growth Around Earlier Fabric w/Void Filled	21 Formal Expansion	22 Company Towns	23 Ideal, Religious, and Worker Towns	24 Colonial Expansion	25 Garden City	26 Early Modern and Fascist New Towns	27 Traditional Movement and the New Urbanism	28 New Modernism
San Francisco	United States	1842														•														
San Francisco	United States	1852																								•				
San Gallo	Italy	[1963]																	•											
San Gimignano	Italy	1990									•																			
San Giovanni Valdarno	Italy	1297																•												
San Giovanni Valdarno	Italy	1800											•																	
San Gregorio da Sassola	Italy	1970																					•							
San Martinoal al Cimino	Italy	1987																		•										
San Miniato	Italy	1963									•																			
San Severino Marche	Italy	1984																	•											
San Vittorino	Italy	[1963]										•																		
Sandusky	United States	1818																								•				
Sansepolcro	Italy	1963											•																	
Sansevero	Italy	[1963]										•																		
São Paulo	Brazil	1913																	•											
Sarzana	Italy	1486											•																	
Sauveterre d'Aveyron	France	[1974]											•																	
Sauveterre-de-Béarn	France	[1974]									•																			
Sauveterre-de-Guyenne	France	[1974]											•																	
Savannah	United States	1733														•														
Savannah	United States	1735																•												
Savannah	United States	1790																•												
Savannah	United States	1799																•												
Savannah	United States	1801																•												
Savannah	United States	1815																•												
Savannah	United States	1841																•												
Savannah	United States	1856																•												
Scarperia	Italy	1800											•																	
Scherpenheuvel	Belgium	1661																					•							
Schrobenhausen	Germany	[1963]										•																		
Sciacca	Italy	1984																	•											
Seaside	United States	1984																											•	
Sedan	France	1702												•																
Selinus	Italy	628 BC			•																									
Sergovia (Ségovie)	Spain	1920									•																			
Sérignac	France	[1974]											•																	
Sessa Aurunca	Italy	1984									•																			
Seville	Spain	1906															•													
Shaker Heights	United States	1990																									•			
Sheffield	England	1800																	•											
Sherston	England	1946																•												
Shincliffe	England	1946									•																			
Siena	Italy	1909									•																			
Soest	France	[1974]										•																		

City	Country	Date of Plan	1 Early Cities	2 Greek	3 Greek Colonial	4 Imperial Rome	5 Roman Colonial	6 Islamic	7 Indian, Asian	8 Medieval on Early Fabric	9 Medieval Linear, Spinal, or MultiArms	10 Medieval Circular or Free Growth	11 Medieval New Town	12 Renaissance on Earlier Fabric	13 Renaissance Ideal	14 Colonial Grid	15 Early New World Settlements or Late Renaissance	16 Grid Expansion	17 Grid Expansion Graphed onto Earlier Fabric	18 New Baroque	19 Growth Around Earlier Fabric w/Walls Removed	20 Growth Around Earlier Fabric w/Void Filled	21 Formal Expansion	22 Company Towns	23 Ideal, Religious, and Worker Towns	24 Colonial Expansion	25 Garden City	26 Early Modern and Fascist New Towns	27 Traditional Movement and the New Urbanism	28 New Modernism
Solarolo	Italy	[1963]											•																	
Solomiac (da Lavedan)	France	[1974]											•																	
Soncino	Italy	[1963]																	•											
Sonoma	United States	1875																								•				
Southampton	England	1800																	•											
Spalato	Croatia	[1963]											•																	
Spello	Italy	1984										•																		
Spisska Nova Ves	Czech Republic	[1974]									•																			
Spoleto	Italy	1909																	•											
Sroda Slaska	Poland	1860											•																	
Stanislawów	Ukraine	1792													•															
Stia	Italy	[1974]									•																			
Stockholm	Sweden	1838																					•							
Stockholm, Competition for the Royal Chancellery	Sweden	1922																										•		
Stralsund	Germany	1904																	•											
Strassbourg	France	[1974]																	•											
Strassbourg	France	1909																					•							
Stribro (Mies)	Czech Republic	[1974]											•																	
Stuttgart	Germany	1902																					•							
Sulmona	Italy	[1984]																	•											
Syracuse	Italy	1909									•																			
Szczecin-proposed	Poland	1630													•															
Tabor	Czech Republic	[1974]										•																		
Talamone	Italy	1255											•																	
Tallmadge Center	United States	1874																								•				
Tanger	Morocco	1909						•																						
Taormina	Italy	1984								•																				
Tappahannock	United States	1706														•														
Taranto	Italy	1940																	•											
Tarquinia	Italy	1990																•												
Tarragona	Spain	1906																	•											
Teggiano	Italy	1984										•																		
Terezín	Czech Republic	1870													•															
Termoli	Italy	[1984]																	•											
Terra del Sole	Italy	[1963]													•															
Terramara of Castallazzo	Italy	[1963]	•																											
Terranuova Bracciolini	Italy	1800											•																	
Thaxted	England	1946									•																			
Thoune	France	[1974]										•																		
Timgad	Algeria	100					•																							
Tivoli	Italy	1990																					•							
Todi	Italy	[1984]									•																			
Toledo	Spain	1906																	•											
Tolentino	Italy	1984										•																		

City	Country	Date of Plan	1 Early Cities	2 Greek	3 Greek Colonial	4 Imperial Rome	5 Roman Colonial	6 Islamic	7 Indian, Asian	8 Medieval on Early Fabric	9 Medieval Linear, Spinal, or MultiArms	10 Medieval Circular or Free Growth	11 Medieval New Town	12 Renaissance on Earlier Fabric	13 Renaissance Ideal	14 Colonial Grid	15 Early New World Settlements or Late Renaissance	16 Grid Expansion	17 Grid Expansion Graphed onto Earlier Fabric	18 New Baroque	19 Growth Around Earlier Fabric w/Walls Removed	20 Growth Around Earlier Fabric w/Void Filled	21 Formal Expansion	22 Company Towns	23 Ideal, Religious, and Worker Towns	24 Colonial Expansion	25 Garden City	26 Early Modern and Fascist New Towns	27 Traditional Movement and the New Urbanism	28 New Modernism
Torino (Turin)	Italy	28					•																							
Torino (Turin)	Italy	1590								•																				
Torino (Turin)	Italy	1620												•																
Torino (Turin)	Italy	1670												•																
Torino (Turin)	Italy	1720																	•											
Torino (Turin)	Italy	1914																					•							
Toul	France	1938												•																
Toulon	France	1840												•																
Toulous	France	1909																					•							
Tournai	Belgium	1695												•																
Tournay	France	[1974]											•																	
Tournon d'Agenais	France	[1974]											•																	
Tours	France	[1974]																	•											
Trani	Italy	[1984]																					•							
Tremadoc	England	1946									•																			
Trento	Italy	1913																	•											
Trevi	Italy	1984										•																		
Trevi nel Lazio	Italy	1980									•																			
Trie-sur-Baïse	France	[1974]											•																	
Tripoli	Libya	1929						•																						
Troyes	France	[1974]										•																		
Truscania	Italy	1984																	•											
Udine	Italy	[1963]										•																		
Unicov	Czech Republic	[1979]										•																		
Urbino	Italy	1963										•																		
Utrecht	Netherlands	1927																			•									
Vailhourles	France	[1974]										•																		
Valence-d'Agen	France	[1974]											•																	
Valence-sur-Baïse	France	[1974]											•																	
Valenciennes	France	1906																	•											
Valentine	France	[1974]											•																	
Vallejo	United States	1850																								•				
Valletta	Malta	1963												•																
Vasto	Italy	1984																	•											
Vaux-le-Vicomte	France	1990																					•							
Velletri	Italy	[1984]										•																		
Venice	Italy	1950										•																		
Venosa	Italy	1984																•												
Venzone	Italy	1255											•																	
Verdun	France	1906												•																
Verdun-sur-Garonne	France	[1974]											•																	
Verfeil-sur-Seye	France	[1974]																•												
Vergt	France	[1974]											•																	
Verneuil-sur-Avre	France	[1974]										•																		
Verona, municipium	Italy	49 BC					•																							

City	Country	Date of Plan	1 Early Cities	2 Greek	3 Greek Colonial	4 Imperial Rome	5 Roman Colonial	6 Islamic	7 Indian, Asian	8 Medieval on Early Fabric	9 Medieval Linear, Spinal, or MultiArms	10 Medieval Circular or Free Growth	11 Medieval New Town	12 Renaissance on Earlier Fabric	13 Renaissance Ideal	14 Colonial Grid	15 Early New World Settlements or Late Renaissance	16 Grid Expansion	17 Grid Expansion Graphed onto Earlier Fabric	18 New Baroque	19 Growth Around Earlier Fabric w/Walls Removed	20 Growth Around Earlier Fabric w/Void Filled	21 Formal Expansion	22 Company Towns	23 Ideal, Religious, and Worker Towns	24 Colonial Expansion	25 Garden City	26 Early Modern and Fascist New Towns	27 Traditional Movement and the New Urbanism	28 New Modernism
Verona	Italy	1925												•																
Versailles	France	1746																		•										
Vianne	France	[1974]											•																	
Vicchio	Italy	1366											•																	
Vicenza	Italy	1920										•																		
Vienna	Austria	1547																			•									
Vienna	Austria	1833										•																		
Vienna (Hofburg)	Austria	1914																				•								
Vigevano	Italy	[1963]										•																		
Villafranca di Verona	Italy	[1963]											•																	
Villafranca Veronese	Italy	[1963]										•																		
Villarreal	Spain	1274											•																	
Villefranche de Belves	France	[1974]											•																	
Villefranche-de-Lauragais	France	[1974]											•																	
Villefranche-de-Longchapt	France	[1974]											•																	
Villefranche-de-Rouergue	France	[1974]											•																	
Villefranche-sur-Mer	France	[1974]										•																		
Villefranche-sur-Saône	France	[1974]											•																	
Villeneuve-de-Berg	France	[1974]																•												
Villeneuve-l'Archevêque	France	[1974]											•																	
Villeneuve-le-Comte	France	[1974]											•																	
Villeneuve-sur-Lot	France	1264											•																	
Villeneuve-sur-Lot	France	[1974]																•												
Villeneuve-sur-Yonne	France	[1974]											•																	
Villenouvelle	France	[1974]																•												
Villeréal	France	[1974]											•																	
Villingen	Germany	ca 1200											•																	
Viterbo	Italy	1909										•																		
Vitoria	Brazil	1767										•																		
Vitoria	Spain	[1974]										•																		
Vitry-le-Francois	France	1545													•															
Vodnany	Czech Republic	[1974]										•																		
Völkermarkt	Austria	1234											•																	
Volterra	Italy	1909									•																			
Vysoke Myto (Hohenmauth)	Czech (Germany)	[1963]											•																	
Warsaw	Poland	1600											•																	
Warsaw	Poland	1780																					•							
Warsaw	Poland	1831																					•							
Washington DC	United States	1792														•														
Washington DC	United States	1791																		•										
Washington DC, L'Enfant	United States	1791																		•										
Weissenhofsiedlung	Germany	1927																										•		
West Wycombe	England	1946									•																			
Wethersfield	United States	1640									•																			

City	Country	Date of Plan	1 Early Cities	2 Greek	3 Greek Colonial	4 Imperial Rome	5 Roman Colonial	6 Islamic	7 Indian, Asian	8 Medieval on Early Fabric	9 Medieval Linear, Spinal, or MultiArms	10 Medieval Circular or Free Growth	11 Medieval New Town	12 Renaissance on Earlier Fabric	13 Renaissance Ideal	14 Colonial Grid	15 Early New World Settlements or Late Renaissance	16 Grid Expansion	17 Grid Expansion Graphed onto Earlier Fabric	18 New Baroque	19 Growth Around Earlier Fabric w/Walls Removed	20 Growth Around Earlier Fabric w/Void Filled	21 Formal Expansion	22 Company Towns	23 Ideal, Religious, and Worker Towns	24 Colonial Expansion	25 Garden City	26 Early Modern and Fascist New Towns	27 Traditional Movement and the New Urbanism	28 New Modernism
Wickham	England	1946																•												
Wielun	Poland	[1974]											•																	
Wiesbaden	Germany	1896																	•											
Williamsburg	United States	1782														•														
Winchester	England	1800								•																				
Winterthur	Switzerland	[1974]											•																	
Woodstock	United States	1869									•																			
Worchester	England	1800									•																			
Writtle	England	1946										•																		
Wurtzburg (Würzburg)	Germany	1800												•																
Würzburg (Wurtzburg)	Germany	1895																			•									
York	England	1800								•																				
Ypres	Belgium	1906															•													
Zamosch (Lublino)	Poland	1650													•															
Zanesville	United States	1815																								•				
Zara	Italy	1924																	•											
Zatec	Czech Republic	1843									•																			
Zgierz	Russia	1821																	•											
Zlotoryja	Poland	[1974]											•																	
Zürich	Switzerland	1907																	•											
Zutfen	Germany	1963																	•											
Zutphen	Netherlands	1868																	•											
Zwolle	Netherlands	1868																			•									

Sources for City Plans

"Aerial Map of Beijing." Washington, D.C.: CIA, 1950.

Baedeker, Karl. Baedeker editions. Leipzig, 1837–1937.

Bartholomew, J. G. *Literary and Historical Atlas of Europe.* New York: E. P. Dutton, 1936.

Baynton-Williams, Ashley. *Town and City Maps of the British Isles, 1800–1855.* London: Studio Editions, 1992.

Benevolo, Leonardo. *The History of the City.* Trans. Geoffrey Culverwell. Cambridge, Mass.: MIT Press, 1980.

Berlin: Aus den Ersten Zeiten. Berlin: Königlichen Bibliothek, 1910.

Bertarelli, L. V. *Italia Méridionale Sicile et Sardaigne.* Paris: Hachette, 1935.

Beaulieu, Sébastien. *Les plans et profils des principales villes et lieux consid,rables du Comt, de Flandre, avec les cartes générales et les particuliéres de chaque gouvernement.* Paris, ca. 1700.

Braunfels, Wolfgang. *Monasteries of Western Europe.* Princeton, N.J.: Princeton University Press, 1973.

"Bufalini Plan." In Allen Ceen, *La Pianta Grande di Roma di Giambattista Nolli, 1748.* Amsterdam: Architectura & Natura Press, 1991.

Burelli, Augusto Romanero. "Berlin, Potsdam Platz." *Materia* 11 (Sept.–Dec. 1992): 40–45.

Canina, Luigi. *Gli edifizj di Roma antica cogniti per alcune reliquie.* Rome, 1848–56.

Chambry/Zaniso/Pascoe Architects. Milan Plan, 1988–98.

Chipperfield, David. *Theoretical Practice.* London: Artemis, 1994.

Città da scoprire: Guida ai centri minori, Italia settentrionale. Vols. 1–3. Milan: Proprieta del T.C.I., 1983–85.

Cunliffe, Barry. *The City of Bath.* Gloucester: Sutton, 1986.

Cooper, Wayne W. "The Figure/Grounds." Master's thesis, Cornell University, 1967.

Dennis, Michael, and Jeffrey Clark. Carnegie Mellon Master Campus Plan. Carnegie Mellon University Competition (First Prize & Commission), Pittsburgh, 1988.

Dennis, Michael, and Klaus Herdeg. *Urban Precedents.* New York: J. Rietman, 1974.

Duffy, Christopher. *Fire and Stone: The Science of Fortress Warfare, 1660–1860.* New York: Hippocrene Books, 1975.

Eisenman Architects. *Five Westside Stories: Five Possible Futures for the West Side of Manhattan.* Montreal: Canadian Centre for Architecture, 2000.

Fantozzi, F. *Pianta geometrica di Firenze,* 1843.

de Fer, Nicolas. *Introduction à la fortification. . . .* Paris: Chex L'Autheur, 1705.

de la Feuille, Daniel. *Atlas Portatif, ou le Theatre de la Guerre en Europe.* Amsterdam, 1702.

Fong, Stephen. "London, Marylebone District Development." *Cornell Journal of Architecture* 2 (Aug. 1993).

Frase, Douglas. *Village Planning in the Primitive World.* New York: Braziller, 1968.

Friedman, David. *Florentine New Towns: Urban Design in the Late Middle Ages.* Cambridge, Mass.: MIT Press, 1988.

Furttenbach, Joseph. *Gewerb-Stattgebäw.* Augsburg, 1650.

Galantay, Ervin Y. *New Towns: Antiquity to the Present.* New York: G. Braziller, 1975.

Gelsomino, Luisella. *La Cultura Della Citta: Lazio.* Faenza: Edizioni C.E.L.I., 1992.

———. *La Cultura Della Citta: Toscana.* Faenza: Edizioni C.E.L.I., 1992.

Graves, Michael, ed. *Roma Interrota.* London: Architectural Design, 1979.

Gromort, George. *Choix de Plans de Grandes Compositions.* Paris: A. Vincent, 1907.

Gruber, Karl. *Die Gestalt der Deutschen Stadt: Ihr Wandel aus der Geistigen Ordnung der Zeiten.* Munich: Callwey, 1983.

Guida Breve. Milan: Proprieta del T.C.I., 1951–53.

Guida D'Italia/IT Cent. Vols. 1 and 3. Milano: Proprieta del T.C.I., 1922–23.

Guida D'Italia/Italia Meridionale. Vols. 1 and 3. Milan: Proprieta del T.C.I., 1926–28.

Guida D'Italia/Le Tre Venezia. Vol. 1. Milan: Proprieta del T.C.I., 1939.

Guida D'Italia/Liguria, Toscana Settentr, Emilia. Vol. 2. Milan: Proprieta del T.C.I., 1916.

Guida D'Italia/Piedmonte, Lombardia, Canton Ticino. Vol. 1. Milan: Proprieta del T.C.I., 1926.

Gutkind, E. A. *International History of City Development.* Vols. 1–8. New York: Free Press, 1964–72.

Helmer, Stephen D. *Hitler's Berlin: The Speer Plans for Reshaping the Central City.* Ann Arbor, Mich.: UMI Research Press, 1985.

Herdeg, Klaus. *Formal Structure in Indian Architecture.* New York: Rizzoli, 1990.

———. *Formal Structure in Islamic Architecture of Iran and Turkistan.* New York: Rizzoli, 1990.

Hillairet, Jacques. *L'Ile de la Cite.* Paris: Editions de Minuit, 1969.

Hoepfner, Wolfram, and Ernst-Ludwig Schwandner. *Haus und Stadt im Klassischen Griechenland.* Munich: Deutscher Kunstverlag, 1986.

Holl, Steven. *Anchoring: Selected Projects, 1975–1991.* Princeton, N.J.: Princeton Architectural Press, 1989.

Hurtaut, Pierre-Thomas-Nicolas. *Dictionnaire Historique de la Ville de Paris et ses Environs.* Paris: Moutard, 1779.

Katz, Peter. *The New Urbanism: Toward an Architecture of Community.* New York: McGraw-Hill, 1994.

Koetter Kim & Associates: Place/Time. Intro. Alan J. Plattus. Essays by Colin Rowe and Fred Koetter. New York: Rizzoli, 1997.

Krier, Léon. *Léon Krier: Houses, Palaces, Cities.* New York: St. Martin's Press, 1984.

Kuyper, J. *Gemeente Atlas.* Leeuwarden, Netherlands, 1865–70.

Latham, Ian, and Mark Swenarton, eds. *Jeremy Dixon and Edward Jones: Buildings and Projects.* London: Right Angle, 2002.

Lavedan, Pierre, and Jeanne Hugueney. *L'urbanisme au moyen age.* Paris: Arts et metiers graphiques, 1974.

Le Corbusier. *Le Corbusier et Pierre Jeanneret: Oeuvre Complête.* Zurich: Erlenbach, 1964–70.

Le Doux, Claude Nicolas. *Architecture de C. N. le Doux: Collection qui rassemble tous les genres de bâtiments employeés dans l'ordre social.* Paris: Lenoir, 1847.

Maps of the Society for the Diffusion of Useful Knowledge. 2 vols. London: C. Knight, 1849.

Mariani, Riccardo. *E 42: Un Progetto per L'ordine Nuovo.* Edizioni Comunita, 1987.

Meier, Richard. *Richard Meier, Architect: 1992/1999.* New York: St. Martin's Press, 1999.

Metrogramma SRL Arch. Andrea Boschetti, Arch. Alberto Francini. Prints in author's collection.

Monmarche, Georges. *France Automobile et un Volume: La France Entiere, Sites et Monuments, Sous la Main.* Paris: Hachette, 1938.

Morini, Mario. *Atlante di Storia Dell'urbanistica: Dalla Preistoria All'inizio del Sccolo XX.* Milan: Editore Ulrico Hoepli, 1983.

Moore, Charles W., William J. Mitchell, and William Turnbull Jr. *The Poetics of Gardens.* Cambridge, Mass.: MIT Press, 1988.

Muirhead, Findlay, and Marcel Monmarch. *Southern France.* London: Macmillan & Co., 1926.

Piranesi, Giovanni Battista. *The Complete Etchings.* Intro. Luigi Ficacci. New York: Taschen, 2000.

Plan of the City of Cleveland. City of Cleveland Planning Department, 1990.

Plan of the City of Shaker Heights. City of Shaker Heights Planning Department, 1990.

Plan of Rome, 1942. City Planning Department, Esposizione Universale, Rome, 1995.

Plan of Vaux-le-Vicomte. Institut Géographique National, Paris, 1990.

Plan of Venice. Instituto Geografico Militare, Firenze, 1950.

Powell, Kenneth. *City Transformed: Urban Architecture at the Beginning of the 21st Century.* New York: te Neues, 2000.

Rasmussen, Steen Eiler. *Towns and Buildings Described in Drawings and Words.* Cambridge, Mass.: MIT Press, 1969.

Reps, John W. *The Making of Urban America: A History of City Planning in the United States.* Princeton, N.J.: Princeton University Press, 1965.

Rocque, John. *A New and Accurate Survey of the Cities of London and Westminster, the Borough of Southwark: With the country about it for nineteen miles in length and thirteen in depth.* London, 1751.

Sharp, Thomas. *The Anatomy of the Village.* Harmondsworth: Penguin, 1946.

Spain Blue Guide. London: MacMillan & Co., 1929.

Stockdale, John. *A Speculative Picture of Europe, Translated from the French of General Dumouriez.* London, 1798.

Stockdale, J. *Plans and Maps of European Cities and Countries.* Piccadilly: J. Stockdale, 1800.

Strickland, Roy, ed. *Post Urbanism and Reurbanism: Peter Eisenman vs. Barbara Littenberg and Steven Peterson: Designs for Ground Zero.* Ann Arbor: University of Michigan, 2005.

Tschumi, Bernard. *Cinégramme folie: Le Parc de la Villette, Paris nineteenth arrondissement.* Princeton, N.J.: Princeton Architectural Press, 1987.

Unwin, R. *Grundlagen des Städtebaues: Eine Anleitung zum Entwerfen Städtebaulichen Anlagen.* Berlin: Otto Baumgärtel, 1910.

Venturi, Robert. *Learning from Las Vegas: The Forgotten Symbolism of Architectural Form.* Cambridge, Mass.: MIT Press, 1977.